Gautier on Dance

Théophile Gautier.

Gautier on Dance

Théophile Gautier

Selected, translated and annotated by

Ivor Guest

DANCE BOOKS
CECIL COURT LONDON

First published 1986 by Dance Books Ltd.,
9 Cecil Court, London WC2N 4EZ.

ISBN 0 903102 94 3

Distributed in the USA by Princeton Book Co.,
P.O. Box 109, Princeton, N.J. 08540.

British Library Cataloguing in Publication Data
Gautier, Théophile
Gautier on dance.
1. Ballet—France—Reviews
I. Title II. Guest, Ivor
792.8'45   GV1649

Designed by Tina Dutton; design and production in association with Book
Production Consultants, Cambridge.

Typeset by Millford Reprographics International Ltd, Luton

Printed by Billings and Sons Ltd., Worcester

To the memory of Ed Binney
in gratitude for a friendship
that began, so appropriately, in
the Bibliothèque de l'Opéra,
and for his unfailing generosity
as a colleague.

ALSO BY IVOR GUEST

Napoleon III in England
The Ballet of the Second Empire
The Romantic Ballet in England
Fanny Cerrito
Victorian Ballet Girl
Adeline Genée
The Alhambra Ballet
La Fille mal gardée (editor)
The Dancer's Heritage
The Empire Ballet
A Gallery of Romantic Ballet
The Romantic Ballet in Paris
Dandies and Dancers
Carlotta Zambelli
Two Coppélias
Fanny Elssler
The Pas de Quatre
Le Ballet de l'Opéra de Paris
The Divine Virginia
Letters from a Ballet-master
Adeline Genée: a pictorial record
Designing for the Dancer (contributor)
Adventures of a Ballet Historian
Jules Perrot

Contents

List of Illustrations xiii
Translator's Note xvii
Introduction. xix
The Reviews 1

1836

1   Marie Taglioni dances at the Palace of Compiègne.   1
2   The Statuette of Fanny Elssler   3

1837

3   The Spanish Dancers   5
4   Opéra: *Les Mohicans*.   9
5   Opéra: Return of Fanny Elssler in *La Tempête*   15
6   Opéra: Revival of *La Muette de Portici*; Dolores Serral.   17
7   Opéra: Revival of *Nathalie*.   20
8   Fanny Elssler.   22
9   Opéra: *La Chatte métamorphosée en femme*.   25
10 Opéra: Revival of *Le Dieu et la bayadère*.   29

1838

11 Reflections on Fanny Elssler.   31
12 Opéra: *La Volière*   33
13 Opéra: *Le Diable boiteux*   37
14 Opéra: Début of Lucile Grahn   38
15 The Devadasis, or the Bayaderes   39
16 Th. des Variétés: The Bayaderes.   47
17 Opéra: Revival of *La Sylphide*, with Elssler   51
18 Opéra: Revival of *La Fille du Danube*, with Elssler   56

1839

19 Opéra: *La Gipsy*.   58
20 Opéra: *La Tarentule*   66
21 Th. de la Renaissance: *El Marcobomba*   76

22 Opéra: Lucile Grahn in *La Sylphide* 78
23 Opéra: Début of Augusta Maywood...................... 79

1840

24 Opéra: Benefit of Fanny Elssler 82
25 Th. de la Renaissance: *Zingaro* 86

1841

26 Opéra: Revival of *Les Noces de Gamache* 91
27 Opéra: *Giselle*... 94

1842

28 Opéra: *La Jolie Fille de Gand*........................... 103

1843

29 Opéra: *La Péri* 112
30 Opéra: Début of Caroline Fjeldsted...................... 122

1844

31 Opéra: *Lady Henriette* 124
32 Opéra: Lola Montez 130
33 Opéra: Return of Marie Taglioni in *La Sylphide*............. 131
34 Opéra: Marie Taglioni in *Le Dieu et la bayadère* 134
35 Th. de la Porte-Saint-Martin: Thoughts on seeing Risley and
   his sons 138
36 Opéra: Marie Taglioni's Benefit......................... 140
37 Opéra: Début of Tatiana Smirnova 144
38 Opéra: *Eucharis*....................................... 146
39 The Death of Clara Webster............................. 153

1845

40 Opéra: Début of the Viennese Children 155
41 Th. de la Porte-Saint-Martin: Lola Montez 159
42 Opéra: Début of Adeline Plunkett....................... 161
43 Opéra: Début of Elena Andreyanova 163

1846

44 Her Majesty's Th., London: Lumley commissions a ballet
    from Heinrich Heine 164
45 Opéra: *Paquita* 166
46 Her Majesty's Th., London: *La Bacchante* and *Lalla-Rookh* .. 171
47 Opéra: *Betty* 175

1847

48 Opéra: *Ozaï* 178
49 Opéra: *La Fille de marbre* 182

1848

50 Opéra: *Griseldis* 189
51 Opéra: *Nisida* 198
52 Opéra: Return of Fanny Cerrito. 201
53 Opéra: *La Vivandière* 204

1849

54 Opéra: *Le Violon du Diable* 207
55 The Ballet at Her Majesty's Theatre, London 212
56 Opéra: *La Filleule des fées* 215

1850

57 Opéra: *Stella* 222

1851

58 Opéra: *Pâquerette* 225
59 Opéra: Revival of *La Vivandière* 228
60 Opéra: *Vert-Vert* 230

1852

61 Opéra: Revival of *La Sylphide*, with Priora 234

1853

62 Opéra: *Orfa* 236
63 Th. Lyrique: *Le Lutin de la Vallée. La Sténochorégraphie*..... 239
64 Opéra: Revivals of *La Fille mal gardée*, with Besson, and
    Giselle, with Forli..................................... 244
65 Th. du Gymnase: Petra Cámara........................... 247
66 Opéra: *Aelia et Mysis* 250
67 Th. Lyrique: *Le Danseur du roi*......................... 257
68 Opéra: *Jovita* 259

1854

69 Opéra: *Gemma*... 265
70 Th. du Gymnase: Manuela Perea. Th. du Palais-Royal:
    Josefa Vargas 270

1855

71 Opéra: *La Fonti* 273
72 Opéra: Revival of *Le Diable à quatre*, with Beretta 277

1856

73 Th. de la Porte-Saint-Martin: *Esmeralda* 279

1858

74 Opéra: *Sacountala* 281
75 Bolshoi Theatre, St. Petersburg: *Eoline*.................... 288

1863

76 Tribute to Emma Livry 295

1864

77 Opéra: *Néméa* 297
78 Opéra: Léontine Beaugrand in *Diavolina*.................. 307

1865

79 Opéra: Revival of *La Muette de Portici*, with Fiocre 309

1866

80 Opéra: *Le Roi d'Yvetot* 311
81 Opéra: Revival of *Le Dieu et la bayadère*, with Salvioni 315
82 Opéra: Début of Grantzow in *Giselle* 317
83 Opéra: Revival of *Néméa*, with Grantzow 319
84 Opéra: *La Source* 320

1867

85 Opéra: Revival of *La Source*, with Grantzow 324
86 Opéra: Revival of *Le Corsaire*, with Grantzow 325

1868

87 Opéra: Return of Grantzow in *La Source*. 327

1869

88 Opéra: Revival of *Le Prophète* 329

1870

89 Opéra: Revival of *Robert le Diable*, with Fonta 330
90 Opéra: *Coppélia* 332

1871

91 Opéra: Revival of *Coppélia*, with Beaugrand 335

Appendix: Notices not translated in full 337
Index 351

Illustrations

FRONTISPIECE
1 Théophile Gautier.

BETWEEN PAGES 70 AND 71
2 The Paris Opéra that Gautier knew.
3 The interior of the Opéra during a performance of *Robert le Diable*.
4 Marie Taglioni in *La Sylphide*. Statuette by Jean-Auguste Barre.
5 Fanny Elssler dancing the *Cachucha*. Statuette by Jean-Auguste Barre.
6 Los Dansadores. Mariano Camprubí and Dolores Serral.
7 Lise Noblet and Mme Alexis Dupont dancing *El Jaleo de Jerez*.
8 Nathalie Fitzjames.
9 Fanny Elssler in *La Chatte métamorphosée en femme*.
10 Louise Fitzjames as the Abbess in *Robert le Diable*.
11 Louise Fitzjames caricatured as an asparagus in a Ballet of Vegetables.
12 Fanny Elssler in *La Volière*.
13 Fanny Elssler dancing the *Cachucha* in *Le Diable boiteux*.
14 Fanny Elssler in *La Sylphide*.
15 Fanny Elssler dancing the *Cracovienne* in *La Gipsy*.
16 Therese Elssler as Mab in *La Gipsy*. Statuette by J.-J. Elshoecht.
17 The bayadere Amany. Statuette by Jean-Auguste Barre.
18 The Bayaderes in *The Malapou*.
19 Fanny Elssler dancing the *Tarentella* in *La Tarentule*.
20 Albertine and Louis Bretin in *Les Pages de duc de Vendôme*.
21 Lucile Grahn in *La Sylphide*.
22 Augusta Maywood.
23 *Giselle*, Act I.
24 Carlotta Grisi in *Giselle*, Act II.
25 The dance of the three-legged man in *La Jolie Fille de Gand*.
26 The villagers' dance in Act III, Scene III of *La Jolie Fille de Gand*.
27 The opening scene of *La Péri*.
28 Lucien Petipa and Carlotta Grisi in *La Péri*.

BETWEEN PAGES 166 AND 167
29 Caroline Fjeldsted dancing the *Redowa*.
30 Clara Webster.
31 Henri Desplaces, Adèle Dumilâtre and Lucien Petipa in *Lady Henriette*.

32 Lola Montez: hissed at the Porte-Saint-Martin and the Opéra, and horsewhipping a Prussian gendarme.
33 Professor Risley and his two Sons.
34 Marie Taglioni, as the dying Sylphide.
35 Marie Taglioni dancing the *pas de l'ombre* during her farewell season in Paris.
36 Marie Taglioni and Prosper-Nicolas Levasseur in *Le Dieu et la bayadeere*.
37 Tatiana Smirnova.
38 Elena Andreyanova.
39 Adèle Dumilâtre in *Eucharis*.
40 Adeline Plunkett in *La Péri*.
41 The Danseuses Viennoises in the *pas des moissonneurs*.
42 *Paquita*, Act II, with Lucien Petipa, Carlotta Grisi and Georges Elie.
43 Fanny Cerrito dancing the *pas de chibouk* in *Lalla Rookh*, with Arthur Saint-Léon.
44 Sofia Fuoco and Lucien Petipa in *Betty*.
45 *Ozaï*, Act II, Scene I, with Adeline Plunkett, Georges Elie and Henri Desplaces.
46 Arthur Saint-Léon and Fanny Cerrito in *La Fille de marbre*, Act I.
47 Episodes from *Nisida*.
48 Carlotta Grisi and Lucien Petipa in *Griseldis*.
49 Fanny Cerrito and Arthur Saint-Léon in *La Vivandière*.
50 Arthur Saint-Léon and Fanny Cerrito in *Le Violon du Diable*.
51 Jules Perrot in *Zingaro*.
52 *La Filleule des fées*, Act II, with Carlotta Grisi and Jules Perrot.
53 Fanny Cerrito dancing the *Sicilienne* in *Stella*.
54 Fanny Cerrito in *Pâquerette*.
55 Esther Aussandon.
56 Olimpia Priora.
57 Adeline Plunkett in *Vert-Vert*.
58 Olimpia Priora in *Vert-Vert*.

BETWEEN PAGES 262 AND 263
59 Petra Cámara.
60 Arthur Saint-Léon and Marie Guy-Stéphan in *Le Lutin de la vallée*.
61 Josefa Vargas dancing the *Madrileña*.
62 Manuela Perea, la Nena, and her company.
63 *Orfa*, Act I, Cerrito's entrance.
64 *Aelia et Mysis*, Act II.
65 Arthur Saint-Léon in *Le Danseur du roi*.
66 Carolina Rosati in *Jovita*.
67 Louis Mérante and Fanny Cerrito in the *valse magnétique* in *Gemma*.

68 Caterina Beretta as Autumn in the ballet in *Les Vêpres siciliennes.*
69 Amalia Ferraris.
70 *Sacountala,* Act I. The *pas de deux* by Amalia Ferraris and Lucien Petipa.
71 *Sacountal,* Act II.
72 Théophile Gautier demonstrating steps for *Sacountala* to Amalia Ferraris.
73 Amalia Ferraris and Lucien Petipa in *Sacountala.*
74 Théophile Gautier and Alexandre Dumas *fils* in St. Petersburg.
75 Playbill for the St Petersburg production of *Eoline.*
76 Emma Livry in *Le Papillon.* Statuette by Jean-Auguste Barre.
77 Martha Muravieva in *Néméa.*
78 Louis Mérante in *Néméa.*
79 Eugénie Fiocre in *Néméa.*
80 Léontine Beaugrand in *Le Papillon.*
81 Eugénie Fiocre in *La Muette de Portici.*
82 Adèle Grantzow.
83 Caricatures by Marcelin of *Le Roi d'Yvetot.*
84 Guglielmina Salvioni in *La Source.*
85 Louis Mérante in *La Source.*
86 *La Source,* Act III, Scene II, with Salvioni, Mérante and Eugénie Fiocre.
87 The roller-skating ballet in the 1869 revival of *Le Prophète,* led by Elliot and Frederika.
88 Giuseppina Bozzacchi, the first Swanilda in *Coppélia.*

PROVENANCE OF THE ILLUSTRATIONS

Bibliothèque de l'Opéra, Paris, Nos. 1, 2, 3, 7, 14, 20, 21, 31, 36, 37, 50, 52, 54, 56, 60, 62, 68, 71, 77–80, 85.
Bibliothèque Nationale, Paris, Nos. 11, 81.
British Library, Nos. 35, 42, 47, 48, 55, 57–59, 63, 68, 70, 72–74, 83, 86, 87.
Harvard Theatre Collection, No. 4, 8, 33.
Leningrad Theatre Museum, No. 75.
Musée des Arts Décoratifs, Paris, Nos. 10.
Soviet Archives, No. 82.
Theatre Museum, Copenhagen, No. 29.
Theatre Museum, London, Nos. 15, 19, 30, 34, 43, 61.
Collection of the Author, Nos. 5, 6, 12, 13, 18, 23, 25, 26, 41, 44, 45, 49, 51, 64, 76, 84.
Collection of Edwin Binney 3rd, Nos. 9, 17, 24, 27, 28, 32, 38–40, 46, 53, 65–67.
Collection of Parmenia Migel Ekstrom, No. 22.

Collection of Leo Kersley, No. 69.
Collection of Jean-Louis Tamvaco, No. 16.

PHOTOGRAPHIC CREDITS

Photographic Service, Bibliothèque Nationale, Nos. 11, 50.
Service Photographique, Musée des Arts Décoratifs, No. 10.
Sylvia Chaban, Brunoy, No. 60.
Max Erlanger de Rosen, Paris, Nos. 14, 20, 37.
Felix Fonteyn, London, No. 76.
John R. Freeman & Co (Photographers) ltd, London, Nos. 34, 35, 42, 43, 61, 73.
Bent Mann, Rødovre, Denmark, No. 29.
Godfrey New Photographics Ltd, Sidcup, Kent, Nos. 3, 5, 6, 12, 13, 15, 18, 19, 22, 23, 25, 26, 41, 49, 51, 71.
Pic, Paris, Nos. 7, 21, 36.
M. Rigal, Paris, No. 85.
Rodney Whitelaw, Orleans, Mass., Nos. 9, 17, 24, 27, 28, 32, 38–40, 46, 53, 65–67.

Translator's Note

In order to keep the length of this book within reasonable limits, this selection of Gautier's writings on the dance has had to be limited to the reviews of theatrical performances that he wrote for the press. For that reason the articles on *Le Diable boiteux* and *Giselle*, which he contributed to the album, *Les Beautés de l'Opéra*, and his biographical essay on Carlotta Grisi in the *Galerie des Artistes Dramatiques* have been deliberately excluded. Again for reasons of space, emphasis has been laid on his ballet reviews, only the more important of his writings on ethnic dancers being included—notably his two important articles on the Bayaderes and a small selection of his articles on Spanish dancers, all of which are relevant to his attitude towards the element of *couleur locale* that played an important part in Romantic ballet, as it did in Romantic art in general.

The texts used for the translation have been those of the newspaper articles themselves. During Gautier's lifetime a number of these, covering the period from 1837 to 1849, were reprinted in a six-volume collection of his dramatic criticism entitled *Histoire de l'art dramatique en France depuis vingt-cinq ans*, and a few reappeared in other compilations, references being given in this book at the end of the relevant item, following the title and issue of the newspaper in which it first appeared. The reference number given in the Vicomte Spoelberch de Lovenjoul's definitive *Histoire des oeuvres de Théophile Gautier* (Paris, 1877) is also to be found there, preceded by the letter L.

The task of annotating these reviews has at times been complicated by the fact that they were written at short notice and to a deadline, having to be delivered to the newspaper in time to be published in the Monday issue. Tied to this schedule, Gautier did not always have sufficient time to check his references, and there seem to have been occasions when the printers misread his manuscript and the error went undetected when the proofs were corrected. The interested reader will find several instances of this in the notes. In the translated text I have taken the liberty of correcting obvious errors and amending the spelling of names where necessary.

For further reading the following works are recommended: Joanna Richardson's standard biography, *Théophile Gautier, His Life and Times* (London, 1958); the chapters on Gautier in Andrei Levinson's *Meister des Ballets* (Potsdam, 1923), Deirdre Priddin's *The Art of the Dance in French Literature* (London, 1952), and Margit Weinholz's *Französische Tanzkritik im 19. Jahrhundert als Spiegel ästhetischer Bewusstseinsbildung* (Bern and Frankfurt/M., 1974); and Edwin Binney 3rd's comprehensive work, *Les Ballets de Théophile Gautier* (Paris, 1965). A detailed account of the ballet of the period will be found in my chronicles of the ballet at the Paris Opéra, *The Romantic Ballet in Paris* (2nd. ed., London and New York, 1980) and *The Ballet of the Second Empire* (2nd. ed., London and Middletown, 1974), which between them span the years from 1820 to 1870.

Finally, I must record my gratitude to many generous friends and colleagues who have taken trouble to help me in various ways. To David Leonard, my publisher, I owe the initial suggestion that launched me on this project. My friend and colleague, Edwin Binney 3rd, read the work in draft, making many suggestions that have improved the text, and has been invaluable in advising on illustrations and allowing me to reproduce items from his vast collection of ballet prints. My cousin, Odile Tweedie, elucidated a number of points in the translation, and I am indebted to Michael Carey for help in locating classical references. Specialists in various fields have generously responded to my queries: in particular Pamela Woof and Claire Lamont of the University of Newcastle, Professor Norma Rinsler and Dr. Michael Heath of King's College, London, Miss C. R. Pickett and Mrs Meera Dawson of the India Office Library and Records, and Dr. A. P. McGowan of the National Maritime Museum. My thanks are due too to the staff of the various libraries which I have haunted in my endeavour to elucidate every allusion that I considered worthy of a footnote: in London, the British Library and the London Library, and in Paris, the Bibliothèque Nationale, the Bibliothèque de l'Opéra and the Musée de la Conservation du Louvre. Finally, I have to acknowledge my debt to my wife, who has borne my affair with a word processor with great understanding and endured many hours listening to me reading the text.

Holland Park,
London.   IVOR GUEST

Introduction

B orn in 1811 at Tarbes, within sight of the Pyrenees and only a few miles
from the Spanish border, Théophile Gautier remained all his life a
southerner at heart: a Frenchman first and foremost, but irresistibly drawn
towards Spain, the mysterious land beyond the mountains with its savage
passions and exotic culture tinged with harsh undertones resulting from its
long subjection to the Moors and the proximity of Africa. His parents settled
in Paris when he was a child, and that city became his centre, but whenever
circumstances allowed he would escape abroad—not only to Spain, his most
frequent destination, but to Russia, North Africa and the Near East too—
becoming in the process unusually well travelled for a man of his time.

He presents himself, therefore, as a Parisian, educated and plying his
writer's craft in that city, earning his livelihood as a prolific journalist but
carving his reputation as one of the most influential poets and original
novelists of his age. Such a diversity of literary activity not unsurprisingly
produced its strains, and there were times when the daily grind of his
profession became almost unbearably irksome, but he was a compulsive
writer—and indeed a natural journalist, producing his copy rapidly and with
hardly a correction—and as a commentator on art, travel and the theatre,
unsurpassed. His press coverage of the annual Salon filled many newspaper
columns over a period of several decades; the accounts of his travels, many of
them later collected into books—his *Voyage en Espagne*[1] (1843) and his
Voyage en Russia (1865) remain classics to this day—reveal the fascination
that other cultures exerted over his imagination and his urge to soak himself
in their unfamiliar, exotic atmosphere, or their *couleur locale*, to use one of
the Romantics' favourite phrases; and his theatrical reviews convey an
enthusiasm and an immediacy that enable a reader of a century later to
recapture some of the ephemeral magic of those hours passed in gas-lit
theatre or opera house.

His reputation as a writer was by no means confined to his skill in reporting
events. Growing up in the intoxicating atmosphere of Romanticism, he
absorbed its philosophy with all the fervour of a champion. As a young man
he joined the band of writers and artists who basked in the glory of Victor

---

[1] Originally published in the form of articles in *La Presse* and other periodicals, and
later collected in book form under the title *Tra los montes*. The definitive title of
Voyage en Espagne dates from the second edition of 1845.

Hugo, and played a conspicuous part, clad in his pink waistcoat that became part of the Romantic legend, in the celebrated fracas at the Théâtre Français during performances of Hugo's drama, *Hernani*, which breached all the rules and conventions of classical tragedy. The famous pink waistcoat reveals him in the limelight at a crucial moment in literary history, but his contribution to the literature of his time was far more profound, being wrought in the seclusion of his study, in the creative writings on which his enduring fame is based, in his sensitive and beautifully crafted verse and in the vivid and elegant prose of his novels, and in the principle of art for art's sake, that beauty is supreme in itself, which he propounded in the preface to his novel, *Mademoiselle de Maupin*.

In the pages that follow the focus is narrowed to Gautier as theatre critic, and, more precisely, as an observer of the ballet. His writings on the dance are for the most part scattered among the succession of newspapers for which he wrote unceasingly from his twenties until the end of his life. The earliest—a notice of Taglioni's appearance before King Louis-Philippe at Compiègne— appeared in *La Presse* in October 1836, but this was no more than a news item with comment, for he had certainly not been present at the performance. His next two dance notices appeared anonymously in the short-lived paper *La Charte de 1830*, but although more important, they were still no more than occasional pieces. His real début as a regular critic occurred in July 1837, when he wrote his first review as dramatic critic of *La Presse*, describing *Les Mohicans*, a wretched ballet that survived for only four performances. For several months his reviews appeared above the initials G.G., which concealed a collaboration—or rather, a sharing of the post—with his friend and former school-mate, Gérard de Nerval. Thanks to the diligence of Gautier's bibliographer, Spoelberch de Lovenjoul, it is known with some certainty which articles each collaborator contributed, the "G.G." articles reproduced in this selection (Nos. 4 to 7, 9, 10 and 12) being those that Gautier implicitly claimed as his own by allowing them to be included in his collected dramatic criticism, published under the title, *Histoire de l'art dramatique en France depuis vingt-cinq ans*. In June 1838 Nerval withdrew from this arrangement, and thereafter Gautier's contributions appeared above his own name. Except for periods when he was away on his travels he was to review theatrical events of all kinds in *La Presse* until the end of March 1855. He then accepted the post of dramatic critic of the government paper, *Le Moniteur Universel*, but his scope there was at first more limited, since opera and ballet fell into the preserve of the regular music critic, Pier Angelo Fiorentino. Consequently there was a gap of several years in Gautier's ballet criticism, which with very few exceptions was resumed only after Fiorentino's death in 1864. In the beginning of 1869 Gautier transferred to the new government paper, *Le Journal Officiel*, and from 1871 his notices appeared in another new paper, the *Gazette de Paris*. His last ballet review appeared on

October 23rd, 1871. He died in his house in Neuilly-sur-Seine a year later to the day.

Gautier's view of ballet was that of a poet and an artist, supported by his accumulating experience as an author of ballet scenarios, of which no less than six were to see fruition on the stage—*Giselle* (1841), *La Péri* (1843), *Pâquerette* (1851), *Gemma* (1854) and *Sacountala* (1858) at the Opéra, and *Yanko le bandit* (1858) at the Porte-Saint-Martin.² This gave him an insight into the craft of constructing a ballet that was unique among the critics of his day. In someone else such an involvement might have implanted an exaggerated idea of the scenarist's importance, but with engaging modesty Gautier maintained that the scenarist was the servant of the choreographer, his task nothing more than to produce the canvas on which the latter, to whom all the credit would be due, creates his three-dimensional moving picture.

At that time it was common for ballets to be produced to sometimes quite complex dramatic scenarios that, if dialogue were added, could equally well serve for a melodrama or an *opéra comique*, but Gautier recognised the dangers in this trend, likening such *ballets d'action*, with their overladen themes, to dramas played by deaf-mutes. In his own scenarios he endeavoured to follow a less pedestrian path, bringing into play his vision as a poet and devising situations that would develop naturally within a framework of dance and movement. This was no easy task, for it involved an approach that transcended the superficial story-telling of pantomime and spoke to subtler emotions through the plastic form of the dance created by the choreographer.

The notion of a plotless, abstract ballet was of course for a much later generation to discover and exploit, but Gautier's vision at least foresaw, even if darkly, the direction that ballet would take in the next century. He had the perception to realise that the obstacle that prevented ballet from realising its full potential was the attitude of the Paris public, which was "too rational to admit that any pleasure could be derived from the rhythm and construction of the movements apart from the interpolated *pas*" and "not artistic enough to be satisfied with the plastic content of . . . the dance". Demands for "a clear-cut meaning, a theme, a logical dramatic development, a moral, a well defined ending", he plainly saw, were leading ballet astray. *La Sylphide*, the work which had initiated the Romanticisation of ballet when produced at the Opéra in 1832, was for him the ideal model with its simple and easily

---

² In addition to these Gautier wrote or sketched out six other ballet scenarios: *Cléopâtre* (1838), for which X. Boisselot wrote the music and Elssler was envisaged for the leading rôle; *La Statue amoureuse* (c. 1853); a ballet written for the English Opera House, London (1848), which Binney suggests may have been based on Goethe's *Wilhelm Meister*, and was to have had music by Berlioz; *Le Mariage à Séville* (before 1870); *Le Preneur des rats de Hameln* (1870–71), for which Massenet was to write the music, but which was not produced on account of Mérante's opposition; and *La Fille du roi des Aulnes* (1870–71), also offered to Massenet, who was reluctant to risk comparison with Schubert.

understood plot developing out of "a moving and poetic conception", and he adopted a similar formula in *Giselle*. For him the very essence of ballet was its inherent beauty, conveyed in the plastic forms produced by the dancers in movement and repose. His ideal ballet, he once wrote, would have the quality of a dream, a series of chimeras dissolving into one another, and it would be created, not by a dramatist, who would tend to produce a play without words, but by a conjunction of poet and artist, the first conceiving the idea and the latter transcribing it into a series of outline sketches, depicting moments in the action. To illustrate what he had in mind, he drew attention more than once to the line drawings of Moritz Retzsch illustrating moments in Goethe's *Faust*.

While Gautier seems never to have envisaged the choreographer being his own scenarist, he always saw him as the dominant author of a ballet, "poet, musician and drill sergeant combined". He was familiar with Stendhal's eulogy of Salvatore Viganò, the celebrated Italian choreographer of the early years of the century who prepared his ballets "like an Athenian sculptor trying out poses on his models", striving meticulously to produce a homogeneous stage picture, but he always regarded the choreographer's task as that of giving plastic form to the conception provided by the poet–artist collaboration. In Gautier's view this underlying conception was the essential ingredient that transformed a mere collection of dances into a ballet. In his later years he became concerned that this concept of ballet was being ignored, and was moved to protest, asking, "What would the immortal Viganò . . . have said of those modern ballets which are no more than a succession of *pas* that lead out of nothing and have no connection with one another?" But strangely, while recognising Viganò to have been a powerful creative artist, Gautier did not press for a tighter collaboration between scenarist and choreographer, nor apparently did he himself involve the choreographers who worked to his own scenarios in the original conception of the work. On a more technical level, Gautier never attempted any serious analysis of the choreography in his reviews. Almost certainly this was due to his lack of technical knowledge, for while he had made a serious study of painting as a young man and was himself a talented artist, his knowledge of dance technique was not based on direct personal experience. Ballet dancing in his day was very much an exercise practised by professionals, and it was unheard of for a critic or indeed anyone not following a stage career to participate in a ballet class. His knowledge was therefore gleaned piece-meal through his personal contacts with dancers. His main source must have been Carlotta Grisi, from whom he undoubtedly learnt a great deal about the dancer's craft and the ways of the world of ballet. His involvement in a number of productions as scenarist would have added to his specialised knowledge, giving him a vocabulary that enabled him to add an impressive, if somewhat superficial, gloss to his descriptions of dancers in action, although not enough to enable him to attempt a serious analysis of the choreographic process.

Choreographers consequently received little attention in his reviews, and on some occasions none at all. In his lengthy review of *Giselle*, for example, Coralli was mentioned only in passing and Perrot completely ignored, notwithstanding that Gautier was closely concerned not only with the production, but also with its gestation, having witnessed the ballet taking shape in Adolphe Adam's *salon*, when Perrot was moulding the rôle of Giselle on Carlotta. Gautier's attitude towards Perrot, whom he certainly held in very high regard, is revealing. While praising his ability to design dances as skilfully as he once could dance them, he never gave him specific credit for his genius in producing ballets that were theatrical spectacles resting on their own merits. Another prominent choreographer of the time, Joseph Mazilier, whose ballets were renowned for their strong dramatic content, did not rate a mention in the reviews of *La Gipsy* and *Paquita*, two of his most successful works, and it was only when describing a later ballet, *La Fonti*, that Gautier acknowledged his skill at producing mimed action. Perhaps the greatest compliment to a choreographer to be found in Gautier's writings is his tribute to Lucien Petipa for the originality and freshness he brought to his production of *Sacountala* and his "feeling for plastic form in groups and [his] ease in handling masses".

Consistently with his attitude towards art in general, Gautier was obsessed with the idea of beauty in his outlook on ballet, and for him ballet's main attraction was the grace in the motion of the dancers' bodies and the development of lines that were a delight to the eye. Ballet he saw as "silent rhythm, music made visible", and dancing as a "pagan, mysterious and sensual" art, a glorification of woman idealised in the ballerina. An unashamed admirer of beautiful women, he was provided with a succession of superb models for his vivid pen. It was his good fortune to live in a period wonderfully rich in ballerinas. His earliest impressions centred on the two most brilliant dancers of the century who at that time were contending for supremacy at the Paris Opéra, the ethereal Taglioni and the warm and womanly Elssler, symbols respectively of poetry and passion, whom he distinguished in a memorable passage as the Christian dancer and the pagan. Then followed another ballerina who seemed to combine the gifts of her illustrious predecessors—Carlotta Grisi, to Gautier "the incomparable Giselle . . . with the golden hair and violet eyes" who became his muse and life-long friend. For her he wrote the scenarios of *Giselle* and *La Péri*, true poems in dance that earned her immortality in ballet's gallery of fame. The 1830s and 1840s were a golden age of the dance which Gautier chronicled in colourful detail, but his ballet-going days were far from over when Carlotta retired. Other ballerinas, each one charming in her individual way, succeeded her; the ebullient Fanny Cerrito, whom he first saw in London in the mammoth Indian ballet, *Lalla Rookh*; Amalia Ferraris, who had initially come to his notice in Naples, curiously supported by a corps de ballet in absurd green petticoats imposed by royal command, whom he was later to see many times in Paris, and who was guest star in St. Petersburg when he was in Russia in 1858; the fragile Emma Livry, white hope of French ballet, so cruelly cut down in the flower of her youth; the gentle Adèle Grantzow; and finally the two ballerinas he saw in *Coppélia*, their performances separated by the trauma of the Franco-Prussian War and the Commune—first, the touching, ill-fated Giuseppina Bozzacchi and then her bird-like successor, Léontine Beaugrand.

Of course such a very human man had his favourites, chief of whom was Carlotta Grisi, into whose family he was admitted as a sort of brother-in-law, for he lived for many years with her sister Ernesta, who bore him two daughters. In his later years his greatest pleasure was to visit his adored Giselle on her Swiss estate as a cherished friend and faithful chevalier, and Carlotta's name was to be the very last word formed by his dying fingers.

An earlier passion, less personal but more keenly felt by a younger heart, was for Fanny Elssler, who seems to have become in his imagination a reflection of the heroine in his novel *Mademoiselle de Maupin*, a character who first makes her appearance as a young man of great beauty, arousing strange emotions in the story-teller, and later turns out to be a woman. It was this dual attraction that Gautier imagined to illustrate his theory that beauty is to be admired for itself alone. A few years later he found, in Fanny Elssler, a dancer who personified this ideal as no other ballerina ever would, perceiving in her that same ambivalent sexuality that was the secret of the attraction of Madaleine de Maupin. In one of his ballet reviews he commented on her somewhat undeveloped hips and unpronounced bosom and discerned the mysterious appeal of the hermaphrodite of antiquity—superficially, a surprising judgment when it is recalled how deeply Fanny Elssler stirred masculine passions, in a way that her great contemporary, Taglioni, never did, but on reflection, surely a logical example of his perception of beauty as a quality transcending sexual considerations and in no way inconsistent with his admiration of Elssler as a woman. Gautier embarked on his career as a theatre critic at the very moment that Elssler was delighting Paris with her ardent and sensual rendering of the *Cachucha*. The rudiments of this dance she had learnt from Dolores Serral, a member of a group of Spanish dancers who had recently introduced Paris to the *escuela bolera*, the classical style of Spanish dancing then at the height of its development. A few years later, in 1840, Gautier paid his first visit to Spain. There, in Granada and Seville, he saw Spanish dancing in its natural surroundings, and ever afterwards he was a self-confessed *aficionada*, letting no opportunity slip of writing a vivid word-portrait of any Spanish dancer who appeared on the Paris stage. Such renewals of contact were always acutely felt experiences, and whenever the sound of castanets rang in his ears he had only to close his eyes to imagine himself back in his beloved Spain.

His interest, not only in Spanish dancing but in ethnic dance generally, was a reflection of the Romantic yearning for *couleur locale*, and one of the greatest experiences of his life, to which he reverted many times in his writings, was when his path crossed that of a small company of Indian dancers, the Bayaderes, who visited Paris in the summer of 1838. He was among the privileged few who were admitted to a private display of their art in the house they had taken in the Allée des Veuves, and despite language difficulties, he struck up a touchingly paternal relationship with the principal dancer, Amany, a girl of great beauty. It was to Amany and the Bayaderes that he looked back, twenty years later, when he was adapting Kalidasa's *Sacountala* for a ballet.

Fanny Elssler, Carlotta Grisi, Fanny Cerrito, Amalia Ferraris; Dolores Serral, Josefa Vargas, Petra Cámara, La Nena, Amany—it is very noticeably a gallery of beautiful women that is celebrated in Gautier's reviews. As for his attitude towards men in ballet, that was very typical of his time, being coloured by a certain amount of prejudice and conditioned also by the low standard of male dancing on the Paris stage. In his early reviews he openly admitted this prejudice—for example, in welcoming the absence of male dancing in *La Volière* (1838) he declared his revulsion at the sight of "a man showing off his red neck, great muscular arms, and parish beadle legs, and the whole of his heavy frame shuddering with leaps and pirouettes." A month later he qualified this as applying to *danseurs nobles*, allowing that strength was the only grace that a man might be permitted to possesss and citing Mazurier as a performer whom he could have accepted and enjoyed watching. Whether he saw that great comic dancer and acrobat, who died when Gautier was sixteen, we do not know for certain, but Gautier certainly saw Jules Perrot, who first made his name by imitating Mazurier and then went on to become the star male dancer of the Opéra. Perrot's years at the Opéra were already over when Gautier began reviewing, but seeing him at the Renaissance with Carlotta Grisi in 1840, he was delighted to observe that he had "nothing of that feeble and inane manner that usually makes male dancers so unbearable". Some years later he praised him as "the last man to have danced".

However, Gautier was not so blinkered as to be incapable of admiring talent when he saw it, and he always found pleasure when watching Lucien Petipa. When he first saw him in *La Tarentule* (1840), he noted that he was "not too repulsive for a man", but this grudging admission was soon transformed into a genuine admiration of the man whom he was to call "the tenor of the dance" and who created the leading rôles in most of his own ballets, Albrecht in *Giselle*, Achmet in *La Péri*, Massimo in *Gemma* and Douchmanta in *Sacountala*. Gautier greatly admired his warm, expressive miming, his "ardent and chivalrous grace" and his modesty of manner. Another male dancer who made a favourable impression on Gautier was Arthur Saint-Léon, "the india-rubber man", possessor of a spectacular technique. But dancers of the calibre of Perrot, Petipa and Saint-Léon, able to impose themselves on a disinterested public, were rare at a time when opportunities for male dancers were few and far between. Louis Mérante, who performed worthy services as principal male dancer of the Opéra thoughout the Second Empire, seldom drew a word of praise from Gautier, who could still accurately report in 1856: "Today the public no longer takes notice of men in ballet".

Were it possible to fly back in time to the Paris of Louis-Philippe and Napoleon III, we could not ask for a better guide to the ballet than Théophile Gautier, the only major literary figure of his period to write both for and on the dance and be proud of it. Gautier loved the dance for its own sake, he had seen the art of ballet blossom under the influence of Romanticism, he had personal contacts in the profession, he knew the musicians, writers and artists who collaborated in the productions, and he himself was an experienced hand at writing scenarios and held definite and original ideas about the potential of ballet as an art. No other critic of his time had such a wide span of qualifications, nor the poet's perception and the gift of verbal imagery that enabled him to convey the magic of a performance on the printed page. So let us, in our imagination, settle ourselves comfortably by his side in the stalls of the long-vanished opera house in the Rue le Peletier, to enjoy his company and indulge in the privilege of sharing his vision of a rich lifetime of ballet and dance.

1

Marie Taglioni dances at the Palace of Compiègne

Palais de Compiègne,
September 29th, 1836.

B eing in the mood for amusement, His Majesty summoned Mlle Taglioni, the chaste and divine dancer whom you well know, to Compiègne. Happy the king who can call on Mlle Taglioni[1] to dance for him alone, when and where he pleases! It makes one envy him for being king and understand how disagreeable it is not to have been elected oneself.[2] Taglioni danced, or rather hovered awhile in the air, with such languid abandon, with such sensually yearning poses, such artistry and naturalness, and such simplicity and decency that the delighted king expressed his satisfaction by presenting her with a magnificent sapphire brooch, surrounded by brilliants of great price, that did honour both to the hand that bestowed it and to the hand that received it.

This revival of ancient royal customs gives us special pleasure, for we do not hold the commonly accepted belief that a constitutional monarch should be no more than the first servant of our kingdom.

What is more, this favour could not have been better placed, for Taglioni is one of the greatest poets of our time. She has a wonderful understanding of

---

[1] Marie Taglioni (1804–84) had been promoted principal ballerina of the Opéra by Dr. Véron when he became Director in 1831, and established her supremacy by creating La Sylphide in 1832. At this special performance at Compiègne Taglioni danced a pas de deux with Mme Alexis Dupont and appeared in extracts from Le Dieu et la bayadère.

[2] Louis-Philippe had become King of the French as a consequence of the Revolution of 1830. He had been elected as Lieutenant-General of the Kingdom before accepting the throne. The Palace of Compiègne, situated about fifty miles north-east of Paris, had been built during the reign of Louis XV, and remained one of the sovereign's residences until the end of the Second Empire.

the ideal side of her art, and it can be said of her, as was said of Garat,[3] that she is not just a dancer, but the dance itself. The name of the muse Terpsichore will inevitably fall into oblivion and be replaced by that of Taglioni. She is as great a genius, using the word to mean a faculty carried to its furthermost limits, as Lord Byron. Her *ronds de jambe* and the undulations of her arms are, by themselves, the equal of a long poem.[4]

La Presse, October 13th, 1836.
L:147.

---

[3] The allusion is to Pierre-Jean Garat (1764–1823), one of the finest singers of his time. When, at the beginning of his career, he was commanded to sing before Marie-Antoinette at Versailles, the Comte d'Artois (later King Charles X) made the comment that he needed further study. To this the composer Salieri, who had been accompanying Garat, retorted: "He study music, sire! But he is music itself."

[4] *Un sonnet sans défauts vaut seul un long poème.* (Boileau, *Art poétique*, chant II, line 94.)

2

2

The Statuette of Fanny Elssler

One of the most successful attempts to have been made in miniature sculpture has been inspired by the loveliest of all the ballerinas who have ever trodden the boards of the Opéra. To console us for the absence of Fanny Elssler, who has very nearly died of a serious illness,[1] a young sculptor, who, as can be seen, is full of intelligence and ingenuity, has had the idea of representing this ravishing creature as she appears in *Le Diable boiteux*.[2] M. Barre[3] went to the Opéra for relaxation, not for inspiration; for pleasure, not for ideas; and was overwhelmed by such grace! As an artist he is better qualified than anyone else to appreciate the harmonies of the figure, the contours of arm and shoulder, the distinguishing shape of the head, the lines of the neck, the oval form of the face, all the qualities of beauty and charm that transform the dancer into a woman. Mlle Elssler was dancing the famous *Cachucha*, a difficult test of taste and fascination that her intelligence enables her to surmount so successfully. M. Barre has taken as his model one of those attitudes in which, with arms curved, head tilted and leg stretched, Mlle Elssler is playing her castanets and seems to be regarding the spectator through a circle formed by her arm. He has succeeded beyond measure in conveying all the provocative decorum that resides in the bend of the body, all

---

[1] Fanny Elssler (1810–84) was the antithesis of Taglioni, projecting herself through her style of dancing as a woman of earthly passions in contrast to the ethereal style of Taglioni. She made her début at the Opéra in *La Tempête* in 1834, and in 1836 created a sensation with her *Cachucha*, a stylised Spanish dance inserted in the ballet *Le Diable boiteux*. Towards the end of October she caught a chill when her carriage broke down while conveying her from Bordeaux to Paris. Complications set in, her life was despaired of for a few days, and it was six months before she appeared again on the stage.

[2] Ballet-pantomime in 2 acts and 3 scenes, sc. Burat de Gurgy, chor. J. Coralli, mus. C. Gide, f.p. June 1st, 1836.

[3] Jean-Auguste Barre (1811–96), frequently mentioned by Gautier, is now remembered for his statuettes of Taglioni, Fanny Elssler, the bayadère Amany, and Emma Livry, but he also portrayed in the same manner the Duc d'Orléans and the Prince de Joinville, sons of King Louis-Philippe, and sculpted a fine bust of Napoleon III.

the suppleness of the shoulder movements, the ardour in the legs, the soft curves of the neck. So much for the inspiration! As for the statuette itself and its detailed execution, it is quite beyond reproach and of excellent workmanship. The accessories are ingeniously done, the lace and the effect of satin being admirably rendered, and the head, which is treated with remarkable delicacy, reproducing the delightful shape of the original and the arrangement and styling of the hair of which Mlle Elssler alone seems to have the secret. It was an excellent idea of M. Barre to let everyone share the good fortune of viewing this charming portrait, which is being exhibited in their shops by the two Paris dealers who are in the forefront in following the latest trends in novelties, M. Rittner, the print dealer of 25 Boulevard Montmartre, and M. Susse of 31 Place de la Bourse.

La Charte de 1830, November 28th, 1836.[4]

[4] This article was unsigned. It was identified as being by Gautier by Jean Richer (*Bulletin des Bibliophiles*, 1976, I).

3

The Spanish Dancers

Unless you are a fossilised dugong[1] or manatee buried deep below the tertiary layer, you have undoubtedly seen the Spanish dancers—that charming couple, Camprubí and Dolores Serral.[2] If you made the dreadful mistake of not booking a stall or a box at the Variétés when those two sparkling butterflies were brushing the tips of their wings in a burst of sequins on the dusty boards that had nearly given way beneath the heavy clogs of that great beast Odry, the Antinoüs of the cooks,[3] you can only beat your breast with a rock like St Jerome as a sign of repentance, and hang yourself firmly on a strong nail with a noose around your neck to teach your head the weight of your feet, for you have missed one of the most ravishing and poetic performances in the world.

You know what a hideous sight an ordinary male dancer is—a great awkward creature with a long red neck swelling with muscles, a stereotyped grin that is as irremovable as a judge, expressionless eyes like the enamel eyes of mechanical dolls, the thick calves of a parish beadle, arms like carriage shafts, and then the great angular movements with elbows and feet placed at

---

[1] The text, both in *La Presse* and in *Fusains et eaux-fortes*, gives "drigoug", clearly a printer's misreading of the manuscript.

[2] Dolores Serral and Mariano Camprubí were two of the four Spanish dancers who had made a sensational appearance at the Opéra balls in 1834. In 1837 they were again engaged for the balls, and appeared also at the Théâtre du Palais-Royal and the Théâtre des Variétés, where they enchanted the Parisians from February until early in May.

[3] Charles Odry (1781–1853) had recently given a hilarious parody of the *Cachucha* in *Les Saltimbanques* at the Théâtre des Variétés (f.p. January 25th, 1838). One of the most popular low comedians on the Paris stage, he was celebrated for his nonsensical repartee. His ugliness was an asset, as the ironical epithet Gautier here uses bears witness. The name of Antinoüs, the Bithynian slave who became the favourite of the Emperor Hadrian, has become synonymous with a man of surpassing beauty.

right angles, the airs of Adonis and Apollo, and the *ronds de jambe*, pirouettes and other gestures of mechanical puppets. Nothing could be more
dreadful, and I really cannot resist throwing a shower of apples and hard
boiled eggs instead of the rain of flowers customary at the Opéra. The
dancing of Señor Camprubí is as pleasing a sight as that of a woman, yet he
preserves a heroic and gentlemanly expression in his poses that has nothing in
common with the foolish affectation of French male dancers.

And ballet girls, what a sad lot are they! There is enough ugliness, misery
and poverty of form to move you to pity. They are as thin as lizards that have
been fasting for six months, and when you inspect them without your opera
glasses, their bosoms, which are hardly perceptible amid the fragile swirling
of their arms and legs, make them look like spiders disturbed in their webs
and madly scuttling away. I do not know if you have taken it into your head
to make a special study of a ballet girl's neck and chest. When lit from below,
the clavicles form a ghastly transverse projection, attached to which, like the
strings on the bridge of a violin, are four or five tendons stretched to breaking
point on which Paganini could easily have played a concerto. The larynx,
given greater prominence by the lack of flesh, forms a protuberance resembling the lump in a turkey's neck that stands out like a nut that has been
swallowed whole, and one looks in vain for the slightest rise in the flat plain
of their charms that suggests the presence of what poets in their jargon call
"the twin hillocks", "the two little snowy mountains" and other fine and
vaguely anacreontic expressions. As for lower limbs, they are so absolutely
disproportionate in their thickness that it seems as if the upper part of a
consumptive girl's body has been sawn off and attached to the legs of a
Grenadier guardsman.

Dolores has a plump bosom, rounded arms, slender legs and tiny feet, and
in addition to being a very good dancer, is very pretty. If any woman is
rigorously required to be beautiful, it must surely be a dancer. Everyone has
the right to be ugly with the exception of actors and actresses and dancers. A
very talented actress can get away with being merely pleasingly attractive and
graceful, but it is absolutely essential for a dancer to be very beautiful. Dance
is a wholly sensual and material art that speaks neither to the intelligence nor
to the heart, but is directed only to the eyes. Stand on the tips of your toes,
spin like a top for quarter of an hour, raise the leg towards the ceiling—what
will all that mean to me if I am shocked by the sight before me?

A woman who appears half-naked in a flimsy gauze skirt and tights to pose
before your opera glasses in the glare of eighty footlights with no other
purpose than to display her shoulders, bosom, arms and legs in a series of
attitudes that show them off to best advantage, seems amazingly impudent if
she is not as beautiful as Phaenna, Aglaïa or Pasithea.[4] I am not very

[4] The Graces in ancient Greek legend.

interested in seeing an ugly figure morosely jigging about in the corner of some ballet. The Opéra should be a sort of gallery of living statues in which all types of beauty are combined. Dancers, through the perfection of their figures and the grace of their attitudes, should serve to maintain and develop the sense of beauty that is vanishing day by day. They should be models, selected ·as carefully as possible, whose task is to appear before the public and instruct it in the ideas of elegance and good grace. To be a dancer it is not enough to know how to perform the steps, jump high and manipulate a scarf. Agility is only a secondary quality.

Dolores and Camprubí have nothing in common with our own dancers. They have a passion, a vitality and an attack of which you can have no idea. They give the impression that they are dancing, not just anyhow so as to earn their fee, like other dancers, but for their own pleasure and personal satisfaction. There is nothing mechanical in their dancing, nothing that appears copied or smacks of the classroom. Their dancing is an expression of temperament rather than a conforming to a set of principles; every gesture is redolent of the fiery Southern blood. Such dancing as this with blonde hair would be a complete contradiction.

How is it that such hot-blooded and impetuous dancing, with its exaggerated movements and its free gestures, is in no way indecent, whereas the slightest *écart* of a French ballet girl is shockingly immodest? The answer is that the *cachucha* is a national dance of a primitive character and such barefaced simplicity that it has become chaste. It is so openly sensual, so boldly amorous, and its provocative coquetry and delirious exuberance are so full of the joys of youth that it is easy to forgive the very Andalusian impetuosity of some of its mannerisms. It is a charming poem written in twistings of the hips, sidelong expressions, a foot advanced and then withdrawn, all joyfully accompanied by the chatter of castanets and having more to say on its own than many volumes of erotic verse.

There is one position that is ravishingly graceful. It is the moment when the dancer, half-kneeling, with back proudly arched, head thrown back, a large red rose unfolding in her beautiful half-loosened black hair, arms dreamily extended and only gently shaking the castanets, smiles over her shoulder at the lover who is approaching to steal a kiss. A more prettily designed group could not be imagined. It has nothing of the ridiculous and insipid grace of comic opera. The cavalier has in his movements a facility and an alert and proud nonchalance. He is as supple, precise, sinuous and lively as a young jaguar. The lady is young, light, free in her poses, forming her attitudes with admirable clarity, producing her sparkling smile only when the moment is opportune, barely raising the sequined folds of her basquine[5] above the knee,

---

[5] The outer skirt as worn by a classical Spanish dancer, usually decorated with lace and often with a weighted hem.

and never indulging in those awful *écarts* of the leg that make a woman look like an open compass.

It is strange that this delightful couple has not been engaged at the Opéra, for it would have been very easy to find employment for them. Those national dances, so original in character, would have introduced a wonderful variety into the choreographic repertory, which by nature is so monotonous. In my opinion the Opéra should seek out the finest dancers in the world, anyone with a reputation in this field. Can one believe, for example, that a bayadère rôle would not assume a very lively attraction if performed by a genuine bayadère from Calcutta or Masulipatam? Why not have almehs in the theatre in the Rue Le Peletier?[6] Our new relations with the East should enable us to obtain a few without any great expense or difficulty.

M. Lubbert,[7] who was once Director of the Opéra and, having visited the Gateways to the Levant, is a good judge of such matters, declares that nothing can compare with the perfection of their dancing girls. However, do not jump to the conclusion that we are asking that Chinese rôles should be played exclusively by Chinese, for our acceptance of convention in art is too deeply ingrained to descend to such puerilities. But certainly the choreographic art, being a mute and positive art, lends itself more than any other to an innovation such as this, which can only add spice to the deadly boring framework of ballet. The *saltarello* and the *tarantella* danced by Romans and Neapolitans, the *cachucha*, the *jota aragonesa* and the *zapateado* by Spaniards, and the scarf dances of almehs and bayadères would surely offer an attraction that is lacking when they are performed by ordinary dancers. But while waiting for the almehs, the Opéra should have retained the Spaniards and brought more of them from Madrid, where, it is said, there are even better dancers to be found.

La Charte de 1830, April 18th, 1837.
(*Fusains et eaux-fortes*, pp. 91–98.) L:222.

---

[6] The street in which the Paris Opéra was then situated.

[7] Emile-Timothée Lubbert (1794–1859) had directed the Opéra from 1827 until 1831, being Dr Louis Véron's immediate predecessor.

4

Opéra: *Les Mohicans*

Les Mohicans, ballet-pantomime
in 2 acts, ch. A. Guerra, mus.
Adam, f.p. July 5th, 1837.

We are losing no time in reviewing the ballet of *Les Mohicans*, for it will probably not last long on the playbills, and we could well be saying with prophetic foresight, "I only had to pass by, and it was already no more."[1]

The second performance[2] was violent and stormy. The discordant sound of whistling—something quite unheard of in the harmonious surroundings of the Opéra—frequently made piercing inroads into the music of the orchestra, adding a part that M. Adam[3] never dreamed of writing. Crude exchanges of invective broke out between the pit and the proscenium boxes, and the gentlemen of the pit were in the wrong, for never was whistling more deserved.

The choice of subject is most unfortunate. Soldiers and savages have little to offer choreography. Naked redskins and other characters in buffalo skins provide nothing for the eyes to feast upon.

A ballet demands brilliant scenery, sumptuous festivities and magnificent courtly costumes. Fairyland is the place where the action of a ballet can most easily be developed. Sylphides, salamanders, undines, bayaderes and nymphs of every mythology are the obligatory characters. For a ballet to be at all

---

[1] Gautier added a new opening when this review was reprinted in *Histoire de l'art dramatique*: "The first steps we took in our career as a theatre critic were marked by an unfortunate omen. We arrived on the dramatic battlefield just in time to record a defeat and gather the bodies of those slain the day before. So let us lose no time in reviewing the ballet of *Les Mohicans* . . . ."

[2] It was also the last.

[3] This was the second ballet score composed for the Opéra by Adolphe Adam (1803–56). He had written the music for *La Fille du Danube* in the previous year. His score for *Giselle* was to establish him as the foremost composer of ballet music of his time. Other ballets with his music which Gautier reviewed were *La Jolie Fille de Gand*, *La Filleule des fées*, *Orfa* and *Le Corsaire*. He also wrote a number of successful *opéras comiques*.

convincing, it must be entirely unrealistic. The more fabulous the action, the more chimeric the characters, the less will be the shock to authenticity, for it is easy enough to believe that a sylphide can express her sorrow in a pirouette and make a declaration of love with a *rond de jambe*. But all that is not very convincing, despite optical illusions and theatrical conventions, when it comes from a person in a powder-blue silk dress whose father is a rather portly colonel in white leather breeches and riding boots.

We saw this savage ballet of *Les Mohicans* through to the bitter end with the most profound and sustained concentration, making desperate efforts at understanding something of it. We did not want to demean ourselves by consulting the scenario except in the last resort.

This is what we made of it. It seemed that the Mohicans wanted to recover from the English a little violin to which, from all appearances, they ascribed magical powers. The English defended the little violin as best they could, but not well enough to prevent the Mohicans from carrying it away at the end through the intervention of Hawk Eye, the good fairy in this Mother Goose tale, and so the little violin was finally restored to its rightful owners. This seemed a very suitable struggle for a ballet.

But when we read the scenario, we found we had completely misunderstood the whole thing. This is no reason why we should not describe the ballet. By reviewing something that is incomprehensible, we shall ourselves be incomprehensible, but that will be the fault of M. Guerra,[4] the author of this fine production, who certainly dances better than he writes.

The scene is set in a picturesque site in North America which was served up to us a short time ago in the ballet *Brézilia* as a virgin forest in South America. The site, *pace* MM. Devoir and Pourchet, is neither picturesque nor American, nor is it even a site.[5] However, the scene painters were given a wonderful opportunity of depicting one of those vast American forests, with giant trees, strangely shaped bushes, tall plants ruffled by the passing of wild animals, remote glades illuminated by shafts of sunlight, and pools of shimmering water to which deer nervously come to immerse their black muzzles. This virgin land, which has been so well described by Cooper,[6] lends itself to the composition of a set of grandiose and exotic character, but MM. Porchet and Devoir have been content to line up a few trees like panels of a screen,

---

[4] This was to be the only ballet that Antonio Guerra (1810–46), an Italian dancer and choreographer, produced at the Opéra.

[5] *Brézilia, ou le Tribu des femmes*, ballet in 1 act, ch. F. Taglioni, mus. Gallenberg, f.p. Opéra, April 8th, 1835. It was common practice at this time for scenery and costumes to be used again, as the scene-painters Pourchet and Devoir did here, touching up a set originally painted by Philastre and Cambon.

[6] James Fenimore Cooper (1789–1851), on whose novel, *The Last of the Mohicans*, the ballet was very loosely based.

rounding the whole thing off with an unpleasant grey sky and rocks that are to be found nowhere in the world and ought not to appear at the Opéra.

On the right can be seen an incredible cabin made of wood and leaves, guarded by two sentries. As day breaks, many people can be seen lying on the ground. The sight of all these sleeping figures, some lying on their backs, others on their stomachs and a few on their sides, is far from voluptuous and makes one think instinctively of the cattle market at Sceaux. Three or four redskins in violet tights emerge from the wings and cross the stage, taking great care not to step on the horizontal figures—such delicate thoughtfulness! According to the scenario, they seem to be planning an attack. Oh, triumphantly assertive scenario! But they do not look as if they are plotting anything, and seem quite happy to cross from left to right making terrible faces as they go.

"To the sound of drum rolls and bugle calls," everyone gets up. The major comes out of the cabin, reviews his troops, and announces that they are to break camp. The soldiers spend the time that remains before they leave indulging in "various pastimes". The moment seems badly chosen. Soldiers hardly indulge in pastimes when about to set off on a march of eight to ten leagues in the day. However, these "various pastimes" merely consist of a ball that the soldiers give to the "savage" Indian women. Alice, who has come out of the incredible cabin wearing an improbable dress of sky-blue silk, opens the dancing herself so as to overcome the shyness of the young native girls; Major Arwed dances too, very neatly in his boots, spurs and sword; and to music provided by Jonathas, the comic character of the piece and possessor of the little violin, everyone joins in.

At this juncture we shall interrupt this poetic description to make an observation on the subject of costume. The young Red Indian girls, several of whom look old and starving, are wearing a sort of muslin loincloth—imagine, muslin in the impenetrable forests of America!—adorned with ribbons and feathers that give the impression that they are naked to the waist. Their shoulders, neck, bust and arms—yellow, red or blue, or even, less usually, white—give the appearance of being bare, but where the flesh ends, fleshings, designed to continue the flesh, begin—an absurd idea, for fleshings are usually bright pink or light violet and nothing could be more indelicate or ugly. Since nudity is unacceptable by current moral standards and it is impossible to present the Graces and Cupid on the stage in their natural costume, and since we no longer appreciate pure form and beauty sufficiently to accept it unveiled, it would be better to choose subjects that do not require such scanty costuming. Representing women's bosoms and backs by pink corsets is an offence against good taste, truth and decency. This is all by the way. Nor do we believe that savages braid their hair in the Greek fashion, but that is a minor complaint. So let us return to our soldiers indulging in "various pastimes".

Leaning on his long rifle, Hawk Eye views the dancing with an expression of concern. His opinion of the expedition is nothing like so high as that of the Major, to whom he confides his anxiety. The Major replies, we know not exactly how, that he has no fear since his fiancée is with him and he is ready to die in her defence. Only a Major in spotlessly white leatherskin breeches could come out with such an explanation. But, Major, it is just because Alice is with you that you have cause for alarm; what do you find so reassuring in flaunting a girl, with only a simple sky-blue dress and a few wretched supers for protection, before this horde of Mohicans in zebra-striped and tattooed fleshings of such an unsociable red?

While Hawk Eye is pensively absorbed in these reflections, the dancing continues. The soldiers amuse themselves by plying Jonathas, a dancing master with fantastic legs who is wearing a suit shaped like a gigantic tulip, with drink. Alice climbs on to a litter and the company parades before her, while Jonathas alone is sound asleep, his head resting on a rock of a shockingly garish hue that gave us eye-strain throughout this act, which, alas, was so long!

A savage creeps up to Jonathas and steals his snuff box and watch. The latter wakes to find himself face to face with a flaming red visage of a most menacing aspect. The savage dashes into the wings, and Jonathas, terrified by this encounter and the surrounding solitude, begins to tremble all over and goes down on his knees to pray for divine assistance. Happily he sees Hawk Eye, who reassures him and blows his horn to summon the Colonel's escort. The escort arrives, and the Colonel, touched by Alice's prayers, agrees to take Jonathas with them. Laughingly, the soldiers hoist him astride a dusty horse (the horse really is dusty), and the little caravan sets off. A loud fusillade is then heard; the caravan is being attacked by the Mohicans. Hawk Eye comes out of the cabin again, and sees a pumpkin coming towards him, decorated with long stripes of various colours. This pumpkin, or wooden mask, is none other than the juggler of the enemy tribe, "a venerated personage". Hawk Eye pretends to be dead, and when the juggler approaches to rob him, he runs him through with a dagger, and strips him of wooden mask, tomahawk, mocassins, scalping knife and all his incongruous accoutrements. Alice and Jonathas are taken prisoner. So ends the first act.

The second act is much the same, and we shall not bother to describe it in detail. The scenery changes and now represents the temple of the fetish. We must ask MM. Devoir and Pourchet why they have placed a Tahitian *marae*[7] in a scene of North America. Jonathas is to be eaten alive—he will make a frugal meal!—and Alice is to be given to the chief. Hawk Eye, wearing the wooden mask, is protecting them as much as he can without giving himself away. Jonathas, having found his violin, makes the savages dance. Alice,

[7] A temple enclosure used for worshipping and sacrificial ceremonies.

forced to wear Indian dress, namely a gauze petticoat decorated with ribbons, which is more suitable for dancing than the fine robe she wore in the first act, dances a pleasant little *pas* with Jonathas with the intention of saving Arwed, her fiancé, who has also been captured by the savages. Jonathas relieves the Mohicans of their clubs and bows under the pretext that these weapons will be an incumbrance when they are dancing, and at a prearranged signal, a pistol shot fired by the Major who has worked himself loose, a body of English troops that has been lying in wait nearby comes on to the scene and frees the prisoners. General rejoicing and outrageous *cabrioles*! Jonathas is rewarded for his exceptional bravery by being appointed drum-major. Sounds of drum-rolls and whistling.

The whole of the comic effect of the piece rests on the cowardice of Jonathas, the dancing master. A dancing master need not be a hero, on the contrary, and furthermore, Jonathas's terror is not at all imagined or exaggerated. He has every reason to be frightened, for he is to be scalped, cut up into pieces, put into the pot, roasted and eaten, a very serious prospect and certainly no laughing matter. We shared his anxiety and fully understood the unpleasantness of his situation. Even a Colonel of the Gymnase would have been afraid, and a Sergeant of the heroic Franconi would have been worried sick at the thought of being carved up and seasoned with various sauces by Mohican cannibals.[8] If the terror of a comic character is to be amusing, the danger must exist only in his imagination, but in this case it is real, very real, and his position ceases to be funny and inspires pity. However that may be, Elie,[9] who is cast in this rôle, played it with a witty feeling for the fantastic. Elie is like those strange tailors and enthusiastic wigmakers in the Tales of Hoffmann who wear exaggerated costumes with reflecting buttons and breeches of yellow satin with leafy designs. There is something about him of Peregrinus Tyss, the candid and naïve lover of little Elisa Doertje.[10]

As for Mlle Nathalie Fitzjames,[11] who was making her début, it is unfortunate that she had to appear in such a wretched piece. She is very young, with pretty features and an air of distinction, and remarkably elegant. Although in

[8] At one time the Gymnase had acquired a reputation for staging plays with military men in the cast. More recently, *Le Colonel d'autrefois*, a comedy-vaudeville in one act by Mélesville, Gabriel and Angel, had been produced there (f.p. April 12th, 1837), in which a regiment receives as its new colonel a fifteen-year-old lad whose father, a Duke, has purchased his commission for him. The "heroic" Franconi was Laurent Franconi, then head of the family that had established the circus in France. Franconi's circus, at this time known as the Cirque-Olympique, specialised in military pantomimes with equestrian acts.

[9] Georges Elie (1800–c.83) was a member of the Opéra ballet from 1824 to 1848.

[10] Characters in *Meister Floh* by E.T.A. Hoffmann (1776–1822).

[11] French ballerina (b. 1819), younger sister of the dancer Louise Fitzjames, danced at the Opéra from 1837 to 1842.

13

appearance somewhat frail, she is agile and strong. She seems destined to take her place among our finest dancers; her movements are designed with clarity and candour, she jumps well, and her *pointes* are strong and firm. Notwithstanding the insignificance and lack of character of the *pas* in this ballet, Mlle Nathalie found ways of displaying her valuable qualities, and she only needs a better part to be fully adopted by the public.

La Presse, July 11th, 1837.
HAD I, 5–11. L:246.

5

Opéra: Return of Fanny Elssler in *La Tempête*

La Tempête, ou l'Ile des génies,
ballet-faery in 2 acts, sc. Nourrit
(anon), ch. J. Coralli, mus.
Schneitzhoeffer, f.p.
September 15th, 1834.

Mlle Fanny Elssler has just made her reappearance in the rôle of Alcine in *La Tempête*. The ballet of *La Tempête* is a ballet, and that is the only good thing to be said about it. It also has the distinction of spoiling one of the finest operatic subjects one could wish for. Why Oberon is to be found in this piece instead of Prospero is a complete mystery. Oberon is inseparable from *A Midsummer Night's Dream* and cannot appear without his wife, Titania. Alcina, that prestigious creation of Ariosto, seems completely out of place on the Island of Tempests alongside Caliban, and I very much doubt whether Fernando will make her forget the brilliant knight, Ruggiero.[1] But we shall not press our observations on the intrinsic merits of the scenario any further, for the literature of the legs is hardly a subject for contention. So let us quickly turn our attention to Fanny Elssler. A volley of applause broke out when her gauze veil parted, allowing us to see the seductive enchantress, and no one doubted that the virtuous Fernando would soon be unfaithful to the memory of Léa, Oberon's protégée.

The dancing of Fanny Elssler is completely independent of academic principles. It has a character all its own which sets her apart from other ballerinas. Hers is not the ethereal, virginal grace of Taglioni, it is something much more human which appeals more sharply to the senses. Mlle Taglioni is a Christian dancer, if one can use such an expression about an art that is proscribed by Catholicism. She floats like a spirit in a transparent mist of

[1] In the epic poem, *Orlando furioso*, by Ariosto (1474–1533) the knight Ruggiero is conveyed to the island of the enchantress Armida, where he falls under her spell before eventually making his escape.

white muslin with which she loves to surround herself, and she resembles a contented soul scarcely bending the petals of celestial flowers with the tips of her rosy feet. Fanny Elssler is a completely pagan dancer. She recalls the muse Terpsichore with her tambourine and her tunic slit to reveal her thigh and caught up with clasps of gold. When she fearlessly arches her back, throwing her voluptuous arms behind her, she evokes a vision of those beautiful figures from Herculaneum or Pompeii standing out in white relief against a black background and accompanying their steps with sonorous, echoing *crotala*. Virgil's verse,

Crispum sub crotalo docta movere latus[2]

instinctively springs to mind. The Syrian slave girl he so loved to see dancing beneath the pale trellis of the little inn must have had much in common with Fanny Elssler.

Undoubtedly spirituality is something to be respected, but in the dance a few concessions can be made to reality. After all, dancing has no other purpose but to display beautiful bodies in graceful poses and develop lines that are pleasing to the eye. It is silent rhythm, music made visible. Dancing is ill suited for expressing metaphysical ideas; it expresses only the passions. Love, desire with all its coquetries, the aggressive male and the gently resisting woman—these are the subjects of all primitive dances.

Fanny Elssler has grasped this truth perfectly. She has dared more than any other dancer of the Opéra. She was the first to introduce the audacious *Cachucha* to these modest boards without sacrificing anything of its native flavour. She dances with her whole body, from the top of her head to the tips of her toes, and so she is in the true sense a beautiful ballerina, whereas the others are nothing but pairs of legs thrashing about beneath static torsos.

La Presse, September 11th, 1837.
HAD I, 38–39. L:257.

---

[2] The verse comes from Virgil's poem, *Copa*, which opens:
Copa Syrisca, caput Graia redimira mitella,
Crispum sub crotalo docta movere latus,
Ebria sumosa saltat lasciva taberna,
Ad cubitum raucos excutiens calamos.
(Syrisca, the inn-keeper, her head bound with Greek kerchief, trained as she is to sway her tremendous limbs to the notes of her castanets, within her smoky tavern tipsily dances in wanton wise, shaking against her elbow her noisy reeds. Trans. by H.R. Faircloth.)

6

Opéra: The Revival of *La Muette de Portici*; Dolores Serral

La Muette de Portici, opera in 5 acts by Auber, f.p. 1828, revived September 25th, 1837.

A triple attraction drew a large crowd to the revival of *La Muette de Portici*—first, the début of Duprez in the rôle of Masaniello, formerly played by Nourrit[1]; then that of Fanny Elssler, to whom Mlle Noblet, with a generosity that may have been a trifle perfidious, has yielded the rôle of Fenella;[2] and in addition to that, the titbit of a new Spanish *pas* danced by Mme Alexis Dupont[3] and her sister, and the wish to judge M. Auber's music after hearing the grand and solemn scores of *Les Huguenots, Guillaume Tell* and *La Juive*.[4] As you can see, this performance was a most delicious and exquisite feast. And in consequence the huge auditorium of the Opéra proved to be too small and three or four of the pit benches had to be converted into orchestra stalls . . .

Let us move on to the dancing. The great success of the evening was the

---

[1] Louis-Gilbert Duprez (1806–96), one of the most celebrated tenors of his day, sang at the Opéra from 1836 to 1849. His predecessor in the rôle of Masaniello, and its creator, was the no less distinguished singer, Adolphe Nourrit (1802–39), who sang at the Opéra from 1821 to 1837 and was the anonymous author of the scenario of *La Sylphide*.

[2] The heroine of the opera, the dumb girl Fenella, had been created by Lise Noblet (1801–52), in her prime one of the leading ballerinas in Europe, who danced at the Opéra from 1818 to 1841.

[3] Mme Alexis Dupont (1807–77) was Lise Noblet's sister, born Félicité Noblet. She danced at the Opéra from 1826 to 1841. After her marriage to the tenor Alexis Dupont, she used her married name.

[4] Three of the most celebrated grand operas in the repertory, composed respectively by Meyerbeer (1836), Rossini (1829) and Halévy (1835).

Spanish dance by the Mmes Noblet. Their entrance was eagerly awaited. They appeared in white satin basquines, threaded and bespangled with silver, with roses in their hair, and wearing the high ceremonial combs—in fact, the whole fantastic costume of Dolores Serral. Then, to the strains of a melody that was as naïve as all folk tunes are and fragmented into equal divisions by the babble of the castanets, they danced the most daring and brazen *pas* ever to have been seen at the Opéra. It was phenomenal, outrageous, unimaginable, but it was charming. Imagine swaying hips, spines arching back, arms and legs thrown into the air, the most provocatively voluptuous movements, a hot-blooded fury, and a diabolical attack—truly, a dance to awaken the dead.

The impression made by this dance on an audience accustomed to the *pointes* and *entrechats* and the angular poses of French ballet technique certainly surpassed the wildest expectations of Mlle Noblet's partisans. The two sisters were applauded as never before, and—perhaps an unheard-of honour in the splendours of the Opéra—they were called back and made to start the *pas*, *El Jaleo de Jerez*, all over again.

Mlle Noblet gave Fenella to Mlle Elssler, but she has stolen the latter's *Cachucha*. Neither of these ladies is in debt to the other, or rather both of them are very much indebted to Dolores Serral, who was the first to import the *Cachucha* to Paris and has been imitated, first by Fanny Elssler and now by Mlle Noblet. In spite of the great reputation and higher standing of her rivals, Dolores Serral is still to the best of our knowledge the leading exponent of the *cachucha* and the *bolero*.

Her talent has a character all its own. In the most exaggerated *écarts* of this unrestrained and animated *pas* she was never immodest. She is full of passion and voluptuousness, but true voluptuousness is always chaste. She seems spellbound before the gaze of her partner. She weaves her arms as though swooning from love, and bends back her head as if intoxicated by the scent and unwilling to bear the weight of the large rose that blooms in the mass of her black hair. Her body curves with a nervous shudder as if she were turning on the arm of her lover, then she sinks down, brushing the floor with her arms while still playing the castanets, only to spring up, quick and alert as a bird, darting a sparkling laugh at her partner.

For Dolores the *Cachucha* is a faith, a religion. It is obvious that she believes in it, for she performs it with all the emotion, passion, guilelessness and seriousness that it is possible to summon up. Fanny Elssler and Mlle Noblet dance it a little like unbelievers, more to satisfy a whim or cheer up the opera glasses of that bored sultan, the public, than out of any real conviction. Also, they are both spirited flirts, amusing but not erotic, which is an unpardonable sin in a *cachucha* or a *bolero*.

Why has Dolores Serral, whose dances obtain such success thanks to the legs of Fanny and Noblet, not been engaged at the Opéra, where there has for long been room for her, as there has also for Camprubí.

Mlle Elssler's efforts were not among the happiest. The rôle of Fenella, being set among a host of characters who are not dumb, seems somewhat out of place and tedious. It makes one think of the histrion in Roman farces who used to mime the speech being declaimed by an actor alongside, or those fairground shows at which only a single actor was permitted to speak.

When she made her first entrance, with a pale and frightened look, her brown eyes like two dark splashes in her long white features, and her lustrous black hair smoothed down on her head like a taffeta headband, she reminded me—oh, forgive me, Terpsichore!—of Jean-Gaspard Deburau,[5] the Pierrot of the Funambules, and this resemblance struck several other people too in the same way. However, drawing such a parallel is in no way damaging to Mlle Elssler, for Deburau, who many people believe is a witty paradox invented by Janin,[6] is really the greatest mime on earth. Mlle Fanny Elssler, who made the most of a thankless rôle, had one magnificent moment when, rejected by the guards of the chapel where her seducer's marriage is taking place, she sits down on the ground and lets her head fall into her hands as she dissolves into a flood of tears. She could have been a figure by Bendemann, the painter of *Jeremiah*,[7] or one of the Trojan women of Euripides. She was as beautiful as an antique statue. Her Neapolitan costume, which was completely authentic and severe, fell in large austere folds that were incomparably stylish. One would like to have designed it oneself. Mlle Fanny plays her rôle without any show of coquetry towards the audience, concentrating entirely on her desperate situation, and this conscientious approach might have prejudiced her success, which was not uncontested.

La Presse, October 2nd, 1837.
HAD I, 40–43. L:263.

[5] Jean-Gaspard Deburau (1796–1846) was the supreme mime of his generation. He appeared at the tiny Théâtre des Funambules in the Boulevard du Temple, where Parisians flocked to see him. He was renowned for his touching rendering of the character of Pierrot.

[6] The critic Jules Janin (1804–74) immortalised Deburau in his *Histoire du théâtre à quatre sous*, published in 1832. He began writing for the *Journal des Débats* in 1836 and inaugurated a more personal style of dramatic criticism that spoke more directly to his readers.

[7] Eduard Julius Friedrich Bendemann (1811–89) painted his *Jeremiah on the Ruins of Jerusalem* in 1834.

7

Opéra: Début of Nathalie Fitzjames in *Nathalie*

Nathalie, ou la Laitière suisse, ballet in 2 acts and 3 scenes, ch. F. Taglioni, mus. Gyrowetz and Carafa, f.p. November 7th, 1832, revived October 11th, 1837.

The ballet of *Nathalie* belongs to the simple category: in it the "chalet"[1] plays an important part, as one might expect. The only thing I could understand was that Nathalie has been abducted by a gentleman in a red suit, who is accompanied by a number of Amazons (Amazons in the mountains!). The red gentleman installs a statue in his place, and Nathalie, who is shut up in the castle, gradually becomes accustomed to its stupid expression and scarlet jacket. The gentleman then takes the place of the statue and receives the girl's kiss, whereupon the parents enter, the Amazons return, and Nathalie marries the lobster-coloured young lord. All this is interspersed with the comical despair of that excellent mime, Elie, whose mournfully skinny legs repel all the girls to whom he pays court with inexhaustible patience.

Mlle Nathalie[2] made the most of an insignificant rôle, which she was playing for the first time. She dances in a manner that is not lacking in originality. She rebounds from the stage as if it were a racquet, and shows promise, with a little more training, of becoming a remarkable dancer. Her only shortcomings are that she is still too angular and that she wears a sad and cross expression when dancing that detracts from the charm of her features. Ballerinas' smiles are undoubtedly stupid and more horrible than the emaciated grin of death itself, but a merrier, more serene physiognomy would be much more appropriate in a simple, playful girl like a little Swiss milkmaid.

The ballet of *Nathalie* is not new, and so we shall not embark on a long

[1] Presumably a reference to Adam's popular one-act *opéra comique, Le Chalet,* f.p. Opéra-Comique, September 25th, 1834.

[2] Nathalie Fitzjames. See No. 4, note 11.

discussion about it, but merely say in passing that we take little pleasure in naïve and simple ballets, *ballets champêtres* and Florian.[3] The only thing that amused us during the performance was the regular return of an oil spot on the waterfall.

La Presse, October 16th, 1837.
HAD I, 51–52. L:267.

---

[3] This sentence of the final paragraph was omitted from the version reprinted in *Histoire de l'art dramatique*. Jean-Pierre Claris de Florian (1755–94) was celebrated in his time as a writer of fables and some charming but somewhat superficial comedies in the style of the *commedia dell'arte* for the Comédie Italienne, mostly constructed around the rôle of Harlequin.

8

Gallery of Beautiful Actresses: Fanny Elssler[1]

Journalists, when writing about actresses, concern themselves with little more than their talent and acting. They do not analyse their beauty, and never judge them from the purely plastic point of view. Sometimes they speak of their grace or their charm, but that is all.

However, an actress is like a statue or a picture that is offered for your inspection, and it is permissible to criticise her without any scruples of conscience, to reproach her for being ugly just as a painter might be rebuked for faulty drawing (any question of pity for physical defects is out of place here), and to praise her for her charms with the same calm detachment shown by a sculptor standing before a marble statue who might exclaim, "Now here is a beautiful shoulder" or "What a well shaped arm".

But reviewers never dwell on this important aspect, with the result that the reputations of pretty actresses are made by chance, and most of the time are far from justified. And furthermore, many of these reputations linger on for half a century or so, which in all honesty is too long!

A host of heroic Generals and charming civil servants from the days of the Empire,[2] and no less charming provincials and even full-blooded Parisians, still admire the traditional and mythological freshness of Mlle Mars,[3] the inimitable Célimène, that harks back to the age of legend.

[1] This was the first essay in a series entitled *Galerie des belles actrices*, which appeared in *Figaro* between October 1837 and January 1838, the other subjects being Giulia Grisi, Mlle George, Jenny Colon, Mme Damoreau and Cornélie Falcon. Gautier commenced a second series, *Galerie des actrices d'esprit*, of which only two essays appeared, on Suzanne Brohan and Marie Dorval.

[2] Napoleon's Empire had finally ended in 1815, twenty-two years before, and men who had served France in those stirring times were now entering middle or even old age.

[3] Mlle Mars (1779–1847), the most distinguished actress of the time, was playing young parts at the Théâtre Français until shortly before her retirement in 1841. Célimène in Molière's *Le Misanthrope* was one of her most celebrated rôles.

Generally speaking, beautiful actresses are quite plain. This is fair comment, and if they did not have the stage for a pedestal, no one would pay them any attention, and they would merge into the crowd of plain everyday women who have no particular asset apart from not being men, as is obvious when they discard the costume of their own sex to adopt that of ours.

These remarks do not apply to Mlle Fanny Elssler, who is in the full flower of youth and beauty, and has the advantage of not having been admired by our grandfathers.

Mlle Fanny Elssler is tall, supple and well-proportioned; her wrists are slim and her ankles delicate. Her legs, which are purely and elegantly shaped, recall the strong, slender lines of those of Diana, the virgin huntress. The kneecaps are neat and well defined, and the whole knee beyond reproach. Her legs are very different from those of the ordinary dancer, whose body seems to have shrunk into her stockings and settled there. They are not the legs of a parish beadle or a knave of clubs that stir the admiration of the elderly gentlemen in the stalls and set them busily polishing the lenses of their opera glasses, but two beautiful legs from an antique statue worthy of being cast and lovingly inspected.

We will be forgiven, I hope, for dwelling at such length on the legs, but we are speaking of a dancer.

Another point for praise: Mlle Elssler has rounded and well shaped arms that do not reveal the elbow bones and have none of the wretched shape of her companions' arms, whose frightful thinness makes them look like lobster claws dabbed with wet-white. Even her bosom is full, a rare thing in the world of *entrechats* where the "twin hills" and "snowy mountains" so much extolled by students and minor poets seem to be completely unknown. Nor is there any sign of those two bony triangles that quiver in the back like the roots of torn-off wings.

As for the shape of her head, we confess that it does not appear as graceful as it has been made out to be. Mlle Elssler has superb hair framing her temples, as shiny and glossy as the wings of a bird. Its dark colouring seems a little too Mediterranean for the Germanic set of her features. It is not the right hair for the head and the body. The oddity about it is jarring, and disturbs the harmony of the whole. Her very dark eyes, the pupils of which are like two little jade stars in a crystal sky, do not match her nose, which, like her forehead, is rather German.

Mlle Elssler has been called "a Spaniard from the North", which was intended as a compliment. It is, however, a defect. Her smile, the whiteness of her skin, the set of her features and her calm brow are German, while her hair, her tiny feet, her dainty tapering hands and the somewhat bold arch of her back are Spanish. Two natures and two temperaments are struggling inside her, and her beauty would have been greater had one of them predominated. She is pretty, but does not fit into any distinct national category; she wavers between Spain and Germany. And this same uncertainty is to be found in her sexual characteristics. Her hips are somewhat undeveloped, and her breasts are no fuller than those of a hermaphrodite of antiquity. She could equally well be a charming woman and the most charming boy in the world.

We shall close this sketch with a few words of advice. Mlle Elssler should produce her smile more openly and more often. It is sometimes held in check and restrained, and she shows her gums too much. In certain *attitudes penchées*, the lines of her features are badly presented; the eyebrows become tapered, her mouth turns up at the corners, and her nose becomes pointed, giving her a sly expression that is not pleasing. Also, Mlle Elssler should dress her hair with more of it behind the head. If her hair were arranged a little lower, it would break the sharp line of her shoulders and the nape of her neck. We also advise her not to paint her pretty fingernails such a deep shade of pink. That is an unnecessary vanity.

> *Figaro*, October 19th, 1837.
> (*Les Belles Femmes de Paris*,pp. 40–45;
> *Portraits contemporains*, pp. 372–375.)
> L: 268.

9

Opéra: *La Chatte métamorphosée en femme*

La Chatte métamorphosée en femme, ballet in 3 acts and 7 scenes, sc. Duveyrier, ch. J. Coralli, mus. Montfort, f.p. October 16th, 1837.

*L*a *Chatte métamorphosée en femme* did not reap all the success that had been anticipated. There is nothing very divine in the scenario of M. Ch. Duveyrier,[1] the poet of God and brother of M. Mélesville. The plot is taken from a vaudeville by M. Scribe,[2] in which the leading rôle was played by Mlle Jenny Vertpré,[3] but the action no longer takes place in Germany, but in China, a setting that comes naturally to fantastic and preposterous imaginations.

Oug-Lou, a well-read young man, has a passionate obsession for his cat and leads a solitary life with an aged servant in a woefully run down cabin. He has a horror of women, to whom he prefers his white cat—"it is a taste like any other, it is his nature".

---

[1] Charles Duveyrier (1803–66) was a disciple of Father Enfantin, the leader of a pseudo-religious sect inspired by the socialistic philosophy of Henri de Saint-Simon. After Enfantin's death he went into seclusion at Ménilmontant, designing his costume with the words "Charles, poet of God" inscribed on the front. He was a younger brother of the celebrated playwright Mélesville (1787–1865).

[2] Eugène Scribe (1791–1861), the most prolific dramatist of his time, whose works ranged from comedies to opera libretti and ballet scenarios. The original version of *La Chatte métamorphosée en femme* was a one-act folie-vaudeville written by him in collaboration with Mélesville and first performed at the Théâtre de Madame on March 3rd, 1827.

[3] Jenny Vertpré (1797–1865), a diminutive beauty and a witty actress, was one of the most popular performers on the French stage in the 1820s.

The Princess of China, who has fallen in love with Oug-Lou (why?), decides, while going for a ride on an elephant, to take the bit between her teeth (or should it be trunk?) and manages things in such a way as to be rescued by Oug-Lou, who, taken in by her contrived faint, takes her into his cabin and revives her.

We most humbly beg the pardon of M. Duveyrier, the poet of God, but how does one manage to be carried off to a prearranged spot and know that a man called Oug-Lou, who is passionately in love with his cat, will be standing just there by the roadside to perform the rescue?

That seems a difficult thing to do, even for the daughter of the Emperor of China, a comical country to judge from screens, ballets and mimodramas.

Princess Kié-Li tells her tutor, Kiang-sse-Long (or *qui en sait long*),[4] the head of the Court of Mathematics, that she wants to marry Oug-Lou, and commands him to see that Oug-Lou and Kan-Kao come to the fête that is to be given in the Imperial palace. Before leaving, the Princess gives her hand to the handsome Oug-Lou and expresses the tenderest interest in him, but Oug-Lou, a slave to his fixation, soon returns to his cat. The Princess is astonished and annoyed, and for good reason—imagine abandoning Mlle Elssler for a frightful stuffed rabbit[5] that has a totally misguided idea that it looks like a white cat! The old nurse tries to smooth things over, telling the Princess about Oug-Lou's excessive passion for his cat and his no less excessive horror of women. Kié-Li smiles and gets into her litter, confident that when Oug-Lou realises that she is the daughter of the Emperor of China, he will readily abandon his cat to the first alley tom he comes across. So, at least, the Princess believes. Happy innocent Princess!

The scene changes to reveal, according to the scenario, a vast amphitheatre in the Emperor's palace. We give the scenario's definition in default of any other, for we were never able to discover for ourselves what the stage is supposed to represent. On the left are two enormous crags joined by a bridge, and a sun that looks rather like a fried egg. Add to that the obligatory accompaniment of floating banners and porcelain towers with umbrella-shaped roofs. This set is very brightly coloured, but has the disadvantage, common to many stage sets, of being uninhabitable.

All kinds of dances are performed, and an infinite number of standards and parasols are paraded around. Oug-Lou and Kan-Kao, who is carrying a rather unChinese-looking basket containing the same poorly stuffed white rabbit we spoke of earlier, are placed to the audience's right. The sun (note this well) continues to shine on the left, and still looks like a fried egg. The Princess refuses hordes of uncouth princes, whom her father wants her to

---

[4] He who knows a lot.

[5] In later notices Gautier scornfully referred to this ballet as *Le Lapin blanc métamorphosé en femme.*

marry. The sound of a gong at the entrance announces the arrival of Kiang-sse-Long, tutor of the Princess and head of the Court of Mathematics, to tell the Emperor that the sun is about to be consumed by the dragon. This, according to the scenario (oh blessed, fantastic, sacrosanct scenario!), is the material conception that the Chinese have of an eclipse, and the Princess must marry the first man she will meet after the darkness ends. Indeed, a blob of black sealing wax is beginning to advance over the disc of the sun, the footlights dim, and what the theatre deigns to call darkness reigns over the scene. Kiang-sse-Long, who is not so stupid as his prodigiously decorated red chimer and his pot-belly might lead one to believe, escorts the Princess to Oug-Lou's side. The sealing wax disappears, and the light of the sun, which has now fully emerged from the dragon's throat, shines down on the beautiful Princess Kié-Li as she gives her hand to the young student, Oug-Lou.

In the following act we are in a forest, inhabited by a bear with its head under its arm for a reason we were never able to understand, even with the aid of the scenario. QUI EN SAIT LONG, chancing to be in this forest, gives Oug-Lou a strangely shaped bonnet that has the property of transforming cats into women. But here there is a problem. If Oug-Lou loves cats and cannot bear the sight of women, why does he so readily accept a bonnet that is going to turn an animal he adores into a being he loathes? But the ballet does not bother itself with such details.

This bonnet has been invented by the Princess Kié-Li, who really has much too much imagination for a girl of her age. Oug-Lou cannot wait to try the bonnet out on his cat. He lifts the cover of the basket that serves as a nest for the grey rabbit that the scenario persists in calling a white cat. Surprise! He sees Mlle Elssler crouching down, rubbing her snout with one of her paws. Mlle Elssler jumps out of the basket and performs every imaginable feline antic. She leaps on to the furniture, plays with balls of thread, opens the birdcages, drinks milk from a plate, arches her back, abandons her lover for a mouse that she hears scuttling behind a cupboard, and escapes on to the rooftops. The Princess Kié-Li wanted to prove to the young student that cats are not as worthy as women, and are even more insufferable, if that is possible. The scene changes to represent a terrace overlooking the city of Peking. Pages are indulging in all sorts of pastimes. The Princess, whom the young Oug-Lou still imagines to be his cat in human form, flirts outrageously with the young Imperial pages. Oug-Lou is miserable, when suddenly the real white rabbit, which old Kan-Kao has sold in a moment of distress, comes out of a drainpipe and runs across the stage with both legs on each side moving in turn. All is now revealed, and Oug-Lou marries the Princess in a splendidly illuminated palace.

This is as conscientious a description as it is possible to write, and as conscientiously boring. How much nicer it would have been for both us and our readers if we had talked about Mlle Elssler, who was as charming as ever and displayed a real cat-like suppleness in the *pas* that was added at the second performance! The frightful inadequacy of the plot could not have been more gracefully concealed.

La Presse, October 23rd, 1837.
HAD I, 53–56. L:270.

10

Opéra: Louise Fitzjames in *Le Dieu et la bayadère*

Le Dieu et la bayadère, opera in 2 acts, mus. Auber, libr. Scribe, ch. F. Taglioni, f.p. October 13th, 1830, revived November 24th, 1837.

There surely could not have been a more unfortunate idea than to cast Mlle Louise Fitzjames[1] in the rôle of the Bayadere. There is not the slightest connection between Mlle Fitzjames and a bayadere. *Figaro*, that witty journal of shattering truths, declares that Mlle Fitzjames would be very well cast as an asparagus in a ballet of vegetables. Maybe that is a trifle excessive, but it is quite clear that Mlle Louise Fitzjames dances the rôle of the Bayadere very badly.

It is always unpleasant to condemn a woman for her physical defects, and it grieves us to speak the gloomy truth to Mlle Fitzjames. We are well aware that it is no fault of hers that she is not fatter, but the very sight of such lack of flesh is most painful.

It should never be forgotten that the principal quality required of a dancer is beauty. There is no excuse for not being beautiful, and it is permissible to reproach her for ugliness just as one may criticise an actress for faulty delivery. Dancing is nothing more than the art of displaying elegant and correctly proportioned bodies in various positions favourable to the development of line. It is essential for a dancer to have a body which, if not perfect, is at least graceful. Mlle Fitzjames has no body at all. She would not even be substantial enough for ghost parts, for she is as diaphanous as the horn of a lantern, and the ballet girls bobbing about behind her show through her completely. Dancing is essentially pagan, materialistic and sensual. Mlle Louise Fitzjames' arms are really too spiritualistic and her legs too aesthetic;

---

[1] Louise Fitzjames (b. 1809), the elder sister of Nathalie Fitzjames, danced at the Opéra from 1832 to 1846.

she is as skinny as a lizard or a silkworm, and skinnier than the celebrated Mlle Guimard, who nevertheless enjoyed a good income from the stipends of M. de Jarente.[2] If we were in her shoes, we would go on a six months' diet of *kaiffa*, analeptic sago, and the *racahout* of the Arabs.[3]

The only reason we can think of for casting her in this rôle is that Lafont[4] was such a heavy God that it was felt wise to pair him with a weightless ballerina to make sure that he would be lifted off the ground when the time came for him to ascend to the heaven of Indra.[5]

We should add that Mlle Fitzjames, who has no excuse for not being light, stumbled so clumsily two or three times during a *pas de zéphyr* that she was quite loudly hissed.

In this opera-ballet the bayaderes are divided into singing bayaderes and dancing bayaderes. These two categories are then subdivided into flesh-coloured bayaderes and coffee-coloured bayaderes. The latter (what a disastrous sacrifice in the interests of local colour!) wear *filoselle*[6] stockings over their arms and silk or cotton gloves of an undefinable colour on their hands. Their faces are carelessly daubed with ochre or liquorice juice, which makes them look more like chimney-sweeps than those voluptuous charmers, gilded by the sun, who tinkle the silver bells on their bracelets on the steps in front of the temple doors. Anyone would think it a simple matter to invent a dye of a warm enough pallor to convey the lovely amber-yellow colour of oriental complexions in which the eyes open like black flowers. If that could be achieved, that awful chocolate colour and those *filoselle* stockings that offend even the most short-sighted eyes could be dispensed with. Or, simpler still, it could quite simply be agreed that negresses are white. So far as we are concerned, such a convention would have our support. The redskins in *Les Mohicans* and the yellow skins of *La Bayadère* have quite put us off colour.

La Presse, November 27th, 1837.
HAD I, 72–74. L:280.

---

[2] Madeleine Guimard (1743–1816), the leading ballerina of the Opéra in the years just prior to the Revolution. Monsignor de Jarente, Bishop of Orleans, was one of her many lovers.

[3] *Kaiffa*, a concoction of potato flour, ground rice, roasted cocoa, sugar, sago, salep, lichen jelly and gelatine, spiced with vanilla; sago, a food starch prepared from the pith of palm tree-trunks; *racahout*, a mixture of starches, including cocoa, acorns and rice—all very fattening foods.

[4] Marcellin Lafont (1800–38) was then taking over the tenor rôles of Adolphe Nourrit, who had retired. Lafont died after a short illness in 1838. He was the younger brother of the actor, Pierre Lafont, who married the ballerina Pauline Leroux.

[5] Hindu god, the lord of heaven in the Brahmanic Dharma.

[6] Coarse silk.

11

Reflections on Fanny Elssler

Mlle Fanny Elssler holds the golden sceptre of beauty in her white hands. She only has to appear to draw a passionate murmur from the audience that is more flattering than all the applause in the world, for it is addressed to the woman, not the performer, and beauty which is God-given is always a source of greater pride than the talent that comes from oneself.

It can be emphatically stated that Mlle Fanny Elssler is the most beautiful of all the women appearing on the stage today. Others may have a few points that are more perfect, eyes that are larger or a mouth that lights up more happily, but none is so completely lovely as Fanny Elssler. What is fascinating about her is the perfect harmony of her head and her body. She possesses hands that match her arms, feet that match her legs, and shoulders that are indeed the very shoulders for her torso. In a word, she is all of a piece (forgive this picturesque slang), and no single part is beautiful at the expense of another. Looking at her, you do not exclaim, as you do with other women, "God! what beautiful eyes!" or "What beautiful arms!" Instead you cry, "What a desirable and charming creature!" For since every part is elegant, pretty and well proportioned, nothing compulsively catches the eye, and your gaze wanders like a caress over those smooth, rounded contours that might have belonged to some divine marble from the age of Pericles. That is the secret of the utter pleasure that is provoked by the sight of Fanny Elssler, the Ionian dancer whom Alcibiades might have invited to his suppers dressed in the costume of the Graces, her girdle loosened, her crown of myrtle and lime lying on the table, and her gold *crotales* chattering at the end of her tapering hands.

Fanny Elssler has often been compared to Diana the Huntress, but this is not a fair comparison. In spite of her divine nature, Diana has a certain look of a sour old maid. The boredom of eternal virginity has given to her profile, noble and pure though it is, a touch of severity and frigidity. Notwithstanding the assertions of evil-minded mythologists that she had fifty children by her pallid lover, Endymion, she gives the appearance, in the snow-white marble out of which she was fashioned, of a virgin *alpestre e cruda*,[1] to use the phrase of Petrarch, which is not to be found anywhere in Mlle Elssler's features. Moreover, the great rage into which she flew when she caught Actaeon watching her bathing proves that she had some hidden defect, such as a flat chest or a poorly shaped knee, for a beautiful woman taken by surprise does not react with such savage modesty. Mlle Elssler would have no need to change anyone into a stag. The legs of Diana are thin, slender, and a little on the long side, as befits the legs of a rustic divinity whose mission is to run through coppices putting deer to flight. Those of Mlle Elssler, however, are heavier in shape, yet very firm, combining strength with voluptuous curves with which the hunting Goddess was not endowed.

If Mlle Elssler resembles anyone aside from herself, it must be the son of Hermes and Aphrodite, the hermaphrodite of antiquity, that ravishing chimera of Greek art.

Her admirably shaped arms are not so full as those of the average woman, but plumper than a young girl's. There is a supple, vivacious quality in their contours that conjures up the image of a marvellously beautiful and somewhat effeminate young man such as the Indian Bacchus, Antinoüs or the Apollo Belvedere. The same relationship extends to every other part of her beauty, which is rendered all the more attractive and piquant by this delightful ambiguity. Her movements too are impressed with this duality. Beneath the amorous languor, the intoxicating sensuality that yields to the heat of passion, and the feminine sweetness and all the gentle fascination of a ballerina, can be sensed the agility, the sudden speed and the steely muscles of a young athlete. Also, Mlle Elssler appeals to everybody, even to women who cannot endure ballerinas.

Le Messager, May 4th, 1838.
(*Souvenirs de théâtre, d'art et de critique*, 51 54.) L:348.

[1] Quoted from a poem by Petrarch (*Rime*, LII), describing Diana bathing as "a wild hill girl" (N. Kilmer's translation).

12

Opéra: Benefit of Mlles Elssler

La Volière, ou les Oiseaux de Boccace, ballet-pantomime in 1 act, sc. Scribe (anon.), ch. T. Elssler, mus. Gide, f.p. May 5th, 1838.

One benefit performance follows another these days, giving the lie to the axiom that one day follows another but is never the same. Just as the price of the seats is doubled, so too is the boredom, for instead of finishing at eleven o'clock, the performance is dragged out until one o'clock in the morning to the great annoyance of porters.[1] Those taking their benefit do things very conscientiously and do not want to cheat the public. It might be good to offer a benefit to the public one day soon, but no one ever gives much thought to their convenience.

This daunting introduction is not directed to the Mlles Elssler, who had arranged their benefit in an amusing and witty manner, adding to the hot-pot of celebrated figures from the legitimate stage and the ballet, the seasoning of a ballet première . . . .

Mlle Therese Elssler's ballet, *La Volière*, though a little infantile and Florianesque, was nonetheless graceful. Here is the plot:

Thereza d'Alcazraza, owner of an estate in San Domingo, has been seduced and abandoned by Don Alonzo de Montreal, a Spanish grandee. She has consequently conceived a hatred for those monsters, those horrors, that are men, and in order to protect her young sister Zoé from the danger of being seduced, she keeps her shut up in a high-walled house in the company of several of her young companions.

A large birdcage with golden bars contains birds of every kind of song and

---

[1] In addition to the new ballet, *La Volière*, the performance included an act from *Le Mariage de Figaro* with Mlle Mars, Mme Cinti-Damoreau and Rosa Dupuis, an act from *Lucia di Lammermoor* with Duprez, and *Le Concert à la cour*. This last piece included a series of *tableaux vivants* based on well-known paintings, in which Fanny Elssler portrayed the principal figure in Baron Gérard's painting, *Corinne au cap Mysène*, now in the Musée des Beaux-Arts, Lyon.

plumage. Gunima the cook has no use for these birds—hummingbirds, waxbills, parrots—and would like to see them all released, but for the young prisoners they afford entertainment. And a meagre entertainment it is, for a thousand songbirds are not worth one quarter of a lover.

The negress Gunima shares her mistress's opinion of men, for her drunkard of a husband, Domingo, sold her to a European for a barrel of brandy, and her soured view of mankind is quite understandable. Young Zoé, although segregated from the outside world and kept in the most chaste ignorance, is no less a woman for all that. She is tormented by vague desires, she feels she is missing something that she cannot define (that something being, of course, love), she is bored by dressing up, and tired of playing games with her companions. It is all the same to her whether she dances or not, and her sister has to set her an example to persuade her. Admittedly, she then acquits herself to perfection.

But after a few moments a persistent knocking is heard at the door. Thereza, after much hesitation, decides to open it.

A young man enters, followed by an old negro carrying two guns. He is lost, and unable to locate his fellow hunters. He is dropping with fatigue, and just wants to sit down and take some refreshment. Thereza, finding the very sight of a man intolerable, and, moreover, anxious for her young sister Zoé, orders him to leave immediately without giving him time to recover his breath. But she cannot turn him out quickly enough to prevent him from catching a glimpse of the captive flock, a sight that makes him yearn to return to that splendid cage.

Zoé is returning to the house for lunch when, by chance, she observes the young hunter Fernand perched in full view in the foliage of one of the trees that overhang the garden, planning how to get in again. "Look," she cries to the cook Gunima, "What is that up there in the tree?" "It is a bird of the great open spaces," replies Gunima, who is probably aware of Plato's definition of a man as an animal with only two feet and no feathers, "a very wild, subtle and mischievous bird, whose only pleasure is doing evil, and who is to be avoided at all costs." It is quite obvious that Zoé's only wish now is to meet this dangerous creature at close quarters.

With his fishing rod Fernand lifts a bunch of keys that someone has left lying on a table by the gate, and choosing a moment when Zoé is alone in the garden, he enters the estate.

Zoé, who takes him for a young chick—or for a bird, we wanted to say— behaves towards him as if he were an innocent young warbler. She breaks up a biscuit and throws little pieces as to a real canary. The canary quickly gobbles them up, and to catch him, she ties a piece of thread around his foot and drags him into the cage, quickly slamming the door shut. Delighted with her prize, she goes to look for her friends to show them the rare bird that has been added to the collection.

The negro Domingo, who is looking for his master, is astonished to find him shut up in the cage, and bursts into laughter which the imprisoned Fernand finds uncalled for. Domingo's merriment at length abates, and he frees his master, only to be pushed into the cage in turn as a punishment for those roars of laughter.

Zoé returns with the young creoles, who shriek in terror at the sight of this black-feathered bird pitifully beating its wings and making faces behind the golden bars of the cage. It is no nightingale, as was promised, but an owl of the most hideous aspect!

Fernand then returns, frees Domingo, and flirts with the girls. Hiding behind a tree, Zoé begins to feel jealousy gnawing into her heart with its rat-like fangs, and determines to use the large cutlass that Gunima has given her and quietly slit the throat of the wayward bird. When the dancing is over, Fernand sits down on a bank of moss and falls asleep. Zoé then approaches to cut his throat, but like Psyche on the point of stabbing Cupid, she lets the carving knife drop from her hand. The sleeper is awakened by the noise, and with the aid of a few caresses has no difficulty in stifling the budding jealousy of the charming creole.

While everyone is performing *pirouettes* and going into the cage, Fernand's uncle, Don Alonzo de Montreal, the man who seduced Thereza, realising that the moment for decision has come, makes a very well-timed entrance and after a few passages of mime and some marching and countermarching in the dark, marries his former mistress. After Domingo has been caught in a trap by the mischievous girls, Gunima forgives him for having once sold her for a barrel of brandy. Fernand wins the hand of Zoé, and with that the company indulges in a surfeit of *entrechats* to celebrate the happiness of the three couples. The curtain falls.

We will not offer the slightest literary criticism of the framework of this ballet, which is the product of the intelligent legs of Mlle Therese Elssler. It is quite an adequate excuse for amusing and varied dances. We shall begin, therefore, by praising Mlle Therese Elssler for the taste she showed in not giving the male performers anything to dance in her choreography. Indeed there is nothing more disagreeable than a man showing his red neck, great muscular arms, parish beadle legs, and the whole of his heavy frame shuddering with leaps and pirouettes. We were spared that tedium at the performance of *La Volière*.

The *pas* that Mlle Therese Elssler and her sister performed is charmingly designed. There is one moment in particular, when the two sisters run forward from the back of the stage holding hands and shooting out their legs in unison, that for its harmony, correctness and precision surpasses the imagination. It is as if one were the shadow of the other, or there were only one dancer, advancing alongside a mirror that reflects her every movement. There could be no more delightful or harmonious sight than this dance, which was performed with great speed and precision. The audience's satisfaction was expressed in a storm of applause, accompanied by a chorus of canes and stamping of feet.

Fanny, to whom her sister Therese had, as always, given the most prominent rôle, displayed a childlike grace, an artless rapidity, and a quite adorable sense of mischief. Her creole costume suited her to perfection—or, we should say, she suited her costume to perfection.

A well supplied salvo of bouquets was aimed at the stage from every corner of the house. Flower sellers must love benefit performances! If this continues camellias will become unobtainable and extinct . . . .

El Jaleo de Jerez, danced by Mmes Noblet and Dupont, gave great pleasure. Just to see the fantastic, sparkling costume beneath its shower of sequins is enough to put anyone in a good mood. Mmes Alexis and Noblet danced with much fire and spirit, but it was a long way from the serpentine suppleness and the intoxicating passion of Dolores Serral, whom the Opéra has had the singular clumsiness to let escape. How ravishing the *Jaleo* would have been if danced by her and Fanny Elssler! We applaud the invasion of Spanish dancing with all our might, for the Spaniards have always been, and always will be, the best dancers in the world.

La Presse, May 7th, 1838.
HAD I, 129–132. L:349.

13

Opéra: *Le Diable boiteux*

Le Diable boiteux, ballet-
pantomime in 3 acts and 10
scenes, sc. Burat de Gurgy,
Nourrit (anon), ch. J. Coralli,
mus. Gide, f.p. June 1st, 1836.

*L*e *Diable boiteux*, which is a witty ballet (and intelligence is a rare quality in a ballet, as it is in everything), is still drawing full houses. The *Cachucha* continues to arouse the liveliest applause. The public cannot tire of it, and Mlle Elssler is always forced to repeat it, which she does with charming good grace. On the most recent occasion she danced it admirably, with unimaginable fire, attack and suppleness. Her poses were given with a proud, arched accent and a bold, sensual quality that would be the envy of the most fanatical dancers of Seville. Her *Cachucha* is becoming more and more Spanish every day, and responding to the encouragement of the audience, she is abandoning herself more and more to the languors and the passionate exuberance of this divine dance. Let us hope that this trend will be catching, and that the ladies of the corps de ballet will be fired with some of this completely Southern ardour. It is quite extraordinary that Spanish dancing has been revealed to us by a German, but then genius knows no frontiers.

Figaro, May 21st, 1838.
L:352.

14

Opéra: Début of Lucile Grahn

Le Carnaval de Venise, ballet-
pantomime in 2 acts, ch. Milon,
mus. Persuis, Kreutzer, f.p.
February 22nd, 1816. Revived to
include *pas de deux* for début of
Mlle Grahn, August 1st, 1838.

The Danish *débutante*, Lucile Grahn, brought new life to the old *pas de Zéphyre*, which she danced with Coustou, through her lightness and brilliance. She is tall, slender, loose-jointed and well proportioned, but would look much prettier if she did not smile so persistently. A dancer's smile should play about her mouth like a bird hovering above a rose, unable to land without damaging it. Smiles, which are never found on the marble lips of goddesses of old, contort the features and destroy their harmony. The cheeks swell, the skin creases at the corners of the nose, crow's feet appear alongside the eyes, and the lips lengthen and narrow as they stretch. Nothing is more inimicable to beauty. A beautiful woman should keep her face almost immobile. The play of her eyes is enough to animate and illumine it.

This serious reproof should not scare Mlle Lucile Grahn, whom we found very charming, and who was most favourably received by the public. She will be an excellent acquisition for the Opéra.

La Presse, August 7th, 1838.
HAD I, 155–156. L:365.

15

The Devadasis, otherwise known as Bayaderes

The very word bayadere[1] evokes notions of sunshine, perfume and beauty even to the most prosaic and bourgeois minds. At the lilting cadence of that word Philistines start jumping on to one foot and singing *Tirili* like Heinrich Heine's Berliner.[2] Imaginations are stirred, and dreams take shape of latticed pagodas, monstrous idols of jade and porphyry, transparent pools with marble steps, bamboo-roofed choultries,[3] palanquins hung with mosquito nets, and white elephants with vermilion howdahs on their backs. There is a sensation of dazzling light, and through the pale smoke of burning incense appear the unfamiliar silhouettes of the East.

You will also be reminded of the slender legs of Mlle Taglioni beneath billowing clouds of muslin, the rosy shades of her tights plunging you into dreams of the same hue. Inevitably, the very unIndian bayadere of the Opéra will merge with the *devadasi* of Pondicherry or Chandernagore.

Until now bayaderes had remained a poetic mystery like the houris of Muhammad's paradise. They were remote, splendid, fairylike, fascinating, vaguely placed in a swirl of sunlight in which dark eyes and jewels vied with one another in their sparkle. The tales of travellers, who are always preoccupied with the study of some insect or stone, have given us very inadequate ideas in this respect, and, apart from Haafner's ravishing story of Mamia,[4] we knew nothing of the dancers of India, not even their name, for the word

---

[1] The word is derived from the Portuguese *bailadeira*, a female dancer.

[2] The Berliner was the narrator's companion in the section on Italy in the *Reisebilder* of Heinrich Heine (1797–1856). When he was told of the plan to visit Italy, "he suddenly leaped from his chair, pirouetted three times on one foot, and trilled 'Tirili! Tirili! Tirili!'" (*Reisebilder, Italien*, chapters V and VI).

[3] Caravanserais found in India for passing travellers.

[4] Relying no doubt on his memory, Gautier wrote "Hummer" for the author of this true story of a European traveller's love for an Indian bayadere. It is to be found in Jacob Haafner's *Lotgevallen op eene reize van Madras over Tranquebaar naar het eiland Ceilon* (Haarlem, 1806), which Gautier knew either in its French translation, published in 1811, or in the brief extract published in *Le Monde dramatique* (1835, vol. I, pp. 161–162, and see also p. 416).

bayadere is Portuguese. In actual fact they are called *Devadasis* (the favoured ones of God), a name that derives from a fable in the Hindu mythology that has provided the subject for *Le Dieu et la bayadère*.

This scented poetry that, like all poetry, existed only in our dreams, has now been brought to us lazy Parisians who never stray from the gutters of the Rue Saint-Honoré and for whom the world ends at the suburbs. India, realising that we would not go to her, has come to us, like the Prophet who decided to go to the mountain when it did not come to him. For India, wild and remote as it is, cannot dispense with the opinion of Paris. It is imperative that Paris should pass judgment on its *devadasis*, and India should know what impression the priestess-dancers Amany, Saoundiroun and Ramgoun will make alongside the sisters Elssler and Noblet.

In the absence of their sacred river, the Hoogly or the Ganges, the Devadasis have established their bungalow a few yards from the Seine, in the Allée des Veuves,[5] in a house set among greenery that is doing its best to represent an Indian habitation. Knock on that green-painted fence with shutters behind it as a protection against prying eyes. You have arrived, and an old soldier standing guard at the door will enable you to recognise the mysterious abode. The old soldier is not there for nothing, for apparently attempts have been made to kidnap these exotic beauties, and over-enthusiastic lovers of Eastern dancing have been climbing the wall into the garden.

After establishing our identity at the gate, we were admitted into a low room, the end of which was closed by a door with large flaps. A vague aroma of Oriental perfumes permeates the house, aromatic sticks of benzoin and amber burn slowly in a corner of the room, and on the other side of the door can be heard the tinkle of little bells on the dancers' feet.

Only a door now separated us from the realisation of one of our life's dreams, one of our last poetic illusions, and we felt strangely moved, half in expectation, half in anxiety. At a sign from the master, the flaps opened and the troupe, consisting of five women and three men,[6] came towards us and

---

[5] Now the Avenue Montaigne. The house occupied by the Bayaderes was No. 23, a small single-storeyed building standing in its own grounds.

[6] The contract between the bayaderes and their French impresario, E.C. Tardival, was published in the theatrical journal, *Le Courrier des Théâtres*, on September 15th, 1838. In it their names and ages were given as follows: Tillé-Ammalle, aged 30, of the weaver caste; Ammany-Ammalle, aged 18; Ranga-Ammalle, aged 14; Soundra-Ammalle, aged 13; Ramalinga-Modely, aged 40, of the weaver caste, director of the dance or Nattonven; Saravanapoullé, aged 25, of the agamoudir caste, a singer or "pattagan"; Devanayagapoullé, of the agamoudir caste, musician or "mattalacaran". Amany, Saoundiroun and Ramgoun were sisters. The contract was for a term of eighteen months, and each of them was entitled to receive 10 rupees (27.70 francs) a day and in addition two lump sums of 500 rupees, one at the outset of the engagement and the other on returning to India. Amany and her sisters, Ramalinga and Saravanapoullé, were described as coming from Tiruvendipuram, a Vishnu shrine near Pondicherry.

made their salaams, to which we replied to the best of our ability with a Parisian bow.

The salaam consists of lowering the head to the feet, with the hands held alongside the ears. They then rise, alternately displaying the whites and blacks of the eyes, and accompanying all this with a little wriggle that defies description.

This salutation has the seal of humble grace and pride that is peculiar to Orientals, outshining our own as apples pale alongside oranges and gaslight weakens in the glare of the sun.

Before going on to describe the bayaderes and their dances, let us hasten to record that they are charming, unimpeachably authentic whatever certain minor journals may have said, and they coincided exactly with the idea we had formed of them. We were very flattered to find how accurate had been our intuition, for in a novel of ours entitled *Fortunio*[7] ... we introduced a number of Hindu characters whom we described so accurately and true to life that, having seen the real *devadasis*, we would not wish to change one word. So, after this tribute to our instinctive perspicacity, let us return to the bayaderes.

We shall start with Amany, the most beautiful and the tallest woman in the troupe.

Amany might be eighteen years old. In colour her skin is like a Florentine bronze—a shade that is a mixture of olive-green and gold, very warm and very gentle, and not at all like the black of the Negroes or the brown of the Mulattos, but a shade that is as tawny as gold and brings to mind one of the colours found in the coat of a deer or a panther. To the touch this skin is silkier than rice paper and cooler than a lizard's underbelly. Amany has blue-black hair, long, fine and flowing like the hair of a dark European. Her hands and feet are extremely tiny and refined. Her ankles are slender and bare, the big toe being separated from the others like the foot of a lark, and as in ancient Greek statues. For delicacy and elegance, the sides and front of her torso and her back could compete with the most perfect surviving examples of the art of antiquity. Her arms are charming, unequalled in their rounded form and slenderness. The entire nature of her body bespeaks a force and a purity of blood that is unknown in our civilisation, where the intermixture of races has destroyed and corrupted every physical type.

Her head is oval in form, with a well proportioned forehead, straight nose, firm chin and cheeks that are somewhat prominent—the face of a pretty Frenchwoman. The only difference is to be found in the mouth, which is pretty, it is true, but a little more radiant than a European mouth, the blue-

---

[7] *Fortunio*, Gautier's first novel, had been published in instalments in the newspaper, *Figaro*, between May 28th and July 24th, 1837, under its original title of *L'Eldorado*. Reentitled *Fortunio*, it came out as a separate volume in May 1838.

dyed gums and teeth that she outlines with black lines giving it an alien, Asiatic character. As for her eyes, they are incomparably beautiful and brilliant. They are like two jade suns revolving in a crystal sky. They have a transparency, a limpidity, a creamy, velvety brilliance, a sensual, exotic languor that are beyond one's power to imagine. All the vitality of the features seems to have settled in those miraculous eyes, for the rest of her face is as immobile as a bronze mask, only a suspicion of a smile slightly parting the lips to give life to such tranquillity. Amany's adornment is as strange and charming as her person. A yellow line, drawn with a brush and renewed every day, stretches down her forehead from the parting of her hair to the meeting of her eyebrows. The deep black of her hair, parted in coils and plaited in the fashion of the Swiss, throws into relief the sparkling brilliance of the tinsel and glass jewellery with which she is bedecked. A brass cap engraved with the form of a snake sits on the crown of the head, where our own women are wont to pin their chignons. This cap is held in place by a cord ending in a transverse circlet. The tresses are intertwined with threads of gold and silk tassels. A more extravagantly graceful or coquettishly alien hair style cannot be imagined.

Enormous pendants, strangely worked, sparkle and quiver at the ends of her ears, which are pierced with enormous holes large enough to put one's thumb through. The upper lobe is also riddled with openings, which are stopped up with little wooden pegs to prevent them from closing.

And again, quite contrary to our ideas of elegance, the left nostril has been pierced, together with the nasal septum, to allow a silver ring, encrusted with precious stones, to pass through it and rest on the upper lip. At first this ornament seems in barbaric taste, but one quickly becomes accustomed to it and finally discovers a depraved and piquant grace in it. Set against her swarthy complexion, this ring, sparkling brightly in the light, produces a fine effect, lighting up the features and somewhat tempering the bejewelled brilliance of the eyes that perhaps otherwise would appear fierce and stand out too blatantly in a face that is uniformly dark.

Five or six strands of gold filigree encircle Amany's neck, two or three copper circlets dangle on her wrists, and her upper arm is enclosed by a sort of bracelet in the form of an upside-down V that compresses the flesh rather tightly. Large rings resound above her ankles, accompanying every movement with a clink of metal, and silver rings sparkle on her toes, for it is on their feet that Indian women wear their rings. Amany's hands are striped with black tattooing, done with great taste, that extends half way up the forearm, for all the world resembling lace mittens.

Wide Oriental trousers, held above the hips by a tightly strapped leather belt, fall in wide folds down to the ankles. A little bodice with very short sleeves encloses and compresses the breasts. This bodice is very pretty, with sequins, tinsel, glass jewellery and silver and gold decorations forming the most capricious and elegant arabesques. While on this subject, let us remark that countries we regard as barbaric show exquisite taste in all their decorative art, and that the most skilful haberdashers of Paris are far from being able to match the purses, tobacco pouches, wallets, fans and other bric-a-brac that people bring back from the Levant, and which are handmade by poor devils who are eaten away by vermin and beaten black and blue.

Between the bodice and the trousers is a large expanse of flesh that is completely bare and unadorned. There could be no more charming sight than that pale golden skin, so smooth and tender, which could be mistaken for a satin corset, and on which the light plays and shimmers with a bluish glow. The chemise, it must be said, is unknown among the bayaderes.

A wide scarf of striped material, its ends falling in front and floating on the stomach, completes this highly original costume.

Saoundiroun and Ramgoun are dressed in exactly the same way, apart from the scarf which in their case is made of white muslin brocaded with gold. Saoundiroun and Ramgoun are about fourteen years old. They wear round their necks the little gold jewel that is the sign of their betrothal to the temple. Saoundiroun is the prettier of the two, at least by European standards. Their exuberance and the joyful brilliance of their smiles contrast with the expression of plaintive resignation of Amany, who looks like a statue of Melancholy brought to life. Tillé, the old lady of the troupe, is not much above thirty, although she looks fifty. As for Veydoun, she is six. Imagine Cupid dyed black. She is the most charming, mischievous and brightest little devil.

The men have a great beauty. They have black sparkling eyes, noses of aquiline cut, little moustaches, and as their only covering, trousers held up by a belt in the fashion of Turkish breeches. Their headwear consists of a piece of striped material, gracefully wound round. The centre of the forehead is illumined by a small bright yellow patch, the size of a seal. In delicacy and purity of form their bodies resemble that of Duret's Neapolitan dancer.[8] They are also the same colour, a beautiful shade of fresh bronze, plain and warm. One of them, Ramalingam, has a white beard that makes the most picturesque impression in contrast to his dark face, giving him the appearance of an old man out of Homer, although he claims to be only forty-two. Ramalingam has three white stripes above the eyes, three more on his side as well as others on the arm. He is the minstrel of the troupe, the one who chants while Saoundiroun and Ramgoun perform, somewhat in the manner of those plays of antiquity in which one actor recites the words while another makes the gestures. Instead of a lyre Ramalingam has only two bronze cymbals, somewhat like castanets, which he clashes together to mark the rhythm. This utterly primitive music is accompanied by Savaranim on the pipes and

---

[8] Francisque-Joseph Duret (1804–65). The Musée Fabre in Montpellier possesses two of his sculptures, *Danseur Napolitain* and *Napolitain dansant la tarentella*.

Deveneyagorn on the drum. The pipes, made out of bamboo, are joined together with wax like the pipes of an Arcadian shepherd, and there is nothing to prevent you from mistaking Savaranim for one of Theocritus's shepherds, except that the pipes are blocked up, we know not how, in such a way as to emit only a single note, which greatly restricts the melody. Deveneyagorn's drum is made of stretched rice leaves. It is shaped like our tambourine, but played with the fingers instead of drumsticks as is the custom here. In the centre of the skin a black circle is drawn with burnt rice that has to be constantly reapplied like the white on a bandsman's leatherskin apron or the chalk at the end of a billiard cue.

So much for the orchestra. One can imagine nothing simpler, more patriarchal, more antediluvian; it is like children's music or a nurse's lullaby whose sole purpose is to send her charge to sleep with its monotonous moan.

Now that we have given you a detailed picture of the musicians and the dancers, let us describe them at work.

Ramalingam, standing at the back of the room, recites a poem, at the same time clashing his cymbals. To each verse he gives a strong emphasis, showing white teeth that are pointed like those of a Newfoundland dog. Imperturbably, Savaranim blows the single note from his pipe, and Deveneyagorn teases his drum with fingering as if he were playing the piano. From time to time the three virtuosos roll their eyes in ecstasy, like music lovers listening to Beethoven's Symphony in C.[9]

With a vivacity and exuberance that remind one of the sudden frisky movements of a young chamois, Saoundiroun and Ramgoun dance a *pas* representing *The Robing of Vishnu*. This dance has nothing in common with our dancing, being a highly stressed pantomime rather than an actually choreographed *pas*. We noticed a certain movement of the head, to and fro like a bird regurgitating, that was exceedingly graceful but, in manner of performance, incomprehensible to our eyes. Then add to this an unbelievable rolling of the eyes more dazzling than the brightest of French glances and the most meaningful of Spanish winks, swaying hips and extraordinary supple arm movements, and you have a performance that is most piquant and original.

What is strange is the noise that the bayaderes' small feet make on the floor. They might be dancing a mazurka with heels and steel spurs. The clear, dry sound they produce when beating out the rhythm makes one wonder whether they are shod with iron.

They also have a way of stopping abruptly in their tracks, making their glass ornaments and necklaces tinkle like a Turkish Jingle.

This dance, by Saoundiroun and Ramgoun, is followed by a sort of *jota*

---

[9] Beethoven's First Symphony in C major.

aragonesa performed by the four dancers, including old Tillé, in which Amany displays a grace that is absolute.[10]

After the "*jota*" comes the *Dance of the Doves.*

The *Dance of the Doves* will be a roaring success, matching that of the *Cachucha*. It is enough to make a fortune for the Indian dancers. Amany stands between her companions, Saoundiroun and Ramgoun, and with gestures and poses of profound melancholy and voluptuousness, recites a sad tale of love and betrayal, something like the Song of Songs, the romance of Saul, or the *pantoum* of Patani's dove.[11] She lifts her arms and dreamily throws them back before allowing them to fall languorously like garlands of flowers wilting in the heat of the day. She makes her lovely brown pupils float in the glutinous limpidity of her large eyes, while keeping up a guttural murmur that is drawn out with endings in "a" and childlike vowels. Meanwhile, Ramgoun and Saoundiroun are whirling with frightening speed. Then something white sparkles and hovers in the midst of the whirlwind. It is a scarf which the waltzing girls are crumpling and tormenting between their fingers. The wild waltz continues; old Ramalingam clashes his cymbals with redoubled ardour, the working of the scarf goes on, and in the centre of the flickering cloud you perceive the beak of a bird. Then its head forms, its body takes shape, and wings appear and begin to beat. After the bird comes the nest and the palm tree with its leaves formed by bunched up material. The music ends, and the waltzing girls come to a stop and kneel before you to offer their graceful handiwork.

[10] This dance was entitled *The Malapou*. Malappu is a Tamil word meaning a dance performed in the presence of a deity, and this dance, incorporating the use of scarfs to form the shape of a dove, is more likely to be Malay in origin than Indian.

[11] A *pantun* is a quatrain of Malay verse, and Patani (or Pattani) is a minor sea-port on the Gulf of Siam about sixty-five miles north of the Malay border. The *pantun* that Gautier here refers to may be the last quatrain of the series entitled "Unique among Girls", published in *Pantun Melayu*, collected by R.J. Wilkinson and R.O. Winstedt (Singapore, 1923):

> In Patani their feathers fall,
> Two score tail of doves.
> Never like this a lass of them all,
> To steal hearts' loves.

The poem on which the *Dance of the Doves* was based was printed in *L'Entr'acte* of August 16th, 1838, as follows:

"I have seen on a palm tree two doves, balancing in the evening breeze; they were reflected in the marble pool; nothing is sweeter than yesterday's loves.

"But a vulture seizes one of the doves, carries it away, tears out its heart, drops it into the sea; the vulture is oblivion; nothing is sadder than yesterday's loves.

"I have seen a flower open at the teardrops of the dew; it blushed at the kisses of the rising sun, quivering on its stalk with passion; nothing is more tender than today's loves.

"Let my beloved look on me with his limpid eyes, and my heart brightens; my beloved is as brilliant as the sun; I blush at the sight of him, I quiver at the sound of his voice; nothing is more tender than today's loves."

What is most surprising is that at the end of this delirious waltz, which lasts for nearly half an hour, the bayaderes show no signs of fatigue. Their breathing is no heavier than normal, not a drop of perspiration dampens their brows. And those bronze bodies, set in motion by nerves of steel, remind one of the finest breeds of horses that never sweat.

After the *Dance of the Doves* the troupe withdrew, leaving behind the sweet scent of amber and sandalwood. The doors closed, and we were brought back to earth from the temple of Pondicherry to find ourself in Paris, in the Allée des Veuves.

P.S. It is reported that the Bayaderes will make their début at the Variétés. Their proper place is at the Opéra, in *Le Dieu et la bayadère*. Is M. Duponchel, who has let Dolores slip away, going to allow Amany to be carried off too?

La Presse, August 20th, 1838.
(*Caprices et zigzags*,
pp. 339–350.) L:368.

16

Th. des Variétés: Début of the Bayaderes

First appearance in Paris, Th. des
Variétés, August 22nd, 1838. 26
performances until September
18th. Later appeared twice at the
Tivoli.

The public's curiosity was whetted to the highest degree. The wonderful
descriptions of the few privileged journalists who were admitted into the
mysterious retreat in the Allée des Veuves had stirred the imagination of their
readers, and everyone was talking and dreaming about the Bayaderes.

"Have you seen the Bayaderes?" was the question that had taken the place
of the banal "How are you?" But how to set about seeing them? Will they be
dancing at a theatre? At the Opéra, the Variétés, the Porte-Saint-Martin, or
the Palais-Royal, where the sound of Spanish castanets still echoes? Who will
win the day—M. Duponchel, M. Dumanoir, or M. Harel?[1] There is a rumour
that *Le Dieu et la bayadère* is being arranged for them—an excellent idea. It is
said they are black. Rubbish! Yellow, red? No. Chocolate brown? What a
dreadful idea! and what about Mlle Taglioni, who is so white and pink?

A few people who are used to tales of sea spiders, intelligent rats, the sky
raining frogs, negresses playing the rôles of Mlle Mars and other inventions
that fill the newspapers during the literary season were even claiming that the
Bayaderes were just a hoax like Kaspar Hauser,[2] the theft of the pictures from

---

[1] Henri Duponchel (1795–1868), Dumanoir [Philippe-François Pinel] (1806–65)
and François-Antoine Harel (1794–1846), at that time respectively directors of the
Opéra, the Variétés and the Porte-Saint-Martin.

[2] The mystery of Kaspar Hauser was a source of curiosity for several years. He
appeared, where from no one knew for certain, completely uneducated, having
apparently been brought up in a dark cellar, unable to stand upright and deprived of
any social contact. There was a rumour that he was the eldest son of the Grand Duke
of Baden. Doctors and educators interested themselves in his case. He was murdered
in mysterious circumstances in 1833. A few weeks before seeing the Bayaderes Gautier

47

the Museum and the division of France. The most sceptical even claimed that old Ramalingam had been a porter in their house, that Amany was simply a shopgirl who had dyed her skin with liquorice juice, and that fifteen years ago Saoundiroun owned a café in Lyon (Saoundiroun is fourteen, by the way!). As for Deveneyagorn, he was said to be a drummer in the suburbs, and Savaranim a regimental fife player. For there are some readers who are easy to convince and others who will only believe if they can stick their finger into the wound, like the late St Thomas of pyronic memory. There are even people who are still convinced that the Osages[3] were the inhabitants of Lower Brittany in full colour.

When the doubters read the account of the Bayaderes' reception at the Tuileries, they began to believe that it was quite probable that the Bayaderes were not shopgirls and that they really did come from the temple of Tiruven-dipuram. However, there were still a few who cited the false Siamese embassy sent to the Great King.[4] But when they saw on the playbill of the Variétés:

THE BAYADERES.

THE SALUTATION OF THE PRINCE, by Veydoun;
THE ROBING OF SHIVA, by Saoundiroun and Ramgoun;
THE DANCE OF MELANCHOLY, by Amany;
THE DOVES, by Amany, Saoundiroun and Ramgoun;
THE MALAPOU, by Tillé, Amany, Ramgoun and Saoundiroun;

MUSICIANS.

Ramalingam, Savaranim, Deveneyagorn.

they could not wait to send their servants to book boxes and stalls, which they did in such numbers that the first six performances are sold out.

On the day of the first performance the public was in a state of great

had reviewed a drama by Anicet Bourgeois and Dennery called *Gaspard Hauser*, f.p. Ambigu-Comique, June 4th, 1838, writing: "Gaspard Hauser, whose mysterious destiny has created such a flutter in the hearts of sensitive and romantic folk, is nothing but a joke of M. Méry. No joke was ever more successful, not even the sea-spider, the dilletante rat, the theft of the pictures from the Museum, those priceless inventions of the mind of our friend Gérard."

[3] A party of Osage Indians, a tribe belonging to the Siouan peoples, including a chief, had visited Paris in the summer of 1827, and created something of a sensation. Many theatres put on special performances for them, and their simple dignity and gentle demeanour were greatly admired. It was reported that a deputation from their tribe had visited Paris during the reign of Louis XIV and that their impressions had been handed down in the oral traditions of their race.

[4] The Siamese embassy that was received by Louis XIV in 1684 was perfectly genuine. The then King of Siam, Narai, was seeking French assistance to counterbalance the influence of the Dutch, and for a few years Bangkok was ceded to the French.

agitation, for at last they were going to see something strange, mysterious and charming, something completely unknown to Europe, something new! And the less enthusiastic spectators could not avoid being moved by that timid curiosity that takes hold of you when suddenly the long impenetrable doors of the harem open before you.

The audience was so impatient that it would not hear out a very amusing little prologue that was well acted by Rébard and Mlle Flore, and forced the curtain to be lowered after the first few scenes.

The curtain rose again, and standing in front of a scene that was as Hindu as it was possible to make it, the five Bayaderes came into view in all their sparkling finery.

They made their salaams with their customary grace and suppleness, and then Ramalingam began to clash his cymbals and recite the poem of the robing of Shiva, accompanied by Savaranim's bamboo pipes and Deveneyagorn's rice-leaf drum.

At first the dancers' movements, so rapid and sudden as to seem more like the shivering of frightened gazelles than the attitudes of human beings, the prodigious winks in which the whites and the darks of the eye vanish in turn, and the outlandishness of their costume caused astonishment among the audience, which was taken aback rather than charmed.

But when the lovely Amany recited her melancholy plaint, the antique beauty of her poses, the supple sensuality of her figure, the sorrowful languor of her gestures, and the plaintive sweetness of her half-smile aroused general applause. She could have been the dark-skinned Shulamite of the Song of Songs, swooning with love, and seeking her beloved on a mountain of balsam or in a garden full of aromatic plants.

The Dance of the Doves had an enormous success. Indeed it is difficult to imagine how two dancers spinning round with frightening speed could form a dove on a palm tree out of a large piece of white muslin whose very size must have been awkward for them. When Saoundiroun and Ramgoun had accomplished this task, they went over to the proscenium boxes to offer it gracefully to the ladies there. This *pas* is far superior to the *pas de châle* and all the other "Indian" scarf shaking that we are accustomed to admire. Its basic idea is charming. Amany writes a letter to her beloved on a palm leaf, and her companions Saoundiroun and Ramgoun make doves out of their scarf to carry her message. Nothing could be fresher or more gracefully simple.

The *Dagger Dance* has a wild and tragic intensity that makes the most striking impression.

The *Malapou,* or the Dance of Delight, is a little like the *Jota aragonesa.* Its movements are lively and full of joy, with the dancers bending back and lifting their arms over their heads with infinite suppleness.

This is the pose that has been chosen by M. Barre, who is engaged in making a statuette of Amany. There could not be a more adorable pendant to the delightful figurine of Fanny Elssler. Mme la Duchesse de C* * is busy with a statuette of Saoundiroun. The Bayaderes are therefore lacking no type of illustration. Art, society and fashion are all combining to pay tribute to them; they are truly the lions of the season.

Talking about fashion, Mlle Fanny Elssler, who had paid a visit to her sister artists, the Bayaderes, in the Allée des Veuves to see if tinier and lighter feet than her own really did exist, was greeted with a salvo of applause when she entered her box, without doubt her due as Queen of the Dance.

Had we been there, we would have clapped more vigorously than anyone else, for there is no greater admirer of Mlle Fanny Elssler than ourself. However, we do wish people would reserve a little of their enthusiasm for great poets or great composers. We would like them to applaud Lamartine, Victor Hugo or Rossini as well when they appear in the theatre. Let us have a little less admiration for the legs and the throat, and a little more for the creative mind.

La Presse, August 27th, 1838.
HAD I, 162–165. L:370.

17

Opéra: Revival of *La Sylphide*

La Sylphide, ballet-pantomime in
2 acts, sc. Nourrit (anon), ch. F.
Taglioni, mus. Schneitzhoeffer,
f.p. March 12th, 1832. Revived
for Elssler, September 21st, 1838.

The Opéra, it has to be said, is short of ballets and does not know how to
employ its army of ballerinas and pretty ballet girls. It appears that
writing for the legs is the most difficult form of literature, for no one has ever
managed to make a success of it. *Les Mohicans*, in spite of headdresses made
of cut-out pumpkins, feather aprons, tomahawks, scalping knives, salmon-
pink tights and the blaze of local colour that was lavished on it, made only a
brief appearance in the theatre. *La Volière* seemed much too childish, and a
few graceful touches could not make up for the weakness of the work as a
whole; *La Chatte métamorphosée en femme*, in spite of a scenario written by
Charles Duveyrier, "poet of God and glorifier of the face of the Holy Father",
and scenery and production that were magnificent in a curious and vaguely
Chinese manner, obtained only a declining success that not even the talents of
Mlles Fanny Elssler and Nathalie Fitzjames could reverse; the revivals of *La
Fille mal gardée*, *La Somnambule* and *Le Carnaval de Venise* had a nostalgic
interest, which made no impression on the box office; but then, as Joshua, the
gaoler in *Marie Tudor*,[1] says, one should no more reconsider opinions one is
prepared to fight for than renew acquaintance with women one has loved at
the age of twenty. Both women and opinions seem very old and ugly, very
bald and toothless, and very stupid. And what is true of women and opinions
is truer still of ballets.

Seeing these ancient pieces which charmed our fathers and whose tunes,
churned out on barrel organs at street corners, used to rock us to sleep in our
early childhood, brings a lump of fragrant sadness into the throat such as is
aroused by the discovery in the corner of some dusty drawer of pigeon-
breasted dresses, yellowed lace, a broken fan with a song by Jean-Jacques

[1] Drama by Victor Hugo, f.p. Th. de la Porte-Saint-Martin, November 7th, 1833.

Rousseau on one side and a gouache of a shepherdess on the other, forgotten relics of a long dead grandmother or great aunt.

But something more than poetic nostalgia, whatever its fragrant charm, is needed to fill the house at the Opéra. And what is more, the dilapidated condition of scenery that has faded completely and cracked along its folds ought to prevent the exhumation of these balletic mummies, which twenty years or so ago may have been fresh young bodies, full of charm, and with smiling countenances, but will now always be slightly ridiculous, old-fashioned, a relic from one's parents' generation.

Consequently the Opéra had only a single ballet, *Le Diable boiteux*, the very amusing and witty ballet by M. Burat de Gurgy[2] that H.M. the King of Prussia liked so much that he sent the author a magnificent tie-pin representing the "limping devil" with a diamond for his stomach, carbuncle eyes and ruby feet, but this ballet has now been performed fifty times and it is high time to give this success a rest and show the fine ballerina in different rôles and different costumes. Although the *Cachucha* is still encored as furiously as ever, it is not right to applaud nothing but the chatter of castanets and Spanish exuberance, and whatever its popularity, a single piece does not make a repertory.

For some time there has been talk of reviving *La Sylphide* and *La Fille du Danube* with Fanny Elssler in Mlle Taglioni's rôles. The Taglionists were up in arms, crying sacrilege and the abomination of desolation. Anyone would have thought someone was putting his hands on the holy Ark. Mlle Elssler herself, with a humility that goes so well with talent, was fearful of tackling rôles in which her illustrious rival had attained such perfection, but *La Sylphide* was too charming a ballet to be dropped from the repertory on account of excessive scruples. There are a thousand ways of playing a rôle and, specially, of dancing the same thing, and the pre-eminence of Mlle Taglioni over Mlle Elssler is a question that can quite properly be open to argument.

Mlle Taglioni, worn out after her interminable travels, is no longer what she was. She has lost much of her lightness and elevation. When she makes her entrance, she is still the same white mist bathed in transparent muslin, the same ethereal, chaste vision, the same divine delight we know so well, but after a few bars signs of fatigue appear, she grows short of breath, perspiration dapples her brow, her muscles tense up with strain, and her arms and bosom become flushed. She who a few moments before was a real Sylphide is now a mere dancer—the greatest dancer in the world, if you wish, but no more than that. The princes and kings of the North, in their imprudent and

[2] Apart from his scenario for *Le Diable boiteux*, Edmond Burat de Gurgy (1809–85) wrote a number of minor works for the stage and a biographical dictionary of actors. He also edited the *Journal de Commerce*, and wrote political articles, mainly of an anti-socialist nature, for *Le Constitutionnel*.

merciless admiration, have applauded her so much, bemused her so with compliments, buried her under such a shower of flowers and diamonds that they have weighted down those intangible feet that, like the amazon Camilla's,[3] bend not the blades of grass that she walks upon. They have laden her with so much gold and precious stones that Marie-full-of-grace is unable to take flight and can do no more than skim the ground timidly like a bird whose wings are sodden.

Today Mlle Fanny Elssler is in the full force of her talent. She can only vary her perfection, she cannot surpass it, because beyond the very good is the too good, which is nearer the bad than one thinks. She is a man's dancer, just as Mlle Taglioni was a woman's dancer. She has elegance, beauty, an intrepid and exuberant vigour, boldness to excess, a sparkling smile, and above all an air of Spanish vivacity tempered by a German simplicity which makes her a very charming and adorable creature. When Fanny is dancing, a thousand happy thoughts enter your mind, your imagination strays into palaces of white marble flooded with sunlight and standing out against a deep blue sky, like the friezes of the Parthenon. You imagine yourself leaning on the balustrade of a terrace, with roses above your head, a cup of Syracuse wine in your hand, a white greyhound at your feet, and beside you a beautiful woman in a dress of flesh-coloured velvet, with feathers in her hair. And your ears are filled with the chatter of tambourines and the silvery tinkle of bells.

Mlle Taglioni made you think of cool and shaded valleys, whence a white vision suddenly materialised from the bark of an oak tree before the gaze of a surprised and blushing shepherd. She might have been taken for one of those Scottish fairies of whom Walter Scott writes, and who roam in the moonlight by a mysterious fountain, with a necklace of dewdrops and a thread of gold about her waist.[4]

If I may express it thus, Mlle Taglioni is a Christian dancer and Mlle Elssler is a pagan dancer. The girls of Miletus,[5] those beautiful Ionians who were so celebrated in antiquity, must have danced like her.

[3] Camilla, queen of the Volscians, was brought up in the woods and dedicated to the service of the goddess Diana as a child. She was so swift that she could run over a field of corn without bending the blades, and make her way over the sea without damping her feet.

[4] Scott frequently refers to fairies in his poems and novels, and Gautier may have been thinking of the White Lady of Avanel in *The Monastery* who rose out of a fountain and bade Halbert:
> Look on my girdle—on this thread of gold—
> 'Tis fine as web of lightest gossamer.
Another spirit associated with a fountain appears in the novel *The Bride of Lammermoor* and in Donizetti's opera based on it, *Lucia di Lammermoor*, which Gautier saw and reviewed when it was staged at the Théâtre Italien on December 12th, 1837. In the opera the second scene is set by the fountain and the heroine's first aria recounts the legend associated with it.

[5] A town on the borders of Ionia and Caria.

So Mlle Elssler, while Mlle Taglioni's rôles may not be suited to her temperament, can replace her in anything without risk or peril, for she is sufficiently versatile and talented to adapt herself and assume the particular guise of the character. Friday's test showed that Mlle Elssler did not overestimate her ability to understand the repertory of her formidable rival.

The subject of *La Sylphide* is one of the happiest ballet subjects that it is possible to come across. It comprises a moving and poetic conception, a rare thing in a ballet and indeed in anything else, and we are delighted that it has been restored to the stage. The action is self-explanatory, can be followed without difficulty, and lends itself to the most graceful scenes. Furthermore, there are practically no dances for the men, which is a great blessing.

We shall not describe the ballet, which everyone knows better than we do, and will speak only of the manner in which it was performed. It was carefully staged, featuring, among the men, Mazilier,[6] the elegant Cléophas of *Le Diable boiteux*, Elie, the amusing simpleton who is not used enough, Simon,[7] who is very good at *saltarellos*, *mazurkas* and other character dances, and among the women, Mlles Fanny and Therese Elssler, Noblet, Dupont and the prettiest *rats* of the theatre.

All we ask for is the refurbishment of the first set, which is showing its age. In many places the backcloth has lost its paint and can be seen through like a worn-out dish cloth. It is not worthy of the Opéra's reputation for splendour.

Mlle Elssler's costume was ravishingly fresh. Her dress might have been cut from dragonfly wings, and her slippers made of satiny lily petals. A crown of convolvulus, of a perfect shade of pink, encircles her brown hair, and behind her white shoulders two little wings of peacock feathers quiver and shimmer, wings that are superfluous with the possession of such feet.

The new Sylphide was wildly applauded. She displayed infinite delicacy, grace and lightness throughout her performance. She appeared and vanished like an impalpable vision, now here, now there. In the *pas* with her sister she excelled herself; they could not have been more graceful. Her miming in the scene where her lover catches her in the folds of the enchanted scarf, expresses sorrow and forgiveness, and the sense of fall and irreparable error, with a rare feeling for poetry, and her last long look at her wings as they lie on the ground is a moment of great tragic beauty.

A little accident occurred at the beginning of the work that had no untoward consequences but at first caused us a moment of alarm. At the

[6] Joseph Mazilier (1797–1868) had been engaged at the Opéra in 1830 and at this point had not embarked on his distinguished career as a choreographer. Gautier was to review many of his ballets: *La Gipsy*, *Lady Henriette*, *Paquita*, *Betty*, *Griseldis*, *Vert-Vert*, *Orfa*, *Aelia et Mysis*, *Jovita*, *La Fonti* and *Le Corsaire*.

[7] François Simon (1800–77) danced at the Opéra from 1822 to 1842, and had the distinction of becoming a member of the Legion of Honour for services rendered in the National Guard.

moment when the Sylphide disappeared up the chimney (a strange route for a Sylphide), Mlle Fanny was carried up too quickly by the counterweight and stubbed her foot quite hard on the wooden base of the mantelpiece.

Happily she was not injured, but this gives us an opportunity to protest against the flying that is a tradition of the old Opéra. We find nothing graceful in the sight of five or six unfortunate girls dying of fright, hooked up high in the air on iron wires that can so easily snap. Those poor creatures thrash their arms and legs about with the desperation of frogs out of water, involuntarily reminding one of those stuffed crocodiles hanging from ceilings. At Mlle Taglioni's benefit performance, two sylphides became stuck in mid-air, and no one could move them up or down. In the end a stage hand took charge and climbed down a rope from the flies to rescue them. A few minutes later, Mlle Taglioni, who has only spoken once in her life (on the stage, mind you) came up to the footlights and said: "Gentlemen, no one is hurt". The next day the two minor sylphides received a gift from the real Sylphide. Another hitch like this will very probably happen soon.

La Presse, September 24th, 1838.
HAD I, 174–178. L:376.

18

Opéra: Revival of *La Fille du Danube*

La Fille du Danube, ballet-
pantomime in 2 acts and 4 scenes,
sc. Desmares (anon), ch. F.
Taglioni, mus. Adam, f.p.
September 21st, 1836. Revived
with Elssler, October 22nd, 1838.

On the occasion of the revival of *La Fille du Danube* something unheard
of happened at the Opéra, where the public normally only applauds
with the tips of their fingers and whistles only through pursed lips. There was
a tumult, a riot, a bacchanale, a battle of fisticuffs, furious bravos and
turbulent whistling, just as in the days of the great conflict between classicists
and romantics. One might have believed oneself back at a performance of *Le
More de Venise* or *Hernani*.[1] It is a glorious thing for Mlle Elssler to have
aroused such lively enthusiasm and no less violent disapproval.

Personally, we cannot understand why the admiration, which is indeed
justly deserved, that certain persons have for Mlle Taglioni should prevent
them from appreciating Mlle Elssler's merits, which they admit only in the
Cachucha and *Le Diable boiteux*.

Mlle Elssler has no desire to encroach on the territory of Mlle Taglioni, for
she is herself well enough endowed to need no one else's spoils. But while
Mlle Taglioni is dancing only for Russian Emperors and Princes, there is no
reason to jettison amusing and graceful ballets that would give variety to the
repertoire and enable us to wait patiently for something new, which is always
a long time in coming . . .

---

[1] Two landmarks in the establishment of Romantic drama on the Paris stage. *Le More
de Venise*, an adaptation of *Othello* by Alfred de Vigny, f.p. Th. Français, October
24th, 1829. *Hernani*, drama by Victor Hugo, f.p. Th. Français, February 25th, 1830,
was the cause of the great fracas between the conservative classicists and the young
Romantics, celebrated by the latter as *la bataille d'Hernani*.

Mlle Elssler ought to be able to assume a rôle of Mlle Taglioni's without committing sacrilege. A ballet is not sacrosanct.

For our taste Mlle Elssler is as good as Mlle Taglioni. First of all, the former has the enormous advantage of being more beautiful and younger. Her pure and noble profile, the elegant shape of her head, and the delicate line of her neck give the impression of an antique cameo of incredible charm. Eyes sparkling with mischief and delight and a simple and humorous smile illumine and animate her happy features. Add to these precious gifts her full, rounded arms, a rare quality in a dancer, her supple figure set well on the hips, legs of Diana the huntress which, were they not mobile, lively and restless like the wings of a bird, might have been sculpted out of Pentelic marble by some Greek artist of the age of Phidias, and to crown all, her allurement and her physical charms—*veneres cupidinesque*,[2] as the ancients called those qualities which are inborn and defy description.

As a ballerina Mlle Elssler possesses strength and precision, clear gestures and vigorous *pointes*, a bold exuberance which shows itself in the very Spanish arching of her body, and a happy and serene facility in everything she does, which makes her dancing one of the most delightful sights in the world. She also possesses something which Mlle Taglioni has never had, a profound feeling for drama. She dances as well as her rival, and acts better.

With a sense of modesty that cannot be too highly praised Mlle Elssler changed all the *pas* that Mlle Taglioni danced. No "profanation" took place, therefore, and when the old Sylphide comes back, she will find all her baggage intact. In the interests of the administration, Mlle Elssler has agreed to take over rôles which were not created for her but which she has succeeded in making her own and rejuvenating. The whistling was thus totally unjust and absurd. The audience protested against it *en masse*, the occupants of all the boxes from the *baignoires* to the uppermost tier rising to their feet and bursting into thunderous applause to assure the charming ballerina that the real spectators were having no part in such an untimely display of disapproval. Mlle Elssler was wildly recalled at the fall of the curtain, and a scented shower of bouquets amply compensated her for the whistling of the cabal.

La Presse, November 2nd/3rd, 1838.
HAD I, 188–192. L:383.

---

[2] A quotation from Catullus's poem on Lesbia's sparrow (*Carm.* III, 1), in which the poet describes qualities by personifications of the feelings of the subject, i.e. loves and desires to denote qualities that evoke those feelings.

19

Opéra: *La Gipsy*

La Gipsy, ballet-pantomime in 3
acts and 5 scenes, sc. Saint-
Georges, ch. Mazilier, mus.
Benoist, Thomas, Marliani, f.p.
January 28th, 1839.

A ballet scenario is more difficult for a writer to compose than you would
think.[1] It is not easy to write for the legs. There can be no proud
bombastic tirades, no fine verse, no poetical clichés, no words for effect, no
puns, no declamations against the nobles, nothing but one situation after
another. So a good ballet is the rarest thing, tragedies, operas and dramas
being nothing by comparison. To devise a plot and order the action in a
manner that is always clear to the spectator, to find events and passions that
can be conveyed by easily understood poses and gestures, to handle considerable numbers of people and make them perform without any confusion, to
select a period and a country whose costumes are brilliant and picturesque
and a locality that lends itself to beautiful scenery, those are the troubles and
difficulties that attach to this futile pastime that is called a ballet and is not
even literature. Many things that are regarded as serious can be done with
much less effort.

Ever since M. Burat de Gurgy's *Le Diable boiteux*, which earned him the
gift of a beautiful pin from the King of Prussia, no ballet had been successful
at the Opéra. *La Chatte métamorphosée en femme*, although coldly received
at first, has been the only one to remain in the repertoire, thanks to the

---

[1] Gautier was writing from some little experience, for at about this time he wrote the
scenario for a ballet entitled *Cléopâtre*, which was submitted to and apparently
accepted by the Opéra. Binney in *Les Ballets de Théophile Gautier* suggests that it was
written with Fanny Elssler in mind for the title rôle; the music was to be composed by
Xavier Boisselot. However, the manuscript gathered dust on the shelves of the Opéra
for several years, and on Gautier's authority was delivered to Boisselot in about 1848.
Unfortunately Boisselot mislaid it, and it has never been found.

splendour of its scenery and production. M. de Saint-Georges, with the assistance of Mazilier and Mlle Elssler, now seems to have broken the spell and solved the problem. *La Gipsy* obtained a resounding success on Monday.

La Gipsy belongs to the type of ballet known as the *ballet d'action*, which infers that pantomime occupies a larger proportion in it than dancing and that the plot is much more complicated than in a *ballet à spectacle*. There had not been a *ballet d'action* produced since *La Somnambule*, *Clari* and *La Fille mal gardée*,[2] so it came across as new, like everything else that has been forgotten.

The scenario of M. de Saint-Georges'[3] ballet has as much action as a melodrama of the good old days.

The curtain rises. Enormous slabs of rock fill the back of the stage, divided in the middle by a torrent. An uprooted fir tree spans the chasm and links the two peaks. Pay attention to that fir tree, which is more dramatic than its log-like appearance suggests. Steps cut in the rock lead to this natural bridge. Beyond are dark forests of pine and larch which ascend the grim mountain-side and dissolve into the misty blue of the distant peaks. On the right rises the castle of Lord Campbell, a splendid, forbidding pile, with balustraded balconies and vermiculated bosses, giving the appearance of aristocratic power. A window is open on the side facing the spectator. Look well at that window. On the left a statue of Charles II can be seen with banners bearing the inscription "Accession of Charles II" in letters of gold. Do not forget the statue. The fir tree, the window and the statue—without them there will be no drama.

To celebrate the accession of King Charles II, Lord Campbell's clan has assembled on the lawn before the castle. A great hunt is to take place, and Lord Campbell and his friends enter, armed with carbines, and set off, all except Narcisse de Crakentorp,[4] who has an aversion for dangerous pursuits and, like Moron in *La Princesse d'Elide*,[5] cannot understand why man should

---

[2] These three ballets had entered the Paris Opéra repertory in the 1820s, Milon's *Clari* in 1820, Aumer's *La Somnambule* in 1827, and Aumer's revival of Dauberval's *La Fille mal gardée* in 1828. All three were based on realistic if simple themes.

[3] Jules-Henri Vernoy de Saint-Georges (1801–75) was a prolific writer for the stage. Today he is known chiefly as the collaborator whom Gautier chose for *Giselle*, but he also produced scenarios for many other ballets, including *La Gipsy*, *La Jolie Fille de Gand*, *Lady Henriette*, *La Filleule des fées* and *Le Corsaire*, all of which Gautier described in his reviews.

[4] Gautier gives the spelling "Krakenthorpe", but I have followed the scenario, un-English though it is.

[5] Moron was the court fool in *Les Plaisirs de l'île enchantée*, a comedy-ballet by Molière, written specially for a fête at Versailles, f.p. May 7th, 1664. The rôle was created by Molière himself. Moron's views on hunting appear in Act I, scene ii.

disturb wild animals that as often as not hunt the hunter. Lord Campbell's little daughter, blonde and rosy, a charming little creature of five who is not so prudent as Sir Narcisse de Crakentorp, also wants to see the hunt and goes to stand by the side of the road. At that very moment, beside the fir tree which we have drawn to your attention, there passes something dark, with paws, that the scenario describes as a wild beast—a bear, a boar, a wolf, a poodle, we are not too sure what. The wild beast, since wild beast it is, attacks the little girl and bites her on the arm, just as Alphonse Karr's dog[6] might have done. Fortunately, one Stenio de Churchill, a Puritan officer on the run, happens to be passing, and snatching up the carbine that Narcisse de Craken- torp, who is half dead with fright, has let fall, kills the beast and saves the child, whose only injury is an arm wound—not serious, but one that will leave a scar eminently suitable for dramatic identification. Lord Campbell invites Stenio to join his friends and himself in celebrating Charles II's accession. The Puritan Stenio sits down uncomfortably at table and picks sparingly at his food, for his Puritan stomach is turned by the Royalist and Cavalier fare.

The clan celebrates the King's feast-day with dances, rejoicing that Camp- bell's daughter has been saved from such a terrible danger. Here there is a pretty *pas de deux* performed by Mlles Maria and Nathalie[7] with incredible grace, unison, precision and lightness. It was a fascinating duel from which neither emerged the winner. Mlles Maria and Nathalie should dance together more often, for they could not be better matched in youth, talent and beauty. The arrangement of the *pas* is original and a credit to Mazilier, who has managed to give it novelty without descending to the bizarre and tortuous.

Lord Campbell, being firmly of the opinion that no meal is complete without drinking and that toasts are obligatory at a political banquet, raises his glass to the statue and proposes the King's health. Stenio, having no desire to drink to the health of Moloch, Dagon, Belial and the Anti-Christ, to use Puritan jargon, dashes his glass to the ground and rises in indignation. The royalist guests, outraged by the Roundhead's insolence, want to kill him on the spot, but Lord Campbell, who has no desire to see the rescuer of his child murdered before his eyes, restrains them. Some gypsies who are present, and who have provided Stenio with clothes for a disguise, join him in protest. Stenio manages to escape in the general confusion, but Trousse-Diable, the gypsy chief, is seized and taken into the castle as a prisoner.

[6] Alphonse Karr (1808–92), journalist and novelist, was editor of *Figaro* at the time when Gautier was contributing to it. Gautier mentioned Karr's black and white dog, Freyschütz—presumably the animal referred to here—in his review of Karr's novel, *Sous les Tilleules* in *La Presse* of March 17th, 1839.

[7] Maria [Jacob] (b. c.1818) danced at the Opéra from 1839 to 1849. She was no doubt a Jewess, and dropped her family name for stage purposes on that account. She married the Baron d'Henneville. Nathalie was, of course, Nathalie Fitzjames.

We have asked you to note a certain window that we strongly suspected would have some dramatic purpose. The window is wide open, and through it Megge, the devoted nurse, can be seen putting the little girl to bed. Trousse-Diable, who is a vindictive fellow, comes into view climbing over the roof, edging his way along the cornice and the entablature, seeking a foothold in the cracks between the stones. In this manner he reaches the window. The sight of the sleeping child gives him a villainous idea. Originally his only intention was to escape, but now he sees an opportunity for revenge. Drawing his great Moorish cutlass, he leaps from the balcony into the room, but then has second thoughts and instead of cutting little Sarah's throat, he carries her off to make a tightrope artist or a street dancer of her.

The child utters piercing screams as she is carried away, but the agile Trousse-Diable has time to reach the bridge over the torrent and, with a kick, sends the fir tree tumbling into the chasm, thus preventing his pursuers from following him. They aim their guns, but holding the little girl's body in front of him as a shield, he backs into the forest of fir trees and disappears.

So there we have a prologue packed with incident. A bear, a bridge, a torrent, a child kidnapped, dancing, a hunt, fights—enough to satisfy the most avid craving for romantic events.

In the second act, for the prologue counts as an act, we are in Edinburgh and ten years have passed. The Puritan officer now balances chairs on his teeth, swallows swords and lifts weights, while Sarah has become a first-class acrobat. Like Goethe's Mignon,[8] she has learnt how to perform the egg dance and spin round with a glass of water. She is the Esmeralda of these modern Truands,[9] an Esmeralda no less charming than the original. The moon, like a blue lamp suspended from the ceiling of the night, casts its azure glow over the streets of Edinburgh from which the window of the Silver Leopard Inn shines out alone like a red star. In this respectable establishment some young noblemen are laughing, singing and drinking, while Trousse-Diable is lying in wait outside for someone to leave so as to rob him at a convenient moment after the patrol has passed. In fact, Narcisse de Crakentorp soon appears in a somewhat inebriated condition. Trousse-Diable, as if wanting to know the time and begging for alms, greets him very civilly and asks, "What time is it?" Instead of replying, "Five francs,"[10] Narcisse takes out his Nuremburg watch, which the shifty Trousse-Diable very deftly slips on to his own fob to the utter astonishment of Narcisse, who finally realises what is happening

[8] A character in Goethe's *Wilhelm Meisters Lehrjahre*, a girl who was exploited as a street performer, the "egg dance" being one of her specialities.

[9] The Truands were the criminal class of fifteenth-century Paris that Victor Hugo so vividly portrayed in his novel, *Notre Dame de Paris*.

[10] Presumably some comedian's quip that had stuck in Gautier's memory—perhaps an example of Odry's repartee (see No. 3, note 3).

and moves to draw his rapier. But Trousse-Diable's companions press round him and rob him with surprising dexterity. The worthy Narcisse de Craken-torp is left nearly as naked as a little St. John.[11]

Fortunately, Mab, the gypsy queen, arrives, wearing a large scarlet man-tilla, and orders Narcisse's belongings to be restored to him. Pickpocketing is one thing, but stealing is quite another. Trousse-Diable's heart bleeds. For a gypsy it is extremely painful to give anything back, which explains why he sidles off, clutching a medallion on a gold chain that he covets. Re-equipped from head to toe, with the exception of the chain, Narcisse bows and leaves, while Mab, seeing Trousse-Diable trying to look inconspicuous in a dark corner, calls him to her and makes him hand over the precious trinket. This chain will serve her to trap Sarah, of whom she is jealous both as queen and as lover, for Mab is in love with Stenio, who in his outlaw existence has preserved his former elegance that sets him apart from the gypsy throng. But she discovers Stenio kneeling before Sarah, and in spite of her rage, has no alternative under gypsy lore but to marry them. She suffers yet another setback, for young Sarah, translating the miracle of Amphion[12] into choreog-raphy, leads the whole tribe after her, like rats on their way to be drowned. But she conducts them, not to the river, as the piper did in the German fairy tale, but to the public square of Edinburgh, where tumblers and fairground merchants foregather. This set is very beautiful, full of open space, sunshine and light. The viaduct with its enormous arches reveal blue crevices of great depth, and the city rises in uneven layers like an enormous madrepore. It is a view which people who have visited the place say is extremely realistic.

In the reproduction of this fine square acrobats tumble and charlatans hawk their wares, and the shrill sound of trumpets and the beat of drums are heard through the laughter of young folk and the chatter of girls in the milling crowd. Adding a touch of Bohemia and Egypt, the whole tribe is dancing, leaping, cabrioling, and the air is filled with the sound of their tambourines, castanets and mandolines, the savage but charming music of a primitive race that exerts such a fascination over sophisticated folk. Mab and Sarah dance one of those ravishing *pas* that suggest the fluttering of dove's wings by the way in which the two sisters[13] shake and gently quiver in a cloud of white muslin. After acknowledging the applause and collecting purses in their tambourines, the two rivals, who only a moment before were so close, separate. A few minutes later Sarah returns alone, wearing the most coquet-tish and cheeky costume imaginable, an officer's tunic all emblazoned with

[11] St John, often portrayed naked in paintings of the Madonna and the Christ child.

[12] According to ancient legend Amphion, the son of Jupiter by Antiope, was the inventor of music, which had been taught to him by Mercury. The walls of Thebes were said to have been erected by the sound of his lyre.

[13] Fanny and Therese Elssler.

buttons, a *vivandière's* skirt, little boots with steel heels, a black cravat framing her delightful chin, and all surmounted by the loveliest little feather, mischievous and triumphant. It is quite impossible to describe this dance. It is a combination of rhythmical precision, charming abandon and an energetic and bouncy speed that surpasses the imagination, and the metallic chatter of her spurs, like castanets worn on the heels, adds a marked accent to the steps and gives the dance a character of joyful vivacity that is quite irresistible. She is now made to repeat this *pas.* We have already protested against this barbaric custom. Apart from interrupting the action, it jeopardises the numbers that follow because if the time allowed for a rest is cut short, the dancer or singer will be tired when their cue comes. We quite understand you might want to take a second look at a passage that has delighted you, but you can always book a box or a stall and come back the following day to applaud the favourite *pas.* We find this enthusiasm to see two performances of the same thing for the price of one on the ground of admiration somewhat penny-pinching and sordid. But here it implies that the *Cracovienne* is all the rage. Seeing difficulties performed with such ease, you would not imagine that the wings of Mlle Elssler, that vivacious, fantastic swallow, could ever tire, and whatever we might say, the *pas* will always be encored. Besides, why dance so well anyway!

In the midst of all those groups that form and disperse before your eyes, you will not have forgotten the medallion. The treacherous Mab has given it to the unsuspecting Sarah, an enemy's gift, a Judas kiss. Sarah slips the chain round her neck, and Narcisse de Crakentorp who begins to flirt with her recognises the stolen trinket.

Stenio and the gypsies put up a desperate resistance, but the forces of law prevail, and after much fighting and scuffling, poor Sarah is brought before Lord Campbell, the chief justice. You will remember Lord Campbell from the first act as a man of haughty mien and resolute bearing, dressed in a red jacket with golden brandeburgs. Now his hair is snowy white. The loss of his daughter has aged him prematurely, and as a mark of his grief, he wears a suit of black velvet with large ivory buttons. A portrait hangs upon the wall, that of the little girl in a sky-blue dress of the first act—the girl, you will recall, whose arm was mauled by the beast and who was abducted by Trousse-Diable when he climbed in through the window.

Sarah defends herself with all the strength of a clear conscience and rejects the infamous accusation, but appearances are against her and Lord Campbell, although troubled by vague memories and the similarity of the prisoner's age to that of his daughter, condemns her to death. Sarah falls in a faint and the nurse, hurrying to her aid, uncovers the providential scar on her arm. All is now explained, there are embraces and tears of joy, and Sarah is beside herself with happiness. Indeed, the transition from gypsy to great lady, from gaol to the drawing room, from darkness to light, is very sudden! What an astonishing turn of fortune, how unexpected the recognition, truly worthy of romantic drama! Throughout this act Mlle Elssler attained the most sublime peaks of tragic acting. The noble pride of innocence, energy, tears, grief, love, intoxicating joy—she ran through the whole gamut of human emotions. Only Miss Smithson or Mlle Dorval[14] could have produced such bursts of pathos, such forceful pantomime.

In the third act we are in Lord Campbell's apartments. The gypsy girl of a moment ago has become a duchess, and truly not much was needed to achieve that. Slender ankles, tapering white hands, small ears—all the signs of good breeding were there already. Surrounded by all this pompous and ponderous luxury, Sarah experiences the same frustrations as Mme de Maintenon's carp[15] that hankered after its mud; she misses dancing in the open air on the acrobat's worn piece of carpet, and above all misses her lover. The minuet, though she dances it with a perfect aristocratic grace, seems very pallid by comparison with the pirouettes she performed on the street. She looks sadly at her poor, fantastic gypsy dress, a tawdry bundle of rags with its holes stopped up with spangles. Like a wild sparrow who is used to pecking and hopping on the roadway, she feels bored in her gilded cage. As she is daydreaming in this way, a window is smashed in, a typical gypsy trick of Trousse-Diable. It is indeed Trousse-Diable and Stenio, who have broken in with the intention of seizing Sarah Campbell. The little troupe that was doing so well out of Sarah's dances has fallen on hard times in the absence of their little comrade and are starving, while Stenio, as can well be believed, is dying of love. Sarah is on the point of being persuaded by these convincing arguments, when Lord Campbell and the society folk are heard approaching. Stenio hides in an adjoining closet that is conveniently situated for lovers caught in the act—an essential adjunct to a theatrical drawing room. Stenio is soon dragged out of the closet and a great scene takes place. The father curses the daughter, the daughter bursts into tears, the lover appears very embarrassed. Sarah declares that she will marry no one else and finally confesses that she was married to Stenio according to gypsy rites and is really his wife. The father is in despair, but is consoled when Stenio reveals his real name. If ever you think you have been involved with a rogue, to find he is just an outlaw is happiness itself. So father Campbell relents and blesses the union of the young couple. Alas, there is many a slip between cup and lip. Like the

---

[14] Two actresses who made a very deep impression on Romantic audiences. Harriet Smithson (1800–54) was an Irish actress who enjoyed a great triumph when she appeared in Paris in 1826 and 1827 and introduced most of the Romantic writers, musicians and artists to Shakespeare, whose plays thus became an inspiring influence in their campaign for the reform of the French theatre. She married Hector Berlioz. Marie Dorval (1798–1849) was, for many, the ideal interpreter of Romantic drama.

[15] Mme de Maintenon (1635–1719), second and morganatic wife of Louis XIV.

appearance of Mona Belcolor in the scene of Franck and Deidamia,[16] Mab's face is seen through the window. Mab has come to take her revenge for Stenio's betrayal and Sarah's beauty. A pistol shot is heard. Stenio falls. Sarah throws herself on her lover's body and faints. Mab is seized, and the curtain falls on this tragic ending, too tragic perhaps for a ballet.

Now that we have come to the end of this rather complicated plot, let us turn to the performance. Mlle Fanny Elssler surpassed herself, creating a mixture of Florinde and Fenella.[17] Mlle Therese Elssler gave the difficult rôle of Mab a suggestion of a Sybil of antiquity that was remarkably effective. Mazilier was graceful and moving, Elie was a delightful Narcisse, and Simon, wearing a very picturesque costume, rendered the character of Trousse-Diable in a manner that was energetic and true to life. The other gypsies looked a little like baker's boys; they ought to have been dressed with greater fantasy and variety. This ballet, Mazilier's first, is gracefully arranged, and the *pas* are novel. The only fault we had to find was that the dances are all placed in the beginning and that the last scenes are devoted entirely to pantomime. The music is by three composers, MM. Benoist, Thomas and Marliani,[18] the act written by M. Thomas appearing greatly superior to the others in the novelty and grace of its arrangement. Everything—scenario, music, scenery and dance—obtained the greatest success. The good old days of *Le Diable boiteux* are back with us again.

La Presse, February 4th, 1839.
HAD I, 220–222. L:398.

[16] Despite an exhaustive search I have not succeeded in identifying this allusion. I have been unable to trace a theatrical piece containing these characters, and indeed the juxtaposition of the names Franck and Deidamia seems so unnatural that I am inclined to suspect a lapse of memory on Gautier's part. Was he referring to the painting by Charlemagne-Oscar Guët (1801–71) of the scene between Adelaïde von Walldorf and Franz in Goethe's play. *Goetz von Berlichingen*, exhibited in the Salon of 1835?

[17] Heroines of *Le Diable boiteux* and *La Muette de Portici*, two of her most celebrated rôles.

[18] Ambroise Thomas (1811–96), better known for his operas *Mignon* and *Hamlet*, also composed some charming music for the dance, as evidenced by his divertissement in the latter work. He wrote the music for two other ballets produced at the Opéra, *Betty* (1846) and, very much later, *La Tempête* (1889). Marco Aurelio Marliani (c. 1803–49), a minor opera composer and pupil of Rossini. François Benoist (1794–1878) was later to write the music for *Le Diable amoureux*, *Nisida* and *Pâquerette*.

20

Opéra: *La Tarentule*

La Tarentule, ballet-pantomime in
2 acts, sc. Scribe (anon), ch. J.
Coralli, mus Gide, f.p. June 24th,
1839.

It is not yet day. The stage is bathed in a velvety blue shadow. However, one young man is already up before dawn and tip-toeing outside a fine-looking tavern. A real Italian tavern, with a brick-built arch, reticulated walls, pillars festooned with fantastic shoots of vine, a sign-board, and most important of all—a balcony, an essential piece of architecture for any dramatic situation. This young man who has risen so early is naturally a lover, for there is no better alarm clock than love. In his capacity of lover, he wishes to serenade his lady. We do not dispute his right to do so, but a serenade is not performed by oneself alone. So our young man, who the scenario informs us is called Luidgi (which is a mistake, by the way, and whom we shall refer to as Luigi to be accurate), goes and knocks on the doors of some of his friends' houses to make the dawn serenade more complete. These gallant young men, all bright and lively, arrive armed from head to foot with guitars, triangles and mandolines to take up their piaces beneath the window of Laurette, the daughter of the post-mistress, and prepare for their sentimental hullabaloo.

Peeping through the vine leaves and the garlands of climbing flowers that brighten the balcony you espy a charming face blooming like a real live flower at the first light of day. The flower is Fanny Elssler, or Laurette. No doubt, like the *belle matineuse* who inspired so many sonnets in the sixteenth century,[1] she wants to cast doubt on which side the sun is rising and to dim the light of dawn with jealousy. The lovely girl leans forward, and seeing the group of musicians, whose intentions are obvious from the presence of Luigi, retires into her maiden's chamber to listen to the serenade at greater ease.

But who is this suspicious character crossing the back of the square, glancing uneasily from side to side? His fierce countenance, his unruly side

---

[1] Claude de Malevile (1597–1647) and Vincent Voiture (1598–1648) both wrote celebrated sonnets on this theme.

66

whiskers, his villainous moustache, the jacket thrown over his shoulders, the pointed hat, and above all the loaded carbine in his hand and the enormous pistols sticking out of his belt leave no doubt as to his profession. He is a bandit, for we have omitted to inform you that we are in Calabria, a countryside that, judging from ballads and *opéras comiques*, is swarming with bandits. This bandit is followed by another, then a third, a fourth and a fifth—a whole procession of them—carrying packages and seemingly involved in some very lucrative business. Behind this first squad of brigands comes a horse to whose back is bound a slim white figure in a straw hat and a tight-sleeved muslin dress, with blonde ringlets falling on her shoulders, the very image of Clarissa and Pamela, one of those romantic heroines who appear in the drawings of Angelica Kauffman.[2] This interesting victim is none other than Mlle Forster,[3] who plays young Englishwomen perfectly for two reasons, first, because she is English, and next, because she is pretty. Her eyes are blindfolded with a black handkerchief, tied round her head as many times as that of Mlle Pigeaire.[4] God knows what fate these bandits have in store for her! Luigi, being a warm-hearted lad, is touched by the poor woman's misfortune and is fired with the generous idea of rescuing her. Throwing aside his guitar, he picks up his rifle. His companions do likewise and dash away in pursuit of the bandits.

While we have been telling you all this, the sun has risen, and we shall take advantage of this break in the action to speak of the scenery, which is very beautiful. It is not one of those sets that arouse the facile enthusiasm of the common herd, such as a fairy palace with fountains and columns of crystal, or a dark underground cavern, or a very blue apotheosis, but merely a very simple landscape with a tavern on one side and on the other a chapel whose

[2] Clarissa and Pamela, heroines respectively of Richardson's novels *Clarissa Harlowe* (1747–48) and *Pamela* (1740), both objects of pursuing males. Angelica Kauffman (1741–1807), painter of the early Neoclassical school.

[3] Caroline Forster was an English-born dancer who was in the ballet company of the Opéra from 1834 to 1844. Two years after this article was written she was to create the part of Bathilde in *Giselle*. In 1840, having met her at a congenial dinner at Nathalie Fitzjames's, Gautier expressed his admiration of her ears and golden hair in some eulogistic verses that begin:
Oui, Forster, j'admirais ton oreille divine
Tu m'avais bien compris, l'éloge se devine
Qu'elle est charmante à voir sur les bandeaux moirés
De tes cheveux anglais si richement dorés.

[4] Mlle Pigeaire was a child reputed to have extraordinary powers when in a state of hypnotic trance. She was brought to Paris by her father to compete for a prize which Claude Burdin, a member of the Académie de Médecine, had offered to the first person who could read a given writing without the aid of eyes and in the dark. Although she gave several successful private demonstrations, the experiment for the prize never took place because her father would not agree to the Académie's requirements on the nature of the blindfolding bandage.

façade is decorated with those grotesque frescoes that gratify the piety of the Italians, a tall umbrella-shaped pine tree, and a few houses scattered about haphazardly. At the back is the road that leads to the mountain, the mountain itself, with its sheer and strangely shaped escarpments, bathed in space and sunshine, and an eternally blue sky smiling down on this beautiful natural scene. That is all. The brushes of the quartet that have given us so many beautiful scenes can be recognised. MM. Feuchères, Séchan, Diéterle and Despléchin[5] could not have chosen a better way of marking their return to the Opéra, from which they had long been excluded through some strange misunderstanding.

Laurette, who has been finding our description too long and is surprised not to hear the music start up again, reappears on her balcony. But all that remains of the serenade is a heap of guitars, mandolines and triangles. There is no one around to play them, which all in all is no great loss, but Laurette cares about her serenade and determines to perform it for herself rather than forgo it. She summons her friends who pick up the abandoned instruments and begin to make a furious din beneath the balcony. Laurette's mother, Matea, an ill-tempered old woman who has little liking for any other sort of music than the clink of money, pokes a very irritated nose out of the window and, unable to see the mischievous girls because of the overhanging wall, goes downstairs in her most offensively maternal manner to put the young suitors to flight. Instead of Luigi, whom she dislikes because he does not have a penny, she finds Laurette and her friends, and not wanting to waste her forbidding expression, bursts into reproaches and scares away the pretty little creatures with her scolding. The sound of gun shots creates a timely diversion. Luigi and his companions are at grips with the bandits. They soon return in triumph, bringing with them the English lady, her baggage and a wounded brigand. The beautiful lady desires to express her gratitude to Luigi, and having found her wallet intact in the baggage, takes out a number of bank notes and gives them to her rescuer to enable him to marry Laurette, for the young man's poverty was the sole reason for Matea's refusal of consent. This abundance of thousand franc notes betrays the hand of M. Scribe,[6] notwithstanding his anonymity, for no other playwright is so care-free in distributing largesse. After rewarding the handsome Luigi in this manner, Clorinde, the beautiful Englishwoman, retires to the nearby convent to wait for a new carriage and horses.

Luigi, who is in a hurry to get married—and such haste is very understand-

[5] Léon Feuchères (1804–57), Charles Séchan (1803–74), Jules-Pierre-Michel Diéterle (1811–89), Edouard-Désiré-Joseph Despléchin (1802–70), all scene painters who worked for the Opéra. Séchan and Diéterle were pupils of Ciceri.

[6] The scenario of *La Tarentule* was written anonymously by Eugène Scribe (1791–1861), the most prolific dramatist of his day.

able when the fiancée is Fanny Elssler—wants the wedding to take place immediately. Mother Matea finds her future son-in-law a little hasty, but she falls in with this hurry and the wedding is arranged to take place that very day. Nothing could be speedier than that.

Suddenly the crack of postillions' whips is heard. Judging from the noise, they must be driving a personage of the highest importance. A post chaise bespattered with a whole firmament of mud comes trundling into the square drawn by two horses bedaubed with muck. The mud and the muck are perfectly represented, M. Duponchel himself having scrupulously supervised the execution of this "natural detail". However, we must point out that in such a climate and such good weather, it would have been more authentic to cover the horses and post chaise with dust instead of manure. Swept-away roads and downpours of rain are needed to get a carriage in a state like that.

With great ceremony the postillions help out of the chaise a perky little old man with a roguish expression, a dissolute smile and a roving eye, swathed in a puce quilted overcoat, the sort that old men used to wear in the time of the Regency, as so well portrayed by Henri Monnier.[7] Who can it be? A duke, a prince, a great nobleman, a banker? Better still! It is the illustrious, learned, marvellous Dr. Oméopatico, who has felt the pulse of all the sovereigns of Europe, a man who can perform miraculous cures, who only begins to treat the sick when their condition is desperate, a doctor who cures the dead—very different from his colleagues who only succeed in killing off the living.

Feeling tired and in need of refreshment, Dr. Oméopatico wishes to break his journey. The post chaise is taken to the stable and the postillions relieved of their high boots. The doctor is fascinated by Laurette's beauty. How charming she is with her red velvet bodice trimmed with gold braid, what pretty little feet she has, what tapering hands, and what a vivacious expression! How he would love to give her a consultation, but Laurette assures him that she is in the very best of health and has not the slightest desire to fall ill. The old rogue pays court to her, taking the liberty of putting his arm round her waist to check her heart beat and taking her hand to feel her pulse, but Laurette is not deceived by this show of medical attention. She slaps his hand and leaves. The doctor, who as is to be guessed from the brand new crepe band on his hat has recently been widowed, bursts into flame like a wick and proposes marriage. Laurette replies by introducing her fiancé to whom she is to be married that very evening. Oméopatico is forced to accept the situation. His old muzzle is no match for handsome young features.

---

[7] The Regency of Louis XV (1715–23), from his succession to his attainment of legal majority, a period notable for a relaxation of morals after the austerity of the last years of Louis XIV. Henri Monnier (1805–77), caricaturist and writer, notable for his creation of the character of Joseph Prudhomme, a personification of the *nouveau riche* bourgeois during the reign of Louis Philippe.

Laurette's young friends come running in. They are impatient for the dancing to begin, their feet are itching, and unable to wait until the ball, they start celebrating the marriage without more ado. Oméopatico sits next to Mme Matea, amorously ogling the girls with a host of old men's coquetries, stretching out his leg to show a well preserved calf, shaking grains of snuff from his lace jabot, opening his diamond-encrusted snuff box, given him by some Northern sovereign, making his ring sparkle in the light, and so on. The sight of all these young people gives him a new lease of life. Laurette goes to change into her ball dress, and while she is away three of her friends, Mlles Albertine, the charming Adèle Dumilâtre and her sister Sophie, who would be really pretty if only she had a little more nose, dance a *pas de trois* of which nothing need be said except that it is a *pas de trois*.[8]

After the conclusion of this *pas de trois*, Laurette reappears. A green bodice with silver ornamentation fits snugly around her supple figure, a very short skirt of white gauze reveals a delicious pair of legs that would be worthy of a Greek sculptor, and she has placed a crown of flowers over her brown hair. Castanets chatter at the end of her fingers. Laurette is going to dance the *Tarantella*! Come, Luigi, what are you doing sitting on a bench? My dear Luigi, don't you know the *Tarantella*? What, you are going to allow your sweetheart to dance with someone else, and you say you are in love and put your hand on your heart the whole act long! You are making a mistake, Luigi, particularly since the young man who is taking your place has a well proportioned figure and is extremely skilful on his legs. You explain that Mlle Therese Elssler was to have danced with Laurette and that Mlle Therese has injured her foot? That is beside the point—the fact is, you are hardly showing any jealousy.

The grace, lightness and precision that Laurette puts into this *Tarantella* is unimaginable. It is a mixture of ethereality and strength, of modesty and intoxication that defies description. Roguishness and passion are combined with unusual success, and the girl's reserve continually surfaces to temper the whole Mediterranean fire of this dance. From now on the *Tarantella* will take its place alongside the *Cachucha* and the *Cracovienne*.

As for M. Petipa,[9] he did not worry the audience at all, being not too

[8] The Dumilâtre sisters, Sophie (b. 1819) and Adèle (1822–1909), were the daughters of an actor and were known as "*les soeurs Demi-lattes*" on account of their thinness. Sophie danced at the Opéra from 1838 to 1845, Adèle from 1840 to 1848. Adèle had the more distinguished career, and was the first Queen of the Wilis in *Giselle*. For Albertine, see No. 26, note 4.

[9] This is Gautier's first reference to Lucien Petipa (1815–98), who had made his début at the Opéra just two weeks before, on June 10th. He continued to dance there until 1862, and he was chief ballet-master from 1860 to 1868. His career was closely linked to Gautier's, for he created the rôles of Albrecht in *Giselle* and Achmet in *La Péri*, and was the choreographer of Gautier's ballet *Sacountala*.

The Paris Opéra that Gautier knew, the theatre in the Rue Le Peletier. Napoleon III and the Empress Eugénie arriving for a gala performance.

The interior of the Opéra during a performance of the ballet of the nuns in *Robert le Diable*. Engraving by Willaeys.

ABOVE: Fanny Elssler dancing the *Cachucha*. Statuette by Jean-Auguste Barre.

OPPOSITE: Marie Taglioni in *La Sylphide*. Statuette by Jean-Auguste Barre.

LEFT: Los Dansadores. Lithograph by A. Bouquet of the statuette by A. de Chevagneux of Mariano Camprubí and Dolores Serral. (*L'Artiste*, 1837, 1st series, part 9.)

BELOW: Lise Noblet and Mme Alexis Dupont dancing *El Jaleo de Jeréz*. Lithograph from a drawing by Louis Lasalle.

RIGHT: Nathalie Fitzjames. Lithograph by Alexandre Lachauchie.

BELOW: Fanny Elssler in *La Chatte métamorphosée en femme*. Lithograph from a drawing by M. Alophe.

LEFT: Louise Fitzjames as the Abbess in *Robert le Diable*. Statuette by A.R. Maréchal.

OPPOSITE: Fanny Elssler in *La Volière*. Lithograph by M. Gauci from a drawing by J. Deffett Francis.

RIGHT: Louise Fitzjames caricatured as an asparagus in a Ballet of Vegetables. Lithograph by Caboche Gregoire. (*Figaro*, April 7th, 1839).

Fanny Elssler dancing the *Cachucha* in *Le Diable boiteux*. Engraving by Jules Collignon. (*Les Beautés de l'Opéra.*)

Fanny Elssler in *La Sylphide*. Lithograph by Wild from a drawing by Franz Krüger.

RIGHT: Fanny Elssler dancing the *Cracovienne* in *La Gipsy*. Lithograph by Joseph Bouvier.

BELOW: Therese Elssler as Mab in *La Gipsy*. Statuette by Jean-Jacques Elshoecht.

ABOVE: The Bayaderes in *The Malapou*. Dancing in the foreground, Amany and Tillé. From a music title.

OPPOSITE: The bayadere Amany. Statuette by Jean-Auguste Barre.

LEFT: Fanny Elssler dancing the *Tarentella* in *La Tarentule*. Lithograph by J. Bouvier.

BELOW: Albertine, in a *pas de deux* with Louis Bretin in *Les Pages du duc de Vendôme*, which she danced in London in 1840.

RIGHT: Lucile Grahn in *La Sylphide*. (Published in the magazine, *La Sylphide*, No. 1.)

LEFT: Augusta Maywood. The earliest print, a lithograph by E.W. Clay, published in New York the year before her Paris début.

ABOVE: *Giselle*, the first act, with Giselle and Albrecht alone on the stage. Engraving by Jules Collignon. (*Les Beautés de l'Opéra.*)

LEFT: Carlotta Grisi in *Giselle*, Act II. (*Album du Théâtre, No. 1.*)

OPPOSITE TOP: The dance of the three-legged man, performed by Eugène Coralli in *La Jolie Fille de Gand*. Anonymous lithograph, from a music title.

OPPOSITE BELOW: The villagers' dance in Act III, Scene III of *La Jolie Fille de Gand*. Anonymous lithograph, from a music title.

ABOVE: The famous leap in the opening scene of *La Péri*, with Lucien Petipa and Carlotta Grisi. Lithograph from a drawing by M. Alophe.

LEFT: Lucien Petipa and Carlotta Grisi in *La Péri*. Lithograph by C.G. and J.H. Lynch.

repulsive for a man. He is young, good looking enough, and has something of the proud elegance of the dancer who partners Dolores. He performed his dangerous task very well.

After the *Tarantella* came a *pas de quatre* performed by Mabille[10] and Mmes Alexis-Dupont, Nathalie Fitzjames and Maria. This *pas*, which was nicely arranged, gave pleasure even though coming immediately after Mlle Elssler's dance. It was performed with great speed, fire and spirit, and drew considerable applause, which was justly deserved, for to shine alongside the sun is a rare achievement.

We did not much care for the garland dance. It reminded us too much of the paper circles that horses jump through at the Cirque-Olympique. The series of arches composed of greenery look just like laundrywomen's hoops decorated with green paper.

When the dancing is finished the happy crowd begins to disperse and go their way. But all of a sudden Laurette reappears, pale, trembling, scared, and in a state of terrified agitation. Everyone crowds around her, asking the reason for her despair. "Luigi has just been bitten by a tarantula." As you know, the tarantula is a species of black spider that is very poisonous, and whose bite causes convulsions and somersaults that can only be cured by music and making the patient dance until his strength is exhausted. Modern medicine rejects this, but the tradition is popular enough to be generally accepted.

At this point the miming of Mlle Elssler attained the very height of sublime tragedy. With terrifying exactitude she conveyed the progress of the bite and the nature of the patient's dance as it grows increasingly convulsive. The most detailed account, loudly declaimed, could not have been clearer than the "speech" she delivered in gestures.

Luigi, restrained with great difficulty by his companions, crosses the stage performing convulsive *cabrioles*, and soon falls exhausted into the arms of Matea and Laurette. Dr. Oméopatico, who, in his currant-coloured greatcoat, with his little stomach compressed in a white-piquéed waistcoat and his watch and chain, is not the good old devil that he seems to be, watches the unfortunate young man struggling and rolling on the ground with complete unconcern. In a few minutes it will all be over. Poor Laurette, who is beside herself with distress, tries in vain to move the pitiless doctor, who, looking on Luigi as a rival, has no desire to let slip such an opportunity of getting rid of him. At the final desperate paroxysm, seeing the man she loves on the point of expiring, Laurette resolves to make the supreme sacrifice. She will offer her

[10] Auguste Mabille (b. 1815) was one of three sons of the founder of the celebrated Parisian dancing garden, the Bal Mabille. He danced at the Opéra from 1835 to 1845, and was briefly engaged as a choreographer, producing the ballet *Nisida* and the skating ballet in the opera *Le Prophète*.

71

hand to Dr. Oméopatico on condition that he saves Luigi's life. Oméopatico then takes a small phial of elixir from a little medicine chest with gold corners and holds it beneath the nose of Luigi, who comes round and looking about him much less wildly, rises to his feet. Oméopatico marries Laurette, and Luigi wishes he had died. Laurette is no less distressed. Dissolving a marriage is difficult, particularly for humble folk who have no friends at court and no one to protect them. Luigi's thoughts turn to the beautiful lady who gave him the thousand-franc notes. Perhaps she can help him in this affair. She is at the Convent of Sainte-Marie, but it is a two-hour journey there and a two-hour journey back, which makes four according to strict arithmetic, and in four hours anything may happen. Suppose Dr. Oméopatico wishes to claim his conjugal rights! Far better to kill him, and then kill oneself! Laurette promises to resist the old man's advances during this time, a difficult task, for beneath his powdered wig Signor Oméopatico is the randiest of suitors—and more-over, in the presence of so charming a wife, even old Priam would have discovered a spark among his ashes. So poor Luigi is devastated.

Now here we are in the wedding chamber, Laurette's bedroom. You see before you a little bed bedecked with flowers, a table with rounded feet, a chair, a mirror, a blue vase of roses, all the simple belongings of a young girl. On the dressing table sparkle the doctor's presents, necklaces, earrings, fine pearls, lace, everything that an infatuated old man might give to his young bride.

The innocent victim is led in. Piece by piece, her wedding dress drops to the floor, and she stands in her simple funnel-shaped corset and gauze petticoat, her crumpled gown lying at her feet. Sorrowfully she crosses her arms in front of her breasts like the ancient statue of modesty.[11] This undressing is performed behind a muslin curtain, a translucent screen interposed by Laurette's companions between the girl's chaste nudity and the exuberance of the old satyr, who can hardly contain himself. He dismisses the pages by giving them money for drink, and with great courtesy and politeness ushers out, one by one, all the friends of his wife, whose courage seems to desert her. Left alone with Laurette, the amorous Oméopatico wishes to sit by her side and take her hand, an extremely modest request for a husband. The poor girl recoils with terror like a doe disturbed by a passing hunter. "Listen," she says, putting her finger to her lips, "can't you hear anything? I think there is someone outside the door." To remove these groundless fears Oméopatico takes a candle and goes into the next room. Laurette slams the door shut behind him and double-locks it. Oméopatico, having tried the door without success, makes his way back through the window.

---

[11] There are two Roman statues in the Louvre in the so-called pose of modesty, one of an unnamed lady, veiled and wearing a diadem, and the other of the Empress Annia Galeria, wife of Antoninus Pius.

Surprise! Laurette is nowhere to be seen! He looks under the bed, behind the curtains, but there is no sign of her. The crafty girl has been moving round the dressing table in the shadow created by the doctor's candle, and sits down very quietly on a chair when his back is turned. Oméopatico asks her why she shut the door. "It was not me, it was the wind." "Come now, the wind cannot double-lock a door." Not knowing what to do next, Laurette asks to say her prayers and goes down on to her knees. While praying, she is struck by an idea. She smiles, gaily raises her head and goes over to the chimney. Suddenly she gives a cry and puts her hand to her foot. Now she has been bitten by the tarantula, and begins to perform the prettiest *cabrioles* you can imagine. Being in possession of the elixir, the doctor is not very worried by this misfortune, whose symptoms he knows how to remove, and he looks on unconcerned as the girl darts and leaps around the room. Laurette's movements become faster. Judging the right moment to stop the spread of the venom, Signor Oméopatico tries to hold the phial beneath Laurette's nose, but she very skilfully sends it flying through the air and it shatters into a thousand pieces. Oméopatico, who is now really worried, tries vainly to grasp his wife, who bounds and spins and darts with ever-increasing speed, every now and then delivering kicks that would not be disowned by Deburau, that master of kicks up the behind.[12]

Oméopatico, out of breath, is wheezing like a pair of asthmatic bellows. He pulls out his handkerchief and collapses into a chair, gasping for breath like a beached whale. Laurette falls on to another chair with a loud cry.

The cry brings all the womenfolk running in. Faced with such a terrible sight, Matea is all confused. The girls press round their friend, who tells them under her breath exactly what she wants them to do. Laurette continues pretending she has lost consciousness. She is dying—she has died, so it is said. Death is quick, for tarantulas, particularly those that have not bitten anyone before, are terrible spiders. The village men give Oméopatico a good hiding with their sticks. He has really deserved it, the old blackguard, the shameless libertine, for being the cause of the death of the prettiest girl in Calabria.

Oméopatico takes to his heels, and Laurette is carried out.

We now find ourselves in a superb landscape, with magnificent mountains, basted, gilded, baked and pickled by the sun. That factory-like building to the audience's left, reached by a ramp of such a life-like colour, is the monastery of Sainte-Marie to which Clorinde, the beautiful Englishwoman, has retired. It is a really lovely retreat. There are long marble terraces, succulent plants that are wonderfully African, and an infinite view over a plain dotted with hills and bestrewn with villages—a charming monastic paradise.

The head of a long procession appears from the wings—first the men, bareheaded and with their arms hanging limp, and then the mourning women.

[12] See No. 6, note 5.

Laurette has died, and here she is laid out in a white veil on a satin-padded bier, borne on the shoulders of four bearers. A crown of white roses, the symbol óf virginity, encircles her diaphanous brow, and her beautiful lashes caress cheeks on which the violets of death have not yet replaced the roses of life. She does not look too bad for a corpse. Luigi, who has arrived to consult Clorinde, comes across the procession and rushes over to the bier, becoming distraught and tearful as he recognises his beloved. Seeing him so upset, the corpse gently raises her head and, giving him the most lively and graceful smile imaginable, motions him to say nothing and not to worry.

The procession continues on its way. The young girls scatter rose petals on the body of their dear companion, whose life seems to have lasted no longer than that of a rose, the space of a single morning. It winds its way up the ramp that leads to the convent, and the body of the beautiful girl is placed at the entrance of the chapel, through whose doors can be seen a splendid blaze of little candles in the Italian fashion. Everyone goes inside, but when Luigi approaches the corpse, it throws its arms around his neck with all the passion of life and gives him a lovely kiss with lips that are rosier than ever. Finally Clorinde arrives in the company of a nun, and comes face to face with Oméopatico, who has put on mourning and does not want to leave without shedding a tear over the tomb of his wife who has, alas, been snatched from him at such an unfortunate moment. At the sight of Clorinde, Oméopatico starts back with a look of alarm, raising his hands to the skies. Clorinde is none other than his first wife, whom, believing she had been murdered by brigands, he has been mourning prematurely. He feels a light touch on his shoulder, and turns to see Laurette, his second wife, who has thrown off her shroud and is looking at him with a mischievous smile. Explanations are now made and all ends happily. Laurette is free to marry Luigi, since her first marriage was a nullity, and Dr. Oméopatico and his wife get back into the post chaise, which the postillions have not thought of washing. Let us wish them a happy journey.

It was a complete success. Barrez[13] gave a very comical touch to the character of Dr. Oméopatico, which he very skilfully prevented from appearing repulsive. He managed, most unusually, to avoid caricature, never once overstepping the limit between exuberance and cynicism.

As for Mlle Elssler, she was graceful, light, touching, witty, as awesome as the Pythia of ancient legend when describing her lover's convulsions after he was bitten by the tarantula, and as mischevious as Columbine in the Italian comedy when she was leading her old Cassandre[14] a dance round her room.

---

[13] Jean-Baptiste Barrez (1792–1868) was a member of the Opéra ballet from 1821 to 1844, and from 1832 principal teacher in the School of Dance.

[14] Cassandre, the fatuous old man, one of the stock types of the Commedia dell'Arte.

She made a comedy out of the ballet, and glossed over everything in the plot that was impossible or risky with admirable delicacy.

The music, so we conscientiously believe, is by M. Gide.[15] We have already given our opinion of the scenery.

La Presse, July 1st, 1839.
HAD I, 267–274. L:426.

---

[15] Casimir Gide (1804–68) had achieved his first success as a composer with his collaboration with Halévy in the opera-ballet *La Tentation* in 1832. As well as *La Tarentule*, he composed the music for *Le Diable boiteux* (1836), *La Volière* (1838) and *Ozaï* (1847), after which he abandoned composition to run the family's bookshop.

21

Th. de la Renaissance; *El Marcobomba o el Sargente Fanfarron*

El Marcobomba, ou le Sergent fanfaron, ballet-pantomime in 1 act by Ragaine, f.p. Théâtre de la Renaissance, August 23rd, 1839.

El Marcobomba[1] is a slender comic interlude that is very bright, amusing and gay. A ballet that makes one laugh is a rarity, a real phenomenon, and the other evening the audience was laughing out loud at the Renaissance. Maybe this is somewhat detrimental to the dance, and maybe there will be some woeful spirits who will object that this Spanish divertissement smacks of the circus and fairground performers, but it is nonetheless true that Señor Piatoli was very amusing in the rôle of Sergeant Fanfaron. Without possessing the force of those two excellent comic mimes, Elie and Barrez, he has verve and spirit and gives a marvellous caricature of the *grand danseur*. His *entrechats* and pirouettes are very witty parodies. Mmes Maria Goze and Fabiani[2] perform the obligatory *cachucha* and various other *pas* with great vivacity and suppleness. There is also another dancer whose name we do not know and who made no impression except that she was charming. She was an even more pronounced Spanish type than her companions—not the Spanish

[1] This ballet turns up, in different versions, throughout the nineteenth century. Jean Petipa, father of Lucien and Marius, produced it at the Bowery Theatre, New York, on November 23rd, 1839; Jules Perrot produced his own version, with music by Pugni, at the Bolshoi Theatre, St. Petersburg, on December 5th (N.S.), 1854; and it was included in the 50th birthday benefit of Lev Ivanov on December 17th (N.S.), 1899. The Russian ballet historian Pleshcheyev also records an amateur production by the dancing master Eberhardt for the Imperial Cadet Corps, performed at a party in 1858.

[2] Gautier wrote "Groze", but the correct spelling seems to have been Goze. Maria Fabiani was probably the daughter of Manuel Rojas Fabiani, teacher of Juan Camprubí.

type that one imagines from poems and ballads, but the type that is to be seen in the paintings of Murillo, with a round, rather flat face, lit by two shining eyes and enlivened by a mouth like a blossoming carnation, a stocky figure, well arched and well set, sturdy legs with nerves of steel beneath their curves, heels that bite, brusque and sharp, into the ground, and over and above it all, a sort of rustic, wild grace, a haughty allure that the other two, who are more exclusively stage dancers, do not possess.

The story of *El Marcobomba* could not be simpler. He is a sergeant who arrives to conscript the young men of a village into the army. The womenfolk will not stand for this, and in a twinkling of an eye all those young lads who a moment before were so alert and lively and exuberant, become, as if by magic, hunchbacks, cripples, paralytics, men with only one arm, epileptics, blind men, shortsighted men, and so on. But Señor Marcobomba is not to be fooled so easily, and he orders his detachment to charge the false cripples, who take to their heels with a speed that augurs well for their continued good health. The lame ones run even faster than the others! The soldiers chase them into the rocks, where a sort of toboggan slide created a very comic effect. In the end everything ends happily. The young men without sweethearts resign themselves to becoming heroes, while the others pay off the majestic Marcobomba to the accompaniment of castanets and heel-tapping.

This interlude will add an agreeable variety to the repertoire of the Renaissance.

La Presse, August 27th, 1839.
L:437.

22

Opéra: Lucile Grahn in *La Sylphide*

La Sylphide (see No. 17), revived with Grahn, November 6th, 1839.

The other evening, quite unexpectedly and without any rehearsal, Mlle Grahn played the rôle of the Sylphide. This substitution was caused by the indisposition of Mlle Elssler, and the young Danish dancer was brave enough to be prepared to appear in a part that has been impressed with the stamp of two great geniuses and rendered sacrosanct against mediocrity.

Mlle Grahn, who is specially suited to play sylphides by being light, young and pretty, allowed herself quite naturally to be pretty, young and light. She was not preoccupied with Mlle Taglioni or Mlle Elssler, making no effort to emulate the misty intangibility of the former or the profound sensitivity and poetry of the latter. She left much to that great guide, chance and the whim of the moment, and as a result succeeded beyond all expectations. Had she had more time to prepare, she would have almost certainly been less successful. Although Mlle Grahn has already displayed a remarkable talent in a number of *pas*, it was in doubt whether she could yet sustain a rôle of this importance from beginning to end.

She passed the test, and the public expressed its satisfaction with warm applause. We shall not disturb the innocent pleasure of this triumph with criticism. Mlle Grahn has already sufficient experience as a dancer to know what she still has to acquire. To be applauded after Marie Taglioni and Fanny Elssler is a wonderful thing for a girl who comes from a most distant country, from the heart of Denmark and Norway—Copenhagen. Luckily for her, the language of the feet is universal and everywhere understood. Mlle Lucile Grahn has taken her place among the most brilliant hopes of the Opéra. Her feet are already fluent in French.

La Presse, November 9th, 1839.
L:446.

23

Opéra: Début of Augusta Maywood

Augusta Maywood's début appearances at the Opéra, in a *pas de deux* in *Le Diable boiteux* on November 11th, 1839, and in *La Tarentule* on November 20th, 1839.

The dance, which has been neglected at the Opéra for so long, and which Mlle Elssler sustained on her own on the points of her tiny feet, seems now to have come into favour again. There has been a string of successful débuts, and following Mlle Lucile Grahn, who comes from Denmark, we now have Mlle Maywood from America. Every corner of the world is sending its own dancer. If this continues the ballet company will soon be the most cosmopolitan in the world. It includes Danes, Germans, Americans, and English—a real Babel with sixty-one tongues but happily the language of the dance can be understood everywhere, and feet do not speak with an accent.

Mlle Maywood[1] has a very distinctive type of talent. There is nothing of the melancholy grace, the dreamy abandon and the carefree lightness of Mlle Grahn, whose eyes reflect Norway's clear blue sky, and who is like a valkyrie dancing in the snow; and there is still less of the matchless perfection, the sparkling assurance, and the allure of Diana of antiquity and the sculptural purity of Mlle Fanny Elssler. She has something brusque, unexpected and fantastic that sets her utterly apart. The daughter of a theatre manager in New York or Philadelphia, we are not sure which, she was all the rage in America, dancing in the most complicated ballets, singing, and acting in

[1] Augusta Maywood (1825–76) was only fourteen (not twelve, as Gautier thought) when she made her Paris début. She was the step-daughter of Robert Maywood, an English actor who became manager of the Chestnut Theatre, Philadelphia. A year after her début she caused a sensation by eloping with Auguste Mabille's younger brother, Charles. Her career did not end there, however, for she went on to become the first American ballerina to achieve international renown, dancing mainly in Vienna and Milan.

tragedy. In a word, she was an infant prodigy. She has now come to seek the sanction of Paris, for the opinion of Paris is important even for the barbarians of the United States in their world of railroads and steamboats. And for a prodigy, Mlle Maywood really is very good.

She is of medium height, supple-jointed, very young (eighteen according to the scandal-mongers), with dark eyes and a bright, wild little face that comes very near to being pretty. Add to that sinews of steel, legs of a jaguar, and an agility not unlike that of a circus performer. And to cap it all, no one could have been less overawed by such a formidable test. She faced the footlights and opera glasses that terrify the strongest hearts, with the calm of an experienced ballerina. You would have thought she was simply dealing with a pit full of Yankees. She covered that great stage from the backcloth to the prompter's box in two or three bounds, performing those almost horizontal *vols penchés* for which Perrot was famous, and then began to gambol, revolve in the air, and perform *tours de reins* with a suppleness and strength worthy of Lawrence and Redisha.[2] She was like a ball bouncing on a racquet. She has excellent elevation and attack, and her small legs, like those of a wild doe, made strides as long as those of Mlle Taglioni. The costume she wore on the day of her first début in *Le Diable boiteux* was very much in the American taste. Imagine a pink bodice with a pink skirt without any white petticoats underneath, and pink tights, the over-all effect being enhanced by frippery and tinsel of various colours. A costume to delight a rope dancer! (This is not a term of scorn—we adore rope dancers.) For her second appearance, in *La Tarentule*, she was dressed as a peasant, with that eternal black bodice and no less eternal petticoat, so hackneyed in ballets with rustic pretensions. If the first costume was too barbaric, this was too civilised. We cannot over-stress the importance for dancers to pay attention to their costumes and avoid simple, tasteful materials that stain easily and need frequent washing. If fantasy is to be permitted anywhere, it is surely in the costumes of dancers, who need frills and the luminous sparkle of spangles and flashy shreds and patches. Mlle Augusta Maywood will be a fine acquisition for the Opéra. She has a style of her own, a very remarkable touch of originality. Connoisseurs who have been to the Coronation festivities in Milan assert that Mlle Maywood has a style that is very similar to that of Mlle Cerrito.[3]

[2] Lawrence and Redisha were a team of "grotesques", famous for their eccentric, acrobatic style of dancing. They had made their début at the Cirque-Olympique in January 1838, and in the summer of that year appeared at the Cirque National des Champs-Elysées, where Gautier saw them and gave them a favourable review in *La Presse* of July 23rd, 1838.

[3] The fame of Fanny Cerrito (1817–1909) was just beginning to spread beyond the frontiers of Italy. Her sensational début in London, from which her international career can be said to date, was only a few months away. However, Paris would not see her until 1847, when she and her husband, Arthur Saint-Léon, were engaged together at the Opéra. Gautier was to write the scenario for her ballet *Gemma* in 1854.

A little accident interrupted the performance for a few minutes. Mlle Paquita, a very pretty girl with dark eyes and jet black eyebrows, fell flat during a *tarantella* in which she was one of the coryphées. Mlle Paquita is so shapely that a fall is not at all compromising for her, and furthermore, not everyone has pink tights like Mlle Maywood! Mlle Sophie, Albertine's sister, who was following Paquita, also fell flat on her face, and we feared that the whole line was going to fall down like a house of cards.[4] There was some laughter at first, but as the public is good-hearted and not as unkind as it might appear to be, the two poor girls, who were covered in confusion and perhaps bruised (which is humiliating for a sylphide), were consoled with a salvo of half-ironic applause.

La Presse, November 25th, 1839.
HAD I, 328–330. L:449.

---

[4] The notorious Albertine (see No. 26, note 4) had two sisters, Fifine and Victorine. The Opéra archives have a record of Victorine, but "Sophie" suggests Fifine.

24

Opéra: Benefit of Fanny Elssler

Performance for the benefit of
Fanny Elssler, January 30th, 1840.
Le Bourgeois Gentilhomme,
comedy by Molière, with
interpolated dances; Act 3 of
Rossini's *Otello*; revival of *Nina,
ou la Folle par amour*, ballet-
pantomime in 2 acts, ch. Milon,
mus. Persuis, f.p. November 23rd,
1813.

We could say that the auditorium resembled an enormous basket of
flowers and the parterre was studded with women, and we could
compose five or six very pretty phrases about the brilliance of the audience,
but in this progressive century it is figures that speak most eloquently, and we
shall merely record that the receipts exceeded 22,000 francs.[1]

The composition of the programme was well worthy of such a gathering.
Among the singers were Duprez, Tamburini, Mmes Dorus-Gras, Pauline
Garcia and Persiani, and among the dancers, Mlles Fanny and Therese
Elssler, Nathalie Fitzjames, Maywood, Forster, and MM. Barrez, Mabille
and Petipa. There was enough to arouse the curiosity of the most lethargic
spectators. . . .

The finale [of *Le Bourgeois Gentilhomme*], the reception of the
Mamamouchi, was certainly never more splendid. Negroes, ichoglans,[2] der-
vishes in glowing turbans, nothing was left out, and we doubt whether the
Grand Monarch himself ever saw it performed with such magnificence.
Interpolated into this reception, without much concern for authenticity, were
a rococo dance as performed in olden times by the famous Dupré and the
illustrious Mlle Anne Cupis de Camargo, the Elssler of the day, to whom M.
Arouet de Voltaire, a gentleman of the King's chamber, did not think it

---

[1] When Marie Taglioni took her benefit in 1837, the receipts were 34,423 francs.
[2] Pages in waiting to the Sultan.

82

demeaning to address a quite detestable madrigal,[3] the *pas de châle* by Mlles Fanny and Therese Elssler, and *La Smolenska* by Mlle Fanny alone, which will attract the whole of Paris society.

The first *pas*, taken from the ballet *Manon Lescaut*, is a perfect evocation of rococo, Watteau and Pompadour. It is a fireplace top in action, a living fan. Lancret, Lépicié and Boucher never did anything better.[4] Imagine amusing old Barrez dressed as a pilgrim embarking for Cythera with crook and haversack, all the trappings of a shepherd of the Lignon,[5] and holding in his hand, like Dame Jacinthe in the game of cards,[6] a posy that he has not the courage to place in the bodice of his shepherdess, a very attractive young person in a paniered skirt, with china butterflies, criss-cross ribbons, powdered wig and patches at the corner of her mouth.

He starts forward, then draws back, expressing his passion by tremendous *entrechats*, rolling his eyes and breathing deep sighs as he offers his posy, but all to no avail. Phyllis is as cruel as a tigress from Hyrcania, and leaves the handsome Thyrsis to indulge in his *gargouillades* and *balloneés*.[7] Luckily love comes to his aid in the form of the god Cupid himself—in pink silk breeches

---

[3] Voltaire's well-known verse contrasted the styles of Marie-Anne de Cupis de Camargo (1710–1770) and her great rival, Marie Sallé (1707–56):

Ah, Camargo, que vous êtes brillante!
Mais que Sallé, grands Dieux, est ravissante!
Que vos pas sont légers et que les siens sont doux!
Elle est inimitable et vous êtes nouvelle:
Les nymphes sautent comme vous,
Mais les Grâces dansent comme elle.

Louis Dupré (1697–1774) was the epitome of the *noble* school of French dancing in the first half of the eighteenth century.

[4] The painter Antoine Watteau (1684–1721) and the Marquise de Pompadour (1721–64), mistress of Louis XV and patron of the arts, personified to Gautier's mind the age of rococo. Nicolas Lancret (1690–1743), who painted both Camargo and Sallé, Nicholas-Bernard Lépicié (1735–84) and François Boucher (1703–70) were three of the outstanding French painters of the same period.

[5] The river Lignon, a tributary of the Loire, figures in the novel *L'Astrée* by Honoré d'Urfé, in which lovesick shepherds paid platonic court to faithful shepherdesses. The shepherd from the Lignon thus became a favourite allusion, found in the writings not only of Gautier, but also of Rousseau and Mme de Sévigné, among many others.

[6] Dame Jacinthe was probably the name given in the Gautier family circle to the Queen of Hearts, who in packs printed before the Revolution was generally depicted holding a flower.

[7] The countrywoman Phyllis and the shepherd Thyrsis are characters who appear in Virgil's seventh Eclogue. Hyrcania was the mountainous region, west of Parthia and south-east of the Caspian Sea, that in ancient times abounded in wild animals, including a species of tiger, now extinct, which is mentioned in Virgil's *Aeneid*, IV 367.

with diamond-studded garters, a *tonnelet à passequilles*,[8] a golden quiver, and a little three-cornered hat, just as he appears in china statuettes and porcelain of the period. From his quiver he daintily draws a very sharp arrow and pierces the heart of the shepherdess through and through, permitting the lovelorn Thyrsis to place the posy in her corsage and steal a kiss.

This scene is acted by Barrez with infinite wit and an excellent sense of comedy. Mlle Forster is a charming shepherdess whom Watteau would have willingly taken as his model. Mlle Albertine[9] is a very roguish and gallant little Cupid.

The *pas de châle* by the two sisters, twin stars of the dance, had the rare merit for a *pas de deux* of being original and novel. It is a series of poses, intertwinings, draperies, be they floating or transparent, that is ravishingly graceful. You could never see anything more noble or more graceful, or better done. Mlle Fanny and Mlle Therese each possesses great talent on her own, but this is doubled when they are together. They attain a fraternal (if we may use the word) perfection and precision that no one else could achieve. Applause that was equally shared told the sisters how much the public loved seeing them reunited.

The *pas de châle* was followed by *La Smolenska*. *La Smolenska* is a sort of *mazurka* or *cracovienne*, full of originality and grace. Mlle Fanny Elssler excels in such dances with their lively bouncy rhythm and their mixture of sensuality and offhand casualness, and this one she danced to perfection. Carried away, the whole house called for an encore, and thunderous applause broke out from all parts. A heavy shower of flowers descended on the forestage in a scented torrent. Her costume had a touch of gypsy coquetry that could not have been more piquant. A velvet necklace with bracelets and gaiters to match gave her a bold and untamed appearance that was very much in keeping with the character of the dance. Thus attired, Mlle Elssler was even prettier than usual, which is saying a great deal. . . .

The ballet *Nina, ou la Folle par amour* must have moved our parents to tears. In it the simple sentimentality of those bygone days blossoms in full flower, and the army shines with all its charm, triumphing with a speed unknown in civilian life. This feeble ballet, which is as faded as the scenery before which it is performed, contains nothing new for anyone apart from the admirable talent of Mlle Fanny Elssler, who rose to the heights of tragedy in the rôle of Nina. In her hands the mad girl of the *opéra comique* has become

---

[8] Gautier occasionally uses the word *passequille* in the sense of excessive ornamentation on a costume. The word does not appear in French dictionaries of his time, but it was probably suggested by the then obsolete word *pasquil*, the name of an ancient marble statue in Rome on which people used to attach ridiculous and often defamatory rhymes.

[9] See No. 26, note 4.

Shakespearean, a worthy sister for Ophelia, a slender white vision whose eyes alone seem to be alive, shining feverishly out of a marble-white face that is as pallid as a Greek statue in the moonlight. At the end of the ballet, when she realises that her lover is not dead, as she had believed, a shining radiance of sublime happiness comes over her features in luminous waves, forming a halo, so to speak. It would be hard to give a better rendering of unexpected happiness and the outpouring of a heart that is overflowing with joy. As a mime, Mlle Elssler has no rival, and we can think of hardly anyone else other than Miss Smithson[10] to compare with her.

In the divertissement Mlle Nathalie danced very daintily in a pretty *pas* with Mlle Maywood, the flying American girl who is bouncing on the racquet of the Opéra with such elasticity. Speaking of America, we very much hope that Mlle Elssler will not be going to dance before the barbarians, and parodying the verses of Voltaire to J.-B. Rousseau, we say to her:

> *Dansez tous vos pas à Paris,*
> *Et n'allez pas en Amérique.*[11]

Have we not given her sufficient praise and applause, and thrown her enough poems and bouquets, to have the right to keep her? She should not, under any pretext, be permitted to go to another continent when she still belongs to this one of ours.

There must have been a revolt of porters that night, for the performance did not end until the following morning, at quarter past one. Things had been done properly, and the pleasure given was good value for 22,000 francs.

La Presse, February 3rd, 1840.
HAD, II 23–27. L:460.

---

[10] See No. 19, note 14.
[11] A parody of the lines in Voltaire's *Le Temple du goût* (1733):
Faites tous vos pas à Paris,
Et n'allez point en Allemagne.

25

Th. de la Renaissance: *Zingaro*

Zingaro, opera in a prologue and
2 acts, libr. Sauvage, mus.
Fontana, ch. Perrot, f.p. February
29th, 1840, for the débuts of Jules
Perrot and Carlotta Grisi.

A t last a success, a real success! M. Anténor Joly[1] has deserved it well, for
he has worked a long time for it with unprecedented zeal. It was not a
matter of a hundred *claqueurs* or so. The whole audience took part, clapping,
stamping their feet and even throwing bouquets—attentions that, in the
manner of great lords, they usually leave to the administration. M. Sauvage's[2]
dialogue and M. Fontana's[3] music played no part in this success—it was
entirely achieved by Perrot's legs. And what legs they are!

Perrot is not good-looking, he is even extremely ugly. Above the waist he
has the physique of a tenor—no need to say more—but from there on down
he is a pleasure to look at. It is not quite good form nowadays to show interest
in the perfection of a male body, but we cannot keep silent about Perrot's legs.
So imagine that I am speaking of a statue of the mime Bathyllus or the actor
Paris that has just been excavated from Nero's gardens or Herculaneum. The

---

[1] Pierre-Paul-Jean-Ariste-Anténor Joly, a former type-setter, had founded the Théâtre
de la Saint-Antoine (later Beaumarchais) in 1835, and for some years edited a
theatrical periodical, *Vert-Vert*. In 1838 the Théâtre de la Renaissance was inaugurated under his direction, being established in the theatre in the Place Ventadour, which
had originally been the home of the Opéra-Comique (1829–32) and later, briefly, had
been known as the Théâtre Nautique (1834). It presented a wide repertory, including
drama and comedy, *opéra comique* and vaudeville, and opened with Hugo's drama,
Ruy Blas. Joly's enterprise was not a financial success, and he withdrew from the
management in 1841. He died in poverty in 1853.

[2] Thomas-Marie-François Sauvage (1794–1877), dramatist and music critic. In collaboration with Castil-Blaze he was responsible for the libretto for *Robin des bois*, the
first French version of *Der Freichütz*, f.p. Th. de l'Odéon, December 7th, 1824, and,
alone, that for Meyerbeer's *Marguerite d'Anjou*, f.p. Th. de l'Odéon, March 11th,
1826.

[3] Uranio Fontana (b. 1815), a composer of little note.

feet and knees are extremely delicately formed, and counterbalance the feminine roundness of contour of his legs, which are both soft and pliable, elegant and supple. The legs of the young man in red hose breaking the symbolic wand in Raphael's painting of *The Marriage of the Virgin* are in exactly the same style.[4] Let me add that Perrot, wearing a costume by Gavarni,[5] has nothing of that feeble and inane manner which usually makes male dancers so unbearable. His success was assured even before he began to dance. Seeing his quiet agility, his perfect timing and the supple movement of his miming, it was not hard to recognise the aerial Perrot, Perrot the sylph, the male Taglioni! And in the *grand pas de deux* of the divertissement, cries of bravo exploded like thunderclaps.

This *pas* is charming, the idea behind it very pretty, and—which is unusual with a *pas*—it had a meaning. The Cassandre[6] of the story wishes to make his ward Gianina dance before the nobleman, but because he has just locked up the girl's sweetheart, she consents with very ill grace. Suddenly she raises her head, her eyes gleam, her features break into a sparkling smile, and her steps become livelier. She has heard the distant chatter of castanets. The sound comes nearer—it is Perrot, Zingaro, who has leapt through the window and alighted on the tip of his elegant foot to join in the village festivities (*opéra comique* style), and now begins one of the most charming *pas* you could possibly behold. In it Perrot displays a perfect grace, purity and lightness. It is music made visible, and if one can express it so, his legs sing most harmoniously to the eye.

Such praise is all the more suspect coming from me because I do not like male dancing at all. A male dancer performing anything other than *pas de caractère* or pantomime has always seemed to me something of a monstrosity. Until now I have only been able to bear men in *mazurkas, saltarellos* and *cachuchas*. With the exception of Mabille and Petipa, the male dancers of the Opéra only reinforce my view that women alone should be admitted into the ballet company.

Mme Carlotta Grisi[7] supports her husband admirably. She knows how to dance, a rare quality. She has fire, although lacking a little in originality. Her dancing is not very distinctive. It is good, but not outstanding. As well as being a good dancer, she is an accomplished singer—two talents that are

[4] Now at the Brera, Milan.

[5] Paul Gavarni (1804–66), painter and lithographer, noted for his elegantly drawn scenes of everyday life of Paris.

[6] See No. 20, note 14.

[7] This was almost certainly Gautier's first sight of Carlotta Grisi (1819–99), although he must have seen Jules Perrot (1810–92) when he was dancing at the Opéra between 1830 and 1835. He was to become a friend of them both, and a devoted servitor of Carlotta. Carlotta and Perrot never married, although a daughter was born of their liaison in 1837.

difficult to combine. Her voice is supple, clear, a little shrill, and weak in the middle register, but she manages it with skill and method. It is a very good voice for a dancer. Many singers who do not dance cannot do as well. As for her features, they are not typically Italian and do not conform to the image evoked by the name of Grisi, the family to which she belongs. She has chestnut-coloured hair, blonde rather than dark, quite regular features, and as far as can be seen under her make-up, a natural complexion. She is of medium height, slender, quite well proportioned. She is not too slim for a dancer, but the shape of her feet is somewhat Italian, or English if you prefer.

This almost phenomenal faculty of singing and dancing at the same time is not the monopoly of Mme Carlotta Grisi. Mlle Nathalie Fitzjames of the Opéra possesses a soprano voice of a very wide range and could play double rôles.[8] There was talk of arranging *Esmeralda*[9] and *Le Dieu et la bayadère* for her.

But let us return to the Renaissance, which is definitely turning into a miniature Opéra, since it has song and dance as its lord and master. The *polacca* was less applauded than the *grand pas*. Mlle Fanny Elssler, whose departure we shall shortly be bewailing, has made us very difficult to please in this area. After the *Cracovienne* and the *Smolenska*, which she performed with such adorable precision, subtlety and haughty grace, nothing can surprise us any more, and surprise is the whole secret of that type of *pas*.

The audience was most brilliant. The critics were there in full force, and the prettiest feet of the Opéra were applauding with all their might.

It has just occurred to me that I have not said a word about the libretto. I must confess that I did not follow it at all, which is a tribute to my sagacity, for I would worry about my intelligence if I could understand such things. The prologue seemed to be all about a chest and a young girl, performed in the manner of *saltimbanques*. I espied a sort of bridge from *Le Torrent*,[10] over which passed a carriage that was fixed on to it, and then came a pistol shot that kills Perrot-Zingaro. The idea of killing off in the prologue the man who is going to dance three important *pas* in the following acts seemed a little premature, but no doubt it was only a toy pistol. For in the next act Perrot-Zingaro, who a moment before had been a corpse, dances a charming *pas de*

[8] Gautier dedicated his poem *L'Ondine et le pêcheur*, written in 1841, to Nathalie Fitzjames. It was set to music by François Bazin, and frequently sung by her at concerts after she had given up her dance career.

[9] *La Esmeralda*, opera by Louise Bertin to a libretto by Victor Hugo, f.p. November 14th, 1836.

[10] As a later reference makes clear (see No. 69), Gautier was here recalling a spectacular scene in a melodrama seen by him some years before. It was almost certainly the scene of the flood cascading down a mountainside that terminated Act I of the melodrama *Le Chasseur noir* by Antier and Nézel, f.p. Th. de la Porte-Saint-Martin, January 30th, 1828.

bouquet with his wife. The chest then reappears, and Perrot goes into an explanation after the manner of that of Théramène,[11] which is not very easy to understand, considering that it was expressed with his hands and feet, and that miming can hardly convey anything outside the present tense. In his capacity as a dancer Perrot is as dumb as Fenella in Auber's opera,[12] added to which Carlotta Grisi sings with such a strong accent that it is impossible to know if she is expressing herself in Italian or in French, and she is equally unintelligible to those of either nation, so you must forgive me for not being very clear in my review. At the end the ridiculous nobleman marries a woman in a yellow and green skirt, whom I thought was Mlle Ozy,[13] although I am not sure, while Perrot married his own wife, who wore a blue skirt. He came off best.

The divertissements are arranged and staged with great taste and clarity. The groups are well designed, and the various evolutions perfectly performed and easy to distinguish. The *pas des Bohémiens* and the Styrian rondo gave great pleasure.

The costumes have been designed by Gavarni. They are varied, original and very picturesque. Gavarni is unrivalled at arranging, producing and designing costumes, and this is only the least of his talents, for there can be few who have not laughed themselves to tears over the witty caricatures which he produces in such profusion, and which seem to give him no more trouble than drawing a capital letter or an initial freehand.

As once happened in a provincial theatre where they omitted the music of *La Dame blanche*[14] because it interfered with the action and replaced it with lively and amusing dialogue, so here they could easily omit the dialogue as

[11] Théramène, the tutor of Hippolyte, son of King Theseus in Racine's tragedy, *Phèdre*. He declaimed, in the last act, the news of Hippolyte's death in the celebrated "*récit de Thélamène*".

[12] *La Muette de Portici*, in which the heroine Fenella is dumb. Zingaro is also dumb.

[13] Gautier was correct. Caroline Ozy played the other leading feminine rôle. The name Ozy is an uncommon one, and one is tempted to wonder if this actress can be identified with Alice Ozy (1820–93), actress and demi-mondaine, who according to her biographer Louis Loviot (*Alice Ozy*, Paris, 1910) made Gautier's acquaintance in 1844. This was the prelude to a long and faithful friendship, "a friendship that was evidently amorous, 'flirtatious' if you wish, but—as Ozy at least maintained, and why should we not believe her?—no more than that". Gautier wrote several short poems eulogising her beauty. During his term as critic for *La Presse* he often took her to premières, but when he moved to *Le Moniteur*, for which he did not review performances at the Opéra for some years, she told Paul de Saint-Victor, who had succeeded him on *La Presse*, how sorry she was to lose the privilege of going to first nights and was assured that she could accompany him whenever she wished. Her real name was Julie-Justine Pilloy, Ozy or Ozi being her mother's maiden name. Her mother, born Charlotte Amédée Ozi (1801–47) and buried with her at Père-Lachaise, would surely have been too old to have been cast as Dorothée, but it is conceivable that Alice had a sister who was briefly on the stage.

[14] A successful comic opera by Boïeldieu, f.p. Opéra-Comique, December 10th, 1825.

"interfering with the action" and keep only the divertissement and the ballet. However, to be fair, we should say that the dance tunes were quite pretty, and that on the whole M. Fontana's music was as good as anything else of its kind.

M. Anténor Joly should take a lesson from this stroke of good fortune. He has three strings to his bow—opera, drama and ballet—and he should now stick to that, and not wear out his actors by making them play a lot of totally insignificant one- and two-act pieces that cannot affect the box office at all. He cannot hope to gain anything from vaudevilles, which are played better at other theatres.

La Presse, March 2nd, 1840.
HAD, II 33–35. L:464.

26

Opéra: Revival of *Les Noces de Gamache*

Les Noces de Gamache, ballet-pantomime-folie in 2 acts, ch. Milon, mus. Lefebvre, f.p. January 18th, 1801, revived January 20th, 1841.

The performance closed with the ballet, *Les Noces de Gamache*. A twenty-year-old ballet[1] is very ancient indeed. However, such an exhumation is good in that it provides us with some excellent arguments against old ballet-lovers who claim that things were better in their day, that everything was then ingenious, delicate, witty, and in good taste, that choreography is currently declining, that artistry is disappearing, that the secret of the *ballet d'action* has been lost, and other gloomy complaints of one kind or another. But surely *Le Diable amoureux* or *La Tarentule* is a hundred times better than *Les Noces de Gamache*. The latter's thin, trembling, quavering music, whose scurrying rhythm allows virtually no time for the action to be developed in pantomime is certainly inferior to the strongly orchestrated music of modern ballets, and we doubt if *Les Noces de Gamache* was better performed at its creation than it was the other evening.

Could you wish for a more delightful Don Quixote than Elie? What a tall, thin, emaciated fellow he is! How gaunt his features, burned by the double tan of insanity and the sun of the Sierra Morena! What a heroic nose, what a knightly moustache! Amadis on the Poor Rock must have appeared more cheerful and happier than that! Cervantes himself could not have imagined the Knight of the Doleful Countenance any differently. And those great sword strokes and parries, those death blows aimed at felling giants and windmills, what of them? This perfect Don Quixote is followed by a no less

---

[1] The ballet was in fact forty years old, but it was twenty years since it had last been performed—on the evening in February 1820 when the Duc de Berry was assassinated as he was leaving the Opéra.

perfect Sancho Panza. No doubt you have seen the engraving of Decamps' drawing showing the hero of La Mancha preceded by his faithful squire.[2] Barrez, the Asmodeus of *Le Diable boiteux*, the Dr. Oméopatico of *La Tarentule* and the Governor of *Le Diable amoureux*, has brought that engraving to life. With his leather jerkin and gaiters, his wide-brimmed hat, his large paunch and short legs, he is the spitting image of that great compendium of proverbs sitting astride his donkey that, for want of a better name, we know as Sancho Panza. Barrez conveys the character's naive greediness, voracious impudence and skill at robbing foodstores in a manner that would have aroused the envy of Deburau, that tall white ghost who is always so half-starved. How well he mimicked, *non passibus aequis*,[3] the great strides of his master, and what a majestic figure he cut on his donkey!

Rosinante was played by a "made up" white horse. To give the illusion of skin and bones, its muscles and flanks were outlined in charcoal, just as a young man would be made up to play the rôle of an older man. Made up in this way as a dignified stage father, with crow's feet at the corner of its eyes, the horse was the most ridiculous sight imaginable. It only lacked jabot, bronzed waistcoat and powdered wig! The donkey was lifelike and free of grease paint.

We ought to have begun by mentioning the ladies—Maria, who plays the rôle of Quitterie, Mlle Blangy and the beautiful Dumilâtre—but the fantastic figures of Elie and Barrez caught our eye first of all.

Mlle Maria was as charming as she could be in her part, which is not very much developed although it is the principal one in the ballet. Mlles Adèle Dumilâtre, Blangy and Albertine danced a Spanish *pas* with great lightness and spirit that was loudly applauded. Castanets, those little tongues of black wood whose chatter comes so fast and furious, never fail to arouse the audience and produce a charming effect. Apart from marking the rhythm and giving accent to the steps, they have the merit of making the dancers use their arms and avoid those semaphoric movements that are meaningless and often unpleasantly distracting. The spangled basquines and silver stripes produce a very beautiful effect. Mlle Albertine,[4] who wore the same costume and hairstyle as her companions, also had on her head a diadem of brilliants of

[2] Alexandre-Gabriel Decamps' watercolour of Don Quixote and Sancho Panza was exhibited at the Salon of 1835. See No. 29, note 18.

[3] "With ill-matched steps," a quotation from Virgil's *Aeneid*, II 724, describing a small boy walking beside his father.

[4] Albertine Albrier, or Coquillard as she was more generally known, was a young dancer who achieved considerable notoriety during her brief career as a dancer. She became a *coryphée* at the Opéra in 1838. Two years later her name was associated with the Duc de Nemours, one of the sons of King Louis-Philippe, an affair that hastened the arrangements for the young prince's marriage. In 1841 Albertine conceived an infatuation for the dancer Edouard Carey, whom she followed to Naples. She died in 1846.

which she seemed very proud. Our advice to Mlle Albertine is that she does not need any additional embellishment to look pretty, and that she should reserve her diadem, which does not go well with her costume, for another occasion.

La Presse, January 23rd, 1841.
HAD, II 95–96. L:495.

27

Opéra: *Giselle*

Giselle, ou les Wilis, ballet-
pantomime in 2 acts, sc. Gautier
and Saint-Georges, ch. J. Coralli
and Perrot (anon), mus. Adam,
f.p. June 28th, 1841.

To M. Heinrich Heine, at Cauterets.

My dear Heinrich Heine, while leafing through your excellent book, *De l'Allemagne*,[1] a few weeks ago, my eyes rested on a charming passage (indeed, one only has to open the volume at random to do that)—in which you speak of the white-robed elfs whose hems are ever damp, the nixes who display their little satin feet on the ceiling of the nuptial chamber, the pallid wilis and their pitiless waltz, and all those delightful apparitions which you encountered in the Harz mountains and on the banks of the Ilse in the velvety mists of German moonlight—and involuntarily I said to myself, "What a lovely ballet that would make!". In a burst of enthusiasm I even took up a large sheet of fine white paper and wrote at the top, in superb rounded characters, "*Les Wilis*, a ballet". But then I began to laugh, and I threw the sheet aside without giving it a further thought, saying to myself, with the benefit of my journalistic experience, that it was quite impossible to transpose on to the stage that misty, nocturnal poetry, that phantasmagoria that is so voluptuously sinister, all those makings of legend and ballad that have so little relevance to our present way of life. That same evening, I was wandering backstage at the Opéra, with my mind still full of your idea, when I met that amusing man who has managed, while adding so much wit of his own, to make a ballet out of all the fantasy and whimsy of *Le Diable amoureux* of

[1] Heinrich Heine (1797–1856), the German Romantic poet who lived in Paris from 1831 and died there, was fascinated by the "elemental spirits" of German folklore. His essay on them forms an important section of his book, *De l'Allemagne*, published in Paris in 1835.

94

Cazotte,[2] the great poet who foreshadowed Hoffmann in the eighteenth century when the Encyclopaedists held sway. I related the tradition of the wilis, and three days later, the ballet of *Giselle* was written and accepted. In another week, Adolphe Adam had sketched out the music, the scenery was nearly ready, and rehearsals were in full swing. As you see, my dear Heinrich, we are not yet so incredulous and prosaic as we appear. You once exclaimed, in a burst of bad temper, "How could a ghost possibly exist in Paris? Between midnight and one o'clock, the hour set aside for ghosts for all eternity, the streets are still bustling with activity. The final bars are then blaring out at the Opéra, happy crowds are pouring out of the Variétés and the Gymnase, people are laughing and frisking along the boulevards, and everyone is going on to some *soirée*. How miserable a poor ghost must feel among this lively crowd!"[3] Well, I only had to take your pale and charming phantoms by the hand and introduce them, and they were welcomed with the greatest respect. The Director and the public offered not the slightest Voltairian objection. The wilis immediately received the freedom of the city in the very unfantastic Rue Le Peletier, the few lines in which you speak of them being placed at the head of the scenario and serving as their passport.

Since the state of your health has prevented you from attending the first performance, I shall, if a French journalist may be allowed to tell a fantastic story to a German poet, try to explain how M. de Saint-Georges made it acceptable and possible for the Opéra, while respecting the spirit of your legend. To achieve greater freedom, the action takes place in a vague part of the world in Silesia, Thuringia, or even in one of Shakespeare's "Bohemian sea ports".[4] Suffice it to say that it is on the other side of the Rhine, in some mysterious corner of Germany. Do not ask more of the geography of a ballet, which is unable to indicate the name of a town or a country in gesture, its sole means of expression.

Hillsides heavy with vines, some red, some yellow, warmed and sweetened by the autumn sun, those fine vines from which hang the amber-coloured grapes that produce Rhine wine, form the background to the scene. Perched on the summit of a bare grey rock, so steep that grass has not grown on it, like an eagle's nest, with encircling walls, pepper-pot turrets and feudal weather-cocks, is one of those castles that are so common in Germany. This is the seat

---

[2] *Le Diable amoureux*, ballet-pantomime in 3 acts and 8 scenes, sc. Saint-Georges, ch. Mazilier, mus. Benoist and Reber, f.p. Opéra, September 23rd, 1840. It was very loosely based on the novel of the same name by Cazotte. Gautier was in Spain that summer, and did not review this ballet.

[3] Heine, *Die romantische Schule*, Book III, Chapter III.

[4] "Our ship hath touched upon the deserts of Bohemia." Antigonus in *A Winter's Tale*, Act 3, Scene 3.

of the young Duke Albrecht[5] of Silesia. That cottage to the spectator's left, all fresh, trim and coquettish, and buried in the foliage, is the cottage of Giselle. The hut opposite is occupied by Loys. And who is Giselle? Giselle is Carlotta Grisi, a charming girl with eyes of blue, a delicate, innocent smile and a lively bearing, an Italian who might pass for a German, just as the German Fanny Elssler resembled an Andalusian from Seville. Her situation could not be simpler: she adores Loys, and she adores dancing. As for Loys, who is played by Petipa, we are suspicious of him for many reasons. Only a moment ago, a handsome equerry, all decked out in gold braid, was whispering a few words to him, cap in hand, in an attitude of servility and respect. A servant of a great house, as this equerry appears to be, would never fail to bow before his master. And so Loys is "not what he seems to be (ballet style), but we shall find that out later."

Giselle steps out from the cottage on the tip of her dainty little foot. Her legs are already wide-awake, and her heart no less so, even though it is morning. She has had a dream, a bad dream. A beautiful noblewoman in a golden robe, wearing a sparkling engagement ring on her finger, appeared to her as she slept as being betrothed to Loys, who was himself a nobleman, a duke, a prince. Dreams can be very strange at times! Loys does his best to put her mind at rest, and Giselle, who is still a little upset, poses a lover's questions to a marguerite. The little silver petals fly off and float to the ground. He loves me, he loves me not. Oh, my God, how unhappy I am, he loves me not! Loys, fully aware that a boy of twenty can make the daisies say whatever he chooses, continues the questioning, this time obtaining a favourable result, and Giselle, delighted by the good augury of the flower, resumes her dancing, ignoring the scolding of her mother, who would much rather see her agile little foot making the spinning wheel hum in the window bay, and her pretty fingers that have been interrogating the marguerite occupied in gathering the grapes that are already over-ripe, or carrying the vintager's wicker basket. But Giselle pays little heed to her mother's warnings, and placates her with a gentle caress. The mother perseveres. "Wretched child, you are always dancing; it will be the death of you, and when that happens you will turn into a wili!" And in expressive pantomime the good woman relates the terrible legend of the nocturnal dancers. Giselle pays no attention. Indeed where is the young girl of fifteen who will believe in a story whose moral is that one should not dance? Loys and dancing, that is her idea of happiness. But such happiness, like any other, wounds a jealous heart in the shadows. The gamekeeper Hilarion is in love with Giselle, and his most

---

[5] It will be noted that in this article, and also in his account of the ballet written in 1844 for *Les Beautés de l'Opéra*, Gautier uses the German form of Albrecht in preference to the French form, Albert, as given in the scenario and used generally in nineteenth-century productions of the ballet.

ardent desire is to injure his rival, Loys. He has witnessed the scene in which the equerry Wilfrid spoke to the peasant Loys in tones of respect. Suspecting that some plot is afoot, he breaks a window of the hut and climbs inside, hoping to find some incriminating evidence. But suddenly there is a sound of horns. The Prince of Courland and his daughter Bathilde, riding a white horse, are weary from the hunt and come to seek a litle rest and refreshment in Giselle's cottage. Discreetly Loys slips away. With a shy and charming grace Giselle hastens to lay the table with shining pewter goblets filled with milk, fruit, and the best and most appetising things in her rustic larder. As the lovely Bathilde raises the goblet to her lips, Giselle approaches with a cat-like tread, and in a rapture of naïve admiration, ventures to touch the soft rich material of which the noblewoman's riding habit is made. Bathilde, enchanted by the girl's simplicity, slips her golden chain around her neck, and expresses the wish to take her back with her. Giselle thanks her effusively, and replies that she desires no more than to dance and to be loved by Loys.

The Prince of Courland and Bathilde withdraw into the cottage for a few moments' rest. The huntsmen disperse. A fanfare on the Prince's horn will summon them when it is time to move on. The workers then return from the vineyards to arrange a festival in which Giselle is the central figure and is proclaimed Queen of the Vintage. The merrymaking is at its height when Hilarion appears, carrying a ducal cloak, a sword and an order of knighthood that he has found in Loys' cabin. There can be no doubt now. Loys is nothing but an imposter, a seducer who has been deceiving the trusting Giselle. A duke can never marry a simple peasant, even in the world of ballet where kings are frequently shown marrying shepherdesses; such a marriage presents unsurmountable difficulties. Loys, or rather Duke Albrecht of Silesia, excuses himself as best he can, replying that after all not much harm has been done and that Giselle will marry a duke instead of a peasant. She is pretty enough to become a duchess and the mistress of a castle. "But you are not free, you are engaged to another," retorts the gamekeeper, and seizing the horn that has been left lying on a table,[6] he begins to blow it furiously. The huntsmen come running in. Bathilde and the Prince of Courland emerge from the cottage and are astonished to see Duke Albrecht of Silesia so disguised. Giselle now recognises Bathilde as the noblewoman of her dream, and is no longer in doubt as to the misfortune that has befallen her. Her heart is breaking, her mind wanders, her feet begin to move and skip in a repeat of the motif that she was dancing with her lover. But her strength is soon exhausted, she falters, and bending down, picks up the fatal sword that Hilarion has brought and would have fallen on its point if Albrecht had not snatched the weapon away in a movement of desperate rapidity. Alas, his action is of no avail, for its

---

[6] The horn is usually hung up by the door of Giselle's cottage.

point has already found its mark. It has pierced Giselle's heart,[7] and she dies, comforted at least by the profound sorrow of her lover and the tender pity of Bathilde.

That, my dear Heine, is the story that M. de Saint-Georges conceived to give us the pretty young corpse we need. In my ignorance of theatrical devices and the demands of the stage, I had been thinking of quite simply setting to action Victor Hugo's delightful *Orientale*[8] for the first act. The scene would have been set in a beautiful ballroom belonging to some prince. The chandeliers would be lit, the flowers arranged in the vases, the tables laid, but the guests not yet arrived. The wilis would appear, momentarily, attracted by the joy of dancing in a room all ablaze with crystal and gilding in the hope of attracting some new recruit. The Queen of the Wilis would touch the floor with her magic wand to fill the dancers with an insatiable desire for *contre-danses*, waltzes, *galops* and *mazurkas*. The entrance of the ladies and gentlemen would make them fly away like insubstantial shadows. Giselle, having danced the whole night through, exhilarated by the enchanted floor and the desire to keep her lover from inviting other women to dance with him, would be surprised by the cold of morning just like the young Spanish girl, and the pale Queen of the Wilis, invisible to all, would have placed her icy hand on her heart. But then we should not have had the touching and well acted scene that concludes the first act in its present form, Giselle herself would have been less interesting, and the second act would have lost its element of surprise.

The second act is as exact a translation as it is possible to make of the page that I allowed myself to tear out of your book, and I hope that when you return, fully recovered, from Cauterets, you will not find it too misinterpreted.

The stage represents a forest by the edge of a lake, overhung by tall pale trees with their roots steeped in the grass and the bullrushes, and with water lilies spreading their broad leaves on the placid surface of the water silvered here and there by the moon with a trail of white patches. Reeds emerge from their smooth brown sheathes to shiver and tremble in the intermittent night breeze. The flowers are half open, languidly spreading their heady scent like those large blooms of Java that madden all who inhale them, and a sort of burning, sensuous atmosphere circulates in this dense and humid darkness. At the foot of a willow tree, lost and embedded among the flowers, lies

---

[7] There has been some controversy about whether Giselle dies from falling on the sword or of a broken heart. On the strength of this description and Gautier's other account in *Les Beautés de l'Opéra*, it is clear that his understanding was that the sword found its mark before being snatched away by Albrecht. The incident was arranged so as to be over in a flash, and perhaps the audience was intended to be left in some doubt.

[8] The poem, entitled *Fantômes* and included in the collection, *Les Orientales*, told of a young Spanish girl who dies from a surfeit of dancing.

Giselle. On the white marble cross that marks her grave hangs, still fresh, the crown of leaves with which she was crowned at the vintage festival.

Some hunters appear, in search of a suitable spot to lie in wait for game, but Hilarion scares them by telling them that this is a sinister and dangerous place, haunted by wilis, cruel nocturnal dancers who are no more forgiving than is a living woman to a tired waltzing partner. Midnight chimes in the distance. From the long grass and the tufts of bullrushes will-o'-the-wisps dart forth in their irregular and twinkling flight, and the frightened hunters take to their heels.

The reeds part and there come into view, first, a little twinkling star, then a crown of flowers, then two beautiful blue eyes, looking gently startled and set in an oval of alabaster, and then finally the whole of that lovely form—slender, chaste, graceful, and worthy of Diana of old—that we know as Adèle Dumilâtre. It is the Queen of the Wilis. With that melancholy grace that is characteristic of her, she frolics in the pale starlight, skimming across the water like a white mist, poising on the bending branches, stepping on the stalks of the flowers like Virgil's Camilla who walked on the corn without bending it,[9] and with a wave of her magic wand summons her subjects, the other wilis, who emerge in veils of moonlight from tufts of reeds, clusters of shrubbery and blooms of flowers to take part in the dance. She announces that a new wili is to be admitted into their band this night. And indeed the shade of Giselle, pale and stiff in her transparent shroud, springs suddenly out of the ground at the bidding of Myrtha (for such is the Queen's name). The shroud falls and vanishes. Giselle, still benumbed from the icy damp of the dark abode from which she has come, takes a few halting steps, casting a glance of terror at the tomb on which her name is inscribed. The wilis take hold of her and lead her to the queen, who with her own hands places on her head the magic crown of asphodel and verbena. At the touch of her wand two little wings, as restless and trembling as those of Psyche, suddenly sprout from the shoulders of the young shade who, however, had no need of them. At once, as if wishing to make up for the lost time spent lying in that narrow bed made of half a dozen long planks and two short ones, in the words of the poet of *Lenore*,[10] she takes possession of the space, bounding and rebounding with the intoxication of liberty and the joy at being no longer confined beneath a thick blanket of heavy earth—all this being sublimely rendered by Mme Carlotta Grisi. The sound of footsteps is heard, and the wilis disperse

---

[9] See No. 17, note 3.

[10] *Lenore* was a popular ballad written by the German poet Gottfried August Bürger (1747–94). The allusion is to Lenore's coffin, "quiet, new and small, six long planks and two short":

> . . .*Still, kühl und klein!. . .*
> *Sechs Bretten und zwei Brettchen!*

and conceal themselves behind the trees. It is a band of young peasants returning from a festivity in a neighbouring village. An excellent prey! The wilis come out of their hiding to entice them into their fatal round. Luckily the young folk heed the words of a wise old man who is conversant with the legend of the wilis, and finally realise that it is tempting fate to encounter, in the depths of a wood and by the edge of a lake, a bevy of young creatures in low-cut bodices and tulle skirts, with stars on their foreheads and butterfly wings at their shoulders. The thwarted wilis go in pursuit, and the stage is left empty.

A young man enters, distraught and crazed with grief, his eyes swimming with tears. It is Loys, or Albrecht if you will, who has given his guardians the slip to visit the tomb of his beloved. Giselle cannot resist the expression of such sincere and profound sorrow. Gently parting the branches, she leans towards her kneeling lover, her charming features aglow with love. To attract his attention she plucks some flowers and placing them to her lips, blows kisses to him. As Albrecht pursues her, the insubstantial spectre begins to flutter coquettishly. Like Galathea, she disappears into the reeds and bull-rushes, *sed cupit ante videri*.[11] The transverse flight, the bending branch, her sudden disappearance when Albrecht wishes to fold her in his arms are original and novel effects that complete the illusion. But now the wilis are returning. Giselle assists Albrecht to hide, for she knows too well the fate that awaits him if he tarries and encounters the terrible night dancers. But they have found another victim. Hilarion has lost his way in the forest. A treacherous path has led him back to the spot from which he had only just fled. The wilis seize hold of him and pass him down their line. As soon as one dancer tires, another takes her place, and all the time the infernal dance is drawing closer to the lake. Breathless and exhausted, Hilarion falls at the feet of the Queen, begging for mercy. But of mercy there is none. The pitiless phantom strikes him with her branch of rosemary, and all of a sudden his weary feet go into convulsions. He rises and makes new attempts to escape. A wall of dancers bars his way; bemused, he is buffeted hither and thither, and letting go the cold hand of the last dancer, he staggers and falls into the water. Farewell, Hilarion, let that be a lesson not to meddle in the love affairs of others, and may the fish gobble your eyes out!

But what is Hilarion but one man among so many dancing women? Less than nothing! Then a wili, with that marvellous instinct of a woman looking for someone to partner her in a waltz, discovers Albrecht in his hiding place. Now here is something, a man who is young and handsome and light of foot. "Come, Giselle, show your mettle, make him dance himself to death." Her pleas, for all their force, fall upon deaf ears, and the Queen threatens to

---

[11] "But eager to be seen before she goes." Virgil, *Eclogues*, III 65.

deliver Albrecht into the hands of less scrupulous wilis. Giselle draws her lover towards the tomb from which she has emerged, telling him to clasp the cross and not leave it, come what may. Myrtha resorts to a diabolically feminine ruse. She commands Giselle, who as her subject cannot disobey, to execute the most alluring and graceful poses. At first Giselle dances timidly and with reluctance, but she then finds herself carried away by her instinct both as a woman and as a wili, and she lightly springs forward and dances with such sensuous grace and such overpowering fascination that the heedless Albrecht leaves the protection of the cross and goes towards her with arms outstretched and eyes shining with desire and love. The fatal delirium takes hold of him, he pirouettes, jumps, and follows Giselle in her most daring bounds. In the grip of this frenzy, he is consumed with the secret desire to die with his mistress and follow his "beloved shade" to the grave. But four o'clock strikes, and a pale streak of light appears on the edge of the horizon. It is daybreak, and the coming of the sun, bringing deliverance and salvation. Now flee, dark visions of night; vanish, wan phantoms! Giselle's eyes shine with a heavenly joy, for she knows that the hour of danger has passed and that her lover will not die. The beautiful Myrtha returns to the petals of her water-lily. The wilis fade away, melt in the air and vanish. Giselle herself is being drawn back towards her tomb by an invincible force. Distraught, Albrecht seizes her in his arms, and carries her, covering her with kisses, to place her on a flower-covered mound. But the earth will not relinquish its prey; the grassy mound opens, the plants bow their heads as though weeping tears of dewdrops and the flowers incline their stalks . . . The sound of a horn is heard, and Wilfrid enters, searching anxiously for his master. A few steps behind him come the Prince of Courland and Bathilde. However, the flowers have now covered Giselle until nothing can be seen of her but a small transparent hand. Then the hand itself disappears. All is over. Never again will Albrecht and Giselle see one another in this world. He kneels before the mound, gathers up a few of the flowers, clasps them to his breast and departs, his head resting on the shoulder of the beautiful Bathilde, who forgives and comforts him.

That, my dear poet, is more or less how M. de Saint-Georges and I have adapted your charming legend with the help of M. Coralli[12], who has invented *pas*, groups and attitudes of exquisite elegance and novelty. We chose as your interpreters the three graces of the Opéra, Mlles Carlotta Grisi, Adèle Dumilâtre and Forster. Carlotta danced with a perfection, a lightness, a boldness and a chaste and delicate sensuality that place her in the front rank between Elssler and Taglioni. In her miming she exceeded every expectation. There was not a conventional gesture, not a false movement; she was nature and alertness personified. It is true to say that she has, for her husband, the

---

[12] Jean Coralli (1779–1854) was chief ballet-master of the Opéra from 1831 to 1850.

aerial Perrot.[13] Petipa was graceful, passionate and moving. Not for long time has a male dancer given so much pleasure and been so well received. M. Adam's music is superior to the music that is ordinarily written for ballet; it abounds in motifs and orchestral effects, and even contains, as a touching concession to lovers of difficult music, a well constructed fugue. The second act successfully solves the musical problem of conveying the fantastic in a way that is graceful and full of melody. As for the sets, they are by Ciceri, who still has no equal in the field of country landscapes. The sunrise which introduces the *dénouement* is magically realistic. Carlotta was recalled amid noisy applause from the entire house.

So your German wilis have had a complete success at the French Opéra. The newspapers will have already told you about it. I would have informed you sooner if I had known your address, but being without it, I am taking the liberty of writing to you in the form of a review in *La Presse*, which will no doubt reach you.

La Presse, July 5th, 1841.
(*Paris Elégant*, July 10th, 1841;
Théâtre, 1st ed., pp. 367–378.)
HAD, II 133–142. L:515.

---

[13] In this roundabout way Gautier hints at Perrot's contribution to the choreography, of which as author of the ballet and friend of the ballerina he must have been fully aware. Although only Coralli's name appeared on the playbills and the scenario, Jules Perrot, who was not on the Opéra payroll and received no remuneration for his work, arranged the whole of Carlotta's rôle. Perrot and Carlotta never married.

28

Opéra: *La Jolie Fille de Gand*

La Jolie Fille de Gand, ballet-
pantomime in 3 acts and 9 scenes,
sc. Saint-Georges, ch. Albert, mus.
Adam, f.p. June 22nd, 1842.

We are in the good city of Ghent, as well you can imagine by looking out through the windows at the stepped roofs of the Flemish houses and the characteristic towers of the Abbey of St. Bavon. And this is the shop of Césarius, the goldsmith, as indicated by those large cupboards filled with jewellery and gold plate.

Beatrix, Césarius's daughter, is taking her dancing lesson, accompanied by her young sister Agnes. We leave you to guess whether the master is pleased with his pupil, for Beatrix is none other than Giselle, the wili, who is no less light for having laid aside her wings. So that good fellow Zéphyros does not hide his satisfaction, showing his delight by a host of comic contortions to which the public, which wholly shares his opinion, adds a storm of applause. Young Agnes, so the scenario says, dances "awkwardly and gracelessly". Mlle Adèle Dumilâtre, who plays this rôle, complies with the authors' directions very inaccurately, for, without making so much progress as her sister Beatrix, she is all charm and grace in her feigned clumsiness. However, Beatrix's thoughts are far away, as the saying goes. She is lost in a dream and preoccupied. A rich foreigner, the Marquis de San Lucar, has been hovering about her like a beautiful butterfly, gleaming with silk, velvet and gold, and his magnificent clothes and his proud bearing have made the meagre suit of her fiancé Benedict appear very drab and humble by comparison. While she is absorbed in these thoughts, her cousin Julia enters, a pretty dark-haired girl with a bright expression, eyes sparkling like black diamonds, and a red mouth that is always breaking into a pretty smile . . . and bad advice. Peeping out from her corsage is the corner of a letter from the Marquis de San Lucar. Benedict arrives too, holding in his trembling hand a bouquet of fresh flowers in full bloom, which Beatrix receives with an indifferent air. Poor Benedict goes into a corner with death in his heart and tears in his eyes, and Julia

103

reckons from the off-hand manner with which her cousin has accepted his flowers that she will be more interested in the Marquis's letter. But Beatrix, being an honest girl, has no wish to accept this improper note. Nevertheless, the little devil Julia reads it to her in a whisper. A virtuous girl can easily refuse to listen to a love letter, but she cannot help hearing it.

Father Césarius, who has no liking for Julia, gives her a very cool welcome and warns his daughters to be on their guard against her. He then informs Benedict that his marriage to Beatrix is fixed for the following day. This news, while filling the young man with joy, makes the girl go pale, realising that tomorrow she will have to embark, for all time, on a humble, bourgeois life and renounce once and for all her dreams of love amid wealth and elegance. Agnes, you may be sure, would never have had such thoughts, and her pretty face glows with joy, for Benedict, although promised to her sister, appears to her as the most charming husband in the world. This does not escape the observant eye of Julia, who is a real little devil in skirts.

But now the street is filling with people, fanfares are sounding from every side, and the whole population is making its way to the town's great kermess.[1] Benedict leaves to get dressed and collect Beatrix's companions. Zéphyros, admirably played by good old Barrez, leaves with him, delighting in the thought that the festival will gives his pupils a fine opportunity to display their skill.

Hardly have they left when the Marquis de San Lucar and his friend Bustamente enter the shop and make some expensive purchases. Julia seizes the chance of pointing out to Beatrix, who has no need to be told, the elegance and good looks of the Marquis. The two strangers give the girls jewels and invite them into their carriage to go to the kermess. Césarius, while finding San Lucar and Bustamente somewhat forward in their manners, has to agree that they are excellent customers. Benedict returns wearing his best suit. Césarius introduces him as his future son-in-law to the Marquis, who does not seem overjoyed at the information. "Have no worry," Julia whispers to him, "she does not love him." The girls and Zéphyros, led by fiddlers, then arrive to join their companions, but Julia climbs into the Marquis's carriage with Beatrix, and if the sympathetic Agnes had not been there to offer him her little white hand, poor Benedict would have had to go to the festival alone.

The scene changes and represents a square in Ghent where the kermess is to take place beneath the tall, age-old trees. At the back can be seen the apple-green poops and red sails of the Dutch and Flemish koffs[2] that lie at anchor in

---

[1] The kermess was an annual fair organised to encourage local commerce. In the nearby town of Bruges there was an even older kermess, which was to provide the setting for Bournonville's ballet, *Kermessen i Brugge*, f.p. Royal Theatre, Copenhagen, April 4th, 1851.

[2] Clumsy two-masted sailing vessels, used particularly in the Netherlands.

the canal. The square is crowded, with men lounging at tables drinking from pewter tankards, indulging in good-humoured banter and flirting with the serving girls. It might be a scene by Teniers or Ostade,[3] but in the manner of the Opéra, that is to say infinitely neat and clean. San Lucar, Bustamente, Julia and Benedict take their seats on a bench to watch the procession of tradesmen pass by. As you know, the Flemish have always had a taste for these interminable processions, in which the guilds march with their banners to the obligatory accompaniment of mythological tableaux on ancient carts. The procession disappears into the wings, and crossbowmen begin shooting at a target, a crown of white roses placed on top of a mast. Bustamente shoots first and misses. The stray arrow finds its mark in the wig of Zéphyros. San Lucar, who is a better shot, carries away the prize, a feat which Julia brings to the notice of her cousin, who is already too prone to find the Marquis charming, dazzled by his aristocratic air, his winning charms and his princely munificence. Happily, the dances are about to begin, and for a moment Beatrix will be removed from Julia's mischievous suggestions. From the very first measures the girl's honest and candid smile returns to her lips and her lovely eyes lose their listless expression and become brighter and gentler. Her innocence has returned. She is no longer thinking of the Marquis de San Lucar and his fine gold-embroidered cloak, its hem lifted by a slender rapier, nor of long velvet robes held up by a little black page, nor of white marble staircases and amber-scented love letters slipped into lacquer caskets filled with jewels, for she is entirely absorbed in the pleasure of dancing with her sweetheart whom she is to marry tomorrow. See how she flies, leaps and glides, and how at ease she is in the air! When from time to time the tip of her tiny foot brushes the ground, you can see that it is purely out of consideration so as not to drive to despair those who have no wings. It must be added that the music for this *pas* is deliciously original. Over the tracery of the orchestra burst, like clusters of fireworks, the sparkling notes of a carillon, giving a wonderful imitation of those Flemish clocks that inspired Victor Hugo to write some lovely verses in *Les Rayons et les Ombres*.[4]

Carlotta is the very incarnation of the aerial dancer whom the poet imagined descending and mounting a crystal stairway of melody in a glow of sonorous light. She reaches, without a falter, the uppermost rung of the ladder of silver filigree that the musician has constructed as if to defy her lightness, and when she descends, the marvelling audience applauds her furiously, already consoled for the loss of Taglioni, who is in the snows of Russia, and Fanny Elssler, who is in the equatorial heat of America. It is quite impossible to dance with greater perfection or more strength and grace, a

---

[3] David Teniers the younger (1610–90) and Isaak van Ostade (1621–49), genre painters who specialised in scenes of everyday life in the Netherlands.

[4] No. XVIII, "*Ecrit sur la vitre d'une fenêtre flamande.*"

more profound sense of rhythm and timing, or a happier and sunnier expression. She betrays no fatigue, no effort; there is no sign of perspiration or breathlessness. Having accomplished these marvels, she returns to her bench, escorted by her partner, as if she had just been dancing a *contredanse* in the ballroom. The *pas* being now at an end, Julia comes up to whisper I know not what in the ear of her cousin, whom she wants to drag down into the abyss into which she herself has fallen, for she is already the mistress of Bustamente. "Hush," says Beatrix, all confused, "we can be overheard. See, here is the key to my bedroom. Come this evening and let us talk about it then." This little incident passes unnoticed by everyone save the Marquis in the general rejoicing. A grand Flemish cotillon is formed, and the entire square is filled with dancers. The beer froths and flows and the festival is at its height when large raindrops begin to fall from the leaves of the trees, the sky darkens, a storm breaks, and the kermess is brought to an end as everyone takes to their heels. Benedict accompanies Beatrix home, to the disappointment of the Marquis, who profits from the confusion by stealing the key that the girl has entrusted to her cousin Julia. The devil is content, for he now has the key to paradise.

Next we find ourselves in Beatrix's modest little bedroom, a real dovecot, recalling Marguerite's little room before her fall.[5] A bed with twisting columns and serge drapes, a tapestry-covered armchair in which the white-haired old father is wont to sit and gaze at his sleeping child, a table for a mirror and many flowers, vases of them everywhere, mainly roses, the natural friends of young girls. And crucifix, prie-dieu, wooden clock—nothing is lacking.

Beatrix enters with her father and Benedict, still wearing the crown won by the Marquis. Her thoughts seem far away, and she pays hardly any attention to poor Benedict, who is at a loss to understand why she is so cold on the eve of her wedding. Césarius notices this too, and then Beatrix, who is tender-hearted, offers the young man her hand as a sign of reconciliation. He smothers it with kisses. But it is getting late, and soon Beatrix is left alone.

She hangs the white crown of which she is still worthy on her prie-dieu, undoes her bodice, steps out of her skirt and slowly undresses, uncovering her beautifully rounded arms and her pearly shoulders with shy modesty. Suddenly a key is heard turning in the lock. At first Beatrix thinks it is Julia, but it is the Marquis de San Lucar who enters the bedroom with that air of gallant authority and respectful familiarity that is the hallmark of the professional Don Juan. Trembling to find herself exposed defenceless before his bold gaze, the chaste girl quickly covers herself with her veil, as a startled sylphide might conceal herself behind a lily leaf. With the passion of a consummate actor, the Marquis utters the familiar commonplaces about undying affection and

[5] In Goethe's *Faust*.

unquenchable love that have been, and always will be, the undoing of so many girls. Julia then appears, putting on a wonderful show of astonishment. The Marquis continues his fine declarations, and when Beatrix refuses to allow herself to be persuaded, pulls out his dagger and threatens to kill himself. You can imagine the terror of Beatrix, who takes all this seriously. There is a knock at the door, and the Marquis has to make his escape through the window, but promising that he will be back. It is Agnes, who has come to remind Beatrix that the wedding is to take place at one o'clock and telling her to have a good night's sleep so as to look fresh. Beatrix falls to her knees, happy to think she is out of danger. She kisses the medallion with her father's portrait, stretches out on the little bed and is soon sleeping the deep sleep of innocence.

Now we are far away from Ghent—in Venice, in the palazzo of the Marquis de San Lucar. And who is this charming lady in a beautiful satin robe brocaded in gold, whose face has the delicate complexion of a Bengal rose and is framed by ringlets of the softest light brown hair? She is now rising, and there can be no mistaking those delicate and charming gestures and that gazelle-like walk—it is Beatrix, it is Carlotta Grisi, and the public, after hesitating for a moment, proves that it has recognised her by bringing the house down with applause. Alas, poor Benedict, what use your nice new sky-blue suit! Your chaste fiancée is lost forever! Insolently respectful young noblemen compliment San Lucar on his good fortune and Beatrix on her beauty. Vendors of fine material and jewellers uncover their wares and display them, and the Marquis buys everything and smothers Beatrix with presents. For this is the way to treat such creatures; since you cannot offer them respect, you ply them with gold, the extent of your love being measured by the sum total of the money spent on them. It is the height of fashion to ruin oneself. San Lucar is very much in love with Beatrix, and rightly so, for never can a more divine pearl have fallen from the casket of Heaven into the earthly mire. Julia, whose life seems linked to her cousin's, has become a dancer at the Teatro La Fenice,[6] now managed by Zéphyros. But it is no longer Don César Bustamente who gives her his hand and carries her fan and her cloak, it is the young Count Leonardo. Beatrix notices this and expresses surprise. Julia laughs at her for being so naïve. Zéphyros is to give a ball *a giorno* at the theatre that evening, and while he is distributing tickets to the young noblemen, Diana, the prima ballerina of La Fenice, exchanges words with Julia and a quarrel breaks out between them which is only ended when San Lucar promises to give his applause to both the rivals. The Marquis's free and easy manner with Zéphyros's dancers strikes a chill in Beatrix's heart. A look of sadness comes over her face, and her blue eyes are on the point of dissolving in tears, when San Lucar returns to her side with tender looks and loving words,

---

[6] The opera house of Venice.

and this little cloud is quickly chased away. Everyone is now occupied in choosing costumes for the masked ball, and naturally and without hesitation the brightest and most extravagant of them are selected.

The scene changes to represent the foyer of La Fenice illuminated *a giorno*, swarming and sparkling with an immense, tightly packed crowd. Among them can be recognised the characters of Pantalone, Scaramuccia, Tartaglia, the Bolognese doctor, Trivelino; Europe, Asia, Africa and America, Night and Day (a very fine Day), a handsome Lady Fortune with blindfolded eyes that see no less clearly for that. And do you hear that burst of laughter, spreading from the stage to the auditorium, as a three-legged grotesque, a classification not envisaged by Cuvier,[7] comes leaping in with three red leather boots. And now here come Mlle Sophie Dumilâtre and Mabille in costumes of blue velvet edged with swansdown, she clicking her steel-heeled shoes in a recollection of the *Cracovienne*. The *mazurka* is followed by a scarf dance performed by Diana and her companions. Scarf dances have, in our opinion, the disadvantage of reminding us too much of the lengths of material fluttering in the breeze that are displayed outside draper's shops.

San Lucar, who is surely the most fickle of men, hangs about the dancers, paying compliments that are so passionate as to arouse Beatrix's jealousy and wound her self-esteem. She leaves the stage for a moment, and shortly afterwards reappears as Diana, wearing a tunic bespattered with silver stars, a crescent of precious stones in her hair, quiver slung over her shoulder and bow in hand. Shouts of admiration greet this graceful mythological vision. Beatrix imitates the poses of Diana of antiquity, pricking up her ears and conveying the impression of a frightened deer fleeing from her over leaves dampened with the dew. Then, curving her arm, smooth as alabaster, she draws a deadly arrow from her quiver, places it to her bow, and looses the string with a vibrating twang. Having killed the deer, she throws down her arms. No longer is she the huntress Diana, the cruel virgin running in the depths of great woods, followed by her white hounds; she has become the Diana of moonlight, the silvered smile of fine spring nights, the bearer of a divine kiss that finds its way, through leaves disturbed by passion, to the transparent brow of the sleeping Endymion.

Beatrix is unanimously declared the fairy of the dance and the queen of the ball. San Lucar, overcome by love and pride, places a crown of roses—not white this time—on the head of his young mistress, to whom he swears eternal devotion. Beatrix, touched by this repentance, detaches a rose from her bouquet and offers it to him. San Lucar pins it to his domino.

All of a sudden a dull murmur spreads through the merry throng. The masked revellers recoil and disperse in terror. A domino of imposing and

---

[7] Baron Georges Cuvier (1769–1832), celebrated for his zoological studies and his work on animal classification.

sinister aspect comes forward with a heavy measured tread like that of the marble boots of the Commander[8] and comes to a halt before the group containing San Lucar, Julia and Beatrix. With an authoritative and commanding gesture he sweeps Beatrix's crown from her head and tramples it beneath his feet. Enraged by such insolence San Lucar rushes at the impudent stranger with rapier drawn. But the latter, throwing back the hood of his cloak, discloses to the astonished company the white-haired head of Césarius, the goldsmith of Ghent. Devastated by the old man's curse, Beatrix falls to the ground in a swoon. Benedict is about to challenge the Marquis, but Césarius restrains him and leads him away, advising him to allow public scorn to complete his revenge.

In the following scene, we are transported at the whim of the scenario to a magnificent villa on the banks of the Brenta. The set, one of the prettiest of the piece, has a fresh, humid, mellow quality that commands admiration.

An orgy is in full flow. Lamps of coloured glass sparkle beneath the trees, casting a multitude of prismatic reflections on the crystal fringes of the fountains. Gold goblets of Cyprus and Sicilian wines are being handed round by pages. Courtesans in tiger-skin tunics, their hair entwined with ivy, are fondling in their laps the heads of young noblemen who are lying at their feet among the flowers that sprout from the mossy sward. The dances grow more and more passionate, and Julia's skirt, which becomes shorter with every act, flies about her, quivering like a butterfly's wing displaying its charms. Beatrix, still trembling after the recent scene, scared by the dissolute licentiousness expressed in word, gesture and glance all around her, and feeling isolated in this world of corruption into which the error of her ways has plunged her, looks on at this bacchanalia without participating, filled with pained shock and increasing horror, like a victim of nightmarish hallucinations.

Supper and dancing are followed by gambling, the only passion that produces neither satiety nor fatigue. San Lucar plays *biribi*[9] with Bustamente, and loses continually. He scatters coins on the table by the fistful, then banknotes, and when his banknotes are exhausted, the title deeds of his vast estates. And when all that has been lost, he tears off Beatrix's necklaces, earrings, bracelets, even the diamond ring with their initials engraved on it, casting his all into the bottomless pit. Luck is against him, and still he loses. What is left to enable him to take his revenge? Nothing but his mistress, and by God, he will wager her, and win her back later. So the stake is that rose of a woman, the gentle and sad figure of Beatrix, her eyes still glistening from the

[8] The statue of the wronged father in the legend of Don Juan who arrives in response to an invitation to dinner as a harbinger of the Don's final retribution. Mozart used the theme for his opera *Don Giovanni*, which had entered the repertory of the Opéra in a French version on March 10th, 1834.

[9] A game of chance popular among gamblers in the eighteenth century. It was not unlike roulette except that the winning numbers were picked out of a bag.

tears of contrition, a rose that has not yet begun to fade in the button-hole of San Lucar. Five, six—seven, eight! Bustamente wins again, and Beatrix must be handed over. But the Marquis and Bustamente are wearing identical dominos, their features concealed by their Venetian masks, so that at first the poor girl will not notice the substitution, but when she does, her indignation at San Lucar's behaviour will stifle every vestige of love in her heart.

Bustamente leads Beatrix back into San Lucar's palazzo, of which he himself is now the possessor. They sit down on a couch. Bustamente puts his arm round Beatrix's waist and ventures a few caresses, to which the poor girl submits with an instinctive feeling of dread. "Take off your mask," she says, "you are frightening me." And when Bustamente refuses, she tears it off herself! There follows a struggle between Bustamente and Beatrix, and she is on the point of being overpowered when the Marquis de San Lucar, mad with remorse and jealousy, arrives in the nick of time to draw his sword on Bustamente, who vainly asserts his rights under their contract. This duel is one of the best produced and most energetic ever to have been seen on the stage. The duellists rush upon one another with indescribable fury, in spite of the efforts of the terrified Beatrix to separate them. Finally, with a skilful thrust, San Lucar strikes Bustamente's sword from his hand. Bustamente retreats towards the window and, pierced through the heart, falls backwards on to the ledge of the balcony, and from there into the Grand Canal. There is a dull splash as his body strikes the water.

Distraught and dishevelled, Beatrix flees from a lover who has become an assassin, and staggers out of the cursed palazzo.

Now come back with us, please, from Venice to Ghent—a journey that is accomplished by a mere whistle from the machinist. Here once again are the serrated gables in which storks make their nests, the tall trees and the fresh, damp atmosphere that has been so beautifully rendered by Dutch painters.

A wedding procession crosses the square. It is that of Benedict who, having completely forgotten Beatrix, is now to marry the gentle Agnes. Gypsies come running in from the other side. Beneath their bizarre and ragged costumes, you may recognise the dancing master Zéphyros and the dancer Julia. She is still pretty after all that has happened, and what else matters! The coarse petticoat is very becoming on her. She has courageously accepted her fate, and without a trace of melancholy she performs the dance of the eggs[10] on a wretched piece of carpet in the centre of the square. But who is this stranger with features lined by grief and suffering, in a straw hat and a wretched grey dress? It is Beatrix, exhausted by fatigue, whom Zéphyros and Julia press to join their troupe, an invitation she rejects with horror. The wedding procession emerges from the church. Beatrix cannot face the sight of a happiness

[10] See No. 19, note 8.

that should have been hers, and runs to the canal to throw herself into its waters.

Here ends the dream, or rather the nightmare. Houses, trees, canal, all disappear, and we are back in the little bedroom, where Beatrix wakes, sick with dread and terror. But she realises that it has all been a dream and, filled now with happiness and quite cured of her ambitious yearnings, throws herself into the arms of her friends who have come to escort her to her wedding. The Marquis's head appears at the window, but he is too late. Beatrix is now safe from his advances.

No one had any doubt that Carlotta would dance her *pas* to perfection, for she is now the leading dancer in Europe. But there might have been fears that the dramatic and violent scenes of the narrative, conceived entirely in pantomime, would not suit her simple, poetic nature. She surpassed every expectation. Her demure shock at the sight of all the orgies and quarrels, her keen sensitivity, her energetic reaction in the duel scene, her horror, depicted with such realism and pathos, at her father's curse, left nothing to be desired. Mlle Maria was ravishingly witty and bright, and made a charming gypsy. Albert appeared elegant, noble, with a haughty and refined allure, and ruined himself like a true nobleman. Elie, who up to now had played only comic rôles, showed that he is equally suited to serious parts. As for Barrez, he is as perfect a natural grotesque as he ever was, and able to make people laugh at the Opéra, which is no small merit.[11]

M. Adam's score is written with the care which he gives to all his ballet music. There are enough themes in it for three *opéras comiques* The *pas des clochettes*, the kermess act, the *galop* in the masked ball, which will be as popular as the *galop* from *Gustave*, contain charming melodies and merry rhythms. A whole article would be needed to list all the delightful phrases that abound in *La Jolie Fille de Gand*. Such profusion is all the more commendable in composers of ballet music, who are paid relatively little even though a very considerable amount of work is involved.

The success was complete. Albert[12] and Carlotta were called before the curtain by a unanimous salvo of bravos. *La Jolie Fille de Gand* can boldly compete with thirty degrees of heat and will make the summer just as profitable for the Académie Royale de Musique as the winter.

La Presse, July 2nd, 1842.
HAD, II 252–253 (much
reduced). L:568.

[11] Elie played Bustamente; Barrez performed the three-legged dance.

[12] François Decombe (1787–1865), professionally known as Albert, danced at the Opéra from 1808 to 1831 and was the last specialist male dancer of the *genre noble*. He was reengaged in 1842–43, when he staged and appeared in *La Jolie Fille de Gand*.

29

Opéra: *La Péri*

La Péri, ballet fantastique in 2
acts, sc. Gautier, ch. J. Coralli,
mus. Burgmüller, f.p. July 17th,
1843.

To my friend, Gérard de Nerval, in Cairo.

I would love to have joined you over there, as I promised. I would much
rather be strolling and chatting with you by the banks of the Nile, in the
gardens of Shubra, or climbing the Moqattam hills, from which there is such
a beautiful view,[1] than polishing the soles of my shoes on the various kinds of
bitumen and asphalt that stretch from the Rue Grange-Batelière to the Rue du
Mont-Blanc. But who can do what he wants, except perhaps you? Like Don
César de Bazan[2] you are seeing women of every colour—yellow, black, blue,
green—and the ibis and rats of Pharaoh, lucky man! As for me, a thousand
cares have prevented me from leaving Paris. My foot seems to be permanently
attached to some invisible wire that tugs me back whenever I want to fly
away. Apart from my *feuilleton*,[3] that tub of the Danaïdes[4] into which I have
to pour an urn full of prose every week, there is always a page to finish or one
to begin, dashing one's hopes every day, as well as all the charming worries
that life is full of. So in the end I stayed behind, and being unable to follow
you, I constructed my own Orient, my own Cairo, in the Rue Le Peletier, at
the Académie Royale de Musique, ten minutes walk from my home.[5]

---

[1] The Shubra gardens, to the north of Cairo, was a fashionable recreational area for
Cairo society in the nineteenth century. The Moqattam is a hill to the south-east of
Cairo, commanding an impressive view.

[2] The impoverished nobleman in Hugo's drama, *Ruy Blas*, f.p. Th. de la Renaissance,
November 8th, 1838.

[3] A *feuilleton* is an article occupying the strip at the foot of the first page or pages of a
newspaper. It was the normal position for theatre criticism.

[4] The Danaïdes were the fifty daughters of Danaüs, King of Argos, who ordered them
to murder their husbands on their wedding night, having been informed by an oracle
that one of them would be his killer. For their crime the sisters were condemned to
eternal punishment, filling a vessel full of holes with water that ran out as soon as it
was poured in.

[5] Gautier was then living at No. 27 rue de Navarin.

There are times when people feel they do not belong to the country of their birth, and begin searching high and low for the place of their true origin. Those who are made that way feel like exiles in their home town, strangers among their family, and are tormented by an inverted home-sickness. It is a strange affliction. You turn into a sort of caged bird of passage, but when the time comes to be off, you are stirred by great desires and then seized with apprehension at the sight of the clouds rolling in to cover the clear sky. If one wished, one could easily assign to each one of today's celebrities not only the country but also the century in which he should be passing his true existence. Lamartine and de Vigny are modern Englishmen, Hugo an inhabitant of the Spanish Netherlands at the time of Charles V, Alfred de Musset a Neapolitan in the days of the Spanish rule, Decamps a Turk from Asia, Marilhat an Arab, Delacroix a Moor.[6] Such an exercise could be carried still further, right down to the smallest detail and even confirming the facial types. As for yourself, you are a German, while I am a Turk, not from Constantinople but from Egypt. I really feel I have lived in the East, and when I dress up in a caftan and an authentic tarboosh at Carnival time, I seem to be donning my everyday clothes. It has always surprised me that I cannot understand fluent Arabic—I must have forgotten it! In Spain, everything that reminds me of the Moors interests me as passionately as if I were a son of Islam, and I am even on their side against the Christians.

Being thus preoccupied with the Orient on a grey day of rain and cutting wind, I had begun, perhaps out of reaction, a kind of little Turkish or Persian poem, and had already written twenty verses when I was suddenly struck with the sensible thought that if I wrote any more, nobody would read them anyway. Poetry is the language of the gods, and read only by the gods, to the great despair of publishers. So I threw my stanzas into the waste-paper basket, and taking a fresh sheet of paper, I dedicated my subject to those same dainty feet that created the last act of *Giselle* out of four lines by Heinrich Heine.

That is more or less my excuse for this fantasy, to which I attach no importance. Each puff of opium, each spoonful of hashish evokes images more beautiful and marvellous than the last.

Inside a harem with little marble columns and mosaic paving and walls fretted like lace, through a rising haze of perfume and jets of water dropping back in a pearly dew, a young man, as handsome and rich as any prince out of *The Arabian Nights*, is discovered in a nonchalant day-dream, his elbow deep in a lion's mane, his foot resting on the throat of one of those Abyssinian cats whose skin is always cold, even when the fiery wind is blowing across the

---

[6] All important figures in art and literature of the period: the writers Alphonse de Lamartine (1790–1869), Alfred de Vigny (1797–1863) and Alfred de Musset (1810–57) and the artists Alexandre-Georges Decamps (1803–60), Prosper-Georges-Antoine Marilhat (1811–47) and Eugène Delacroix (1798–1863).

desert—a sort of oriental Don Juan whose sensual pleasures, but not his desires, are sated. His catalogue of women does not include the chance encounters—the great lady and the grisette, the courtisan and the school-girl—who are inscribed among the triumphs of the European Don Juan. It is not intrigue, adventure, complications and deceived husbands that my Don Juan is seeking, but the possession of beauty in all its forms and aspects. Had he been a Christian, he would have been a great painter, but since he belongs to a religion that proscribes the portrayal of the human face for fear of idolatry, he can only fix his gaze on reality. In this unique seraglio is to be found every type of feminine beauty—the regal Georgian, the Greek with profile sharply chiselled as in a cameo, the pure-bred Arab tawny as bronze, the opal-skinned Jewess floating in a mass of red tresses, the slender arch-backed Spaniard, the vivacious and pretty Frenchwoman, and a hundred living masterpieces to which Phidias, Raphael or Titian would have put his name. And yet Achmet murmurs under his breath the melancholy *ghazal* that the Sultan Mahmud[7] cast into the air of the Bosphorus from the heights of the harem terraces: "I have four hundred wives, and I know not love".

Indeed what is the body without the soul but a lamp without light, a flower without scent? What meaning is there for the disspirited Achmet that the most beautiful odalisques are writhing in despair on tiger-skins, that the tears of the Cadine[8] are disturbing the reflection of her charming features in the water of the pool? He is coldly unmoved amid the love that he inspires. In vain has the eunuch who ministers to his pleasures purchased the rarest slaves for their weight in gold. Nothing can capture his faraway look, even for an instant. He is repelled and wearied by material things. Like all great voluptu-aries, he is in love with the unattainable; he wishes to fly into the realm of the ideal in search of faultless beauty; no thrill can satisfy him, he must have ecstasy, and through opium he seeks to weaken the bonds that bind the soul to the body, demanding of hallucination what reality refuses him. So all those eyes that are as blue as the sky or as black as night, those pearly shoulders, those smooth arms, those satiny breasts swelling with the breath of life, all that youth and splendour is powerless to charm away the boredom that lies heavily on his insatiable heart. Surrounded by the purest forms that human beauty can offer, he asks himself: "Is that all there is to it?" What he cries out for with all his strength is the spirit, the soul, the light. He wants a love with

---

[7] Sultan Mahmud I (1696–1754) was a patron of music and literature, and a poet himself. His yearning for a pure love inspired Gautier to write a poem, which he included in his *Poèmes complètes* (1845):

> Que ne suis-je un esclave,
> Un pâtre obscur
> Savourant sans entrave,
> Un amour pur.

[8] The wife of the Sultan.

wings of flame, a burst of radiance soaring into the infinite and the eternal like a bird in flight.

The earth, symbolised by Achmet, stretches its arms up to the sky, which looks tenderly down on him through the azure eyes of the Peri. Indeed, if mortals have dreamt since time immemorial of divine unions, so has Heaven, in the endless boredom of its happiness, frequently sought its distractions on earth. Such is the pleasure of loving, suffering, shining for a brief moment and then disappearing for ever, that the angels have been deserting Paradise and coming down here to commune with the daughters of men. All mythologies are full of that. To say nothing of the innumerable *avatars*[9] of Brahma and Vishnu, the story of Jupiter is no more than a perpetual incarnation. And what is more, when he tires of assuming the forms of men, he turns himself into an animal to make his success more certain. Matter laments the weight of its chains and the corruptibility of its substance, and aspires to the ideal, the infinite, the eternal, while the spirit, on the other hand, in its abstract melancholy, desires sensation, emotion, even sorrow; it is sick of having no body and is tormented by a need for sacrifice and passion.

Toujours les paradis ont été monotones:
La douleur est immense et le plaisir borné,
Et Dante Alighieri n'a rien imaginé
Que de longs anges blancs avec des nimbes jaunes.
Les Musulmans ont fait du ciel un grand sérail;
Mais il faut être Turc pour un pareil travail.

Notre Péri là-haut s'ennuyait, quoique belle;
C'est être malheureux que d'être heureux toujours.
Elle eût voulu goûter nos plaisirs, nos amours,
Etre femme et souffrir ainsi qu'une mortelle.
L'éternité c'est long.—Qu'en faire à moins d'aimer?
Leila s'éprit d'Achmet; qui pourrait l'en blâmer?[10]

Achmet and the Peri—or in other words, mind and matter, love and desire—meet in the ecstasy of a dream, as on neutral soil. It is only when the eyes of the body are asleep that the eyes of the soul awake. The carnal bonds are then loosened, and the invisible world is revealed; the spirits of heaven descend, those of the earth rise up, and mysterious unions are formed in a vague twilight in which the dawn of eternity can already be sensed. But every

[9] The descent of a Hindu deity to the earth in an incarnate form. The term is not applicable to Brahma.

[10] These verses are by Gautier himself, being all that he wrote of the poem he referred to earlier in this article. Entitled *La Péri*, they were not included in his *Poésies complètes* until the edition of 1875–76.

initiation demands a trial, every faith calls for its martyr. It is not enough to have seen the spirit clothed in the whiteness of snow and flame by which ghosts are to be identified on the symbolic Mount Thabor; the spirit must be recognised in all its incarnations, even in the modest disguise of the flesh, in the fragile and perishable envelope of life. Having comprehended it through the brain, it must be understood by the heart. Desire is nothing without love; that ethereal essence must acquire a body, and she whom you loved as a peri must now be loved as a woman, deprived of wings, crown and magic power.

What a wonderful gift to believe in a divinity surrounded by splendour and seated on a dazzling throne with a sun for its footstool! Sacrifice yourself for the spirit, as the spirit sacrifices itself for you; forsake the earth as it has forsaken Heaven, and from the union of those two devotions will be born the complete angel, that is to say, a being of which each half has renounced its happiness for the well-being of the other. The egotism of both mind and matter will have been overcome, and out of this double annihilation supreme happiness will ensue. The earth is the dream of Heaven, and Heaven the dream of the earth—that is the underlying idea of this poem expressed in *ronds de jambe*. So you see, my dear friend, *La Péri*, a ballet-pantomime in two acts, which can be purchased at the Widow Jonas's[11] in the Passage du Grand-Cerf and Tresse's, the printer and bookseller, is crammed with enough myth to satisfy the demands of a German professor of aesthetics. I should be very upset if I were accused of lacking profundity in ballet matters, and if anyone were to think I had not read Creuzer's *Symbolik*.[12]

Now that I have explained the idea of the poem I wanted to write, I shall give you a few details about the ballet that has been performed at the Académie Royale—and without in any way offending my modesty, for *La Péri* is the work of Coralli and Burgmüller, Carlotta and Petipa, and I can sing its praises as something quite separate from myself. Forgive me for writing to you confidentially in my *feuilleton*, but it is possible that you have now left Cairo and are already on the way to Beirut or Acre, perched on the humps of a dromedary. A newspaper will be more certain of reaching you than a letter, for the tree of publicity today scatters its leaves all over the world and I am sure you will find *La Presse* on the divan of some progressive pasha who subscribes to the European press.

But first I must thank you very much for the local information you sent me, which only reached me when my work was completed. But how the devil could I have introduced among the supers of the Opéra those Englishmen in

---

[11] The Widow Jonas published most of the Opéra's ballet scenarios at this time.

[12] Georg Friedrich Creuzer (1771–1858), author of *Symbolik und Mythologie der alten Völker, besonders der Greichen* (1810–12), in which he propounded his theory that Greek mythology derived from Oriental sources, containing elements of an ancient revelation.

rubber suits, with pricked cotton hats and green veils to protect them from ophthalmia, or those strange Frenchmen proudly wearing ragged remnants of clothes that were in fashion in 1816, or those ridiculous Turks decked out in Mahmud's uniform,[13] in Polish style with brandeburgs but with tarbooshes pulled down over the eyes? And the dress of the fellahin women, which you say is so graceful, consisting of a tunic slit on both sides from the armpit to the heel, could hardly have been realised except with modifications that would have taken away all its character. However, when you return I think you will be pleased with the scenery for the first act, which represents a room in Achmet's harem. It is not like those Turkish cafés adorned with ostrich eggs[14] that are designed to give an idea of oriental magnificence in operas and ballets. It is a genuine interior, well observed, and completely authentic. There are stucco walls, panels of glazed tiles, the ceiling made out of coffers of cedarwood, the vaulting worked in a bee-hive pattern, and long-handled vases filled with roses and peonies. And over there, at the back, in the cool and contemplative shade, is a long divan that invites repose and a golden cabinet with rows of cups, coffee pots and pipes. It is a habitable setting, one in which a true believer might feel at home.

If you have frequented the cafés of opium smokers and dropped the smouldering paste into the porcelain bowl,[15] I doubt if a more brilliant mirage could have materialised before your slumbering eyes than the fairy oasis painted by MM. Séchan, Diéterle and Despléchin, who seem to have rediscovered the misty palette of Brueghel the elder, the painter of paradise.[16] Here are the same fabulous tones, ideally tender and fresh. A mysterious radiance emanating from neither moon nor sun bathes the valleys, brushes the lakes with a light silvery mist, and penetrates the glades of the magic forests; the dew glistens like diamonds on strange flowers whose blooms burst into smiles like rosy lips, and pools and waterfalls shimmer beneath the

[13] Mahmud II (1785–1839), Ottoman Sultan from 1808, who reformed the Turkish army on the European model.

[14] These eggs were suspended at the end of wires from a ceiling beam at the apex of a dome.

[15] Gautier confessed to the Goncourts that he had written his novel *Militona*, published in 1847, in ten days under the influence of five grains of hashish. This may have related to his experiments with the drug that he recounted in *Le Club des hachichins* (published in *Revue des Deux Mondes* in February 1846). These sessions took place in the rooms of the painter Fernand Boissard in the Hôtel Pimodan on the Ile Saint-Louis. Gautier himself never became addicted. "After about ten experiments," he wrote, "we gave up this intoxicating drug for good, not that it caused us any physical harm, but a real writer has no need of dreams other than his own natural ones, and he does not like the idea of his mind falling under the influence of some exterior agency."

[16] Jan Brueghel the elder (1568–1625), called "Paradise Brueghel" to distinguish him from his brother, Pieter Brueghel the younger, whose obsession with grotesque scenes of goblins earned him the nickname of "Hell Brueghel".

117

branches—it is a real dream of Araby, all verdant and fresh. Perhaps never before has the Opéra achieved such a brilliant effect with so little. A few yards of canvas, a few pots of paint, a row of gas footlights, and that is all. The brush, when wielded by a skilful hand, is a great magician.

Whatever charms might be displayed by oriental peris with their gold-striped trousers, bejewelled bodices, parrot's wings, red-painted finger-nails and darkened eyelids, I doubt if any would be lovelier than Carlotta or, what is more to the point, dance as well as she.

When the curtain rises on the second act, you are given a bird's eye view of Cairo from the top of a terrace, and you would not believe that neither M. Philastre nor M. Cambon[17] have ever been in Egypt. The fortress, the mosque of Sultan Hassan, the frail minarets resembling ivory rattles, the cupolas of tin and copper that gleam here and there like giant helmets, the terraces surmounted by cedarwood cabinets, and in the distance below, the Nile overflowing its banks, and the Pyramids of Giza, their marble flanks thrusting through the sand of the desert—nothing is lacking, it is a complete panorama. I could not have seen more if I had gone there myself.

It is in the great hall of the harem, which momentarily opens out for the appearance of the Peri, and on the terrace of Achmet's palace that the action of the ballet takes place, being deliberately simplified to give full scope to the choreographer. I shall not mention a small corner of a prison, which is only introduced to give time to set the lighting for the splendours of the apotheosis and put the clouds in place. From a window of this prison Achmet is thrown on to the hooks for refusing to give up the slave girl whose body the Peri has taken. You can guess that she will not let him dangle from the terrible hooks, and will carry him away to her beautiful kingdom of blue and gold. I would have preferred the original set, which was reminiscent of the picture by Decamps[18] and left all that distressing sight on the stage. Perhaps there was an element of surprise in making the flung-out body rise and not fall, and end up in Paradise itself. But the wise men decided that ballet is not suited to such violence, and perhaps they were right. However, all that is of little importance; the main thing in a ballet, whether it be Scottish, German or Turkish, is the dancing, and in this respect no ballet has ever been so successful as *La Péri*. The *pas du songe* was a real triumph for Carlotta. When she appeared in that luminous glow with her childlike smile, her eyes shining with astonish-

[17] One of the leading partnerships of scene-painters, employing a considerable staff. Both painters, Humanité-René Philastre (b. 1794) and Charles-Antoine Cambon (1802–75), the latter a pupil of Ciceri, were also talented artists in their own right.

[18] Alexandre-Gabriel Decamps (1803–60), one of the most gifted painters of his time, had been sent on a mission to Greece and Turkey as a young man, and at the time of this article enjoyed the patronage of the Royal family. The painting which Gautier refers to is *Le Supplice des crochets*, exhibited in the Salon of 1839 and now in the Wallace Collection, London.

ment and delight, posing like a bird trying to alight but carried away by its wings, the whole house broke into unanimous cheering. And what a wonderful dance it is! How I should love to see it danced by real peris and fairies! You just have to see her skimming the ground without touching it; she is like a rose petal wafted by the breeze, and yet what nerves of steel are enclosed in her frail legs, what strength there is in her feet, which are so small that they would be the envy of the most daintily shod lady of Seville! And you have to see her alighting on the tip of her slender toe like an arrow piercing the ground with its barb.

Carlotta Grisi's dancing is both correct and daring; it has a very special character, resembling neither Taglioni's nor Elssler's. Every pose and movement is stamped with the seal of originality. It is wonderful to be novel in an art that is so limited! In this *pas* there is a certain fall that will soon become as famous as those of Niagara. The audience waits for it with bated breath. At the moment when the vision is about to end, the Peri lets herself fall from a cloud into the arms of her lover. If it were no more than an acrobatic feat, we would not mention it, but this dangerous flight forms a group that is full of grace and charm, giving the impression of a dove's feather drifting down in the air rather than a human body hurtling from a platform. And here, as on so many other occasions, we must pay tribute to Petipa. How devoted and attentive he is to his ballerina, and how well he supports her! He does not seek to attract attention to himself, he does not dance just for himself. And in spite of the sometimes unjust disfavour in which male dancers are held today, he is completely accepted by the public, for he does not put on the artificial graces and the revolting mincing manner that have turned the public against male dancing. A very intelligent mime, he always holds the stage and never overlooks the smallest detail. His success was therefore complete, and he can lay claim to a fair share of the applause that was produced by that admirable *pas de deux*, which from now on will become a companion piece to the *pas* in *La Favorite* and the *pas* in *Giselle*. There is no need for me to describe the *pas de l'abeille*, which you must have seen performed in Cairo in its native purity, if that prudish Mehemet Ali has not turned out all the almehs from the Darfur, as I have just been told by a returning traveller.[19]

I wish you could see for yourself the embarrassed modesty with which Carlotta removes her long white veil; the way in which she poses as she kneels beneath its transparent folds, like the Venus of antiquity smiling from her

[19] "The Darfur" is probably a reference to an establishment in the Copt district of Cairo—possibly the "Gavour house", the *maison de rendezvous* mentioned by Charles Didier in his chapter on prostitution in *Les Nuits du Caire* (Paris, 1860)—that was frequented by almehs, whose dances were notoriously erotic. These dancers were rigorously banned by the Viceroy, Mehemet Ali (1769–1849), and when Didier visited Cairo it was virtually impossible to arrange for them to visit a European house, for while they were safe when inside, they could expect to be arrested on leaving, whipped and deported from the city.

pearly shell; the childlike fright that seizes her when the angry bee emerges from the flower, and all the hope and the anguish, and the changing fortunes of the struggle that she conveys as tunic and scarf, and the skirt which the bee has tried to penetrate, are rapidly discarded right and left and vanish in the whirl of the dance, before she drops at Achmet's feet, breathless, exhausted, smiling through her fear, and desiring a kiss far more than the golden sequins that her master's hand places on the brow and the breast of his slavegirl.

If my name did not appear on the playbill, what praises would I lavish on this charming Carlotta! I am truly sorry to have contributed those few lines of scenario that now prevent me from writing about her to my heart's delight. I am in an embarrassing situation. If you were here, you would spare me this difficulty, but I cannot go and find any old journalist to perform this task. So I am forced to review my own work, and I must admit that if I were to say anything in the slightest way derogatory, I should demand an explanation on the spot. I am very touchy on this point, and leave it to my friends to pick on the author's faults, which they will do perfectly. As a reporter I am permitted to bestow unreserved praise on the choreography and groupings of Coralli, who has never shown such freshness, grace and youthful vigour. The kiosk of the Kashmiri women is a charming conception, and the *pas de quatre* in the second act is full of originality and colour, both in the music and in the dance, and is also perfectly performed by Mlles Caroline, Dimier,[20] Robert, and Dabbas, who is very pretty.

The *pas de trois* by Mlles Sophie Dumilâtre, Pauline Leroux[21] and Mabille had only one fault, it was twenty measures too long. But these have now been cut.

In the part of the disgraced favourite, Mlle Delphine Marquet[22] gave proof of real dramatic talent and great promise. She looked ravishing in a delightful costume, taken from a drawing by Marilhat,[23] that suits her noble and severe

[20] Caroline Lassiat (c.1820–85) was later to become celebrated as the teacher, Mme Dominique, who formed Emma Livry, Léontine Beaugrand, Adèle Grantzow and Giuseppina Bozzacchi. The intrepid Aurélie Dimier was to gain laurels in South America and Australia.

[21] Pauline Leroux (1809–91) danced at the Opéra with distinction from 1826 to 1837 and 1840 to 1844, but owing to uncertain health never achieved the success her talents deserved. She created the leading rôle in *Le Diable amoureux* in 1840.

[22] Delphine Marquet (1824–78), the eldest of three sisters all of whom danced at the Opéra. Her career extended from 1842 to 1846. For her sisters Mathilde and Louise, see No. 56, note 6 and No. 51, note 4.

[23] Prosper-Georges-Antoine Marilhat (1811–47) spent several years in Egypt, where he painted the portrait of Mehemet Ali. He was a friend of Gautier, who in writing the scenario had apparently sought his advice on costumes. However, the costume designs for this ballet now preserved in the Bibliothèque de l'Opéra contain no designs by him. Binney in *Les Ballets de Théophile Gautier*, concludes that Marilhat did not design any of the costumes for the ballet, and this passage suggests that the Opéra merely based the costume for Delphine Marquet's rôle on one of his drawings.

beauty to perfection. As for Barrez, he managed, through sheer talent, to make something out of a wretched little rôle that I freely admit is very bad.[24] Regarding the music, it is elegant, delicate, distinguished, and full of happy, lilting melodies that linger in the memory like the waltz in *Giselle*. I only have one fear—that M. Burgmüller[25] will be dogged by pianos and barrel organs and be forced to emigrate from this beautiful land of France, where he has just been naturalised, not having foreseen this furore.

La Presse, July 25th, 1843.
(*Théâtre*, 2nd. ed., pp. 293–301.)
HAD, III 76–85. L:623.

[24] The chief eunuch of the harem.
[25] Frédéric Burgmüller (1806–74) had written the music for the *pas de deux* for two peasants interpolated into the first act of *Giselle*. As well as composing the entire score for *La Péri*, he wrote some of the music for *Lady Henriette* and the polka which Maria and Eugène Coralli were to introduce on the Opéra stage in 1844.

30

Opéra: Début of Caroline Fjeldsted

Début of Mlle Fjeldsted, August 23rd, 1843.

Denmark is an eminently choreographic kingdom, in spite of its icy situation only a few short steps from Norway, the Laplanders and the North Pole. Copenhagen has already sent us Mlle Lucile Grahn and Mlle Nielsen, and now from the same city comes Mlle Fjeldsted, whose name is not easy to pronounce.[1] To judge from the three examples we have already met, Danish women are a characteristic physical type, for Mlles Lucile Grahn, Nielsen and Fjeldsted are strikingly alike. Mlle Lucile Grahn, whose career was interrupted early by a painful knee injury after a quite brilliant début, is the prettiest of the three and is the same type as the others—tall, slender, fair, with sky-blue eyes that are somewhat cold, like the Northern sky, and cheeks whose rosy blush seems to have been borne upon a breeze suffused with polar snow. Mlle Fjeldsted has abused the dancer's right to be thin, and has really joined the band of the Elves, the Nixes and the Valkyries. Her legs could not be more idealised, and her arms are just as vaporous. Mlle Fjeldsted ought to spend some time in a harem on a diet of *nafé, kaiffa* and *racahout*,[2] for she is light enough as it is, without having to keep herself in such an excessive state of training.

The *pas* she danced with Petipa, without being in any way very original,

---

[1] Augusta Nielsen (1822–1902) and Caroline Fjeldsted (1821–81) succeeded Lucile Grahn as Copenhagen's principal ballerinas when the latter left Copenhagen in 1839. Nielsen took over Grahn's rôle in *La Sylphide*, the two of them created the two leading rôles in *Toreadoren*, and Fjeldsted was the first Teresina in *Napoli*. Nielsen had come to Paris in 1841, in defiance of Bournonville's wishes, and after studying under Jules Perrot, made her début at the Opéra on May 20th, 1842. She was offered an engagement, but preferred to return to Copenhagen, where she continued her career until her retirement in 1849.

[2] Fattening Arab dishes. *Nafé* was a paste made from the fruit of the ketmia, a type of hibiscus. See No. 10, note 3.

proved that she has had a good training and knows how to dance. Her *pointes* are neat and firm, and thanks to Petipa, who is very conscientious and helpful to dancers who ask him to partner them, her *temps penchés* and *enlevés* were well performed. But her arm movements have a jerkiness that is lacking in grace, and the young Dane would benefit by working at this and acquiring greater smoothness. It is said that, for her second début performance, Mlle Fjeldsted is to dance a Spanish *pas* with Coralli's son which is very original and novel in character.[3]

La *Presse*, August 30th, 1843.
L:629.

[3] Caroline Fjeldsted danced this *pas de caractère*—the theatrical press did not specify it any further—at her second appearance at the Opéra on September 18th. She left Paris to return to Copenhagen two days later.

31

Opèra: *Lady Henriette*

Lady Henriette, ou la Servante de Greenwich, ballet-pantomime in 3 acts, sc. Saint-Georges, ch. Mazilier, mus. Flotow, Burgmüller and Deldevez, f.p. February 21st, 1844.

M. de Saint-Georges, who seems to have succeeded M. Scribe as the purveyor of operas, *opéras comiques* and ballet scenarios, is the author of the new choreographic work presented last week at the theatre in the Rue Le Peletier with, let us hasten to add, complete success.

The scene is set in England, a country of which M. de Saint-Georges appears very fond, and in which he often sets the action of his pieces. Every author has, so to speak, a country of his dreams towards which his thoughts turn before anywhere else. For some it is Spain, for others Turkey, the North or the East. Every imagination has its mysterious pole. England, however, is not one of the most choreographic of countries, and lends itself more to drama than to ballet properly so-called. So M. de Saint-Georges' work belongs more to the form that is termed *ballet d'action*, or putting it in another way, in which dancing occupies only a secondary place. In doing so the author is merely obeying instincts that have earned him so many successes in the theatre, but perhaps he sometimes overlooks the fact that a ballet should be a picture before being a drama. But let this be said without in any way diminishing the merit of *Lady Henriette*.

Lady Henriette is a young lady at the court of Queen Anne. Although beautiful, charming, adorable and adored, she is as bored as some blasé nabob or a journalist writing his article. Nothing interests or amuses her. She has even lost her feminine love of finery, regards her newest pieces of jewellery with indifference, and no longer has any taste for music or for reading, and the insipid gallantries of her future husband, Sir Tristan Crakford, give her the vapours and get on her nerves. Her head throbs with the hammer strokes of the blue devils,[1] and one can really understand her

[1] "The blue devils," a now obsolete phrase meaning depression.

condition, for Sir Tristan is the most pretentious imbecile, the most unbearable fool imaginable. So the young lady amuses herself tormenting him by every manner of means: "Pick up my handkerchief," "Fetch my fan," "Open the window," "Close it," and countless other contradictory orders which soon send the unlucky cicisbeo,[2] as red in the face as an angry turkey cock, puffing and groaning on to the corner of a sofa. But all this is not much fun for Lady Henriette, for tormenting a fool is a pastime that quickly palls in a young woman of spirit.

The sound of a rustic march is heard. "What is that, Nancy?" Lady Henriette asks her faithful companion, who is leaning over the balcony. "Young girls who are unemployed, coming to the servants' fair to look for a master and a situation." On the orders of Lady Henriette, the procession comes into the room. The servant girls seeking jobs wear pointed caps, and carry little "bouquets" of straw, as the ever elegant, ever flowery M. de Saint-Georges calls them.[3] Someone more vulgar would have called them whisks of straw, but such a graceless image is not acceptable in a ballet, and "bouquet" is a better word.

Lady Henriette is suddenly struck by a crazy idea. The short skirt, little cap and straw bouquet would suit her to perfection, and she has the sudden whim to dress up as a young village girl and, accompanied by her companion Nancy, go and look for a situation in the servants' fair. A writer once said, "A nun's desire is all-devouring,"[4] but a great lady's desire is much more intense. It is so rare that bored and blasé folk have any whims at all that when one of them chances to have one, it has to be carried out at once even at the cost of turning everything upside down. So now the great lady is leaving with her servant, to the great disapproval of Sir Tristan, who accompanies them and, not without reason, finds the whim extremely misplaced.

Henriette and Nancy have no difficulty in becoming the queens of the fair. Everyone wants to ask them for a dance. Lyonnel, a young farmer, appears particularly taken by the beauty of Henriette.

But now the critical moment approaches. The young girls form a line, each holding an attribute of their calling, a spindle, a broom, a sickle, and so on. The Countess and her companion are forced to take their place in the ranks. The peasants approach and choose the girls who suit them. Lyonnel, as you

---

[2] An ironic term for a lady's devoted admirer. In eighteenth-century Italy a lady was permitted to have a cicisbeo, who was approved by her family and her husband, and would escort her to balls and fêtes.

[3] Gérard de Nerval in his review of the ballet (*L'Artiste*, February 25th, 1844) clearly thought this a misprint, referring to it as "bouquet de paille (livret Jonas, lisez bouchon)".

[4] Slightly misquoted from the poem by Jean-Baptiste Gresset (1709–77), *Ver-Vert*:
Désir de fille est un feu qui dévore,
Désir de nonne est cent fois pire encore.

can imagine, is not going to let such an opportunity slip, and his choice is soon made. He engages Lady Henriette who, thinking that such a contract cannot be serious, puts her signature to the conditions in the presence of an alderman in full dress who sanctions contracts of this sort. A short, fat, thick-set farmer with a complexion like a nut, a friend of Lyonnel by the name of Plunkett, engages Nancy, the companion of the Countess of Derby.

When the time comes for them to follow their new masters, the false servants try to escape, but their attempt fails, they are caught by the peasants and given a warning by the alderman. So, not wishing to create a greater disturbance, they are forced to resign themselves to their lot until another opportunity to escape arises. See where a whim can lead you! Who would have dared say to Lady Henriette that morning that by evening she would be serving a peasant at table with her white hands, and be treated as stupid, not without good reason. We next find our two rash ladies in the farmhouse of Lyonnel and Plunkett. "Take my hat," one says. "Take my cloak," says the other. "Bring me a plate." "Go and fetch a bottle from the cellar. Come along, get a move on! Do we have to serve ourselves?" To all these orders Lady Henriette returns such a haughty look of aristocratic pride, while Nancy responds with such a disdainful little pout and a slap so lightly applied, that Lyonnel and his fat friend are left speechless. But Lyonnel then approaches Henriette with such a respectful and tender expression that she begins to unbend and forget her anxiety about the consequences of her escapade. "Have I lost my head," the young farmer wonders, "or my heart? Such slender and delicate hands were never made to hold a broom. Instead of being servant, you shall be mistress. Yes, I love you and wish to marry you." "But you are already engaged to another." "What does that matter! From now on I can only live for you, and I shall tear up my marriage contract with Mina."

Lady Henriette is both charmed and embarrassed by such a show of passion, but her whim does not extend to marrying a country bumpkin, however good-looking he is. Fortunately, as she is opening the window, she sees Sir Tristan Crakford only a few paces outside, looking very melancholy and standing by a post chaise, all ready and harnessed. For the first time Crakford appears as a welcome sight. As soon as darkness has fallen, Henriette and her servant make their escape, and Lyonnel is just in time to see them climb into the post chaise and set off with all the speed of four galloping horses. Alas, poor Lyonnel! The charming vision who appeared to shine for one brief moment in his shadow has vanished for ever, fled, leaving his heart broken by the poisoned arrow of unrequitable love! And all because a great lady was bored and wanted a minute's amusement, his whole life will be disrupted and discarded, and he will suffer until he goes out of his mind!

In the following act we are in the royal forest at Windsor. Good Queen Anne is out hunting. Tally ho, tally ho! The hounds are barking, the horns are sounding, and the pink riding habits sparkle in the green depths of the wood. But who is this pale, good-looking fellow who looks so well in his uniform? It is Lyonnel, who has sought employment to drown his sorrow, but still cherishes perhaps the secret illusion of finding the one woman he cannot forget. Plunkett, who has found employment with him, offers him something to drink, but all he wants is to kiss the young servant's little bouquet of straw, which he treasures next to his heart. Queen Anne then arrives with her suite, among whom is Lady Henriette, who is tired and begs to be excused from following the hunt. Lyonnel, who has meanwhile respectfully withdrawn, has dropped the tuft of corn, his only memento of his vanished love, on the grassy bank where he had been sitting. And it is precisely there that Lady Henriette chooses to rest, and where the eternal madrigals of Sir Tristan Crakford soon send her to sleep. Disappointed and annoyed by this insolent slumber, the old Celadon[5] leaves, muttering about love in general and Lady Henriette in particular.

Lyonnel returns to look for his bouquet, and realises that the Countess, who has taken off her black velvet jacket, is none other than the pretty servant girl from Greenwich. "It is she, it is really she!" he exclaims under his breath as his gaze meets the superb cold stare that the young woman suddenly assumes. "Do you not recognise your former master?" "What are you saying, what madness is this?" "Do you not recognise this bouquet that you carried at the Greenwich fair, when you hired yourself out as a servant?" "Leave me at once," replies Lady Henriette in her great lady's voice, "or I shall have you arrested."

Lyonnel is shattered by such cold self-assurance, but it is she, of that he is certain. The eye may be deceived, but not the heart.

He is absorbed in his thoughts when cries are heard. Queen Anne's horse has bolted. It has taken the bit between its teeth, and is galloping out of control. Lyonnel dashes forward and is fortunately just in time to grasp the maddened animal. Good Queen Anne is saved, and full of gratitude, gives her rescuer a ring, telling him that he only has to present it to her to obtain whatever he wishes, and appoints him one of her guards. Unable to wait to put the ring to the test, Lyonnel asks Her Majesty to order the ladies of her court to remove their masks. In this way he hopes to see Lady Henriette again, but she has disappeared.

The scene changes, and the action moves to Windsor Castle, where a mythological divertissement is being prepared. Queen Anne is dressed as Juno, and drums roll and the sentries present arms as she makes her appearance in her cloud. Sir Crakford (*sic*) plays the rôle of Jupiter, the most amusing bewigged, rococo Jupiter you could find. The character of Venus has

[5] Celadon, the faithful lover. The term is taken from a character in the seventeenth-century novel, *L'Astrée* by Honoré d'Urfé (1568–1625).

fallen to Lady Henriette, who performs it scrupulously well at least from the point of view of beauty, for she shows a Hyrcanian cruelty[6] towards poor Lyonnel, who recognising her when he comes to change guard, loses his head to such an extent that he becomes mad with rage and sorrow and has to be incarcerated in Bedlam,[7] where we find him in the following scene.

Queen Anne has been visiting the hospital with her ladies in waiting, and Lady Henriette finds herself face to face with poor Lyonnel, whose misfortunes have been caused by one of her whims. The sight of him melts her proud ice-cold heart, and she confesses to the Queen how her thoughtlessness has had such dreadful consequences, and that all she wants to do now is to make amends.

The doctor proposes a treatment that is quite homoeopathic, consisting of taking Lyonnel back to his farm and reproducing the scene of the first act in every detail, and in fact this is what now happens. Lady Henriette dresses up again as the pretty servant girl of Greenwich. The bouquet is pinned to her side, she sets a place on the table, eight o'clock strikes, and Lyonnel seems to come out of a dream. Restored to reality, he goes down on his knees before Lady Henriette, who now no longer rejects him. Good Queen Anne arrives with her court, and Lyonnel presents the ring she gave him, asking for the hand of Lady Henriette. "I hope you will honour my royal word," says Queen Anne, turning to the Countess of Derby, "for I promised to give him whatever he asked when he presented this ring." Nancy makes up her own mind, following the example of her mistress, and the curtain falls as she smilingly stretches out her hand to fat Plunkett.

Mlle Adèle Dumilâtre played Lady Henriette. It was the first time that this beautiful dancer had created a leading rôle in an important work, and she came through the difficult ordeal with flying colours. She has a remarkable elegance and distinction, and in her village costumes revealed a charming coquetry and affected artlessness that well befitted a Countess pretending to be a servant. As for her dances, which consist of a *pas de demi-caractère* with Petipa in the first act and a *pas de Vénus* with Henri Desplaces in the second, she was applauded on several occasions, particularly in the mythological *pas*, which she rendered with the nobility of attitude, the aerial lightness and the modest grace that are her particular qualities. There can be no purer profile, nor a more limpid, bluer glance. One of our dreams is to see Mlle Dumilâtre play one of those pale divinities who appear in Northern legends. What a pretty elf she would make in the Harz mountains, and what an admirable Valkyrie in Odin's Valhalla! All of which does not prevent her from being a charming English Countess in M. de Saint-Georges' ballet.

[6] See No. 24, note 7.

[7] The popular name for the Bethlehem Royal Hospital, the lunatic asylum founded in the thirteenth century and, in the reign of Queen Anne, situated in Moorfields in the City of London.

Petipa, who has the most interesting part in the piece, played Lyonnel with remarkable warmth, passion and strength, but was unfortunately given little opportunity to show off his talent as a dancer.

Mlle Maria, by dint of mischief, and Barrez, by dint of good humour, made something out of two scrappy little rôles. Mlle Marquet looks ravishing in superb costumes, and Mlle Sophie Dumilâtre dances to perfection.[8] Coralli's son,[9] in the dance of a ballet master who has lost his reason, shows such sparkling wit and bizarre grace that he avoids any feeling of distress which such a sight might otherwise have caused.

The music of the second act, composed by M. Burgmüller, seemed superior to that of the other two acts, one of which was by M. Flotow and the other by M. Deldevez,[10] both of whom, however, showed themselves worthy of a more important commission.

La Presse, February 26th, 1844.
L:664.

[8] Maria played Nancy; Barrez, Plunkett; Delphine Marquet, Queen Anne.

[9] Eugène Coralli, the son of Jean Coralli, was a member of the Opéra ballet from 1834 to 1870 and *régisseur de la danse* from 1867 to 1870. He was also a highly successful teacher of ballroom dancing, playing a leading rôle in the introduction of the polka, which he was the first to dance on the stage of the Opéra, with Maria, on March 25th, 1844.

[10] Friedrich von Flotow (1812–83), German operatic composer, whose best work was *Martha*, libr. Saint-Georges, f.p. Hofoper, Vienna, November 25th, 1847, which used the same plot. Ernest-Edouard-Marie Deldevez (b. 1807) was later to compose scores for the ballets *Eucharis*, *Paquita* and *Vert-Vert* at the Opéra, and another, *Yanko le bandit*, for which Gautier wrote the scenario, for the Porte-Saint-Martin (f.p. April 22nd, 1858).

32

Opéra: Lola Montez

Appearance of Lola Montez in the
ball scene from *Gustave*, dancing
L'Ollia and *Las Boleras de Cádiz*,
March 27th, 1844.

We would rather not say anything about Mlle Lola Montez, whose
Christian name reminds us of one of the prettiest girls in Granada,[1] and
whose surname recalls the man who enabled us to experience the most
powerful dramatic emotions we have ever felt.[2] There is nothing Andalusian
about Lola Montez except a pair of magnificent dark eyes. She "*habla*" very
mediocre Spanish, and speaks hardly any French and only passable English.
So from what country does she really come? That is the question. We can say
that Mlle Lola has tiny feet and pretty legs, but as for the way she uses them,
that is quite another matter. We must confess we were unimpressed by the
curiosity aroused by Mlle Lola's various brushes with the police forces of the
North and her attack on Prussian gendarmes with her riding crop. Mlle Lola
is much inferior to Dolores Serral, who at least has the advantage of being
genuine, and who makes up for her imperfections as a dancer by a sensual
abandon, a passion, a fire, and a rhythmical precision that command admiration. We suspect, after hearing about her equestrian exploits, that Mlle Lola
is more at home on a horse than on the boards.

La Presse, April 1st, 1844.
HAD, III 174. L:671.

[1] Lola Montez (1818–61) was born in Limerick. In 1846 she was to add to her
notoriety by becoming the mistress of King Ludwig I of Bavaria.

[2] This memory was not theatrical, but derived from the bull ring. Gautier had been
overwhelmed by the artistry and panache of Francisco Montes ("Paquiro") (1805–
51), one of the greatest matadors of his day, whom he saw in Malaga in 1840; he
devoted several pages in Chapter 12 of his *Voyage en Espagne* to a vivid description of
this bull fight.

33

Opéra: Return of Marie Taglioni in *La Sylphide*

La Sylphide (see No. 17), revived
for the return of Marie Taglioni
with a new *pas de l'ombre*,
June 1st, 1844.

Yesterday, Saturday—the Opéra is now giving performances every day—Mlle Taglioni made her return in *La Sylphide*.[1] It requires great confidence in one's talent to dare to reappear after such a lengthy absence on the stage of one's former triumphs. Paris is the most forgetful of cities. So long as you are there, all is well, but when you leave, you can say goodbye! Paris harbours something of a grudge against a celebrity who deserts it out of preference for England's guineas or Russian roubles to the salaries it pays. And is it not a little right to do so when a voice or a pair of legs has no sooner been pulled up out of the common crowd than it wants to go and sing or dance for others without giving a thought for the applause, publicity and reviews to which it owes its good fortune?

It is true that Paris takes its revenge by immediately inventing another celebrity. It takes the first one that comes along and pushes it into the limelight, and nobody gives another thought to the other who has just departed by the stage coach—she might never have existed. That has never been the case with Mlle Taglioni. She never ceased to be talked about during her absence, for she was not merely a dancer, she was the dance itself. The risk she ran was not being forgotten, but leaving too many memories behind. Absence has the effect that the image of the absent one gradually becomes poeticised, her features become blurred in the memory, they conform to a pattern, coming closer and closer to the ideal that each of us carries in our mind's eye. When that person reappears, she herself will not have changed, but she no longer corresponds to the type that has been formed in the mind.

---

[1] Taglioni had left the Opéra in 1837, since when her career had been centred in St. Petersburg. She had, however, made four guest performances in July 1840.

And another thing—ghosts are not so successful in France, because there is always something provincial about ghosts. No one can leave Paris for five or six years with impunity. So, for a moment, we were a little worried for Mlle Taglioni.

We said to ourselves, "What, just for a few performances, and for a miserable handful of banknotes! What is that to a ballerina today? How unwise to come and shatter a sweet rosy dream, a reputation that has become a legend, and to permit comparison with younger rivals! Taglioni! For us she had already become what Terpsichore was to the generation of the Empire, a living madrigal. Taglioni, the Sylphide! Everything about her was on the point of idealisation, a poetic incarnation, an opalescent mist in the green depths of a magic forest. Taglioni was the dance just as Malibran[2] was music; the one with a smile on her lips, arms harmoniously extended and her toe balanced on the stem of a flower, the other a loosened cascade of black hair, a pale cheek resting on a translucent hand, a vibrant harp, eyes shining with tears—two fairies summoned up to inspire others among us Romantics who do not believe in the Muses. Malibran is now dead, along with her beauty, her genius, her gifts, and all her glory, but Taglioni is alive, and here she is to face that terrible ordeal that not even the most beloved of shades has succeeded in overcoming—that of appearing among people whose life has taken another direction and who have acquired other enthusiasms and other loves.

These fears, which arose through our concern for one of the most charming celebrities of our time, vanished completely when Mlle Taglioni took her first step on the stage. The four years that have passed since she left us and have marked the rest of us with wrinkled brows and crow's feet at the corner of our eyes, have not touched her. Happy woman! She still has the same slender and elegant figure, and the same sweet, intelligent and modest expression. Not a feather has dropped from her wings, not a hair has lost its sheen beneath her coronet of flowers! At the rise of the curtain she was greeted with thunderous applause. What lightness, what rhythm of movement, what mobility of gesture, what poetry of attitude, and above all, what sweet melancholy, what chaste abandon!

Nothing could be more delicate or coquettish than her poses in the *pas de trois*, in which she glides between James and his fiancée, but the cheering was then followed by titters when the supers went into a hilarious Scottish jig. Such slipshod execution is quite inexcusable in a theatre like the Opéra, and indeed is high treason, for there the public is king. The supers dance better than that at the Porte-Saint-Martin and the Cirque. This is not the way for the male dancers to overcome the disfavour into which they have fallen. Far

[2] Maria Malibran (1808–36), the greatest contralto of her day, who died at the height of her fame. She created the title-rôle in Donizetti's *Maria Stuarda*.

better to have had an assortment of wooden puppets operated by strings: at least they would have moved in time.

The *pas* in the second act which ends with the dropping of the wings and the death of the Sylphide was wonderfully performed, and Petipa gave excellent support to the celebrated ballerina with his passionate miming. The idea for this very poetic *pas* is no doubt borrowed from the life of insects, from the virgin grasshoppers whose wings drop off as soon as they have made love. Nature has foreseen everything, even the endings of ballets.

Recalled after the fall of the curtain, Mlle Taglioni was greeted with a hurricane of bouquets and a floral cloudburst. For one moment we feared for her life, so heavy, intense and prolonged was the bombardment. The curtain could not descend to the boards for the thick piles of roses, camellias and Parma violets. Mlle Taglioni is to give six more performances—all too few, considering that a million Parisians and three hundred thousand tourists want to see her again.

> *La Presse*, June 3rd, 1844.
> HAD, III 209–211
> (incorrectly dated June 13th).
> L:685.

34

Opéra: Marie Taglioni in *Le Dieu et la bayadère*

Le Dieu et la bayadère (see No. 10), for the second of Taglioni's farewell performances, June 5th, 1844.

The performances of Mlle Taglioni continue, and are drawing unbelievable crowds. The other day *Le Dieu et la bayadère* was given, and the stalls corridor contained the *Débats*, *Le Messager* and *La Presse* in the persons of Jules Janin, Edouard Thierry and your humble servant. Mlle Taglioni has confirmed the following paradox uttered by some critic who was in a bad temper or a bad seat: "*Les entrées ne servent qu'à sortir.*" That is very easily explained. Everyone who has seen her wants to see her again, and anyone who has not takes advantage of a heaven-sent opportunity.

Goethe's ballad, on which Scribe based *Le Dieu et la bayadère* is a poetic masterpiece.[1] It might have been written by a Brahmin in the grottos of Elephanta or in the great temple of Juggernaut,[2] so well did that powerful genius assimilate the style. No Hindu god with an elephant's head and six arms ever possessed the gift of the *avatar*[3] to such a degree. Goethe's supreme gift of fantasy has covered every age and every land; without once ceasing to be Goethe, he has in turn been Homer, Hesiod, Hafiz, Sudraka, Shakespeare,

---

[1] Goethe's ballad, *Der Gott und die Bajadere*, published in 1797.

[2] Elephanta Island, near Bombay, was so named by the Portuguese colonists from a large stone elephant that used to stand there. The island is famous for its cave temples. Juggernaut, or more properly Jagannatha, is a form under which the Hindu god Krishna is worshipped in West Bengal, and the temple of Jagannatha, built in the twelfth century, dominated the town of Puri.

[3] See No. 29, note 9.

Calderón, Beaumarchais, Voltaire, Jean-Jacques and even Cuvier.[4] Everyone knows that M. Scribe, far from treating the subject as a sacred drama, a sort of Hindu auto-ritual, produced something very much like an *opéra comique*. For all his wonderful skill, M. Scribe failed to take full advantage of this delightful legend. Throughout his libretto runs a thread of irony, and it is obvious that he is no great believer in the mystic *tritvam* of Brahma, Shiva and Vishnu; he probably has doubts about the nine transformations of the last of these, and no fixed opinion on the cosmogonies of Shastah and Baghavadam; and perhaps he is unaware that the god who appears in his piece is not Brahma, but Shiva himself under the name of Mahadeva, one of his numerous manifestations, for he is also called Iswara, Budra, Hora, Shambu, etc. But let us put aside all this Hindu pedantry, and come to the performance of Mlle Taglioni.

Some years ago, in a small house in the Allée des Veuves, that for a short time was transformed into an Indian hut, there lived a troupe of bayaderes who had been brought over by a European *mahout*. All Paris flocked to the Théâtre des Variétés to see them perform the *Malapou, The Robing of Vishnu* and other sacred dances, accompanied by liturgical songs. The wonderful beauty of Amany, the perfection of figure of Saoundiroun and Ramgoun were only appreciated by painters, sculptors and artists. But having admired and accepted Taglioni as the typical bayadere, the French public did not appreciate the genuine article. The white gauze tutus and the delicate pink tights of the Opéra ballet were too much for the gold-striped trousers and the spangled brassières of the Bibiaderis, who were not forgiven for being as yellow as a tobacco leaf from Havana or bronzed like Florentine statuettes. Their wonderful eyes, in which ebony stars seemed to float in a crystal firmament, their bare flanks of polished agate, their fabulously tiny feet, their arms curving like the handles of antique vases, created only a slight impression. White powder, rice powder and vegetable rouge had the upper hand. But to have seen *Le Dieu et la bayadère* performed by an Indian company with the bronzed Amany taking the rôle of the white Taglioni would have been a strange and fascinating experience. We are amazed that nobody grasped what was possibly a unique opportunity. But it is true to say that the desire to do something new does not worry a fussy literary man like ourself, who is not like other Frenchmen. Morals, beliefs, governments, religions can be changed, but the substitution of one type of pirouette for another is one of those unpardonable violations. Our pleasures are ruled by etiquette and the

---

[4] A recognition of the towering achievement of Johann Wolfgang von Goethe (1749–1832), whose literary output was extraordinarily diverse in its range. Poetry, the novel, drama and comedy, science—he turned his hand to all these forms with almost equal felicity. All the great figures of literature and science mentioned here by Gautier directly influenced his work at one time or another.

status quo. What must poor Amany, who was a poetess and wrote hymns in the manner of *The Song of Songs*, have thought of a piece which, to her, would have been a national and sacred legend, in which she would have believed as an article of faith? They say that she went into a depression in London and hanged herself, poor girl, no doubt on one of those days of yellow fog when one cannot see the candle in one's hand.[5]

We often went to see her, taking her packets of tobacco which she smoked in a pipe of red earthenware and reeds. Our conversation was rather limited, because our knowledge of Hindustani did not extend beyond "good day" and "good night," while the only French she knew were the numbers from one to ten. So we would say "good day" to her, and she would reply, "One, two, three, four". However, with her few words she made it clear that she enjoyed our visits and counted them, for every day she changed the number with which she responded to our greeting according to how many times we had been to see her. She was a well brought up girl of high caste. The musicians who accompanied her did not have the right to sit down before her, and in her presence they stood with their backs against the wall and their eyes lowered. She had very good manners, full of dignity and grace. Her smile was charming, particularly when she had not drawn indigo lines between her wonderful white teeth, with which she once tried to crunch the glass cherries on Mme Sand's bonnet. It was the only savage action we saw her commit, although admittedly the cherries were absolutely lifelike and as red and shiny as the real thing.

Such were the thoughts that were running through our mind as we watched Mlle Taglioni moving in her cloud of white muslin.

The silent rôle of the bayadere, which has been inserted into a plot in which the characters sing and speak, presents a certain difficulty that would not exist in a piece entirely interpreted in mime. She often has to hold the stage with nothing to do while the other performers are delivering trills and *fioriture*. Such a mixture of conventions is irritating. With some effort one can accept a group of characters expressing themselves by singing or dancing, but to have someone asking a question in song and being answered in dance is much more difficult to digest. It destroys the harmony, and brings you back to reality with a jolt. Mlle Taglioni overcame this difficulty most successfully and skilfully. By all kinds of expressive and moving plays of her features she takes part in the action when it has moved away from her, showing that she understands every word the actors are saying, even if she does not use the same language herself. The new *pas* in the first act, although marvellously danced, was not so effective as the *pas de deux* of the second act, whether it

---

[5] I have not been able to substantiate this. There seems to be no report of Amany's death in the London press of the time, nor does any record of her death appear in the General Register of Deaths.

was the public or the ballerina that was not sufficiently stirred. Mlle Sophie Dumilâtre, who ought to have been trembling with fright at finding herself in such company, played her part in a manner that gave pleasure, even alongside such a formidable rival. She earned her share of the applause, and during the chorus of canes and the stamping at the end Mlle Taglioni, with the kind-hearted sensitivity that she always displays, took her young companion by the hand so that she could share in her triumph. At the end of the piece the cheering of the audience forced Mlle Taglioni to come down from the Heaven of Indra. But is there any woman who would not forsake Heaven for the sake of earthly bravos, especially when Heaven is spattered with spots of oil and has not been dusted for six months?

La Presse, June 10th, 1844.
HAD, III 215–218. L:686.

35

Th. de la Porte-Saint-Martin: Thoughts on seeing Risley and his sons

Le Songe d'une nuit d'été,
divertissement featuring Risley
and his sons, f.p. June 15th, 1844.

Watching [the Risleys][1] covering such a vast space with their leaps and landing from such a height, we reflected how incomplete and backward is the training of ballet dancers. We were talking to Perrot the other day about the superiority of his dancing, and he made the profound remark, "I was a *polichinelle* for three years and a monkey for two," referring to the Mazurier rôles he had played.[2] In fact the exercises of equilibrists and acrobats have a very different purpose, both gymnastically and dynamically, from those of the dance class, being aimed at producing extraordinary suppleness, agility, strength and assurance. Think what a choreographer with imagination could achieve with such strapping fellows as Auriol, Lawrence and Redisha, Ducrow, and Risley and his sons![3] A ballerina who was also an acrobat would be marvellously effective in a faery ballet. The use of a

---

[1] Richard Risley (1814–74), an American acrobat, specialised in acrobatic ballets in which he was accompanied by boys who were presented as his sons, although there is no evidence that they were his offspring. The review from which this item is extracted is quoted more extensively in Marian Hannah Winter's *Theatre of Marvels* (Dance Index, VIII, 1–2 (Jan.–Feb. 1948), pp. 26–29).

[2] Jules Perrot had begun his theatrical career as an acrobatic dancer in imitation of the style of Charles Mazurier. In his early appearances at the Gaîté in Paris, he had appeared as a *polichinelle*, and later in a monkey rôle in *Sapajou*, in both cases echoing similar interpretations by Mazurier at the Porte-Saint-Martin.

[3] All were celebrated acrobats: Jean-Baptiste Auriol (1806–81), celebrated as a clown; Lawrence and Redisha, already mentioned by Gautier in No. 23 (see No. 23, note 2); Andrew Ducrow (1793–1842), famous also as a horseman; and Richard Risley, whose acrobatic ballet featuring himself and his "sons", John and Henry, Gautier was here reviewing.

springboard would produce prodigious jumps, and the art of balancing would give a completely new dimension to groups and *renversées*. Carlotta's famous leap in *Le Péri* gives an idea of what could be obtained by such means, and with the aid of a ballerina with such a broad training it would be a simple matter to invent graceful feats that were even more terrifying and daring. But first of all, dancing masters, who are the most hidebound sticklers for principle and the most stubborn classicists to be found anywhere, must be prepared to relax their insistence on what they call "turn out", one of the most revolting positions that antiquated erudition could have possibly invented. With feet turned out in this way, dislocations and fractures are inevitable because the balance of the legs is no longer controlled from the thighs, and the torso is not resting properly on the hips. Personally, we cannot imagine how lifting the feet parallel to the horizon can possibly be regarded as graceful. No sculptor or painter has ever made use of this position, which is contrary to nature, elegance and good sense. But suggest a change in something as serious as the dance, and you will soon see what a hornet's nest you have stirred up. The classicists of ballet are pig-headed and violent in quite a different way to the classicists of literature.

La Presse, June 24th, 1844.
HAD, III 218–222 (more
extensive than here given).
L:689.

36

Opéra: Marie Taglioni's Benefit

Benefit of Mlle Taglioni: Act 2 of
La Sylphide; two pas from
L'Ombre; and the *pas de Diane*,
inserted in *La Jolie Fille de Gand*,
June 29th, 1844.

Mlle Taglioni's benefit performance took place on Saturday. At the risk of boring you with a cliché, we must begin by saying that the house was packed. Great artists are for ever making us say the same thing, and so long as they are applauded, they do not care if you write deadly dull reviews. There are some artists who are so predictably perfect and so wonderfully consistent that there is nothing to be gained, so to speak, by going to their performances because one can talk about it with complete confidence without having seen it. All one has to do is to write "perfect, inimitable, ravishing", and all their synonyms, and one is sure to hit the nail on the head. During her ballet career Mlle Taglioni must have caused great unhappiness among the critics, who have been forced to compose perpetual variations on the same theme. If anyone can understand the feelings that drove the peasant from Attica to demand that Aristides be ostracised because he was fed up with hearing him called "the just", it is the critic writing his fifth article about a celebrated dancer or singer, for what would the jealous peasant have said if he had to describe Aristides every Monday.

Speaking for ourselves, although criticism is our profession, we would rather admire than rebuke. How pleasant it is to admire—to see someone realising a dream, an idea of yours, with a brilliance and an artistry to which you yourself could never aspire. Admiring a great artist is an act of identification with him, gaining admittance into the recesses of his soul; it is to understand, and understanding is close to creation. That fine poem that you read with such sincere enthusiasm is truly your own until the echo of the last line has died away, and you have the sensation of having yourself painted that beautiful picture you are looking at so passionately, trying to capture its most

140

delicate brush strokes and its most fleeting nuances. What good times we have had, lost in a book or standing before a picture, identifying with the poet or the painter in a kind of mental *avatar*, and if we are filled with sadness when we come to our senses again, at least our soul has not been gnawed by envy. Admiration is specially sweet when it is concerned with a woman, a graceful and charming art such as the dance, and a living poem such as Mlle Taglioni. And although we have difficulty in finding new words of praise, it will be a pleasure to record this triumph, which, alas, will never be repeated.

These farewell performances, which anyway are not always definitive, have a pervasive and melancholy charm, like the scent of the last rose that one is destined to savour. They give you the feeling of accompanying the departing genius on her final journey into posterity, bidding her farewell with your applause, and when the curtain falls at the end, you are filled with the sadness that comes over you when you see a dear friend being borne away in a post chaise. The very first turn of the wheel passes over your heart.

What tremendous boredom must ensue after all this fuss and bother, this dazzle and excitement! How hard it will be for her to tear herself away from this electric atmosphere and return to the cool shadows of retirement, no longer to see at her feet the row of burners separating her from the world of reality and making her greater than a queen, and no longer to hear that rumble from the pit rolling in waves across the chasm of the orchestra pit. To be sure, Lake Como is a sparkling blue, and the white marble of the villa is gilded by the golden rays of the sun.[1] Mignon herself would be happy there, where the lemon trees bloom and the golden oranges glow amid the dark foliage.[2] But will all that make the retiring Sylphide forget her kingdom of gauze and painted canvas? Will the Italian sun be a fair exchange for the lustre of the stage?

And how attentive everyone is! Look at them levelling and focusing their binoculars, not those light country binoculars that fit into a jacket pocket, but large military binoculars, twin monsters, optical howitzers that will make future generations think we were a race of giants! The entrances to the orchestra stalls were packed with strapping fellows who defied the laws of gravity and physics for four hours by standing off balance with their heads in the auditorium and their feet in the corridors. The judas window of every box whose owners had not been so spiteful as to draw the little curtain, framed a face with eyes agleam and fixed. The balconies resembled the Quai aux Fleurs, they were so tightly packed with bouquets. Everyone in the house was

---

[1] Marie Taglioni had acquired a villa at Blevio, on Lake Como, where one of her near neighbours was the prima donna, Giuditta Pasta.

[2] Mignon was the heroine of Goethe's *Wilhelm Meisters Lehrjahre*. Gautier is quoting a well-known passage from this work:
Kennst du das Land, wo die Zitronen blühn?
Im dunkeln Laub die Gold-Orangen glühn ...

moved by a single thought, to try to engrave on their memory the fascinating poses, the noble and graceful movements, and all the fleeting aspects of the fairy who the following day would become an ordinary woman.

Mlle Taglioni danced the Sylphide. That says it all. This ballet opened the door to a whole new era in choreography, and through it Romanticism entered the realm of Terpsichore. After *La Sylphide*, *Les Filets de Vulcain* and *Flore et Zéphyr*[3] were no longer possible. The Opéra was given over to gnomes, ondines, salamanders, elfs, nixes, wilis, peris, all those strange, mysterious creatures who lend themselves so wonderfully to the fantasies of the ballet master. The twelve mansions of marble and gold of the Olympians[4] were relegated to the dust of the scenery store, and artists were commissioned to produce only romantic forests and valleys lit by that pretty German moon of Heinrich Heine's ballads. Pink tights remained pink, for there can be no choreography without tights, and all that was changed was the satin ballet slipper for the Greek cothurna. This new style brought in its wake a great abuse of white gauze, tulle and tarlatan, and colours that dissolved into mist by means of transparent skirts. White became almost the only colour used. The music of *La Sylphide* is a masterpiece, and the man who wrote it would certainly be famous if anybody could pronounce his name.[5] The Sylphide itself has become identified with Mlle Taglioni; her genius is encapsulated in this type, which she had the good fortune to discover at the beginning of her career.[6] This sort of luck happens to all great actresses, for in the same way Giulia Grisi discovered Norma and Mlle Mars Célimène.[7] So the name of this rôle has become in a way a second name for her; to the outside world the Sylphide is synonymous with Mlle Taglioni, just as Giselle is with Carlotta.

How light and subtle is her grace, and what sweet, tender coquetry there is in the *pas* in which she alternatively hides from and appears to her terrestrial

[3] *Les Filets de Vulcain* was the subtitle of Jean-Baptiste Blache's ballet *Mars et Vénus*, mus. Schneitzhoeffer, f.p. Opéra, May 29th, 1826. *Flore et Zéphyr* was the successful ballet by Didelot, produced in its first version in London in 1796, and later staged by its choreographer, mus. Venua, at the Opéra, being first given there on December 12th, 1815. Both were anacreontic ballets, dealing lightly with the adventures of the classical divinities, and Gautier could have seen them before they were dropped from the repertory in the 1830s.

[4] The dwelling places of the major gods and goddesses of Greek mythology.

[5] Jean-Madeleine Schneitzhoeffer (1797–1852), composer of *La Sylphide* and several other ballets, was burdened with a name that the French found very difficult to pronounce. This they did by shortening it to something like "*Chênecerf*". A joke went around that his visiting cards had printed on them, "Schneitzhoeffer, pronounced Bertrand".

[6] Taglioni created *La Sylphide* in 1832, when she was twenty-eight, five years after her début in Paris and ten years after her first stage appearance.

[7] *Norma*, opera by Bellini, f.p. Scala, Milan, June 20th, 1833, and given its first Paris performance at the Th. Italien, Paris, on December 8th, 1835, on both occasions with Grisi as Norma. Célimène was the leading female rôle in Molière's *Le Misanthrope*.

lover! And again, how innocent her fear, how resigned and modest her sorrow when, caught in the folds of the scarf prepared by the evil witch, she sees her wings drop at her feet, wings which she really did not need, but the loss of which brings about her death. Petipa showed himself worthy of his surroundings by the expressiveness and warmth of his miming and the strength of his dancing. Although current fashion is hardly favourable to male dancers, he earned applause several times.

The *pas de l'Ombre*, which she danced after rather too long a musical interlude, is one of the most charming choreographic compositions we have ever seen. And, a rare quality in a *pas*, it had a motif, and the poses did not follow one another at random and without reason.[8] The scenery, skilfully put together with the backcloths of the Wolf's Glen in *Der Freischütz* represents a wild landscape in which a hazy moonbeam filtering through the clouds produces a bluish twilight in which the sequins scattered on the ballet skirt of the shade sparkle like dewdrops. Mlle Taglioni vanishes and materialises again in the mist, glides over the lake like a wisp of fog stirred by the breeze, and displays such fascinating wiles that her lover follows her into the foam of the waterfall with never a thought that no human body, however light, can follow a spirit. Only faith can save him now, for if he believes it possible to walk upon the water, walk upon it he will. So instead of falling into the black maw of the abyss, he drops into a fairy paradise sparkling with light that must have been dreamed up by a lover of Leyden or Haarlem, being filled with enormous, fabulously striped tulips. It is true that maniacs have no fun dreaming up a paradise.

The fairy flits among these tulips, which the designer has undoubtedly constructed to fit her foot, and seems to be offering a reward to her lover in the shape of a chaplet of flowers, which he tries to snatch from her as she withholds it from him for a while with movements of wonderful rapidity. Much applauded was a passage in which, while still dancing, she gathers up the flowers that have been scattered on the ground. However, we much preferred the first part of the *pas* to the second.

The performance ended with an act from *La Jolie Fille de Gand*, in which the beneficiary danced another *pas*. She was given several calls, was applauded to the skies and bombarded with bouquets, one of which, incidentally, fell on our head. It was one of those monster bouquets shaped like a leg of mutton, or a trapeze, that they make nowadays. Even if hurled by two strong arms, it could not have cleared the orchestra pit, and we were nearly flattened by this floral paving stone!

La Presse, July 1st, 1844.
HAD, III 223–227. L:690.

[8] This was extracted from *L'Ombre*, a ballet by Filippo Taglioni, f.p. Bolshoi Th., St. Petersburg, December 4th (N.S), 1839.

37

Opéra: Début of Tatiana Smirnova

Début of Mlle Smirnova in an inserted *pas* in *La Jolie Fille de Gand* (see No. 28), July 12th, 1844.

Mlle Smirnova[1] has made her début in *La Jolie Fille de Gand*. She is a dancer who comes from Russia, as the "ova" at the end of her name reveals. Mlle Smirnova had been provided with a reputation in advance, a mischief that is all too often perpetrated by treacherous friends, but she is not without talent. In St. Petersburg she made a thorough—almost too thorough—study of Mlle Taglioni. That, of course, is an excellent model, but so much so that one is in danger of becoming lost in trying to follow it. How can anyone imitate a passing cloud, or water rippling in the moonlight, or a shade vanishing in a mist of gauze? How can grace be copied? Mlle Smirnova would have done better to turn more to natural inspiration. If she had sought that, she might have found herself, but then Mlle Smirnova has one dreadful fault in the eyes of the Parisians—she is provincial! We are rather superior—in the manner of the Greeks, who despised all other nations as barbarian—and our herb sellers are shocked by the slightest accent, and we use the term provincial to cover everything that originates from outside Paris—be it Carpentras or Montmartre, just as much as London or St. Petersburg.

There is a certain exaggeration in her smile, rather too much emphasis in her gestures, everywhere something that goes a little too far—tights that are too pink, a skirt that is too short or too long, or a hair style attempting to be in

---

[1] Tatiana Smirnova (1821–71), a pupil of Didelot, danced with the Imperial Russian ballet from 1837 to 1854, modelling her style on that of Taglioni and appearing in some of that ballerina's rôles, including the Sylphide. She had also been the first Russian ballerina to appear as the Queen of the Wilis in *Giselle*. For her Paris début she danced a *pas de deux* from *La Sylphide*, partnered by Lucien Petipa. At the end of August and early in September she made four appearances in Brussels, three in *La Sylphide* and the last in *Giselle*.

tomorrow's fashion for fear of looking outmoded. We were all in agreement about this, we and the rest of all you Athenians from the Chaussée d'Antin, the Faubourg Saint-Germain and the Faubourg Saint-Honoré, who found Mlle Taglioni somewhat provincial when she made her first performance[2] because she had not been in Paris for four years. But how quickly the intelligent new sylphide learned, for at her second appearance she had lost even the slightest vestige of a Russian accent.

La Presse, July 15th, 1844.
L:694.

[2] That is to say, the first of this summer's series of performances at the Opéra. She had last been seen in Paris in 1840.

38

Opéra: *Eucharis*

Eucharis, ballet-pantomime in 2
acts and 3 scenes, ch. J. Coralli,
mus. Deldevez, f.p. August 7th,
1844.

However hard one might look, it would be difficult to find a more
appropriate subject for a ballet than that of *Eucharis*, as the new
choreographic work at the Opéra is called, and whose title should more
properly be *Telemachus, Son of Ulysses*. Whether it was due to the baroque
translation of the epic which Mgr. François de Salignac de La Motte Fénelon,
the swan of Cambrai, made for children educated in the Jacotot method, or to
Fourier's witty sarcasms on the Utopian rubbish of the model town of
Salento, that pleasant young man accompanied by his fierce and forbidding
Mentor has always struck us as being slightly ridiculous.[1] Old wallpaper,
crudely hatched and garishly coloured, that is to be found in cafés and taverns
has left us with crude and comic images of the characters of this prose poem
which has been the cause of so many school-children's impositions and tears.
Often a face had been sliced off at the corner for a window or a door, and the
unfortunate Calypso then had to mourn the loss both of Ulysses and her nose.

At the rise of the curtain, the stage represents a landscape by the sea,
elegantly designed and painted by M. Ciceri in a light and brilliant, but

---

[1] Fénelon, Archbishop of Cambrai (1651–1715), was the author of a number of
allegorical works, of which *Les Aventures de Télémaque* (1699) was the most celebrated. This told of Telemachus's search for his father Ulysses, who had been lost at
sea after the capture of Troy and spent several idyllic years on the island of the nymph
Calypso. During his journey Telemachus visits Salento, where he finds an ideal social
order established. Historically, the Salentini were a people who inhabited the Terra
d'Otranto in the heel of Italy before being conquered and absorbed by the Romans in
the third century B.C.

Charles Fourier (1772–1837) was the inventor of a social theory in which society
would be divided into communal associations of producers called *phalanges*, and
which was designed to produce a fairer distribution of wealth. He made several
references to Fénelon's story of Telemachus in his writings, but was naturally scornful
of an amateur's idea of a perfect society.

Named after the educationalist Jean-Joseph Jacotot (1770–1840), the Jacotot
method of "universal education" was based on learning a lesson by heart, assimilating
it by daily repetition, reflecting on it and passing it on to others.

somewhat cold, manner. The green of the trees is a little too reminiscent of Saint-Denis or Saint-Cloud, and Calypso's island looks too much like an island on the Seine.

We would love to avoid that sacred phrase: "Calypso cannot ...".[2] Modesty forbids us to continue, but that in a nutshell is her situation when the ballet begins. Her nymphs are trying to amuse her in the way in which such things are done in ballets, with all manner of pastimes, pirouettes and *entrechats*. Swaying together, they form themselves into a kind of regatta, mounted on shells of mother-of-pearl, waving their scarfs to resemble sails, and—wonders never cease!—navigating in both directions by the same wind. But how can *jetés battus* and *tacquetés* soothe the heart of a goddess who has been betrayed? Calypso and her faithful followers swear hatred against men in general and death to every stranger who sets foot on the island.

No sooner has the oath been pronounced than a storm blows up in a rather half-hearted fashion in the form of a large black cloth cut out in the shape of a crayfish's beard that is hoisted up by thick ropes that are completely visible. A storm like this would at least be acceptable at the Théâtre Français, where negligent production is the rule, but at the Académie Royale de Musique one has the right to expect a few pinches of lycopodium and a rattle of sheet metal and stones to denote thunder and lightning. In a purely ocular spectacle like ballet, particular care must be devoted to stage effects and details. Two strangers then arrive on a broken fragment of mast, a youth and an old man. The nymphs run towards them, armed with javelins, ready to dispatch them. Fortunately Calypso sees in Telemachus such a likeness to Ulysses that she spares him and gives him the warmest welcome. Eucharis and the nymphs lead Telemachus and Mentor to a grotto to change their clothes, for their tunics are heavy and sodden with the briny deep (classical style), although they came out of the canvas waves looking quite dry and with their curls unruffled. Now you may well ask how a self-respecting goddess comes to have man's clothing to hand in her home, but no doubt they were some cast-off things of Ulysses which she had been piously keeping as a memento.

While Telemachus and Mentor are getting dressed, Venus descends from Heaven with Cupid and the Graces in a thick bunch of clouds.

We have a confirmed horror of stage clouds. There is nothing uglier, heavier, more disgraceful, and less realistic, even in a conventional sense, and we are amazed that such a tawdry method, worthy only of the rough wooden stages on which mysteries used to be played, is still in use. How is it that in a century that has seen such progress in mechanisation, optical illusion and painting, the leading theatre in the world still lowers a piece of packing cloth daubed a grubby grey and stitched up with string to represent the lightest,

---

[2] The opening passage in Fénelon's *Télémaque*: "*Calypso ne pouvait se consoler du départ d'Ulysse.*"

softest and supplest material in existence! The diorama can depict a countryside being covered by a blanket of snow, a building transformed from a ruin to a state of completion, moonlight following a fire, and empty galleries filling with people. Is it not possible, by some similar means, or by the use of mirrors, to give an illusion of mist and simulate clouds in the sky on a backcloth?

Enjoying the most singular refinement of comfort, Venus is languidly seated on a Louis XV sofa, with the Graces sitting on tabourets like Duchesses at court.[3] A public less easy to please would have greeted the sight of that canopy and those flying stools with laughter and interminable hoots of derision. We are quite prepared to accept such rags as clouds capable of supporting such fragrant creatures as Venus and her suite, but padded furniture—that is just too absurd!

Venus, who is still annoyed with Ulysses (the gods are unforgiving), tells Cupid to see that Telemachus, that noble counterpart of Japheth[4] who is searching for his father, is detained on the island. Calypso's notorious propensity to fall in love makes this a simple task; she was the lover of the father, bearded though he was and mature in years, and she will now become enamoured of the son. And since the immortals are whatever age they choose, that is to say eternally twenty, the simple-minded Telemachus will be an easy prey to the goddess's charms. Venus is portrayed to the life by Mlle Marquet. It is true that she has little to do except look beautiful, but she performs her part punctiliously. And if Cupid could see himself with the charming rumpled little features and pretty blonde curls of Mlle Maria, he would surely fall in love with himself and shoot an arrow from his quiver into his own breast. It is a shame that Mlle Maria only wears this graceful costume for a few minutes, for in order to carry out her task, she has to disguise herself as a sailor in a little white tunic with a red border and a Phrygian cap coquettishly tipped over one eye. This lad would make a delicious ship's boy in one of those embarkations that Watteau once made fashionable, with floral ropes and coloured lanterns on the poop, bearing pilgrims of both sexes to the shores of some operatic Cythera.

Speaking of Cythera, put this article aside and read in *L'Artiste* a little masterpiece under that title, written by Gérard de Nerval.[5] A softer palette, a more sparkling imagination, a more amusing scholarship and a more limpid style has never been displayed before in an account of a journey.

But now cables are creaking, ropes are being stretched taut, and the whole machine is rising painfully up to the gas-light battens in the flies.

---

[3] Tabourets were folding chairs on which personages of rank were permitted to sit at the French court in the presence of the King and Queen.

[4] Japheth, one of the sons of Noah.

[5] Nerval's article, "*Voyage à Cythère*", appeared in *L'Artiste* of June 30th, 1844.

The nymphs return, and Cupid appears in the guise of a sailor from Telemachus's ship who has escaped with great difficulty from the storm. He is surrounded by the girls, who find him charming and smother him with embraces. A festivity is organised, and the little sailor (so he is described in the scenario) teaches the nymphs a kind of nautical dance in which, by movements of the arms and hips, he conveys the skill of rowing and the rolling of the waves. Telemachus is so carried away by this performance that he takes advantage of a moment when Mentor has his back turned to change his fine purple and gold-embroidered buskins for a pair of black slippers, and returns to dance a *pas* with the beautiful Eucharis—to the great displeasure of Calypso, who thinks that the innocent young man is learning far too quickly and casts an angry look at the nymph. She is therefore very willing to grant Mentor's request to use her divine power to repair the hull of the wrecked boat and enable young Telemachus to continue his search for his lost father. This does not suit Cupid's plans. With the point of one of his golden arrows he fans the flame that has been kindled in Calypso's heart, making her change her mind, and while Mentor is supervising the repair of the boat, he arms the nymphs with flaming torches and leads them to the jetty, which quickly vanishes in a meagre burst of red Bengal fire[6] that would be greeted with the greatest scorn at the Cirque-Olympique.

The scenario expresses the effect of this blaze on the principal characters in these words: "Sorrow of Mentor, joy of Calypso and Eucharis. Hesitation of Telemachus, who does not know whether to laugh or cry. Triumph of Cupid!" There is nothing we can add to this eloquent analysis.

In the second act the stage represents a grotto. Rows of stalactites hang elegantly from the roof, seams of precious metals glitter in the hewn walls of rock, the white sand is mottled with mother-of-pearl and coral, and marine plants with denticulated leaves and strange blooms grow from fissures in the stone. A misty light, like that of the Blue Grotto, gives a magic appearance to every object, enabling one to make out the initials of Ulysses and Calypso carved on the side of the cave. At this point let us indulge in a little show of erudition, which is permitted by such a classical subject, and ask why MM. Séchan, Despléchin and Diéterle have written the initial of Calypso in the Greek form and that of Ulysses in the French form? In Greek the name of Telemachus's father should begin with an O, for in that language he is Odysseus, not Ulysses. But all this does not detract from the original and picturesque effect of these gentlemen's scenery.

This grotto was at one time Ulysses' apartment, and it is a moving experience for his son to enter it, preceded by Eucharis bearing a candle. Eucharis

[6] A type of firework contained in a cylindrical cardboard container, made with a combustible mixture of chemicals that give off a brilliant white or coloured flame.

would like to take advantage of the situation by declaring her love for the young hero, but the little sailor begs her to hold back and wait until Mentor has departed. Once he has got rid of the icy influence of that forbidding personage, Telemachus shows a fondness for Eucharis that is most damaging to Calypso's plans. He is so madly in love that he feels the need to take off his red buskins and put on his black slippers again, and throw himself into a most stirring dance. Right in the middle of his *pas*, Calypso makes an entrance like Lady Macbeth, with a lamp in her hand, and eyes staring out of a pallid face. Here an interesting question of magnetism arises. Is it possible for goddesses to be sleep-walkers? This is a question that we must leave to M. Debay, author of *Les Mystères du sommeil*.[7]

According to the scenario, Calypso is dreaming of Ulysses, and in her sleep she is searching for memories of her former love. She runs her hands over the initials that her hero had once carved, she leans her head on the edge of the couch on which he used to lie, and she wakes to find herself in the arms of Telemachus. At first the goddess does not seem unduly upset by the substitution of this reality for her dream, but the sight of Eucharis awakens her jealousy, for it is hardly seemly for a well brought up nymph to be discovered in a young man's grotto at such an ungodly hour.

She summons her followers and has the culprit who has been discovered in such incriminating circumstances brought before her. Telemachus wants to follow her, but old Mentor, who could teach a thing or two about magnetism to MM. Ricard, Lafontaine and Thilorier,[8] waves his hand before the face of the poor devil, who falls to the ground stiff with boredom. During the exotic sleep induced by this simple hypnotic pass, Telemachus has a dream of the palace at Ithaca, seeing his mother being pursued by the twenty-two suitors, not one of whom can bend the bow of Ulysses. A beggar arrives and his vigorous arm bends the bow until the two horned ends meet, and then proceeds to kill the insolent fellows with his arrows. At the sight of such strength, Eumaeus and the nurse recognise their master, whose identity is placed beyond all doubt by the scar left long ago on the hero's leg by the wild boar of Parnassus.[9]

---

[7] A. Debay, *Les Mystères du sommeil et du magnétisme, explication des prodiges qu'offre cet état de la vie humaine* (Paris, 1844), an expanded edition of his *Hypnologie*, published the year before.

[8] J.J.A. Ricard and Charles Lafontaine were authors of treatises on magnetism. Lafontaine's wife was a medium, whose seances Cerrito attended when preparing *Gemma* (see No. 70). Jean-Charles Thilorier (c.1750–1818) was the author of *Système universel, ou de l'Univers et de ses phénomènes considérés comme les effets d'une cause unique.*

[9] When Ulysses returned to Ithaca after his wanderings, he was first given shelter by his old steward, Eumaeus. Later he was recognised by his old servant, Eurycleia, by a scar above his knee, received in a struggle with a wild boar on the slopes of Mount Parnassus.

The scene fades. Telemachus awakes, deeply stirred. A display of arms miraculously sprouts from the ground. He seizes the sword, puts on the helmet and breastplate, and rushes from the grotto. By the seashore, his eyes meet a pitiable sight. On Calypso's orders Eucharis has been bound to a rock like Andromeda to become the prey of sea monsters. He wants to rescue her, but bonds forged by the gods cannot be loosened by mortal man; the diamond-hard chains resist his every effort. He falls to his knees and implores Calypso to pardon the nymph. Calypso, who is not at heart a spiteful woman and has hardly any fault except that of being immortally boring, allows herself to weaken and forgive Eucharis. The lovers, entwined with garlands of flowers, are about to be married under the auspices of Cupid, "who is leading them to the nuptial grotto," when Mentor arrives, pale, sad and silent. He points to a ship that has appeared on the horizon, and flinging off his cloak, dives into the calm sea. The sight makes Telemachus feel ashamed at his weakness, and risking what in swimming terms is called a "belly flop", he throws himself from the top of a practicable in Mentor's wake.

At the first performance a scene, which has since been cut, then showed the court of Ithaca, with Mentor, assuming the guise of Minerva, and Telemachus helping his father massacre Penelope's suitors.

Such a subject could only have been rejuvenated by a thorough study of local colour and production. This would have been easy with the new interpretations of the ancient world by the modern artists, André Chénier and M. Ingres, but instead the Opéra has stuck to the conventions of the Empire and the Greek style of M. Guérin.[10] M. Coralli displayed unusual talent in the purely choreographic part, and struggled with all his might against the emptiness of the narrative. There are many graceful groups and skilfully arranged *pas* in *Eucharis*. That of the Satyr, danced by Coralli's son with infinite originality, was much applauded, and the *pas de deux* by Adèle Dumilâtre and Petipa, while containing nothing very novel, was nevertheless full of grace and charm, and well performed. The two Fauns and the Dryad, portrayed by Mabille, Hoguet-Vestris and Sophie Dumilâtre, drew down several salvos of bravos. Mlle Sophie Dumilâtre is making progress every day, or rather every evening. She is rising rapidly, and will soon be ranked among the leading dancers. It would be hard to find greater elasticity and strength. Petipa wears antique costume to perfection, and succeeded in making Telemachus a character that is really not too ridiculous. If Mlle Adèle Dumilâtre's

[10] André Chénier (1762–94), a poet of rare talent whose life was brutally cut short when he was guillotined during the Terror in the French Revolution, was greatly influenced by the poetry of ancient Greece. Jean-Auguste-Dominique Ingres (1780–1867) was a pupil of Jacques-Louis David, and followed his master by painting in the neo-classical style, although hints of the Romantic movement are to be detected in his view of classical antiquity. Pierre-Narcisse Guérin (1774–1833) produced a number of paintings inspired by classical subjects, but he was not an artist of the top flight and his work was generally melodramatic and static.

costume had only been as Greek as her profile, she would have made a perfect Eucharis. But why does she have to wear that ungainly gauze troubadour scarf of shocking pink over her tunic? Mlle Pauline Leroux showed so much talent in *Le Diable amoureux* that we have not the heart to tease her about the rôle of a dressed-up doll[11] that she plays in this work.

M. Deldevez's score is carefully composed, and generally well orchestrated, but in many places it is lacking in melody and rhythm, indispensable qualities in ballet music.

La Presse, August 12th, 1844.
HAD, III 246–253. L:701.

[11] Calypso.

39

The Death of Clara Webster

While speaking of English actors, let us spare a tear for poor Clara Webster,[1] who has just been burned alive in her gauze costume. She was a charming girl, and we can still see her dancing at Drury Lane in *La Péri*. Her long blonde hair whipped about her white shoulders as she finished a pirouette, and the English, who were so proud at having a ballerina born in

[1] Clara Webster (1821–44) was the most promising English dancer of her generation. When Carlotta Grisi introduced *La Péri* to London, at Drury Lane in the autumn of 1843, Clara Webster was one of the leading supporting dancers, and Gautier, who was the author of the scenario, obviously singled her out when he paid a short visit to London. She was very severely burned during a performance of *The Revolt of the Harem* on December 14th, 1844, and died three days later.

Although happily he did not witness it, Clara Webster's fate haunted Gautier, who was inspired to use it as an illustration of the "evil eye" possessed by Paul d'Aspremont, the hero of his novel, *Jettatura*, first published in 1856 (chapter VIII):

"In London he often went to Her Majesty's Theatre, where the grace of a young English dancer had particularly impressed him. Without being taken with her any more than one is by a graceful figure in a painting or an engraving, his eyes followed her among her companions of the corps de ballet in the swirl of the choreography. He loved her sweet, melancholy features, her delicate pallor that the animation of the dance never caused to flush, her beautiful blonde hair, silky and lustrous, crowned, according to the part, with stars or flowers, her long look lost in space, her shoulders of virginal chastity that he could see trembling through his eye-glass, her legs reluctantly raising their gauzy cloud and gleaming through the silk like the marble of an antique statue; each time she came before the footlights he greeted her with a little sign of furtive admiration or levelled his opera-glass to see her better.

"One evening, carried away by the circular flight of a waltz, the dancer brushed that row of fire which in the theatre separates the ideal world from the real; her light sylphide costume fluttered like the wings of a dove about to take flight. A gas-jet shot out its blue and white tongue and touched the flimsy material. In a moment the girl was enveloped in flame; for a few seconds she danced like a firefly in a red glow, and then darted towards the wings, frantic, crazy with terror, consumed alive by her burning costume.

"Paul had been very painfully affected by this accident ... Now [some time later, having realised he possessed the evil eye] he was convinced that his persistence in following her with his eyes had not been unconnected with the death of that charming creature. He looked on himself as her murderer; he felt a self-loathing, and wished he had never been born."

their midst, applauded her furiously and made her repeat every one of her *pas*. It was said that she would recover, but her beautiful hair had blazed about her red cheeks, and her pure profile had been disfigured. So it was for the best that she died.

La Presse, December 23rd, 1844.
L:724.

40

Opéra: Début of the Viennese Children

Début of the Danseuses
Viennoises in *La Jolie Fille de
Gand*, January 15th, 1845.

*L*a Jolie Fille de Gand had attracted many people to the theatre in the Rue
Le Peletier on Wednesday. Ballets, with their combination of spectacle,
rapid action and light music, offer a welcome antidote to the operas of the
modern repertory, which are so long, complicated and noisy that it is hard
work rather than a pleasure to listen to them.

So a great crowd gathered. Carlotta, who appears so rarely, was dancing
that evening, and there is no need to say more. The few opportunities of
seeing her have to be seized with both hands.

To such a powerful attraction was added a feature that had aroused the
greatest curiosity: thirty-six little Viennese girls, brought up and trained by
Mme Weiss, the ballet mistress of the Josephstadt Theatre in Vienna, were to
perform three ensemble dances, the *allemande*, the *hongroise* and the *pas des
fleurs*.[1]

We have a natural suspicion, tinged with aversion, of infant prodigies.
Nothing offends us more than to see children who have been raised in a hot-
house and forced to discard their God-given instincts to be endowed with
man-given skill. Substituting instruction for what should come naturally
revolts us to the core, and all we can do is to reflect sadly on the hours of play
that have been sacrificed, the mad games of prisoner's base, shuttlecock and
ball that have never been played, and the reprimands, punishments, dry bread
and cuffs that have been the means by which their precocious knowledge has

[1] The Danseuses Viennoises were a children's ballet company founded and managed
by Josephine Weiss, ballet mistress of the Josephstadt Theatre, Vienna, that aroused
great admiration by the precision of the ensemble dances they presented. After
appearing in Paris, the company went on to enjoy successes in London, the United
States and Canada.

been driven into them. If going to a school that only accepts prodigies is a fate more deplorable and tougher than being sent to a penal colony, what must be the lot of the poor little runt who is forced to study for sixteen hours out of the twenty-four? How sadly must it lift its weary eyes to the sky, thinking of the birds that sing so merrily in the sunshine without having to bother with theory lessons and practising scales.

Apart from this forcing, the process involves over-stimulating the pride, and the unfortunate child puffs itself up in its little skin like the frog who wanted to be bigger than the bull. It frequently bursts, but what does that matter to the slave-driver! Like a grown-up dwarf, a prodigy is difficult to place when it ceases to be an infant.

Pianists who have been weaned from childhood and tragedians and actors of tender years leave us with a feeling of sadness, but the idea of little girls being drilled in dance exercises that are akin to gymnastics and are an amusement to them is nothing if not graceful and fully in accord with childhood. Only the body is being favourably developed, and the mind is not corrupted by a precocious understanding of feelings and passions that belong to later years.

However, the very glimpse of those pretty pink and white faces, those little chubby arms, and those dimpled shoulders is enough to convince you that this troupe of cherubs has not acquired its talents at the cost of torture. Mme Weiss seems to be as good a teacher as she is skilful as a ballet mistress.

It was in the kermess scene, after the number of the Flemish carillon, that this miniature corps de ballet, which seems to have come straight out of Lilliput, made its first appearance to loud applause.

All of them were dressed in pink satin costumes so fresh, so coquettish, so trim that they at once presented a very agreeable sight. The *pas* they performed was composed of a number of figures, rounds and waltzes that intertwined and unwound with extraordinary facility and precision. There were moments when a charming confusion reigned in the fresh bevy of girls and everything was tangled up and jumbled together beyond belief—like a heap of rose petals scattered by some mischievous zephyr with the tip of his wing. Skirts, tresses and ribbons fluttered in the whirlwind. Then, at a given measure, everything fell into place with dazzling rapidity and clockwork precision. In particular, there was a delightful moment when the whole troupe, forming a single line stretching from one wing to the other, advanced from the back of the stage to the footlights balancing on one leg. Not one of those microscopic feet was behind by a thousandth of a second. They alighted as if moved by a single mind.

The *hongroise*, which was interpolated into the ball scene of the second act, gave no less pleasure. Half the troupe, dressed in male costume, served as partners to the others. You cannot imagine the rapidity and daring of these little Hungarians, the majesty with which they clicked the silver spurs on boots that might have been made for pussy-cats, the determination with which they slapped thighs that were decorated with rich trimmings, and the swagger with which they wore their Uhlan bonnets on the sides of their heads. You know full well that a feeling for tempo, an energetic and free rhythm, and a calculated allure are indispensable qualities for these national and popular dances. Every beat must be stressed with heel taps or the clatter of spurs, so that the slightest error would be noticed at once. Well, in this turmoil, in this circular flight, not once did a spur click or a foot touch the ground out of time. The two *coryphées* who are taller than their companions showed, in addition to their skill in ensemble work, a real talent in the *pas* that they performed on their own.

The *pas des fleurs*, which was inserted into the orgy scene of the third act, brought the house down. We were a little apprehensive about this *pas des fleurs*. Ballet masters, anacreontic poets and young schoolgirls who paint watercolours of bouquets have managed to make flowers ridiculous. Flowers have been the pretext for so many madrigals, folderols and affectations of every sort, and provided so many motifs for the fretted and over-ornate decoration of the last century, so many faded comparisons to the poets of the Empire, and so many false descriptions to modern novelists that the mere mention of them makes one expect something pretentious, outmoded and provincial. Happily our fears were unfounded. Nothing could have been fresher, more ingenious and more gracefully arranged.

Everything that Mme Josephine Weiss's young pupils do with their garlands is truly beyond belief. They turn them into double, triple and intertwining cat's cradles, baskets, networks and arabesques through which all these pocket Taglionis, Elsslers and Carlotta Grisis, as fresh as the paper flowers they use in their evolutions, circulate with the rapidity of humming birds. The concentration and application that must be needed to know one's place in such a variety of passes and figures is something quite amazing, and we believe it would be difficult to make the Opéra corps de ballet perform a similar *pas*. We have to admit that our stage is deficient in the area that demands teamwork and the sacrifice of pride in the interest of an overall effect. Everyone wants to stand out from the group and attract attention on his own. Collective applause does not satisfy the vanity of our dancers and singers; every bravo must be addressed to an individual. Every chorist or supernumerary considers herself misunderstood and thinks she is just as good as the leading performer. Those are the modest ones: the others think they can do better. The *pas seul* is the dream of the ballet girl, who apathetically performs the choreographic ensembles that could be so charmingly effective and form such a pleasing contrast to the *pas* of the leading artists. The success of the Viennese Children has shown what an advantage a skilful choreographer could obtain from a corps that is well drilled and motivated with their own outlook, but for such a thing to happen the corps de ballet girls must somehow be regimented and submitted to a unified training in a Conservatoire.[2] But what can be done with children is no longer possible with young adults, and moreover one can only afford to devote time to dancing when one is earning 60 francs a month.

La Presse, January 20th, 1845.
HAD, IV 30–34. L:729.

[2] Interestingly, Saint-Léon made the same point about the need for a specialised training for corps de ballet work in his booklet, *De l'Etat actuel de la danse*, published in Lisbon in 1856.

41

Th. de la Porte-Saint-Martin: Lola Montez

First appearance on March 7th, 1845, in dances interpolated in *La Dansomanie*, ch. P. Gardel, mus. Méhul, f.p. Opéra, June 14th, 1800. Four appearances in all.

On Thursday a multitude of carriages were stationed before the Porte-Saint-Martin. Inside the theatre an atmosphere of animation and festivity reigned. White gloves and bouquets rested on the ledges of the proscenium boxes. Mlle Lola Montez was to make her début in *La Dansomanie*, in the rôle of Doña Serafina.[1] Some time ago the newspapers were full of the adventures of this beautiful Bradamante[2] who nimbly horsewhipped policemen, rode like Caroline,[3] and could bisect a ball on a knife-point at twenty-five paces. To all these talents Lola Montez adds that of the dance. A somewhat unfortunate attempt she made at the Opéra has not discouraged her. As her name indicates, Lola is Spanish by origin, and she has chosen as her speciality the *cachucha*, the *bolero*, the *jaleo*, the *manchegas*, and all the *pas de caractère* from the other side of the mountains. She dances them with uninhibited boldness, a furious ardour and a fantastic vivacity which must shock all classical lovers of pirouettes and *ronds de jambe*, but is dancing such a serious art that it does not allow any innovation or caprice? Is it really necessary to keep rigidly to the rules? Is it not enough for a woman to be beautiful, young, light and graceful?

[1] The name of the ballet's heroine was Phrosine. Presumably the part which Lola played was unconnected with the action. She was partnered, when occasion required, by Gambardini, a ballroom dance teacher.

[2] Bradamante, the warrior maiden heroine in Robert Garnier's tragicomedy of that name (1582), based on Ariosto's *Orlando furioso*.

[3] Caroline Loyo (1816–after 1878), one of the greatest equestriennes of her day, introduced the *haute école* into the circus and was at this time one of the chief attractions of the Cirque Olympique.

Mlle Lola first appeared in the costume of a Spanish lady—a basquine of black silk falling from her hips and weighted at the hem to stretch the folds, a black lace mantilla, a large comb in the chignon of her hair, a red carnation behind her ear, a fan that opened and closed like a butterfly's wing—and with a stance such as Goya might have sketched in a couple of strokes in one of his glowing water-colours. Then she returned, having changed into a fantastic dancing costume, all ablaze with sparkling sequins and flounces, to perform a *cachucha*, in comparison with which the most furious *pas* of Dolores Serral would have seemed like minuets and gavottes.

Never before had the somewhat plebeian boards of the Porte-Saint-Martin received such an avalanche of bouquets and crowns. There was a hail-storm of camellias, Parma violets and other fashionable flowers, of which at least a third were directed to the dancer's pretty feet and the other two thirds to her eyes, which are the most beautiful in the world and are used to ravishing effect. The Spanish verb *ojear*[4] might have been invented specially for her. Her teeth are as white and brilliant as those of a young Newfoundland dog, and shine like a burst of ivory when she smiles.

A *mazurka* brought Mlle Lola back in a costume no less charming than the first, and gave her the chance to gather still more applause. Severe judges will say that she lacks good training, and that she does things in breach of the rules, but does that matter?

La Presse, March 10th, 1845.
L:738.

---

[4] In Chapter 14 of *Voyage en Espagne* Gautier gives a vivid description of the eye-play of Spanish women. "When a woman or a girl passes you," he wrote, "she slowly lowers her eyelids, then suddenly raises them and pierces you with a glance of unnerving brilliance, then rolls her eyes and once again lowers her eye-lashes. No one but Amany the bayadere, when dancing the Dance of the Doves, can give an idea of those inflammatory glances that Spain has inherited from the Orient. We have no word to describe this eye-play; *ojear* has no equivalent in our vocabulary."

42

Opéra: Début of Adeline Plunkett

La Péri (see No. 29), for the début
of Mlle Plunkett, March 17th,
1845.

Mlle Plunkett[1] is young and pretty, well formed, with dainty feet, slender legs and features that are charming though a little delicate for the stage and not easily distinguishable from afar. She has, in short, everything that is needed to make a ballerina. Many people say that she is one already, but that is a little premature. That she will become a ballerina, there can be no doubt, nor shall we be surprised. The rôle of the Peri was chosen by Mlle Plunkett. To dance the Peri after Carlotta is boldness itself, but the boldness was not misplaced. Mlle Plunkett was applauded very frequently for her pretty face, and at times for her talent. The hazardous leap in the dream scene, which Carlotta performs with the lightness of a dove's feather wafted on the breeze, seemed to terrify the *débutante*, who clung to Petipa's neck in a rather earthly way with her two little fists very visibly clenched. She has *ballon* and travels well, but her *pointes* are still a little soft. Her arms are not lacking in grace, her body is supple, but she still has to acquire the precision, perfection of detail and firmness that distinguish dancers of the top rank.

In the second act Mlle Plunkett danced with some partner or other a very lively and exaggerated sort of *bolero*, which was applauded to the echo for reasons that were not always associated with dancing. Here the *débutante* made the same mistake as Carlotta Grisi, who substituted for the characteristic Dance of the Bee a Spanish dance that had nothing at all to do with the action or the intention of the work. A peri dancing the *cachucha* with castanets was something our imagination had not foreseen. Even in a ballet a

---

[1] Adeline Plunkett (1824–1910), sister of the actress Eugénie Doche who created the rôle of the Lady of the Camellias, first attracted notice in London and was the ballerina at Drury Lane on the night of Clara Webster's accident. Her engagement at the Paris Opéra was to continue until 1852, after which she danced in Italy until 1861.

little authenticity is demanded, if not by the intelligence, then at least by the eyes. For its violence of expression Mlle Plunkett's *bolero* surpasses anything that Elssler, Noblet, Alexis Dupont and Dolores ever dared to do. By performing many frenetic and fantastic things that the dancers of Seville, Granada and Cadiz would never have permitted themselves to attempt, she displayed qualities of flexibility and suppleness which, had they been more controlled, could have created a great impression. Such as she is, and although the Opéra has many dancers on its staff who are much more skilful, Mlle Plunkett seems likely to understudy Carlotta during her leaves because of her appearance and a certain resemblance.

La Presse, March 31st, 1845.
HAD, IV 66–67. L:741.

43

Opéra: Début of Elena Andreyanova

Début of Mlle Andreyanova in a
pas inserted in Meyerbeer's opera,
Robert le Diable, December 5th,
1845.

Mlle Andreyanova[1] is a young Russian dancer; it is not for nothing that her name ends in "-ova". She comes from St. Petersburg and will be returning there. The object of her visit to Paris is not to obtain an engagement, but merely to have the opinion of Paris on her dancing. For this she has made a special journey of eight hundred leagues. An artist who has not obtained the seal of approval of Paris cannot be sure of her talent; she is very nervous, not knowing whether she is in any way deficient or provincial, for it is possible to be provincial in London, Madrid, Vienna, Rome, or any other leading capital.

A pupil of Taglioni, Mlle Andreyanova is not unworthy of that brilliant school. She is blonde, has the blue eyes of a daughter of the North, and displays a well turned leg. She lacks neither grace nor suppleness, and the acute attack of stage fright that upset her and made her tremble like a birch leaf did not prevent her from displaying her lightness and elevation and performing graceful *développements*. Her efforts were rewarded with generous applause. Mlle Andreyanova will be dancing a *pas de caractère* to show another side of her talent.

La Presse, December 8th, 1845.
L:781.

---

[1] Elena Andreyanova (1819–57), prima ballerina of the Imperial ballet in St Petersburg, had had the honour of being the first Russian Giselle. She retired in 1855 and died in Paris.

44

Lumley commissions a ballet from Heinrich Heine

The theatrical season in Paris will shortly come to a close, and that of London will begin.[1] Mr Lumley, director of Her Majesty's Theatre, has just commissioned a ballet scenario from Heinrich Heine. By doing so he has given proof of both taste and intelligence, for the very essence of ballet is poetic, deriving from dreams rather than from reality. About the only reason for its existence is to enable us to remain in the world of fantasy and escape from the people we rub shoulders with in the street. Ballets are the dreams of poets taken seriously.

Nearly every ballet is based on those peripatetic species of elfs, sylphides, wilis and undines that usually dwell by the clear waters of a pond or in grottoes bristling with stalactites. The protagonists of ballet are all wings and feet, but with indeterminate bodies. So the cleverest and most astute writers find themselves out of their element in that strange and marvellous world where sylphides emerge from the bell-shaped flowers of the convolvulus, and wilis bathe in the dew and dry themselves in the moonbeams. Heinrich Heine, whose dual nature of being melancholy and mocking at the same time, has a touch of both Candide and Werther, is perhaps the only contemporary poet to have preserved the graceful simplicity of the old German legends. His mind, so sceptical about all things, has a deep-set belief in the old ballads. Only he and the brothers Grimm know how to write a convincing fairy story.

Mr Lumley has not only had the courage to commission a ballet scenario from a genuine poet, but he has placed a composer at the head of his

---

[1] In the space of a few years London had become one of the most important centres of ballet, based largely at Her Majesty's Theatre, then directed by Benjamin Lumley (1811–75). Jules Perrot had been choreographer there since 1842. Heine wrote two ballet scenarios for Lumley, neither of which was to be performed, *Die Gottin Diana* and *Faust*.

orchestra, Mr Balfe,[2] who combines a talent as a distinguished composer with that of an excellent singer. This choice is a credit to the ability of the director of Her Majesty's Theatre. The leading poet in Germany as a ballet scenarist, and the leading maestro in England as conductor—that is a right royal luxury.

Nothing that Mr Lumley does can now surprise us. In a season of five months, and without receiving any subsidy, he has succeeded in gathering around him Carlotta Grisi, Cerrito, Lucile Grahn, Elssler and Taglioni, the five greatest names in ballet. Think of all the diplomacy, expenditure, stratagems pressed to their conclusion, and indefatigable perseverance that must have been needed to provide London with such a marvellous spectacle, quite apart from all the attention and wheedling that must have gone into making the celebrities, and particularly the female celebrities, live side by side in harmony. To have realised such an impossibility is clearer proof even than that of the railways that time, continents, and distance no longer exist. As for us, one of these birds of passage will hardly interrupt its flight to look in at the Opéra, and that is only half Mr Lumley's company, for he has also engaged singers from the Bouffes,[3] and stars on leave from the Opéra.

La Presse, February 23rd, 1846.
L:797.

[2] Michael Balfe (1808–70), operatic composer whose best-known work was *The Bohemian Girl* (f.p. Drury Lane, November 27th, 1843), the libretto of which was adapted from the ballet *La Gipsy*.

[3] This is a reference to the Théâtre Italien, not, as might be guessed, Offenbach's Bouffes-Parisiens, which did not exist at that time. Many of Lumley's singers sang also at the Italiens.

45

Opéra: *Paquita*

Paquita, ballet-pantomime in 2
acts and 3 scenes, sc. Foucher, ch.
Mazilier, mus. Deldevez, f.p. April
1st, 1846.

The performance of the famous Empire ballet—as it was formerly
described—has at last taken place under the definitive title of *Paquita*.
This name tells you at once that the action takes place in Spain, and indeed the
curtain rises on a picturesque set depicting the Valley of the Bulls near
Saragossa, so named because of the great bulls crudely sculpted in stone that
form the outline of the crests. Huge sheer cliffs with steps cut into the rock
and zigzagging up the near-vertical faces reach up to the sky above. At the
foot is a camp of gitanos. The landscape is marvellously wild, and a fitting
spot for tragedy. It is one of those passes lined with crosses bearing solemn
inscriptions—*Aquí mataron a un hombre, Aquí murió de mano airada*[1] that
are so common in the Peninsula, and which the intrepid traveller never
encounters without a feeling of unease.

The place justifies its sinister appearance, for it was here, on May 5th,
1795, that the Comte d'Hervilly was assassinated along with his wife and
daughter. A mason is busy engraving an inscription commemorating this
mournful event on a slab of marble, on the orders of General d'Hervilly,
brother of the deceased and the officer in command of a French division.

It is General d'Hervilly's wish—and the victories of our armies give him the
right to fulfil it—that the tablet be set in the rock at the very spot where his
brother fell under the blows of bandits, and accompanied by Don Luís de
Mendoza, the Spanish governor of the province, Doña Serafina, Don Luís's
sister, Lucien d'Hervilly, his son, and the young man's grandmother, he has
just satisfied himself that everything is being done as he had ordered.

To take their minds off such sad memories, the governor invites his guests

---

[1] "Here a man was slain, Here died one by an angry hand." Gautier had seen crosses
with such inscriptions by the roadside as he crossed the mountains between Granada
and Malaga in 1840 (see Chapter 12 of *Voyage en Espagne*).

Caroline Fjeldsted dancing the *Redowa*.
Drawing by Edvard Lehmann.

Clara Webster. Engraving by G.A.
Turner from a sketch made before her
death and in the costume she was
wearing on the evening of her accident.

Henri Desplaces and Adèle Dumilâtre in *Lady Henriette*, with Lucien Petipa behind them on the right. Lithograph from a drawing by Célestin Deshays. (*Album de l'Opéra*, No. 15.)

ABOVE: Lola Montez. Left: Hissed at the Porte-Saint-Martin and the Opéra. Right: Horsewhipping a Prussian gendarme. (*La Mode*, September 15th, 1847.)

RIGHT: Professor Risley and his two Sons. Lithograph by Victor Prévost from a drawing by Jules Petit.

Marie Taglioni, as the dying Sylphide. Lithograph by T.H. Maguire from a drawing by A.E. Chalon.

ABOVE: Marie Taglioni dancing the *pas de l'ombre* during her farewell season in Paris in 1844. (*L'Illustration*, June 29th, 1844.)

RIGHT: Marie Taglioni and Prosper-Nicolas Levasseur in *Le Dieu et la bayadère*. Engraving by Blanchard from a drawing by Alfred Johannot.

LEFT: Tatiana Smirnova.
Lithograph by H. Schmid.

RIGHT: Elena Andreyanova.
Lithograph from a drawing by
Shchurovsky.

RIGHT: Adèle Dumilâtre in *Eucharis*. Lithograph from a drawing by L. Loire.

BELOW: Adeline Plunkett in *La Péri*. Lithograph from a drawing by Victor Coindre, from a music title.

The Danseuses Viennoises in their *pas des moissonneurs*. Lithograph by John Brandard.

Paquita, Act II, with Lucien Petipa, Carlotta Grisi and Georges Elie. (*L'Illustration*, April 11th, 1846.)

Fanny Cerrito dancing the *pas de chibouk* in *Lalla Rookh*, with Arthur Saint-Léon. Lithograph by John Brandard.

Sofia Fuoco and Lucien Petipa in *Betty*. Anonymous lithograph, from a music title.

Ozaï, Act II, Scene I, with Adeline Plunkett as Ozaï, Georges Elie as Bougainville, and Henri Desplaces as Surville. (*L'Illustration*, May 8th, 1847.)

Arthur Saint-Léon and Fanny Cerrito in *La Fille de marbre*, Act I. Lithograph from a drawing by Frédéric Sorrieu, from a music title.

Episodes from *Nisida*. Caricatures by Gustave Jamet. (*Journal pour rire*, September 16th, 1848.)

Carlotta Grisi and Lucien Petipa in the forest scene in *Griseldis*. Caricature by Lorentz. (*Journal pour rire*, February 26th, 1848.)

LEFT: Fanny Cerrito and Arthur Saint-Léon in *La Vivandière*. Lithograph by Magnier jeune from a drawing by Henry Emy.

BELOW: Arthur Saint-Léon and Fanny Cerrito in *Le Violon du Diable*. Lithograph from a drawing by Janet Lange.

RIGHT: Jules Perrot in *Zingaro*.
Lithograph by Alexandre Lacauchie.

BELOW: *La Filleule des fées*, Act II, with
Carlotta Grisi and Jules Perrot.

Fanny Cerrito dancing the *Sicilienne* in *Stella*. Lithograph by Martinez.

Fanny Cerrito in *Pâquerette*. (*Galerie Dramatique*, No. 546.)

Esther Aussandon
(*L'Illustration*, April
27th, 1850).

Olimpia Priora.
Lithograph by Léon
Noël.

Adeline Plunkett in *Vert-Vert*.
Caricature by Marcelin. (*L'Illustration*,
December 13th, 1851.)

Olimpia Priora in *Vert-Vert*. Caricature
by Marcelin. (*L'Illustration*, December
13th, 1851.)

to a village festival that is to take place on that very day—"on this spot", says the scenario.

We know from experience not to expect a ballet to make complete sense or be entirely logical. But it does seem a little odd, even in the world of ballet, to give a performance of *cachuchas* on ground that has been stained with blood, and in the presence of the victim's brother, grandmother and nephew—a circumstance rendered still more shocking by the wording on the tablet. That the Spanish governor should be moved by a secret hatred for the French to propose such an ungodly festivity to the general is understandable, but it is hardly likely that the general would accept. But after all, what does it matter! Here come the tambourines, the traditional *panderos*, their small copper plates vibrating and purring in the grip of the gitanos; the castanets chatter, and the festivities begin. Away with sad memories! But who is this pretty creature with the delicate complexion, azure blue eyes and golden hair—a white rose set in a bouquet of red roses? Moorish blood cannot possibly flow in those thin blue veins. There must be some secret story of a child lost or believed dead. For she cannot be a daughter of that tribe with copper-coloured skins, hooked noses and slanting eyes, and as you know, gypsies are great stealers of children, particularly on the stage. And one does not have to be very shrewd, my dear little creature, to guess that hidden in your bodice is a miniature or a cross whose purpose is to enable your parents to recognise you.

Spanish dances are charming, particularly when performed by dancers of the Opéra, and Lucien d'Hervilly gazes at Paquita—for such is the girl's name—with a look that is very passionate coming from a man who is betrothed to Doña Serafina. But truly, never did a tinier foot support a more supple body, or castanets click more vivaciously at the tips of such agile fingers. How lightly she bounds, and how nimbly she evades the advances of her two gitano partners—poor devils who thought it would be easy to put their arms around her waist or kiss her hand. She slips from their grasp like a snake, glancing over her shoulder with a mischievous smile, and the pursuit begins again more furiously than ever. At the end of the dance, still trembling with emotion and out of breath, she stretches out her tambourine to catch the shower of coins that pour into it from every side.

The receipts are good, yet Inigo, the poor little creature's master and slave-driver, is not satisfied. He wants her to make another round. Paquita, whose noble feelings find begging repulsive, refuses. The brute is about to strike her. But being a French gentleman and an officer of the hussars, Lucien cannot allow a girl to be mistreated in his presence. He intervenes and threatens Inigo with his anger if he does not treat Paquita more gently in future.

But Paquita could avoid being beaten if she wished. This big fat bandit has a sort of wild and jealous love for her that her resistance has turned to hatred. A kind of hidden pride, an inborn nobility has led her to despise Inigo. She would rather remain the man's slave than become his wife, and at the sight of Lucien, her aversion has redoubled.

The young officer questions Paquita. He cannot believe that she was born among this horde of vagabonds. The girl wishes to show him the medallion she has so carefully treasured, but she is unable to find it, for Inigo, seeing this conversation taking a dangerous turn, has filched the miniature with a skill that does not say much for his honesty.

Becoming more and more infatuated with Paquita, Lucien offers her a well filled wallet and asks her to let him take her away. The girl would be only too willing to follow him, except that her good sense tells her that a gitana picked up on the wayside cannot become the wife of a French officer. "Then at least give me that bouquet as a souvenir," says Lucien. Paquita, knowing full well what the gift of a bouquet means in the language of ballet, refuses this seemingly innocent favour, and Lucien leaves, feeling very put out.

You must now know that throughout this scene the Spanish governor, who dislikes the idea of Doña Serafina marrying a Frenchman, has been observing the blossoming love of Lucien and Inigo's jealousy with growing delight. Against this background he hatches a plot to bring about the undoing of the young officer. Paquita will be the bait to lure Lucien into the trap, and the gitano will be all too willing to fall in with the governor's plan and rid himself of a rival.

Inigo, who has heard or, to be more precise, observed (for that is the only way of hearing gestures) the latter part of the conversation, manages to steal Paquita's bouquet and hands it to a gypsy woman to take to Lucien, who is overjoyed to receive this treacherous gift. The gypsy woman points to the hut where Paquita lives. Believing that the lover's hour of triumph has come, he presses the flowers to his lips and, making some excuse or other, lets the rest of the convoy depart without him, though not before promising to be in Saragossa on the morrow for the grand ball in honour of his approaching marriage.

In the second act we are under the gitano's roof, a questionable hovel, part slum, part cave, furnished with four walls, and what walls! The greatest luxury of the place is a revolving chimney at the back—described in the scenario as an "infernal mechanism"—that leads to the world outside.

Concealed in a cloak, the governor stealthily enters and hands the gypsy a drug that will make Lucien powerless against his assassins' daggers. Paquita, anxiously suspecting dirty work to be afoot, has hidden behind a chest, and overheard everything. She determines to rescue Lucien or die in the attempt.

Soon the gallant officer appears. Inigo welcomes him obsequiously, taking his cloak and sword, and bidding him to be seated at the table. Lucien lingers near Paquita, at first failing to understand what she is trying to signal to him. Inigo, however, keeps a watchful eye on them and gives the gitana a succession of orders to keep her away from Lucien. Luckily Paquita comes and goes with the lightness of a bird and the swiftness of a squirrel. She lays the table cloth, wards off Lucien's kisses, allays Inigo's suspicions, drops a pile of plates, and while Inigo is bending down to pick them up, changes the glasses so that the bandit will drink the drugged wine and the young man the wine that has not been tampered with. Forewarned, Lucien now understands everything, and during the dance that Paquita performs on Inigo's orders, he falls forward on to the table and pretends to be asleep. The bandit rises, believing his moment has come, but the drug is already taking effect, weighing down his eyelids and weakening his muscles. After one last vain effort to throw off this lassitude, he falls on to his chair in an unconscious stupor. Clearly the governor has done his part well. The bandit opens his jacket to breathe, for he is suffocating, and as he does so, the medallion stolen from Paquita rolls on to the table. The girl picks it up, and taking advantage of the passage by the chimney whose secret she has discovered, she and Lucien stand with their backs against the wall, and at midnight, the time fixed for the murder, the revolving mechanism brings two bandits into the room, at the same time conveying the lovers into the street.

The scene changes. From Inigo's hideout we jump to the palace of the French governor at Saragossa. The ball is in full swing. The splendid uniforms of the Empire, the French gowns of the court ladies and the picturesque national costumes of the Spaniards sparkle in the light of a thousand flickering candles. The *contredanse* and the *gavotte* are performed with classical vigour and precision, but a general feeling of unease prevails, for Lucien d'Hervilly has not yet arrived. Suddenly he enters, with his clothes in disarray, followed by Paquita. He explains what has happened and announces that he owes his life to the devotion of the young gitana.

During this scene Paquita's eyes have alighted on a portrait hanging on the wall, the portrait of the Comte d'Hervilly. Great Heavens, the features are the same as those on the medallion! Paquita is the general's niece and Lucien's cousin!

To celebrate this happy recognition, Paquita leaves to change into a dress of white tarlatan and returns to dance a ravishing *pas*.

This ballet, whose action is perhaps somewhat over-melodramatic, was completely successful. The richness and originality of the Empire costumes, the beautiful scenery, and above all the perfection of Carlotta's dancing carried off the honours. Her last *pas* was daring and difficult beyond belief. There were some hops on the tip of the toe combined with a dazzlingly vivacious spin that caused both alarm and delight, for they seemed impossible to perform, even though repeated eight or ten times. The ballerina was greeted with thunderous applause and twice recalled after the curtain had fallen.

The scene in the gypsy's hut was played by Carlotta with surprising intelligence and dramatic sensitivity. She will soon be as good a mime as she is accomplished a dancer. Petipa, charming in his hussar's uniform, and Elie, who was admirably begrimed and costumed, gave her wonderful support.[2]

Much applauded were a *pas des manteaux* in the first act, and in the second a *pas de deux* by Mlles Adèle Dumilâtre and Plunkett, who vied with one another in grace and lightness. To be applauded alongside Carlotta is a difficult and flattering achievement.

The music of M. Deldevez is rhythmical, not too noisy, and abundant in melodies, bearing witness to a fresh and graceful talent. It made its own contribution to the success of the work.

La Presse, April 6th, 1846.
HAD, IV 240–245. L:805.

[2] Playing Lucien and Inigo respectively.

46

Her Majesty's Theatre, London: *La Bacchante* and *Lalla Rookh*

La Bacchante, divertissement, ch. Perrot, mus. Pugni, f.p. May 1st, 1845. *Lalla Rookh, or the Rose of Lahore*, grand oriental ballet in 10 scenes, ch. Perrot, mus. David, Pugni, f.p. June 11th, 1846.

In the middle of the opera a danced interlude . . . entitled *La Bacchante*, was performed by Mlle Lucile Grahn and Perrot . . . . A set all festooned with vines and fantastic garlands twining around white marble columns, their flutings standing out against a sky saffroned with autumnal tints, replaced the Crusaders' camp,[1] and Perrot, clad in a panther skin, springs from the wings with that light elasticity for which he is still unrivalled.

He is searching for a pretty bacchante who is coquettishly trying to escape from him, but only in order to be better caught, for the Galatheas of the ballet never stray very far. They are too much in need of the footlights and their partners to stay hidden for long behind willow trees and vines.

The bacchante is the lovely and expressive Lucile Grahn, whom all dance lovers will remember, even though she flashed only momentarily across the sky of the Paris Opéra.

Mlle Lucile Grahn belongs to the elegant and poetic school of Taglioni. She has its noble poses, its decently sensual grace, its elevation, and its soft arm movements. Experience has enabled her to realise all the hopes that she formerly aroused, and she has established her position on a stage where, a year ago, all the leading figures of the ballet joined forces.[2]

[1] The previous scene in Verdi's opera, *I Lombardi*.

[2] The 1845 season at Her Majesty's Theatre had been notable for Perrot's all-star Divertissement, the *Pas de Quatre*, in which Taglioni, Cerrito, Grisi and Grahn had all danced together.

In vain the male dancer declares his love with *flic-flacs, jetés battus* and *ronds de jambe.* The bacchante is unmoved, and finishes her *écho*[3] with an expression of disdain. The poor devil then realises that he will have to resort to ingenuity instead of getting out of breath in his efforts to please her. So he picks a bunch of grapes, and squeezes it above the bacchante's upturned head. A stream of ruby-red juice flows into her rosy mouth, and the girl, so intractable a few moments before, now falters, blushing and tearful, to lean on the shoulder of the man she has but recently repulsed.

All these varying shades of feeling could not have been conveyed more intelligently or more movingly than they were by Lucile Grahn. A pretty woman's frenzy must always be tempered by modesty.

Would we be seeking subtlety in everything to discover a profound myth in this interlude, which lasts for only a few minutes? Is not the faun or aegipan telling us, as he crushes the grapes into the mouth of the wayward bacchante, that wine is a more powerful seducer than love, and that it is a good thing to precede a declaration of love with a few bottles of Bordeaux or Champagne, or a few flasks of Anisette or Kirsch? Such a theory, which is hardly flattering to Don Juan and Lovelace, has been developed by a number of clever essayists.

As its title indicates, the ballet of *Lalla Rookh* is taken from the poem by Thomas Moore,[4] who is also known as Anacreon or Little Moore, for this great poet is very small. Despite its oriental label and Persian glitter, the subject of *Lalla Rookh* is very like that of *Jean de Paris.*[5] There is a prince who, in accordance with convention, is betrothed to a princess he has never seen, and succeeds in winning her love by disguising himself as the poet Feramorz. In the end it turns out that prince and poet are one and the same, and everyone lives happily ever after. This idea of a young princess being conducted from her father's court to her royal bridegroom, and falling in love with another man as the journey nears its end is perhaps more suited to story-telling than to pantomime, and furthermore it is difficult to represent a journey on the stage.

The first act of the ballet shows us the palace of the Grand Mughal, where the renowned Aurangzeb[6] is seated on a throne shaped at the back like an

---

[3] *Echo,* or sometimes *écot,* was a term then in use to denote a short variation included in a *pas.*

[4] Thomas Moore (1779–1852) was one of the most popular poets in the English language in his time. *Lalla Rookh* was his best known work, a narrative poem written in a florid style that appealed to the taste of the day.

[5] *Jehan de Paris,* a prose romance written in the late fifteenth century, told of a young King of France who, in the disguise of a merchant, travels with a delegation to Spain to view the princess he is to marry. The story was used by Marsollier in a melodrama, *Jean de Paris,* f.p. Th. de la Porte-Saint-Martin, February 26th, 1807.

[6] Aurangzeb (1658–1707), the last of the Great Mughals of India.

enormous peacock's tail glistening with precious stones. The poet Feramorz then arrives to seek the hand of the princess in the name of the king, his master.

The second act, which is set to David's symphony,[7] represents the caravan's journey across the desert. Not a detail is lacking, not even the *kamsin* or the sand storm. Much admired were two worthy camels, whose front legs could have quarrelled with its hind legs in the best of English invective had they lost their temper.

The third act contains the obligatory recognition scene and the celebrations that naturally follow, and enables us to attend the Feast of the Roses so often sung by Persian poets. And everything ends happily with the marriage of the prince and princess by the light of countless lanterns, lamps and chandeliers.

This very adequate canvas has been embroidered Perrot with a mass of charming dances, such as only he can create. But for us the main attraction of this choreographic poem was Mlle Cerrito, whom we had not seen before, since our previous journeys to London had never coincided with the times she was there.

Mlle Cerrito—and this proves how real are her talents—has rabid admirers and implacable detractors. To the former she is the nymph of the dance, while the latter regard her as a third-rate dancer whose reputation cannot be explained. There is no half-way position—she is either completely accepted or utterly rejected.

We were curious to discover the impression she would make on us and make up our own mind about her reputation, on which Paris still has to set its seal.

Let us begin with her *physique*, to use theatrical jargon, and come to her technique later. Cerrito is blonde, with very gentle and tender blue eyes and a pleasant smile that is possibly a little too much in evidence. Her shoulders and bust have nothing of that skinniness that is usually the mark of a ballerina, whose entire substance seems to have sunk into the legs. Her rounded, well-covered arms do not offend the eye with sorry anatomical details, but unfold gracefully and with suppleness. Her charming figure gives no hint of the fatigue of the studio or the sweat of training. She might be a girl snatched from her family only yesterday and pushed on to the stage. Her feet are small and well arched, her ankles slender, and her legs shapely. Her only shortcoming—whether an illusion caused by her belt being fixed too low, or that her body is a little too long—is that her figure is divided by the waist into two perfectly equal parts, which offends against the rules of human proportion

---

[7] Félicien David (1810–76) first achieved fame with his symphonic ode, *Le Désert*, a descriptive symphonic work depicting a caravan crossing the desert. Nearly all the music was included in Perrot's ballet of *Lalla Rookh*, a work of very great length when first performed, although considerably cut after the first few performances.

and is particularly unbecoming in a dancer. In short, she is young and attractive, and makes a good impression.

The costume that Mlle Cerrito wore, although not strictly authentic, suited her to perfection. Her white gauze skirt is embroidered with garlands of brightly coloured flowers which create an impression of freshness that could not have been more charming or more elegant.

As a dancer Mlle Cerrito has little or no "*école*"—that can be seen at once. Let no one take this statement amiss, for we are no more classical in matters relating to the dance than we are in anything else. The only point we wish to make is that Mlle Cerrito owes more to nature than to application. She dances by inspiration, and indeed her qualities would even disappear if she devoted herself to study in the hope of perfecting her technique, for her "gift" would then be lost, not acquired. Her principal qualities are freshness, flow of movement, and a naivety that makes one overlook a fault on account of its grace. At times she seems to be improvising, so happy is the inspiration behind her steps. Just as certain singers have voices whose main attraction lies in the *timbre* which it would be wrong to impair by study, so Mlle Cerrito has, so to speak, a silvery and youthful *timbre* of dancing which fatigue might shatter.

There can be no comparison between her and those ballerinas whose names are so often coupled with hers, Taglioni, Elssler and Carlotta Grisi. Mlle Cerrito's position, if not so exalted, is none the less distinct and honourable.

In an art that, in spite of its apparent frivolity, possesses rigid rules she represents the flowering of natural gifts, fantasy and caprice.

In our opinion Mlle Cerrito would be very successful in Paris, particularly if she were to confine herself to dancing three or four of those brilliant and delightfully vivacious *pas* that she throws off like child's play, as if dancing for her own pleasure in the privacy of her chamber.

That sums up our impressions. Several *habitués* of Her Majesty's Theatre told us, however, that we did not see the charming ballerina on one of her best days or in one of her best rôles. People also claim that she has seemed more pensive since her marriage,[8] and no longer has the same brio than before. You must understand that these remarks are purely choreographic, and do not suggest that her success was in any way diminished or that she received less curtain calls and bouquets.

La Presse, July 30th, 1846.
L:818(II).

[8] Cerrito had married the dancer and choreographer, Arthur Saint-Léon in April 1845.

47

Opéra: *Betty*

Betty, ballet-pantomime in 2 acts,
ch. Mazilier, mus. Thomas, f.p.
July 10th, 1846.

Alexandre Duval's *La Jeunesse d'Henri V*,[1] a play that achieved success in its day primarily because of the performance of the actors, served as the point of departure for the author of the ballet of *Betty*. We have already deplored the custom, which appears to have taken root at the Académie Royale, of dressing up *opéras comiques*, melodramas and comedies as ballets. Ballet is a special form that calls for a very particular range of subjects, in which the use of dance to express the action is natural and unavoidable. A play transposed into the sign language of pantomime and accompanied by a divertissement is not a ballet. This is a truth that is all too often forgotten. Those who are skilled in dramatic construction are mistaken when they apply their customary formulae to choreography. A poet dictating his ideas to a painter who then transposes them into sketches—that is the best combination for producing a good ballet scenario, which is much more of a rarity than is generally believed, for it is difficult to convey through the medium of graceful bodies a narrative that will at all times be understandable at sight. Having made these reservations, let us say that *Betty* is neither better nor worse than what is commonly understood as a *ballet d'action*, or in other words a pantomime in which *pas* of varying brilliance are interspersed.

Here, as concisely as possible, for we must not be long before coming to Mlle Fuoco, is a résumé of M. Mazilier's scenario.

Charles, led on by Rochester[2] and disguised as a sailor, is paying court to Betty, the daughter of an innkeeper of Greenwich or Gravesend, and she in turn is loved by a young page whom she believes to be a dancing master.

[1] *La Jeunesse d'Henri V*, comedy in 3 acts and a prologue by Alexandre Duval (1767–1842), f.p. Th. Français, June 9th, 1806.

[2] Charles is the Prince of Wales, the future King Charles II. The name of Rochester was undoubtedly borrowed from that of the Earl of Rochester who was a distinguished statesman in that king's reign.

Charles is in a rowdy mood, embracing the wives and daughters of everyone and setting fire to the buckets of punch, and in his struggle is clumsy enough to drop his wallet, which is picked up by the young page. When Rabelais' quarter of an hour[3] arrives, Charles turns out his pockets and can find nothing except his watch, which he offers in payment.

But the watch bears the royal cipher in diamonds set on an enamel ground. Now why should a sailor have such a priceless article in his possession? It is all highly suspicious, and the false sailor is seized and locked up in a room in the inn, from whence the page and Betty help him to escape, after exacting a promise that he will behave better in future.

In the following act the innkeeper, accompanied by his daughter, takes the watch which the sailor left as a deposit to the palace. Great surprise of the worthy man when he recognises Charles, Rochester and the page! The end is not hard to guess. Charles is magnanimous and consents to the marriage of the page and the young girl.

Mlle Fuoco, who was making her début, bears a name of happy augury—fire! It is from Milan, which gave us Carlotta Grisi, that this pretty young dancer comes.[4]

Mlle Sofia Fuoco made a distinct impression from her very first entrance. She has the merit of originality that is so rarely found in the dance—a limited art if ever there was one—and we were never reminded of Taglioni, Elssler, Carlotta or Cerrito.

Her *pointes* are particularly astonishing. She performs a complete *écot*[5] without once lowering her heel to the ground. Her feet are like two steel arrows rebounding on a marble pavement. There is not a moment of softness, nor a quiver or tremor. The inflexible toe never betrays the light body it supports.

It has been said of other dancers that they had wings and flew through the air in clouds of gauze. Mlle Fuoco flies too, but by skimming the ground on the tips of her toes, lively, nimble, and dazzlingly quick.

Dancing, it will be said, does not consist exclusively of *pointes* and *tac-quetés*. True, but since in everything that Mlle Fuoco did we observed cleanness, polish and precision, which in dancing are what style is in poetry, we believe she also possesses the other qualities, no doubt to a lesser degree,

---

[3] The time for settling one's bill, and by extension any unpleasant moment. The term was said to be derived from the bad moment that Rabelais experienced when, having no money on him to pay for his lodging, he made up a number of packets with labels such as "Poison for the King", was duly arrested, and taken under escort to Paris, where the King was highly amused (*Dictionnaire de Trévoux*). The incident is most probably legendary.

[4] Sofia Fuoco (1830–1916), who danced at the Opéra from 1846 to 1850, was noted mainly for her extraordinary virtuosity on her *pointes*.

[5] See No. 46, note 3.

but in sufficient measure. And furthermore, Mlle Fuoco is still quite young. She cannot be more than seventeen, as is attested by a certain juvenile slenderness of the arms and shoulders. Her features, without being exactly pretty, are piquant and animated. She dances with a happy expression, and her lips part in a natural smile. In a few months' time Mlle Fuoco will have learnt how to do her hair better, she will dress in greater taste, she will have acquired a few essential touches of French coquetry, and she will be twice as good as she is now. She is deservedly applauded and recalled every evening, for hers has been one of the most brilliant dance débuts we have had to report for a long time.

Mlle Adeline Plunkett, who is so happily endowed with talent, has been studying intelligently to cultivate her skill. She has the rare quality of an Andalusian dancer's suppleness. Mlle Dumilâtre is still living up to her name of "the beautiful Dumilâtre". Mlle Maria and Petipa play the rôles of the page and the prince, the first with much wit and the second with great allure.

The music, although written at great speed, is worthy of M. Ambroise Thomas.

La Presse, July 20th, 1846.
HAD, IV 287–289. L:816.

48

Opéra: *Ozaï*

Ozaï, ou l'Insulaire, ballet-
pantomime in 2 acts and 6 scenes,
ch. J. Coralli, mus. Gide, f.p. April
26th, 1847.

We said last Monday that a kindly wind was blowing in the world of the theatre. The happy month that has just passed has had nothing but successes. Even *Ozaï,* which under other auspices would have certainly had one of the stormiest of existences, has been able to complete its journey from Tahiti to Paris and from Paris to Tahiti without too many mishaps.

In general, and we are not trying to make a bad joke, savages are not a success at the Opéra. The Mohicans,[1] for whom much effort was spent on a search for authenticity and local colour, were not able to become naturalised in the Rue Le Peletier. Tattooing, rings in the nose, necklaces made of bear claws, moccasins embroidered with hedgehog quills, bracelets of red beans and shells, buffalo skin cloaks, and even headdresses of parrot and pheasant feathers, loincloths of pineapple bark and bead aprons hardly lend themselves to the requirements of ballet costume. So it must be accepted that ballet, such as it is understood today in France, should not stray beyond mythology or legend.

Ozaï has an unfortunate theme, which is not redeemed by the excellence of its performance. M. Coralli has produced enough remarkable works in his long career as *maître de ballet* that one can be severe without in any way tarnishing his well deserved reputation.

The scene, says the scenario, takes place on one of the islands of Oceania at the time of M. de Bougainville's expedition.[2] A pretty Tahitian girl has given shelter to a young French sailor who is the sole survivor of a ship that has been

---

[1] A reference to the unsuccessful ballet, *Les Mohicans,* performed in 1837. See No. 4.

[2] Louis-Antoine de Bougainville (1729–1811), French navigator notable for his voyages in the South Pacific. His was one of the first expeditions to reach Tahiti, which he claimed for France. He has given his name to the largest island of the Solomon chain, and also to the magnificent tropical vine, *bougainvillea.*

wrecked on the reefs, and has hidden him in a grotto, whose entrance is concealed by creepers and climbing plants to protect him from the curiosity or hatred of the natives. The sailor is none other than the nephew of M. de Bougainville. Ozaï loves him with all the strength of her little heart that beats beneath no restricting corset, and every day she brings to her beloved captive all sorts of wild delicacies in a little basket: a cut of monkey meat, spit-roasted cockatoos, sweet potatoes, yams, bananas, palm wine and coconut milk. Touched by these attentions and troubled by Ozaï's pretty features and other charms which enable him to appreciate a dress that is totally primitive, Surville (for that is his name) wants nothing more than to return her love and wed her, with the forest and the waterfall acting as witnesses in Nature's registry office.

But he has retained a fond memory for Mlle de Bougainville, and leading men in ballet are unfailingly faithful and chaste. However, he reflects that he is three thousand leagues from his own country, and having no probable chance of ever seeing his cousin again, he has decided to place a sort of reliquary around Ozaï's neck as a gage of a future union. These scenes are interspersed with dances and divertissements by Ozaï and her young companions. M. Coralli assures us that in composing these dances he has been inspired by various traveller's tales. We would like to believe this but there is nothing specially Tahitian about the multicoloured streamers hanging from the top of a mast that are braided by the twelve girls who revolve around it, for we have seen the same exercise at the royal festivities by the Puerto del Sol in Madrid,[3] on the platform where public dances are performed, and it is hardly likely that the festival organisers would have taken the idea from round-the-world travellers.

After Surville has returned to his grotto, a ship appears on the horizon and moves somewhat awkwardly—and sometimes poop forward—towards the island. Although under a full press of canvas, by some miracle of seamanship she was brought up some distance from the shore. A dinghy pulls away from her, and M. de Bougainville, who is searching for his nephew, lands with an escort of officers and sailors. He unrolls his map and soon falls asleep over it. Enter Ozaï, who is astounded by the sight of this powdered gentleman in a red and blue uniform snoring over a scrawl that, to her, is quite unintelligible. She examines him with great curiosity, plays with his three-cornered hat, which has fallen to the ground, fools around with his rifle, touching the trigger and making it go off. When we say go off, we are being polite to the Opéra's armourer, for the weapon misfired pitifully at the first performance.

Ozaï is knocked unconscious by the detonation, and M. de Bougainville wakes. Seeing the girl lying on the ground, he raises her up and with the help

---

[3] Gautier had made a second visit to Spain to attend the festivities celebrating the marriages of Queen Isabel II and her sister in October 1846.

of his officers and sailors, who have come running in at the sound of the shot, brings her round.

Having recovered from her fright, Ozaï is taught to dance the hornpipe, and given necklaces of glass beads and so many little glasses of rum that she becomes tipsy and is taken on board before she knows what is happening.

And what is that goose Surville doing all this time? He is resting in his grotto, from which he ought to have been alerted by the sound of the rifle shot, an unmistakable sign of the presence of Europeans. Pushing his head through the creepers that form the entrance to his home, he sees the ship at anchor on the horizon, but the sight of its irregular construction does not deter him from swimming out to her, and taking off his jacket, he leaps into the water.

The scene changes to the ship's interior. This sort of set is never effective because it is difficult to arrange it realistically. In this case a cross-section shows the captain's cabin. Above is the bridge, and the lower parts of the masts, shrouds, yards and topsails. To the right and left the sea is beating against the sides of the ship. The mistake is that the cabin is lying much too low in the water. If the hatches were opened, it would be flooded.

Ozaï is placed on a bed. When she wakes, she is sober again. She is astonished and amused by everything around her. She spins the globes, plays with the compasses as if they were dancing dolls, and turns the telescopes in every direction. Finding a mirror, she tries to seize hold of her reflection, darting round it like a sprightly little kitten. M. de Bougainville's negro servant arrives at this juncture and joins his own grotesque antics to her graceful skittishness.

The topman in the crow's nest has spotted Surville striking out with all his might only a short distance from the ship. He is dragged out of the water and hoisted aboard—just in time, for his strength was beginning to fail. Ozaï is overjoyed at seeing her friend again, whom all the dancing, red scarfs, beads, globes, telescopes and mirror have nearly banished from her mind. Mlle de Bougainville's portrait falls out of one of Surville's pockets. M. de Bougainville picks it up, and jumps to the conclusion that the two young people must be in love, but he does not react, for such a union does not fit into his plans.

In the second act we are in Paris, in M. de Bougainville's mansion. The young native girl has been initiated in the arts of powder, whalebone and paniers, but she is still charming and receives the attentions of a financier, a marquis and an abbé with amused distraction. Of all the lessons she has received, those from which she has benefited most have been the classes of the dancing mistress, although she has not lost her native simplicity. For example, seeing Surville offering his arm to Mlle de Bougainville, she unaffectedly takes it herself, as if regarding him as her property.

Surville's promotion is being celebrated by a fête, during which a curtain is drawn aside to show scenes of Tahiti, which the young islander finds profoundly disturbing. She pines for her native land, for she realises now that Surville's love, which could have been hers, is promised to another.

M. de Bougainville, who has been granted an audience of the King and been charged with a new mission in Oceania, goes to Marseilles to board his ship. He is on the point of setting foot on the deck, when Ozaï arrives, wearing her native costume again and begging him to take her with him. In this way the poor girl sacrifices herself for the happiness of the man whom she loves and who might have married her, if only to keep his word.

The character of Ozaï was originally to have been played by Mlle Carlotta Grisi, but a knee injury that kept her house-bound for some time, coupled with her imminent departure for London, prevented any postponement until her recovery and resulted in the rôle being given to Mlle A. Plunkett, who had to learn it in five or six days. The presence of a dancer such as Mlle Carlotta Grisi deprived the ballet, which had little merit of its own, of its best chance of success. However, Mlle Plunkett, who bore the entire burden of the work, and for whom Ozaï is the first new rôle she has created, acted very intelligently, displaying much naïvety and grace. Her miming is simple, expressive and intelligible.

In the mirror scene she revealed a childish coquetry that was charming without being affected. She missed none of the effects of her rôle, and her dancing was, as always, crisp, supple and lively. Mlle Plunkett has greatly improved in elevation and her ability to cover the stage. If *Ozaï* does not remain with us very long, it will certainly not be the fault of its graceful interpreter. Coralli *fils* was very funny in the rôle of the negro. M. Gide's music is not an unworthy companion piece to *Le Diable boiteux*.

La Presse, May 3rd, 1847.
L:870.

49

Opéra: *La Fille de marbre*

La Fille de marbre, ballet-
pantomime in 2 acts and 3 scenes,
ch. Saint-Léon, mus. Pugni (after
Costa), f.p. October 20th, 1847.

Young though she is, Fanny Cerrito has long enjoyed a reputation abroad that could not fail to bring her sooner or later to Paris, the modern-day Athens, the hub of fine arts and good manners, and the fact that her appearance has not taken place sooner was due to obstacles or demands that MM. Nestor Roqueplan and Duponchel[1] have managed to remove or satisfy with their customary skill.

It is indeed strange that a ballerina who took part in the famous *Pas de Quatre*, which the theatrical world still regards as a miracle, and of whom the English speak in the same breath as Taglioni, Elssler and Carlotta Grisi, should still be unknown in France. For any diploma of genius that is not sealed in Paris is defective, lacking a certain authenticity. The approval of Italy, Germany and England is not enough to establish the real worth of an artist of exotic reputation, for in matters of art all other capital cities seem a little provincial in comparison with Paris, and it is often necessary to put a damper on the enthusiasm of Naples, Vienna and London. So this ordeal is a solemn moment for an opera singer or ballet dancer, but whether sought or dreaded, come it must. Alboni[2] has been here, and now Cerrito has arrived in our midst. Jenny Lind,[3] whether she wants to or not, will appear in her turn, the policy of the new Direction being to strew the firmament of the Opéra with comets in the form of all the stars of opera and ballet—without prejudice, of course, to the fixed stars.

[1] Nestor Roqueplan and Henri Duponchel had been appointed Directors of the Opéra on July 1st, 1847, in succession to Léon Pillet.

[2] Marietta Alboni (1823–94) was the most celebrated contralto of the time.

[3] Jenny Lind (1820–87), the celebrated Swedish soprano, had made a sensational London début at Her Majesty's Theatre in May 1847. After her marriage in 1852 she retired from the operatic stage, but occasionally sang in concerts and taught at the Royal College of Music in London for several years before her death.

Cerrito made her début in a sort of ballet in the Anglo-Italian manner, devised and arranged by M. Saint-Léon. The French public, which is fundamentally hypercritical, normally demands a more logical and reasoned theme, even as an excuse for *entrechats* and pirouettes, but on this occasion, making allowances for the hurry with which the ballet was produced and the novel lines of its conception, it let itself be naïvely carried away by its pictorial detail and the charm of the execution.

Before analysing Cerrito's talent, let us give a rapid sketch of the scenes in which the ballerina acted and danced.

When the curtain rises, the spectator is introduced into a gleaming, flamboyant grotto, representing the kingdom of the spirits of fire, the Salamanders. The walls are dappled with rich glints of gold, silver and copper, all fused together in the rock. A glittering throng of pretty salamanders in spangled skirts has assembled in this subterranean palace, swarming, scintillating, skipping—even chattering, one might add to continue the assonance, for this ballet, which is not as silent as most, occasionally resorts to words, expressed through the mouths of a chorus, as if the eloquence of gestures were distrusted. These are the words of the salamanders, "grouped", as the scenario explains, "in attitudes of surprise":

> *O puissant génie, écoute,*
> *De la flamboyante voûte,*
> *Satan a suivi la route*
> *Que tu daignas lui montrer.*
>
> *Il ne vient pas solitaire*
> *Dans le séjour du mystère,*
> *Un habitant de la terre*
> *Ose avec lui pénétrer.*

Although this is not its usual concern, a ballet scenario can versify no worse than an opera libretto, as you can see. But what the devil is Satan doing in the kingdom of Salamanders? Is he looking for a fire-brand because the flames of Hell have gone out? Not at all, he is accompanying a young sculptor, Manasses. (Now why this Jewish name, seeing that the Israelites look on the plastic arts as an encouragement to idolatry?) This sculptor, a new Pygmalion, has fashioned from a block of Paros marble a stone mistress that he incautiously desires to bring to life, and to accomplish this he has made a pact with the Devil, who is introducing him to the prince of the Salamanders, possessor of the flame that breathes life into clay, the very spark that fell from the torch of Prometheus when he applied the fire of Heaven to the flanks of his own creation.[4]

---

[4] According to ancient legend Prometheus made the first man and woman out of clay, which he animated by means of the fire that he had stolen from Heaven.

At Satan's request, the King of the Salamanders, who can refuse him nothing, points his sceptre at an enormous rock and utters the following invocation:

> *Qu'à l'instant en ces lieux paraisse la statue,*
> *Qu'un habile ciseau de grâce a revêtue.*

The rock splits apart, and suddenly Manasses' masterpiece is seen, standing out in all its whiteness against a black background. The statue is now to receive its soul, but subject to a condition that the poor sculptor never anticipated. If you are making a contract with the powers of Hell, you have to have a very clever lawyer! The voice of the genie—for, as in the theatre of the ancients, Quériau[5] has a singer to utter the phrases which he expresses in gestures—announces the terms of the pact:

> *J'animerai le corps que Manassès forma;*
> *Vivante sous ma loi que sa femme de pierre*
> *A la clarté des cieux entr'ouvre sa paupière!*
> *Fille de feu, que son nom soit Fatma.*

At the words of the genie's invocation, an angry flame shoots out of a fissure in the cavern and licks the pedestal with its tongues of blue and green. The genie continues his recitatif in Alexandrine verse:

> *Fatma, connais ici ma volonté suprême;*
> *Fascine les mortels par tes charmes vainqueurs;*
> *Mais si tu faiblissais, si tu cédais toi-même*
> *A l'amour, dont ta vue embrasera les coeurs,*
> *Je reprendrai soudain le rayon de lumière,*
> *Le souffle créateur qu'en ton soin j'ai placé;*
> *Et désormais, rendue à ta forme première,*
> *Tu resteras un marbre immobile et glacé.*

The chorus takes this up with solemn persistence:

> *Que son coeur soit de marbre, et, sans rien écouter,*
> *Qu'elle inspire l'amour et sache y résister.*

As soon as these words have been uttered, a revolving device causes the marble figure to be replaced by a woman of flesh and blood who immediately darts on to the stage, crossing it in two or three bounds. It is Cerrito, overflowing with delight that her feet have been released from their pedestal, and giving free rein to her joy. A very natural attraction draws her to the man who has provided her with such charming features, such a deliciously moulded bosom, and such beautifully rounded arms. But poor Manasses

---

[5] Germain Quériau danced at the Opéra from 1835 to 1850.

recoils in alarm, filled with the fearful thought that Fatma can never love him and that she will be reclaimed by the marble out of which he fashioned her. There is nothing he can do, for of what else is a statue transformed into a woman capable than love? But she will fall in love with another! That is all that Manasses can gain. The Devil has cheàted him with this cynical reservation.

At the back of the cave a point of light begins to flicker, increasing in size to reveal a magic tableau of a young Moor sleeping in the shade, and the image of Fatma appearing to him in his dream. The young Moor is Aliatar, a descendant of the Caliphs of Granada who has been dispossessed by the Spaniards. He wishes to capture the vision, but it vanishes and the circle contracts.

So Manasses has been well and truly warned. As you can guess, Satan has acted not out of charity, but to pile the agony of jealousy on to the sufferings of unrequited love.

The magic now over, the action returns to this world, and we see a city, part Gothic, part Moorish, rising from the banks of a river. A notice nailed to a post, announcing that "Gypsies are forbidden to enter Seville", leaves us in no doubt about the geographical location of this act. But here we must pick a little quarrel with MM. Cambon and Thierry,[6] which we do without much misgiving seeing that their set is perfectly painted and imbued with fresh air and sunshine and other effects. The Guadalquivir, whose Arabic name, only slightly Spanishified (Oued-el-Kebir), means River King, is as wide in Seville as the Rhine is in Cologne, the Scheldt in Antwerp, or the Thames in London. The city is actually joined to the outlying district of Triana by a very long pontoon bridge, while the stone bridge that MM. Cambon and Thierry have thrown across the Guadalquivir has only seven or eight arches. Manasses and Fatma have joined a troupe of gypsies. Fatma is sweeping everyone off their feet with her vast range of dances, each one more passionate than the last—frenzied *cachuchas* and satanic *boleros* that no one can resist. The most exalted personages have only to see her to join in the dancing as if bitten by a tarantula, and even *alcades* and *corregidors* forget their dignity. Manasses has laid aside his sculptor's chisel and become a dancer, performing the most prodigious *cabrioles*. However, Fatma's heart has not yet stirred for anyone. Manasses is doing his utmost to ward off danger, but nevertheless, Fatma, without having exactly fallen in love, has already singled out the young Moor, Aliatar, among the crowd of her admirers.

Satan, under a disguise, has revealed to the swarthy descendant of the Caliphs that the charming woman of his dream is even more delectable in real life. Aliatar, who has African blood in his veins, pursues Fatma with the most

---

[6] Joseph-François-Désiré Thierry (1812–66), a pupil of Gros, was associated with Cambon (see No. 29, note 17) in producing scenery for the Opéra from 1847 to 1865.

burning passion, and, marble maiden though she is, she cannot remain unmoved by his ardour. After the great scene of fascination, in which the animated statue charms peasants, soldiers, noblemen, *alcades*, and even a procession of penitents, Manasses escorts Fatma to a boat, which is soon followed by a sizeable fleet filled with frenzied admirers. Aliatar, left on the bank, throws himself into the water, and with desperate strokes follows the vessel that is bearing away the beauty he adores. In the nick of time there appears out of nowhere a fellow whose motto might well be taken from the words of the old ballad which, although not in the *romancero*,[7] is not without merit:

> *Je l'ai par mer,*
> *Je l'aurai par terre*
> *Ou par trahison.*

The next act takes place in Granada, in the Alhambra—an unfailingly appropriate setting for charming scenes—that palace that exerts so powerful an attraction on the imaginations of writers of romance, and whose splendour and elegance have never been surpassed.

Fatma has been rejoined by her admirers, who have sung her praises so loudly that the King wishes to judge the dancer's talents for himself, and has commanded a brilliant fête to be prepared. As usual Fatma arouses the most frenzied enthusiasm.

Manasses is not unduly worried, for in scanning the teeming throng of admirers he has not observed the man who poses the fatal danger to Fatma. However, Aliatar is concealed behind a pillar, following the young girl with a burning gaze. For her he has conceived the desire to recover the throne of his ancestors, and to place his beloved on a throne alongside his own. The insurrection breaks out. The Moors surprise the Spaniards, and once again the standard of the Prophet flies over the Red Towers.[8] The young Caliph proclaims Fatma his queen of beauty. Touched by such love, the marble maiden softens, puts her hand to her breast, and gazes languorously at the valiant Moor. But wonder of wonders! The flush of life disappears from her cheeks, the icy grip of stone is freezing the heart that has only just begun to beat, and in the place of an adorable woman, the Moor finds himself clasping nothing but a masterpiece of sculpture. As for Manasses, whose fate is linked to the statue, he is struck dead and the Devil bears him away.

This ballet, which should not be judged severely for its plot, offers a few

---

[7] A body of Spanish folk ballads, dating from the fourteenth and fifteenth centuries, many of which deal with the conflict between the Spaniards and the Moors.

[8] The *Torres Bermejas*, the Vermilion Towers, are the oldest part of the Alhambra, so named, it is believed, after the red ferruginous concrete or *tapia* with which they are built.

choreographic situations and opportunities in the way of scenery and production, and provides an adequate and very appropriate frame for the ballerina, who otherwise could only have appeared in isolated *pas* in the short time she will be with us.

Fanny Cerrito is happily endowed for the stage. She is blonde, her blue eyes have sparkle and tenderness, and a ready smile lights up her attractive features. Her waist is neat, and her arms are plump and softly contoured, a rare quality in a ballerina. Her well developed bosom avoids the skinniness that is all too prevalent among ballet dancers. Her legs are slender, and she has pretty feet. Physically, she has all that is needed to interpret the poetic imaginations of ballet scenarists; undines, sylphides, salamanders will have nothing to complain about in the way she portrays them.

As a dancer, Fanny Cerrito's principal qualities are the grace of her poses, her unexpected attitudes, the rapidity of her movements, and the speed with which she covers the stage. Her jumps and her *ballonnées* have an ease and an elasticity that command admiration. The whole upper part of her body is charmingly graceful. Her arms, the bane of ballerinas who ought to heed the advice of the servant in *Le Malade imaginaire*[9] and have them cut off as an unnecessary encumbrance, curve and float gently in the air like the pink draperies that waft over the heads of nymphs against a black ground in the frescoes of Herculaneum.

In her whole manner there is a touch of happiness, brilliance, an effortless unfolding, that betrays no toil or fatigue. But her very merits conceal a defect. For along with all her facility, freshness and youthful appearance, there is also to be discerned a lack of style and faulty technique, and without wishing to descend into frivolous erudition, we shall merely remark that she suffers from lack of good training. Nature has done everything for Cerrito, but even the most felicitous gifts have to be cultivated. An artist of her calibre and renown ought not to lay herself open to criticism from dancing masters, who think they have said the last word when they have observed some untidy *pointe* work and placings of the feet that are not fully turned out. These small blemishes disappear quickly in the dazzling whirlwind of her bold, artless, unexpected and graceful dancing, and at the Opéra Cerrito might have imagined herself back at Her Majesty's Theatre, under the wing of Mr. Lumley of London.

Her success was complete and decisive. Cerrito conquered her audience with her very first bounds. Never before had the Opéra seen a more resplendent assembly, the boxes taking on the appearance of jewel caskets and

---

[9] In the famous scene where Toinette disguises herself as a doctor and says to her master, Argan, "What the devil are you doing with that arm? If I were you, I would have it cut off immediately. Don't you see it is taking all the nourishment and starving the whole of that side of your body?"

flower beds. The Spanish dance, *L'Aldeana*, made a great impression. Nothing could have been more supple, livelier, or more frenzied.

Saint-Léon[10] caused astonishment by the taut boldness of his dancing and the strength of his jump. He succeeded in winning applause for himself, not an easy thing at a time when male dancing is out of favour. Apart from his talents as a dancer and a choreographer, Saint-Léon plays the violin in a quite masterly fashion, according to those who have heard him. It would seem a simple matter to find a plot that would show him off both as a dancer and as a virtuoso.

By the enormous box-office receipts the public has expressed its appreciation of the trouble the Direction is taking to provide its pleasures. Extravagance is good business management in the theatre, the money thrown out of the window being returned threefold through the doors. To be sure, when one already has Carlotta Grisi, it seems an unheard of luxury to invite Cerrito as well. But the addition of variety to excellence produces a fabulous combination, and this has just been achieved.

La Presse, October 25th, 1847.
HAD, V 153–155. L:900.

---

[10] Arthur Saint-Léon (1821–70) was a male dancer of exceptional strength and virtuosity. Also, as well as being no less virtuosic on the violin, he was an extremely talented choreographer, producing many ballets for the Opéra, including *La Fille de marbre*, *La Vivandière*, *Le Violon du Diable*, *Stella*, *Pâquerette*, *Néméa*, *La Source* and *Coppélia*, all of which Gautier reviewed. In the last ten years of his life he dominated the ballet both in Russia, where he was engaged as ballet-master in St. Petersburg, and in Paris, where he spent his summers.

50

Opéra: *Griseldis*

Griseldis, ou les Cinq Sens, ballet-pantomime in 3 acts and 5 scenes, sc. Dumanoir, ch. Mazilier, mus. Adam, f.p. February 16th, 1848.

A ballet is a symphony made visible. Gestures, like music notes, have no very precise meaning, and apart from their general significance, can be interpreted by everyone according to individual taste. It is a silent dream experienced in the waking hours, to which one adds one's own words. The audience works on the theme provided by the author or choreographer, and embroiders it with a thousand variations according to its fancy, and this makes ballet at the same time the most material and the most idealised form of spectacle. According to one's outlook, it can be a series of pirouettes and capers of varying grace, or the most ravishing poem—but a poem that has not been committed to words.

Ballet may be enjoyed by natures that are either very simple or very refined. The former allow themselves to be carried away by the movement, the brilliance, and the variety of the figures or the scenery, while the latter, disenchanted with the exaggerated histrionics and bad style of actors, love the silent canvases that can be filled in as they please, guiding rather than dictating their daydreams.

So we are not one of those who go to a new ballet and read the scenario during the performance without once raising their eyes because they prefer to understand it rather than to see it.

One of the charms of ballet is that the characters are really anonymous and resolve themselves into the eternal types that have been the mainstay of dramatic productions ever since the world began. The father, the old man or the *barba*, to use the Spanish term, the lovers, the young girl or the sylphide, the servant, and the good or bad spirit who helps or hinders—these are the pawns, arranged in one way or another, with which all ballets are made.

189

The ballet which the Opéra has just presented is called *Griseldis, ou les Cinq Sens*. Griseldis let it be; it is a pretty name. That charming whirlwind of gauze, smiles and flowers is designated by those pretty syllables. We wish it well in order to make our story-telling easier, and are about to set off for the lands of dreams.

A line of tall columns forms the gallery of some princely or royal residence. Through the arches can be seen the green treetops of the park, lining avenues that stretch into the hazy distance, where marble statues stand like white phantoms. Where are we? In Prague, right in the middle of Bohemia, an excellent countryside for a ballet.

Reclining on a divan, and leaning on his elbow, a young man is sighing with boredom. It is no fault of his father that he is bored, nor of his tutor, for he is surrounded by a bevy of girls who are trying in vain to attract his attention, revolving around him as they dance. But the indolent young man remains unmoved by the languorous poses of their arms, the neat and energetic movements of their legs, and their dark looks and flashing smiles. They smother him with caresses, charm him with music, intoxicate him with perfumes, ply him with exquisite dishes and delicious wines, but nothing can arouse his pleasure. Change his Hungarian boots for buskins of antiquity and he might be Hippolytus himself,[1] just as handsome and just as cold; the forests, where in the clearings the virginal Diana might be glimpsed hunting deer with her pack, is the scene of the only pastime he cares for.

His father, the King, unlike the usual run of fathers, is wise enough to be worried lest this might compromise the future of his dynasty, and he would much rather his son were a little more of a rascal, specially now that a barbaric delegation from the Hospodar has arrived, brilliantly attired and accoutred and creating a great racket, with the object of arranging a marriage between the Bohemian prince and the Princess of Moldavia—an entirely acceptable union required by the politics of the time. On a velvet cushion sparkles an engagement ring and the crown of the duchy that the young Princess has brought as her dowry. The indifferent young man pays no attention to these plans, while his father rubs his hands as if struck by the thought that while his son may not be very passionate, he is at least pliant and obedient, but he has reckoned without a certain Griseldis who, after the ambassador has left, furtively and timidly comes forward on the tip of her tiny little foot, performing little hops like a wagtail in a meadow, with turns of the head as if she were listening to the silence and scanning the solitude. She darts rapidly round the gallery, inquisitively and apprehensively inspecting and touching everything about her. What do we have here, a crown? But this

[1] Hippolytus, son of Theseus by the amazon Hippolyte, repulsed the advances of his stepmother Phaedra, who believed that her husband was dead. The myth was the subject of a lost tragedy by Euripides, and of a celebrated classical tragedy by Racine.

heavy circle of gold, all knobbled with chiselling and precious gems, must surely scratch and bruise the head that wears it. Her pliant little chaplet of cornflowers and daisies, still damp with morning dew, refreshes and perfumes the temples with the gentleness of a caress and is a thousand times preferable. So away with the heavy mass of diamonds and metal, and let the floral garland, quite overcome by such an honour, take the place of the royal insignia on the cushion. And to make the significance of this emblematic substitution doubly clear, Griseldis places alongside it a miniature of herself. Two violet eyes shining out of a pink cloud, a delicate and mischievous smile, a neck cocked to one side like a bird, golden curls, the tip of a shoulder gleaming like silver—this is what the miniature must portray if the Walachian, Bulgarian or Dalmatian artist had the slightest talent. The young prince instantly prefers the circlet of cornflowers to the gold crown, and at the sight of the miniature, will hear no more of the Moldavian marriage. When the bespurred and moustachioed delegation returns, he rebels like the very devil and turns down the political marriage. "What, my son, has a simple shepherdess, a humble peasant, turned your head at a moment like this! Do not expect anything to come of that!" cries the King with some very expressive gestures. "I have a good mind to curse you. But no, I shall not curse you. The girl is so pretty that you are to be excused. But go away for a while, a journey will make you forget and see things in a better light, and in a couple of months you will go to the court of the Hospodar completely cured of your romantic infatuation." So Elfrid leaves with his tutor, just such a sensual and idiotic fool as one would expect the tutor of a fairy-tale prince to be.

Now where is the pretty village with thatched roofs brushed with moss, chimneys exuding wisps of bluish smoke, leaded windows, low doors framed fancifully with hops or virgin vines, chestnut trees giving shade with their leafy branches, and crumbling walls held together by a lacework of creeper? The inn sign will tell us. We are still in Bohemia, and this tavern has the glorious privilege of giving shelter to Prince Elfrid, who is now asleep inside. But the village soon comes to life, and its girls begin to dance in the square, expressing their joy at having the King's son within its walls.

In the course of their dance a girl appears, wearing a charmingly exotic costume, a mandoline slung across her shoulders. Sequins sparkle and rustle in her hair and about her neck. A jacket of yellow morocco leather with edges embossed with coloured rosettes covers her shoulders, a leather belt with wonderful Oriental stitching pinches her slender waist, the seams of her transparent sleeves are embroidered with flowers and all kinds of vivid arabesques, and a striped apron floats before her. You could not imagine anything more picturesque or Bohemian, and Carlotta is to be congratulated on the authenticity of her costume. Only those who have been theatre dressers can appreciate the magnitude, we would almost say enormity, of the task of designing a morocco leather jacket and a leather belt for a ballerina

191

who finds even tulle, gauze, tarlatan and *crèpelisse* too heavy, and would willingly settle for just the fabric of the wind of which Petronius speaks![2] Usually it is as much as one can do, by fines and threats, to force the supers to make a small concession to local colour! Carlotta had her just reward for respecting the wishes of the designer. Never was she more adorable than in this fanciful costume which makes a change from corsets and white skirts, and each time she crossed the stage, she gave the impression of one of those large butterflies from Kashmir, whose wings glow with all the colours of the rainbow.

The peasants crowd round this Esmeralda,[3] who plays the mandoline and dances with such passionate perfection, and is capable of turning the heads of all the Claude Frollos of Bohemia. It is Griseldis, who has put on this disguise to follow the young prince whom she loves, and for whom she wishes to be fairy, angel, ideal and guide.

Elfrid, a sad and disconsolate figure, comes out of the inn, sits down on a bench and gazes with a melancholy expression at the miniature he wears next to his heart. Hiding in the ruins of a Gothic chapel, Griseldis observes him closely. The prince knows nothing of Griseldis but her portrait, his only contact with her having been an emblem, a symbol, an idea, a mental image. Now she wishes to charm him by the most immaterial of means, a sound that vibrates to the beat of her heart and is instilled with the secret of her love. Strings quiver and sigh at the touch of unseen fingers, and a pure, tender melody rises into the silence like a jet of water trembling in the breeze.

The prince is disturbed by the sound of these magic notes. He rises and sets off in search of the owner of the mysterious voice. No one but she could sing like that; only the voice of his beloved could so thrill the heart and melt the soul. Every other sound is but noise by comparison. This, it seems, is how M. Dumanoir's ballet must be understood, for his young prince is neither deaf nor blind, and must have the senses of smell, taste and touch, otherwise he would be a mere simpleton, or worse still, an idiot. Or perhaps by means of some anachronistic clairvoyance Prince Elfrid has heard a lot of modern music by this composer and that at the court of the King, his father, and if that is the case, one can well imagine that he has not much taste for the delights of the ear.

Alas, the prince's pleasure is of short duration. The day's activities chase

---

[2] Petronius, *Satyricon*, 55:
        aequam est induere nuptam textilem,
        palam prostare nudam in nebula linea.
(Is it right for a bride to be clad in a cloud/Or wearing a whisp show off bare to the crowd? Trans. J.P. Sullivan, 1965.) Dancing girls in ancient Rome used to wear costumes of Coan silk so flimsy as to be almost transparent.

[3] Esmeralda, the heroine of Victor Hugo's novel, *Notre Dame de Paris*, was a street dancer for whom the warped archdeacon, Claude Frollo, conceived a fatal passion.

away his waking dreams. The town comes to life with all its trivial clamour—the crowing of the cock, the rhythmical hammering of the blacksmith in the glow of his forge, the sound of horns as the grooms prepare for the day's hunt. Church bells summon the parishioners to prayer, the wheels of passing carts grind over the cobblestones, children shake their rattles, and tambourines are throbbing in the hands of dancers. It is the most terrible din, the most glorious bacchanalia imaginable. How on earth, if you please, can anyone listen to a secret voice in all that hullabaloo! Dazed and distraught, the prince makes his escape, stopping up his ears, followed by his faithful tutor Jacobus. There is a profound philosophical allegory here. It is only in solitude and silence that soul can communicate with soul. Activity and noise deafen the heart as well as the ears.

Now we are in Belgrade, in the palace of Hassan, the governor of the city. Already a flavour of the Orient is in the air. There are heart-shaped arches, verses from the Koran adorn the walls, and the cedar-ceilinged kiosks are decorated with coloured tiles. Hassan, reclining on a pile of cushions, is smoking his pipe and drinking coffee with his women, and in true pasha style is somewhat bored by them. Night has fallen. Lamps shining in luminous globes stand out against the deep green background of the garden, scattering spangled threads on the dark water of the pools.

Suddenly the sound of a horn is heard. Two strangers enter. Elfrid claims hospitality as the son of a king. Hassan offers him the most sumptuous apartment in his palace, but the night is warm and the air scented, and Elfrid prefers to sleep in a hammock or in the kiosk. The pasha withdraws after demonstrating to the prince a machine which controls the lighting in the garden. While openly accepting anachronisms in operatic arias—and also let us forgive Paolo Veronese for the double bass players in his *Marriage at Cana* and Teniers for painting Achilles smoking his pipe beneath the walls of Troy[4]—we find the use of gaslight in the garden of a sixteenth-century pasha from Belgrade a little premature, unless it is supposed to be a prophetic symbol of future civilisation in the East.

The prince settles down in his hammock and almost at once falls asleep. Soon a white figure appears on the threshold of the kiosk. It is Griseldis. She approaches Elfrid, bends over him and notices that he is still wearing her miniature. Griseldis has a vague feeling of anxiety. She does not know if she is truly loved, and she is afraid, not only because her appearances up to now

---

[4] Veronese's *Marriage at Cana* is in the Louvre. It was brought to Paris as part of Napoleon's booty, and was not returned in 1815 because of its size, being exchanged instead for a number of smaller pictures. It is unclear to what painting Gautier is referring as the Teniers. There seems to be no painting in any public collection that fits the description. Bénézit's *Dictionnaire critique et documentaire des peintres etc.* lists a painting, *Achilles discovered by Ulysses*, which was auctioned in 1737. Had Gautier seen this in a private collection?

have been concealed and mysterious, but also because the prince might take her for a dream, a fleeting illusion. Not even the purest of women cares to remain in an ideal state, an abstraction, a disembodied Beatrice.[5] And so Griseldis, who has revealed her presence only through a portrait and a melody, is now to attempt a somewhat less nebulous manifestation. Her lips brush the forehead of the sleeping prince, who wakes and tries to seize the tender phantom of his dream. Then begins one of those coquettish pursuits in which Carlotta has no rival. She darts hither and thither, skimming the stage like a swallow and evading his grasp, now with a sequence of little steps on the *pointe* of unbelievable rapidity, now by a great jump that suddenly leaves her pursuer far behind. But always she remains in an area of alternating light and shade produced by a regulated switching on and off of the gas, so that every now and then Elfrid can catch up with her and realise, by brushing against her warm cheek or her tender shoulder, that touch is a very delightful sense, and that if there is something more precious than an ideal, it is reality. Nevertheless he is unable to catch a glimpse of the features of the shade with the satiny complexion.

So rapidly does the Prince of Bohemia lose his innocence that Griseldis only just manages to escape. The women of the harem, which is as carelessly guarded as the one in the tragedy of *Bajazet*,[6] now find the newcomer very much to their liking and furtively appear before him, like white shades, but the Prince is not deceived. He thrusts aside their gentle hands, and turns away from their rosy lips. Realising that Griseldis is the only woman in the world for him, he makes his escape.

A moment ago we were in a kiosk, and we now find ourselves in a forest. This perpetual journey, which scenery allows us to enjoy for nothing, is not the least of the ballet's pleasures. The dark trunks of the oak mingle with the silvered shafts of the birch trees. Overhead their branches intersect to form a mysterious vault, and through chinks in the foliage sunbeams scatter on the grass like so many pieces of gold fallen from a spendthrift's pocket. Grass and roots spread all around, vying with the watercress for the fresh spring water, whose reflection shimmers on the lowered antlers of the deer. View-halloo! view-halloo! The sound of hunting horns is heard, and the barking of hounds and the pounding of horses galloping over the uneven forest paths.

Who is this intrepid amazon on a prancing steed? It is Griseldis, as daring a horsewoman as she is light on her feet. The hunting party halts. Griseldis dismounts and gathers a nosegay of wild flowers. From a bush of wild roses she plucks a bloom, from the hawthorn a few snow-white blossoms, from the spring some blue-eyed forget-me-nots and lilies of the valley, their flowers

[5] Dante's Beatrice, immortalized in *La divina commedia*.

[6] *Bajazet*, a tragedy by Racine, f.p. Hôtel de Bourgogne, January 5th, 1672. Its action takes place in the harem of the Sultan in Constantinople.

clustered like pearls, while the greensward yields its shy and bewitching violets. Binding them with the stem of a bullrush, Griseldis conceals the small spray in her bosom, its purpose quite obvious. The hunt moves off. Elfrid and Jacobus then enter, and the tutor, choosing this as a suitable spot for a picnic, takes some provisions out of the prince's litter and spreads them on the ground.

Their lunch is interrupted by a rustic festival. It is the gardeners' feast day, and a merry band of girls comes trooping by with flowers in their hair, corsages, hands, and baskets, and with banners flying—a motley of pink, white, blue, scarlet, yellow and green, a veritable flower-bed in motion. The dancing begins. The girls form lines, crossing and interweaving, and then coming suddenly to a stop, letting their garlands drop to the ground to form symmetrical flower-beds with patterns constantly changing with the choreography. The whole house burst into applause at the invention of it all, for it was as elegant as it was ingenious, and so completely unexpected. But the more the girls thrust their flowers under his nose, the less is Elfrid moved by their scented coquetry. Then suddenly, from within the gigantic floral mound of massed baskets, a frail white hand throws a little nosegay, half faded, at the prince's feet. Elfrid picks it up and passionately inhales its scent. Those poor half-dead grasses, those wild flowers that are now shedding their petals, have acquired a penetrating, transcendent aroma from the bosom of the beloved that makes myrrh and cinnamon revolting by comparison. Whatever emanates from the loved one becomes transformed and idealised, acquiring an irresistible charm. The bullrush plucked by her hand smells better than ambergris, benzoin, lily, rose and tuberose, and the mountains of spices celebrated in the *Song of Songs*.[7]

When the girls have gone, Jacobus's thoughts turn again to lunch. The prince is not hungry and wants only to sleep so that he can dream of the charming creature whose brief appearances are a source of both torment and delight. But sleep eludes him, and Griseldis, as if reading his thoughts, stretches her fascinating hands before him, fluttering them in hypnotic passes. Elfrid falls asleep, or rather falls into a trance, and in this blissful slumber hallucinations, evoked by Griseldis's will power, form before his closed eyes. Clouds slowly descend and aerial figures sweep across the stage. Never before has such daring, poetic and successful flying been seen at the Opéra. Imagine *tableaux vivants* performed in the air, not by unfortunate *petits rats* hooked on to wires and making rowing movements with their arms and legs in a canvas sky, but by beautiful women, well posed and grouped, whose roseate pallor is appropriately shrouded by a piece of gauze and a floating scarf. One of them carries a lyre, and the other a bugle—they represent Glory and Poetry. Griseldis is able to evoke these charming apparitions with impunity,

---

[7] *The Song of Solomon*, viii, 14.

for nothing can prevail against love, which, as the Bible tells us, is strong as death.[8] The beautiful phantoms vanish, and Griseldis raises a cup of crystal-clear spring water to her lips before waking Elfrid from his hypnotic trance and slipping away.

Elfrid runs over to the cup, and draining it, has the sensation of drinking the most delicious liqueur. His lips have touched where those of Griseldis have brushed, and for him the tasteless liquid has turned into Cyprus wine, malmsey, lachryma christi, or whatever is most succulent, smooth and fragrant. What a bouquet this plain water has! No bottle of Chateau Laffitte brought back from the Indies ever had the like! In this way taste has been awakened in a prince who until this moment was insensitive to the most skilful preparations of the kitchen, but has now, for the first time in his life, become intoxicated—and on a glass of plain water touched by two beautiful lips.

Alas, he must now leave behind him the sighing voice, kisses that alight in the night, fragrant nosegays, cups that intoxicate the soul, visions of delight, fascinating shades stretching their arms from the cloud tops, all that ideal and fantastic world, and descend from poetry to prose, from love divine to a marriage of convenience! Although he has tarried on his way as long as he could, the prince has at last reached Jassy and the court of the Hospodar, whose daughter he must wed.

The mission of his beautiful mentor is not quite accomplished. She has made the prince appreciate the charms of hearing, touch, smell and taste, but she has not yet made herself visible; in other words, she has given him only an incomplete image of herself. Elfrid gazes forlornly at the miniature and the withered nosegay which he now must discard, for he wears on his finger the ring of the Princess of Moldavia. Then a familiar melody, coming like a refrain from Heaven, falls upon his ears, and suddenly, to his amazement, Griseldis appears before his eyes. It is the woman of his dreams, the original of the miniature! Understanding all that has happened, he clasps Griseldis in his arms and places the princess's ring on her finger. A flourish of trumpets interrupts this scene between the lovers, and with a modest display of fright Griseldis darts into the wings.

The wedding procession is approaching. Elfrid is determined to refuse the hand of the princess outright. But from beneath her veil she softly murmurs the opening phrases of the cantilena that Elfrid has heard twice before, and the material concealing her face falls to reveal the mischievous and smiling features of Griseldis.

Elfrid has the rare good fortune of discovering his ideal woman in his wife, who in common with some of the romantic princesses in German fairy tales,

---

[8] *The Song of Solomon*, viii, 6.

has had the whim to be loved for her own sake. But what excuse will this excessively happy prince have if he later takes a mistress?

The ballet closes with a *pas* danced by Carlotta Grisi with a perfection that has never before been seen. There is a combination of strength and grace, with sudden bursts that are never abrupt, a clockwork precision that does not exclude suppleness and elegance, and a marvellous brilliance and *brio* that realise the ideal of the fully accomplished ballerina, Elssler and Taglioni in one person. In particular there is a movement turned on one *pointe* alone, in which she flashes forward, vigorously impelled by her leg as if it were a bow of steel—the most audaciously charming impossibility that a dancer in command of all the resources of her art could possibly dare. We cannot imagine dancing being taken further than this, and for Carlotta Grisi the creation of the rôle of Griseldis will continue the series of triumphs which *Giselle*, *Le Diable à quatre* and *Paquita* have given her. Petipa deftly handled a rôle that was essentially passive, and Berthier brought a very comical touch to that of Jacobus. The music is by M. Adam—no more need be said. Adam is the most consistently successful composer in this field, which demands melody and still more melody, rhythm and still more rhythm, very ordinary little qualities which are scorned by maestros with grand pretensions, and with good reason, for it is no small matter to fill three hours with continuous melody. Musically speaking, *Griseldis* is worthy of its predecessor, *Giselle*. And—an unusual happening in a ballet, in which the most harmonious voices are condemned to silence—Carlotta, who as everyone knows has a pretty soprano voice that is very pure and true, herself sings the *ritornello* at the end that she has already rendered twice from the wings.

La Presse, February 21st, 1848.
L:919.

51

Opéra: *Nisida*

Nisida, ou les Amazones des Açores, ballet-pantomime in 2 acts and 3 scenes, sc. Deligny, ch. A. Mabille, mus. Benoist, f.p. August 21st, 1848.

*L*es Amazones des Açores seems a little apocryphal in spite of the abundance of references given in the preface of the scenario. The chronicles of the Convent of Sainte-Victoire, written in Latin by the Reverend Father Herrera and published in the collection entitled *Vetera Hispaniae analecta, collegit J.-B. Hicksius, Lipsiae,* 1602, in 8vo, must be extremely rare, and we strongly suspect that the copy which M. Deligny[1] used as his primary source of information is unique, for the book is not to be found in any other library.

Nor do we have any greater confidence in the curious books quoted in support—*Een seer ghenouchlicke ende vermacklicke historie, in neder-duytsch,* by Hans van Hendrick, *Antwerpen, int jaer MDX; La Sociedad de las Mugeres independientes; Derradeira* by Alvares Cabral, Coimbre, 1507, small in-folio; *P. Bertii tabularum geographicarum, libri V, Amstoldodami,* 1602; *Miscellanies of a traveller,* by Jonathan Lovesey, Cambridge, 1661, in-4to—which appear to come from those legendary libraries for which Rabelais delighted to invent illusory works with far-fetched titles.[2]

The new ballet certainly had no need of such erudition. It does not matter where and when the action takes place, or what Mlles Plunkett, Maria, and

---

[1] Eugène Deligny (1816–81), Secretary-General of the Opéra from 1846 to 1854, wrote the scenarios for *Nisida* and, anonymously, *La Fonti.* He also wrote numerous vaudevilles and comedies and a number of novels.

[2] These titles, which have been corrected to accord with the preface to the ballet's scenario, are indeed fanciful. Chapter VII of Rabelais' *Pantagruel* contains an imaginary catalogue of books supposed to be found in the theological library of Ste. Victoire in Paris.

Luigia Taglioni[3] dance; no further geographical or chronological detail is needed.

In the ballet Father Herrera's Doña Mercedes de Casa-Real, the liberator of women, *liberadora de las mujeres*, has become, quite simply, Josefa. As her general she has Mlle Plunkett; Mlles Emarot, Caroline, Barré, Galby, Franck, Théodore, Paulus, James, Aline, L. Marquet,[4] Legrain, Quéniaux and Laurent are her officers, and her army is composed of a crowd of supers who carry out their drill exercises as efficiently as the *vivandières* of the Garde Mobile.

The plot consists of this and nothing more. During the month of May the amazons feel that the presence of roses and violets is not enough to satisfy their hearts, and so they send a ship to a neighbouring island in search of a few individuals of the uglier sex.

For twelve hours these individuals are most gracefully welcomed, caressed and festooned with flowers, and they are then taken back, blind-folded, to where they came from.

When the ballet opens, the ship is discharging its male cargo. Prominent among the temporary captives are the handsome Etur de Guadassé, the leading man, and the vain, hump-backed Don Oscar de Babourda, a grotesque and comical figure.

The festivities begin, and when night casts its mysterious veil over the grouped figures, Queen Josefa, who has selected Don Etur for herself, inadvertently bears off Don Oscar de Babourda, clasping him tenderly in her arms without realising that she has been tricked, for Etur has followed Nisida, her commander-in-chief.

Eventually the error is discovered, and Josefa demands that Etur should choose between her and her subject. The young man, who has fallen in love with Nisida and been somewhat revolted by the prolonged meeting that has taken place between the queen and the hunch-back in the grotto bath, opts for the girl.

In her rage Josefa summons her bodyguard, intending to throw this Spanish Orpheus to those Azorean bacchantes. Fortunately the hunch-back makes his escape and, now no longer blind-folded, jumps into a row-boat to seek male reinforcements. In a short space of time the island is invaded by ships with full complements of men, and a great battle takes place in which they resort to no other weapons than bouquets and kisses, a sure means of

---

[3] Luigia Taglioni (1823–93) was the daughter of Salvatore Taglioni, who was for many years ballet-master in Naples where he produced an incredible number of ballets, and thus first cousin to the famous Marie. She danced at the Opéra from 1848 to 1857.

[4] Louise Marquet (1830–90), the youngest of the Marquet sisters, at this time a humble member of the corps de ballet. She remained a stalwart member of the company until 1879, creating and appearing in many important secondary rôles.

conquering an army of women. Etur marries Nisida, the queen is deposed, and the amazons realise that it is better to have husbands and lovers all the year round than on a single day in the month of May.

M. Deligny, who has given proof of his wit and good taste in a number of vaudevilles, cannot have gone to much trouble in devising this scenario, which serves no other purpose than to provide an excuse for the plastic scene of the bath and the drilling of the women. There is no need to seek anything else in it than that.

Nisida marks the début of M. Mabille as a choreographer. The clarity of his lines, his true feeling for groups and his facility in handling masses are very promising. The actual dancing lacked neither novelty nor grace, but it is a pity that he had such an insignificant theme to work on.

The honours of the ballet went to Mlle Fuoco. As a dancer, she showed herself to be agile, firm and precise. With her toe planted in the stage like an arrow-point, she performed, in particular, a most astonishing pirouette in the form of a rising spiral. Mlle Plunkett, who has nothing to do but pose voluptuously and puff out her chest, somewhat neglects her pretty legs, which must be crying out to show their paces. Looking charming is not everything; it is still necessary to dance. Mlle Luigia Taglioni has a modest grace reminiscent of the illustrious school in which she was formed. As for the men, their rôle is necessarily self-effacing in a work of this sort.

M. Benoist's music is well constructed and conscientiously written, although one might wish for more distinctive melodies and more pronounced rhythms. The scenery of the bathing scene, painted by MM. Philastre, Cambon and Thierry, is very original. Apart from that, the production is not worthy of the usual splendours of the Rue Le Peletier. However, it is true to say that the Théâtre de la Nation[5] is as poverty-stricken as everyone else, and one should not expect too much from a ballet produced during a state of siege and a time of reappraisal.[6]

La Presse, August 28th, 1848.
L:946.

---

[5] The Opéra was renamed the Théâtre de la Nation after the 1848 Revolution.

[6] Paris was the scene of violent unrest that summer, as various forces fought for supremacy in the newly formed Republic.

52

Opéra: Return of Fanny Cerrito

La Fille de marbre (see No. 49),
revived October 4th, 1848.

*L*a Fille de marbre is an old friend, whom it is a pleasure to see again. Maybe the scenario does not have much logical development, but no matter! Choreography only proceeds by leaps and bounds and takes little notice of how the scenes link together.

There is nothing more like a dream than a ballet, and this is the explanation of the peculiar pleasure afforded by this apparently frivolous type of spectacle. It offers, in one's waking moments, the enjoyment of phenomena that nocturnal fantasy traces on the canvas of sleep, a whole world of chimeras moving before your eyes. Infinite perspectives stretch to blue horizons, and mountains, plains, towns, castles, forests follow in rapid succession. Where only a moment ago the sea was unrolling its curling wreaths of foam, there is now a bed of flowers. Trees are transformed into pillars, lilies open out into marble urns, fountains spurt silvery streams into the blue-tinged foliage. Then everything crumbles, and you descend into the fiery depths of Hell or rise into the gilded glory of Paradise, with Bengal fire[1] scattering its strange glints of scarlet and green.

This moving panorama is inhabited by a population of painted, strutting figures, glittering in a shower of sequins, coming and going, seeking one another and then separating in a bizarre confusion. Rose-pink legs, glimpsed through a haze of tarlatan, extend like compasses. Flowers are thrown, kisses blown by finger tip, bodies arched and bent back, and there is a great deal of staring, pirouetting, cabrioling, grasping of waists, "*fromages*"[2] and fluffing up of skirts, all done without uttering a word.

---

[1] See No. 38, note 6.

[2] *Faire des fromages* was defined by Littré in his dictionary as a children's game in which little girls spin round quickly and sink to the ground, making their skirts puff out around them in the form of a round cheese. The theatrical usage relates to the similar effect on skirt and petticoats produced by a rapid turn.

While all this is going on, there comes from the orchestra, which has been providing the rhythmical accompaniment to the vision, the throb of double basses, the soaring strains of violins, the baying of horns, the sighing of oboes, the yapping of clarinets, the whistling of flutes, the thunderclaps of the big drum, the tinkling of the Turkish jingle, the clash of cymbals, and the lowing of saxhorns. The music chases the choreographic fancies through the perpetual din of the transformation scenes, and all the characters—princes, princesses, sylphides, shepherdesses and peasants—advance to the line of footlights that separate illusion from reality, smiling and making eyes at you, and swooning with semaphoric gestures like deaf mutes trying convulsively to speak.

By some evil spell or enchantment, these troubled apparitions, who shake at the slightest sound and go bounding on the springy boards, have been deprived of speech. Their graceful or plaintive poses give the impression that they are imploring an unseen deity to break the chains that bind their tongues. But fortunately the god remains unmoved, and we are spared a host of commonplaces, platitudes, bombast and grammatical faults.

In this kaleidoscopic swarm each spectator sees what he wants to see. It is like a sort of symphony of forms, colours and movement, in which the general meaning is indicated, but the details are left to be interpreted as one pleases, according to one's train of thought, preference or whim.

So every time a ballet is given with a ballerina of some renown, the few members of the elegant and intelligent set who have remained in Paris turn up, unless prevented by cannon fire and barricades,[3] for this type of entertainment that is at the same time so material and so idealised, so positive and so fantastic, so special and yet so universal.

Cerrito was greeted on her first entrance with a long salvo of applause. She is still voluptuous, a *"charmeresse"* to use that old word. Her plump and rounded arms unfold with exquisite grace, she is as light as ever and still has the same facility of covering the stage, and she has greatly improved in correctness of style since last year.

It is plain to see that she has been working under an intelligent teacher. Experience is now being added to her natural gifts. She had a great success in the *pas de la fascination* and the Spanish dance. Saint-Léon can claim his share in the bravos. He has strength, agility and a surprising elevation. He serves his partner with rare devotion, strength and self-effacement, acting as a living spring-board that doubles his ballerina's resources.

---

[3] The summer of 1848 had been marked by a series of disturbances as moderate and communist elements struggled to dominate the new Republic. In June the barricades went up again, and the ensuing uprising was harshly suppressed by General Cavaignac. These events were to be the prelude to the election, in December, of Prince Louis Napoleon as President.

The evening ended with a very abundant scented shower, a downpour of bouquets.

La Fille de marbre is to be followed by a ballet-divertissement entitled *Tartini, ou les Fleurs animées*. In it Saint-Léon will have the opportunity of appearing as a violinist as well as a dancer, for he has the reputation of possessing these two talents in equal measure. Tartini is the musician known for *The Devil's Sonata*, which he heard played in a dream by a cloven-footed Paganini seated at his bedside.[4]

La Presse, October 9th, 1848.
L:955.

---

[4] Giuseppe Tartini (1692–1770) was a brilliant virtuoso who, apart from composing the sonata for which he is famous, was responsible for a number of improvements to violin strings and bows.

53

Opéra: *La Vivandière*

La Vivandière, ballet-pantomime
in 1 act, ch. Saint-Léon, mus.
Pugni, f.p. October 20th, 1848.

Strictly speaking, *La Vivandière* is merely one of those divertissements or danced interludes that are performed between the acts of the opera in London. It affords Mme Fanny Cerrito an excuse to be charming, which is all that is required. However, we feel that in the presence of a Paris audience, the charming ballerina might be running the risk of losing some of her popularity if she were always to appear in ballets arranged with so little regard for the plot. In England and Italy this does not matter very much, but in France the choice of subject is very important.

The French are not artistic enough in the true sense of the term to be satisfied with the plastic content of poetry, painting, music and the dance. They also require a clear-cut meaning, a theme, a logical dramatic development, a moral, a clearly defined ending; few of us look at a picture, read a book, or listen to an aria purely for the beauty of its colour, language or sound, in short for its intrinsic charm. This is both a shortcoming and a merit. This attitude, which has produced one of the most rational dramatic literatures in the world, makes us at times very critical, particularly towards ballets and operas, which three times out of four fail or succeed because of the scenario or libretto and not because the music is good or bad, and since we regard frivolous things so seriously, the slightest fault in the arrangement of a divertissement makes us bristle with shock. If one dared, one would be invoking Aristotle in connection with a *cabriole* that is well or badly executed.

Speaking personally, we can enjoy watching a pretty dancer, however absurd the plot. If her foot is tiny and well arched, and rises on its *pointe* like an arrow, if her leg is dazzlingly pure in shape and moves voluptuously in its mist of muslin, if her arms form supple and flowing curves like the handles of Greek vases, if her smile bursts forth like a rose filled with pearls, we care little for anything else. The story might have no ending, no beginning, no middle, for all we care. The real, unique and eternal theme for a ballet is the dance itself. On this score *La Vivandière* would be an excellent ballet, but unfortunately more importance has been attached to the framework than to the execution, and since the ballerina had only a muted success, it would be as well, we think, to press on with the rehearsals of *Tartini*.

Here, in a few words, is the story of this divertissement. A young *vivandière* of some exotic nationality—Czech, Bohemian, Walachian or Magyar, to judge from the costumes—is courted by a nobleman and a bailiff, the one conceited, the other ridiculous. The girl has a lover, one of those postillions whose horn echoes so sweetly in the melodies of Schubert, and in an attempt to find herself a dowry she bestows inviting smiles on the baron and the greybeard, both of whom are burdened with shrewish and jealous wives. But do not imagine that her virtue is at risk from these two rivals. The *vivandières* of ballet can give the *rosières* of Salency[1] a head's start so far as virginity is concerned. In a night-time assignation, in which her quickness of movement and vivacious pirouettes save her from being kissed and grabbed round the waist, she succeeds in extracting, as tokens of their affection, a golden chain from the bailiff and a signet ring from the nobleman.

Then, by indulging in a somewhat dubious operation, popularly known as blackmail, she threatens to expose her admirers' infidelity to their wives on the strength of this indisputable evidence, unless they buy back the chain and the ring at their value to a trapped husband. The bailiff and the nobleman each throws the *vivandière* a purse, whose weight is proof that their wives must be terrible shrews. With her newfound wealth, the *vivandière* can now marry the postillion, an excellent match, and the happy event is celebrated with that assortment of *pas*—*cabrioles, mazurkas* and *redowas*—that are to the climax of a ballet what Bengal fire[2] is to the climax of a pantomime.

In the rôle of the *vivandière* Mme Cerrito is full of sweetness and roguish grace, tricking her two lovers with all the ease that such a light and supple ballerina can muster, grazing their noses with her spiralling pirouettes, and slipping from their grasp with the agility, rapidity and stealth of a grass snake. All her *pas* were much applauded, particularly the last one, a kind of polka that she dances with great spirit and verve.

Saint-Léon was also much applauded. Not for a long time has a genuine male dancer been seen in France. The marked disfavour into which male dancing has fallen has considerably reduced the share of the choreography assigned to men in ballet. Petipa himself, who is an elegant actor and a mime

---

[1] The ceremony of the *rosière* was first instituted in the fifth or sixth century by St. Médard, Bishop of Noyon, at his birthplace, Salency, a rose being awarded to the most virtuous girl in the village. The libretto of Grétry's *opéra-comique, La Rosière de Salency* (f.p. Fontainebleau, October 23rd, 1773) was based on this tradition.

[2] See No. 38, note 6.

full of fire and passion, seems to be apologising for his dancing by devoting himself exclusively to displaying his partner. Since Perrot retired, Saint-Léon is the only man who has dared to dance at the Opéra for the sake of dancing, and his success has been a surprise to everyone.

La Presse, October 23rd, 1848.
HAD, VI 7–9. L:957.

54

Opéra: *Le Violon du Diable*

Le Violon du Diable, ballet-
pantomime in 2 acts and 6 scenes,
ch. Saint-Léon, mus. Pugni, f.p.
January 19th, 1849.

In the White Horse Inn at Roscoff[1] Bretons are sitting at the tables, some playing cards and others emptying jugs of cider, while the young people dance to the sound of bagpipes.

The inn is full of laughter, light and warmth, but outside it is dark and pouring with rain and the wind is beating against the leaded window panes as if demanding entrance. A vivid flash, followed by a peal of thunder, dims the lights in the room, the house shudders to its foundations, and the door bursts open with a crash, as if shattered by the lightning. On the threshold stands a man, whose black garb highlights the sinister pallor of his complexion, leaning on a stick and sardonically surveying everything about him.

Nothing could be more ordinary than a traveller caught in a storm seeking shelter in an inn, and yet everyone is filled with fear. A feeling of unease weighs down on all present, and it is some minutes before the young men and girls come to their senses and begin dancing again.

Admittedly the stranger does not have a prepossessing appearance. His movements are strange, his gestures abrupt, and there is something super-natural about him. When he sneezes, the windows rattle and the glasses vibrate; when he shakes out his rain-sodden cloak before the fire, the cards of the players scatter like dead leaves in a gust of wind, and the fiddler collapses as the barrel he is standing on breaks apart.

"Who are you?" cries the frightened hostess.

"Doctor Matheus," comes the reply as the man produces a parchment diploma that looks very ancient and authentic.

Gradually the people recover their composure, and are beginning to forget the strange doctor when another visitor enters—a young man in the company

---

[1] Roscoff is a small port on the north coast of Brittany, about forty miles north-east of Brest.

of a servant carrying a valise and a violin case. Urbain, for that is his name, seems to be in a state of great agitation. He asks the hostess if a young girl of extraordinary beauty, travelling with her father, has yet arrived at the post house. The hostess shakes her head. Urbain is in despair, for he has lost track of the girl he loves.

The doctor, who has been silently observing him, approaches and says: "In your impatience you have overtaken the girl you are following. Wait for her here. She will soon arrive."

"How can you know that?"

"I have second sight. Hélène de Vardeck is charming, and you are right to love her."

At that very moment, the doctor's prediction is realised. The sound of carriage wheels is heard, and Hélène de Vardeck, in a smart travelling costume, enters with her father and the worthy Anselm, a Benedictine monk who is accompanying her. You have already guessed that the duality of the drama has now been established, and that this Father Anselm is the natural enemy of Doctor Matheus, for ballets and faery spectacles conform to the doctrines laid down by Zoroaster in the *Zend-Avesta*, which are entirely concerned with the struggle between Ormazd and Ahriman.[2] Here Anselm is the principle of good, and Matheus that of evil; they are light and darkness, the one a creature from Heaven, the other a denizen of Hell. Hélène de Vardeck represents the ideal, the controlling objective, Urbain is man's free will, and Father Anselm symbolises the obstacle to be overcome. They are, as you see, the same stock characters that have taken part, since the world began, in the mystery of the tree[3] and the study of good and evil. This drama has been played out for the past six thousand years with an appeal that never loses its freshness.

Hélène de Vardeck is not in love with Urbain. Her aristocratic looks have never rested on a humble virtuoso. She is unmoved by the triumphs he has just obtained at court, and to add to his misery, Urbain learns that she is about to marry a certain M. de Saint-Ybars, who is probably no relation of the playwright of the same name.[4]

Father Anselm advises Urbain to forget Hélène, but Matheus provides him with the means to obtain her. These means smack of witchcraft and the smell of sulphur, but what lover can ever hesitate?

---

[2] The *Zend-Avesta* is the sacred book of Iranian cults and myths, compiled in about the seventh century B.C., at the time of the prophet Zoroaster. Its commanding theme is the external struggle between good and evil, the two poles of existence, personified by Ormazd and Ahriman.

[3] The apple tree in the Garden of Eden.

[4] Saint-Ybars, the pseudonym of Isidore de Latour, was the author of a number of plays, including several tragedies that were produced at the Th. Français.

The doctor traces a circle on the floor with his stick. The storm increases in intensity, the clock strikes midnight, strange sounds of sighing and rustling are heard, odd forms take shape in dark corners, and worms and lemurs come slithering along the walls, sliding down the chimney and pouring out of the steps of the staircase, pallid, dishevelled, dressed in the grey skin of spiders with bat-like membranes. Matheus asks them for the rose that inspires love, the laurel that comes with fame, and the snake that charms.

These three ingredients are then cast into a cauldron, along with Urbain's violin, which, thanks to this concoction, will acquire a magic power and an irresistible appeal, and repeat the miracles of the lyres of Orpheus and Amphion.

Urbain cannot wait to put his instrument to the test, and never did an Amati or a Stradivarius, even under the bow of Paganini, produce such a pure and vibrant sound. Nor did the Cremona violin, from which Councillor Krespel drew such marvellous harmonies in the tale of Hoffmann, sing with more tenderness or passion.[5]

Hélène, clad in a white nightgown, holding a lamp like Psyche coming to gaze at the sleeping Cupid, appears at the top of the staircase, which she slowly descends, advancing, spell-bound, thrilled and fascinated, towards the virtuoso. Father Anselm, who is watching over her, orders her to return to her chamber, but before she leaves, she lets fall a ribbon, which Urbain picks up and places to his lips. In the language of ballet, the dropping of a rose or a ribbon before a young man is an eternal pledge, and so the violinist, who is not unfamiliar with choreographic usage, understands at once that Hélène de Vardeck loves him.

In his joy he has almost forgotten the existence of Doctor Matheus, who now reminds him with a sardonic smile of the service he has rendered and requests a little acknowledgment in return, as of right, for the doctor is not a man to do a good turn for nothing. He is very willing to be helpful and to place his power and skill at the disposal of friends, but on one little condition that he will reveal later, and you can guess what that will be.

From the inn at Roscoff we jump to the Château de Pouligrein, where Count Vardeck is giving a ball. Urbain arrives at this festivity, and M. de Vardeck, observing the looks that pass between his daughter and the virtuoso, announces Hélène's marriage with M. de Saint-Ybars. Hélène immediately objects and leaves the paternal roof to follow the man she loves (dance style).

Now we are at a picturesque little farm, the home of Hélène's cousin, Solange Cerdick. Emotionally exhausted, Hélène is asleep on a couch in a

---

[5] The Amati and Stradivari families were the most celebrated violin makers in the golden age between the sixteenth and eighteenth centuries. Councillor Krespel is a character in Hoffmann's tale *Rat Krespel*, which tells of a violin with a magical tone that causes the death of his daughter by forcing her to sing against her doctor's orders.

room the walls of which have been cut out to enable the spectator to see in from the outside. Peasants returning home from the fields walk silently by—in other words, they dance in whispers and on tip-toe for fear of waking the young lady.

When the peasants have gone, Doctor Matheus arrives, to Urbain's great embarrassment. The doctor is more sinister and sardonic than ever in spite of the sweet expression that he affects. In exchange for the magic violin that has enchanted Mlle de Vardeck, he demands Urbain's signature to a scrap of parchment, a bill of exchange payable at the expiration of eternity. "Who are you?" cries Urbain in terror. "My young friend, I am the Devil," replies the so-called Doctor Matheus, "and you must have been a fool not to have guessed it". A flash of lycopodium and a stamp on the floor sounding like the shoe of Mephistopheles' horse are proof that Doctor Matheus is no imposter.

"Come, if you do not want to sign, give me back the violin and we can treat our contract at an end. Look, the Baron de Saint-Ybars is already coming to claim his fiancée, who has fallen under a magic spell," says Doctor Matheus. Virtuously Urbain refuses, and a goblin smashes the violin into a thousand pieces. Father Anselm, appearing suddenly through the wall of the room in a *gloire*,[6] thwarts the Devil's plans. The sight of a phantom in the form of Hélène, following the Baron de Saint-Ybars, does not shake Urbain's resolve. He prefers to lose his sweetheart than to sacrifice his soul. Convinced of the purity of Urbain's feelings, Father Anselm approaches him and makes up for the loss of his violin by giving him another that contains a celestial spirit. Urbain loses no time in trying out the instrument, which emits heavenly sounds and puts to flight a charming little demon. From now on Urbain will be cured of his obsession with the Devil and will be master of the heart of Hélène, who throws herself into his arms.

Count Vardeck enters the farm demanding his daughter, but Father Anselm restrains him, pointing out that the second act has come to an end and he has objected long enough to the happiness of the lovers. And to avoid further argument he shows Count Vardeck, who is very proud of his lineage, letters of nobility that the King has just bestowed on the great violinist Urbain.

It only remains to celebrate the happiness of the lovers, which in opera is done by arias and in ballet by a *pas*. Everyone assembles in the ballroom of the Château de Pouligrein, where the divertissement begins.

The scenery depicts a splendid glass-house with arcades of strangely inter-twined trellis-work. Huge tubs of flowers—camellias, dahlias, fuschias and others—are arranged on the steps. Concealed in these flowers are dancers, who dart out to group themselves around a lively young man whose costume

[6] A flying platform, decorated to resemble a cluster of clouds, used in theatrical scenery for the descent and ascent of Gods and suchlike characters.

and watering can proclaim him to be the gardener. The scenery then changes to a luminous perspective, a dazzling landscape all golden and sparkling, with a deep blue horizon like the Edens of "Paradise" Brueghel,[7] where winged girls, balanced on large banana leaves, skim over the transparent waters of an azure lake. The gardener is borne to this fairylike spot, where the girls all dance madly, a few pretty supers rise up in a sort of apotheosis, and the curtain falls.

It is a charming scene, but without being inquisitive, one might well wonder what it means. Although we are well enough versed in the conventions of choreography to unravel the general meaning, this divertissement remained a mystery to us, and we can only quote the words of the scenario, which under the brief heading, *Explanation of the Divertissement*, includes the following two sentences:

"The flowers are rebelling against a gardener who holds them captive beneath the panes of a green-house, and carry him away to the kingdom of the dew."

"The handsome gardener finds favour with the ruler of this magic spot and becomes her husband."

It could not have been more positively put.

One of the most curious features of this ballet is the experience of hearing Saint-Léon play the violin, not as a dancing master scraping his *pochette*, but as a consummate virtuoso. That it becomes a magic instrument in his hands is quite believable.

This double talent cannot fail to have its effect on the box-office, for *Le Violon du Diable* has the appeal of both a concert and a ballet, the violin solos and the dances being of equal merit. Saint-Léon's fingers are as nimble as his legs.

Mme Fanny Cerrito dances like a Grace, if one may pay her an old-fashioned mythological compliment in the year fifty-two of the Republic, to use the red calendar,[8] but this does not prevent her from assuming a devilishly roguish expression in the *pas de lutin*.

In spite of a few forced incoherences, this ballet was a complete success.

La Presse, January 22nd, 1849.
L:975.

---

[7] See No. 29, note 16. Jan Brueghel the elder's painting of the Garden of Eden is in the Mauritshuis in The Hague.

[8] The Republican calendar, introduced in France during the Revolution, dated the years from September 22nd, 1792, the day after France was declared a republic. It was abandoned at the end of 1805.

55

The Ballet at Her Majesty's Theatre, London

The ballet has been somewhat neglected during the reign of Jenny Lind, neglected not by the management but by the public. Carlotta Grisi has never danced better than in *Electra*,[1] in which she plays the part of a star, but it is no longer fashionable to applaud ballerinas. The production was considered sufficiently immaterial, virginal and chaste, the gauzes of Jenny Lind made the pink tights look rather improper, and it was the height of taste among the ladies to get up and withdraw after an opera, leaving the ballet to the crude instincts of the gentlemen. This charming little example of hypocrisy, which has just been thought up, has fortunately stopped short at Jenny Lind.[2]

Ballets in London are not like those in Paris, where pantomime is given prominence. Over there the action is sacrificed, as it is in Italian opera. *Pas* follow one another, motivated with complete indifference to the plot, and no one takes much notice of anything implausible or impossible. The scenery, which is painted in very bold strokes and washed like the water-colours of Turner, Allom or Cattermole,[3] lacks the logical construction of the masterpieces of Séchan, Despléchin, Diéterle, Cambon and Thierry. Everything is garish, sparkling, shot with gold and silver, bejewelled, filled with flowers and fountains that are often real, illuminated by bright red or bluish lights in a

---

[1] *Electra, or the Lost Pleiade*, ballet in 5 scenes by Paul Taglioni, music by Pugni, f.p. Her Majesty's Theatre, London, April 17th, 1849.

[2] Jenny Lind had made her London début in 1847 amid scenes of extraordinary enthusiasm. As Benjamin Lumley put it in his *Reminiscences of the Opera*, "the ballet was no longer the 'town talk'. The ungrateful town could find tongue for one object—Jenny Lind."

[3] Joseph Mallord William Turner (1775–1851), Thomas Allom (1804–72), George Cattermole (1800–68). The English school of watercolour painters used a method of colour-washing a monochrome underpainting that was somewhat similar to tempera-oil technique.

taste that is partly reminiscent of the Lakeland[4] school, partly oriental, and in which the moonlit mists of Scotland often steal over a Turkish cupola or a rose garden of Djinnistan.[5]

The costumes are very fresh and light. There is a great deal of gauze, flowers, sequins and little golden trimmings. Among the girls of the corps de ballet, who on the whole are prettier than those of Paris, one can pick out several charming faces that would worthily grace a Keepsake or a Book of Beauty.[6]

A charming ballerina, who has been promised to us by the Opéra but has not yet crossed the Channel, is Rosati, who is very much liked in London. She is graceful and admirably formed, with shapely legs, small feet, a supple figure, and an easy smile. Her dancing has a playful character. She has something casual and bizarre, in the old meaning of the word.[7] Everything she does exudes joy, pleasure, happiness. There is no seeking after effect, and no apparent fatigue. She dances in the way that Alboni sings.[8] There is also a pretty creature who goes by the name of Marie Taglioni, and who is not too overwhelmed by her formidable name, the greatest in ballet, when her zeal does not outstrip her strength.[9]

We are also pleased to see one of our young compatriots, Mlle Estelle Aussandon, whose beauty can compare with all that is most exquisite, regular, rosy and diaphanous in white Albion, that swan's nest set in the ocean. She is greeted with applause every time she emerges, briefly, in an ensemble or a *pas de trois* to perform some *pas seul* or *écot*,[10] for she poses with much grace and elegance and dances in perfect time, her *pointes* are very clean, and she has the advantage that she never becomes flushed in rapid

[4] Gautier here uses the word *lackiste*, an adjective used to describe the English Lake poets.

[5] An allusion to the Persian classic, *Golestan* (The Rose Garden) by Sa'di (c. 1213–92). Djinnistan means the land of the Djinns. The term is also used by Heine in his essay, *Elementargeister* (Elemental Spirits), following the passage about Avalon: "You know Avalon, but the Persians know it too, and call it Djinnistan. It is the land of poetry."

[6] *The Keepsake* and *The Book of Beauty* were fashionable annuals that sold in large numbers in London at Christmastime. Lady Blessington edited *The Book of Beauty* from 1833 and *The Keepsake* from 1841.

[7] Carolina Rosati (1826–1905), an Italian ballerina of by then an established international reputation, was to be engaged at the Opéra from 1853 to 1859. *Bizarre* originally had the meaning of strikingly handsome and brave, before acquiring that of extravagantly eccentric.

[8] See No. 49, note 2.

[9] Marie Taglioni the younger (1833–91), daughter of Paul Taglioni and niece of the great Marie Taglioni. She had made her début at Her Majesty's Theatre, London, in 1847.

[10] See No. 46, note 3.

movements. No other dancer, not even Cerrito, displays arms that are more beautiful, more rounded, or more harmonious, and you know what a hindrance the arms can be while dancing, and more than one ballet-master would agree with Toinette[11] and want to cut them off. Let us hope that at the end of her engagement Mlle Estelle Aussandon will come to Paris, where a triple success of youth, beauty and talent will be awaiting her.

La Presse, June 4th, 1849.
L:997.

[11] In *La Malade imaginaire*. See No. 49, note 9. In the original the name is given as Roinon, clearly a printer's error.

56

Opéra: *La Filleule des fées*

La Filleule des fées, ballet-
pantomime in 3 acts and 7 scenes,
sc. Saint-Georges, ch. Perrot, mus.
Adam and A. de Saint-Julien, f.p.
October 8th, 1849.

A ballet is a serious thing, and must not be treated lightly. A tragedy, a drama or a comedy is usually created to be judged by one nation alone, and to understand all the beauties of a work of that nature, a thorough knowledge is required of the language in which it is written. There is no necessity for this in a ballet, which speaks in a silent language that can be understood by all. The first pantomime must have been performed the day after the confusion of tongues at the Tower of Babel.

People who were speaking to each other one day and no longer understood one another the next no doubt discovered this as a way of spending the evening before producing authors in their new dialects. The Utopian's dream of a universal language has been realised in the ballet. *La Sylphide* has been performed with equal success in the four corners of the earth. It has pleased the Esquimos, developed the taste of the Patagonians, and drawn only one criticism from the Papuans—that the Sylphide was not black. Practically none of the work's finer points escaped them. But go and play *Cinna* or *Mithridate*[1] to the Hottentots and see how much pleasure they get out of it.

Ballet is therefore the most synthetic, the most universal and the most humanly comprehensible work that can be undertaken. It is mimed poetry, dream made visible, the ideal rendered palpable, love translated into images, grace given rhythm, harmony condensed into shapes, music transmuted from sound to sight. It is a hymn without words to the rotation of the spheres and the movement of the worlds that Plato imagined to be muttering in space; a sacred procession recalling the motions of the stars whose significance, once

---

[1] Two classical tragedies in the repertory of the Comédie Française, *Cinna* by Pierre Corneille (f.p. 1640–41) and *Mithridate* by Jean Racine (f.p. Hôtel de Bourgogne, January 6th or 13th, 1673).

preserved by the mystagogues, has now been lost through the stupifying influence of civilisation. Too much care and attention cannot therefore be devoted to accomplishing a task that is so difficult and carries such a heavy responsibility.

This solemn introduction is not irrelevant, for in the ballet of *La Filleule des fées*, which is so remarkable from every point of view, M. de Saint-Georges has on two or three occasions breached the fundamental laws of choreography. This struck us to the quick, for M. de Saint-Georges has a classical talent. What will the pupils and underlings do if the great masters allow themselves such liberties! But let us not anticipate.

La Filleule des fées belongs, by its subject, to those great traditions that are as ancient as the world itself, full of mysterious and profound meaning, but which short-sighted pedants now downgrade to the level of fairy tales. We are speaking of those Manichean struggles between good and evil that for the past six hundred years have provided the duality of every drama—the gigantic contests between Ormazd and Ahriman recounted in the *Zend-Avesta*. The Izeds are not so disguised by the gold-starred veil of the fairies that we cannot sense their sparrow-hawk wings beneath the transparent gauze.[2] But here a sense of morality is superimposed on the cosmogonic features of the tale, in that all the misfortunes of the heroine derive from the fact that her father was ignorant of the rights of hospitality owed to a fairy disguised as an old woman—a profound lesson which also serves to teach and illustrate the principle of reversability, for it is not the father who is punished, but the daughter, according to the theory of the transmission of sins, a profound myth that inflicts joint responsibility on later generations.

The device employed by M. de Saint-Georges to illustrate these eternal truths is very simple. A daughter has just been born to a farmer, who is giving a feast to celebrate her baptism. One after the other, two old women knock at the door and are patronisingly invited to the table. A third arrives, even uglier, more toothless and sour-faced than the first two. She is not well received, particularly because her presence will increase the number of those at table to thirteen. M. de Saint-Georges, a man who by studying the ballet has acquired a wide knowledge of the occult and is above any petty Voltairean incredulities, acknowledges—as do Cardano, Agrippa, Father Kircher and Iamblicus[3]—the fatal significance of the number thirteen, a fearsome number in which a disorbited unit circles the twelve sidereal mansions. In such circumstances there would be no alternative but to go out and look for

---

[2] See No. 54, note 2. The Izeds appear in the *Zend-Avesta* as benevolent spirits of the second order who defeat the evil Devs.

[3] A clutch of philosophers: Gerolamo Cardano (1504–76), Agrippa (fl. first and second centuries), Father Athanasius Kircher (1602–80), Iamblicus (c.250–330).

the man whom Méry imagined as following the calling of "fourteenth man".[4] No such idea enters the head of the farmer, and the old crone is sent packing, muttering and making menacing gestures.

The other two old women cast off their rags and endow the baby with every possible gift, but the third, who is none other than the Wicked Fairy, prefers to wait until the child is fourteen before presenting gifts that will be worse than those that the Greeks take to their enemies[5]—the presents of the rejected Fairy Carabosse.

It is this Wicked Fairy who has caused M. de Saint-Georges, until today so consistent and correct, to commit a very serious crime against the poetry of ballet, a crime whose enormity, we are bound to say, the public did not seem to notice, and which had no ill effect on the success of the piece.

Instead of describing the fate that lies in store for young Isaure by means that are acceptable in choreography, the Wicked Fairy causes the following phrase to appear in red letters on a cloud:

Tremble for her,
I shall keep back my gifts until she is fifteen!

The only language permitted in ballet is that of signs. To replace this by the spoken word or an inscription destroys the entire harmony of the convention. It is as if someone had stuck a sculpted nose on to a painted portrait. It is a return to those Gothic images in which the painter, because he lacked the ability to draw facial expression, wrote the words he wanted a character to be saying on a scroll coming out of his mouth. No matter perhaps, but those two lines deprive *La Filleule des fées* of its universal character and bring it down to the level of a tragedy. You have to be a Frenchman to understand it.

Up to this point the Englishmen, Spaniards, Italians, Russians, Turks and Persians scattered throughout the house had followed the action perfectly. A young Chinese in the balcony, dressed in the European fashion with his black pigtail tucked into his cravat, who appeared to be following all the beauties of the work, from that moment assumed a puzzled and disappointed expression. That unfortunate red caption made the whole of *La Filleule des fées* unintelligible to him, in spite of M. de Saint-Georges' precaution of writing it in somewhat baroque French for the benefit of those who did not understand this beautiful language. This crime is perpetrated a second time. Addressing

---

[4] Joseph Méry (1797–1866), novelist, poet and journalist, was a close friend of Gautier, who broke his journey to Algiers in the summer of 1845 to stay with him at Marseilles.

[5]   *Equo ne credite, Teucri.*
    Quidquid id est, timeo Danaos et dona ferentis.
(Do not trust the horse, Trojans. Whatever it is, I fear the Greeks even when they bring gifts.) Virgil, *Aeneid*, ii, 48, talking of the Trojan horse, the celebrated subterfuge by which the Greeks conquered Troy.

the Pink and the White Fairies, the Wicked Fairy causes another explanatory caption to appear: "You have made her so beautiful that henceforth no man will be able to look on her without losing his reason." This phrase, which greatly puzzled the Englishmen, Spaniards, Italians, Russians, Turks and Persians, appeared to send the Chinese into a fit of despair.

Oh, Saint-Georges, by allowing yourself to use those inscriptions, did you not realise that you were making your ballet unplayable in Pekin, Timbuctu, Lahore, Stamboul and a thousand other places in the absence of a translation, which is often difficult to do and can alter the beauty of your ideas?

But let us not go on about this fault, which is a small flaw in a diamond, but continue with our account.

Isaure, who had no need of the fairies' gifts to be charming, grows up peacefully in her pretty cottage, a little nest of foliage and flowers, where she is loved, cherished and protected by Alain, her foster-brother and her childhood friend. Naturally, she does not love him. Woman, says the proverb, is like a shadow—she runs away from the man who is pursuing her, and pursues the man who is trying to avoid her. For Alain she feels friendship, which is far worse than hating him, for love can grow out of hate. All her affection is concentrated on a young Prince who lives in the castle whose towers pierce the sky on the backcloth.

The poor peasant boy is in despair, and wants to throw himself down the well. As he leans over the coping to carry out this intention, a little old woman shoots out of the black depths, offering protection for the price of a kiss.

The protection of the Wicked Fairy, for it is she, is not much use, for she is more adept at doing harm than good. Endowed by her with a magic power, Alain tries to frustrate the love of the Prince and Isaure, which has been championed by the Pink Fairy and the White Fairy. He continually seems on the point of finding happiness, but always it escapes him, for happiness cannot come through the power of evil.

Having set eyes on Isaure at the moment when her fifteenth birthday makes her fatal to the human mind, he goes mad and commits all manner of follies. The Prince only escapes a similar fate by being struck blind by the power of Isaure, who has been given a wand by the White Fairy, and prefers her lover to lose his sight than his mind. The spell will only be broken if the Prince, now as blind as Cupid with his eyes bandaged, can pick out his beloved from a bevy of fairies, sylphides, ondines and fantastic beauties who press around him, fondling him with embraces and caresses. At first somewhat troubled by these voluptuous advances, the Prince hesitates, but he soon picks out Isaure, whom he recognises by her heart beat.

The spell is broken; Alain recovers his reason and the Prince his sight, the Wicked Fairy's anger is spent, and the lovers celebrate their wedding in a temple of crystal, encrusted with carbuncles, sapphires, rubies and topazes, like some heavenly Jerusalem seen against a dazzling sun spinning like the wheel of a burning chariot. Everyone is happy except Alain, who looks on the apotheosis with an expression of sadness. Well, he will find consolation. That is always the way in the end.

La Filleule des fées is danced by Carlotta Grisi to choreography by Perrot—that says it all, a double perfection which forms a perfect circle, her execution matching the conception and the conception never eluding the execution, with harmony and grace going hand in hand—the very realisation of the balletic ideal! Perhaps never did the charming ballerina appear more correct, stronger or lighter than in *La Filleule des fées*. She seemed to be flying, as if held in the air by some invisible hand, the tip of her white satin slipper landing with no more sound than a snowflake. Her poses have such charm, and she appears so demure and naive in her enjoyment; she invests her entire rôle, played on the *pointes* virtually from one end to the other, with a poetic simplicity. What abandon she puts into her *tours de force*! What grace she brings to her strength! And how easily she achieves the impossible! A *pas* by Perrot danced by Carlotta—nothing more wonderful can be imagined. It is enough to make Terpsichore herself, if one is still allowed to mention that mythological name, forget her Greek. Muse though she be, she could not have done as much in her antique buskins than our young Italian in her little satin slippers.

Perrot, who is cast in the rôle of Alain, rendered it with that charming feeling that he alone possesses. There is no better actor-dancer than he, even when not dancing, for the *pas* in a ballet belong to the favoured lover, and in *La Filleule des fées* Perrot, who does not win his bride in the end, is reduced to the status of a comic opera bass. He is barely allowed a few little character steps of the waltz and the mazurka. The pleasure of lifting the heroine and making her float for a moment in a haze of gas-light four feet from the ground is reserved for him who might be called the tenor of the dance, Petipa, who performs this task admirably and with an ardent and chivalrous grace that is the secret of his continuing success.

The ensemble dances are arranged with unusual skill and care. It is obvious that the eye of a master has peered into every corner and left no detail to chance. No one can manipulate large numbers of dancers with more facility than Perrot. The whole crowd, from footlights to backcloth, is dancing, and each dancer is performing something pretty and well designed.

The Wicked Fairy is played with much elegance and majesty by Mlle Marquet the second,[6] as one says at the Opéra, where there are dynasties of beauty. We make no complaint about this innovation, for while wicked characters are usually allotted to the uglier dancers, evil in the guise of beauty is a kind of violation of mathematical principles, beauty being a quality associated with goodness.

[6] Mathilde Marquet, the second of three Marquet sisters who danced at the Opéra.

The scenery is very beautiful. To convince our readers, we have only to mention the names of MM. Cambon, Thierry and Despléchin, but that of the second act deserves a special description.

It represents a park, or rather a kind of Garden of Armida,[7] with a truly magical aspect. It is night, and the great trees spread their dark branches over vases mounted on pedestals and groups of statuary. Ramps, with curving balustrades, wind their way down from terraces on which clusters of flowers bend their heads. An ornamental pond spurts a jet of water high in the air that falls like a sparkling rain, and the moon casts its argent light through the foliage, vaporous and cloudy as an opal.

The moonbeams sparkle in the fountain, water pours from the urns, spirits that seem part mist and part woman dart across the pond, swans glide silently in their reflection, the light that just now was shining white on the marble breasts of the statues turns pink, and the sculpted nymphs seem to come to life at the touch of the fountain like so many Galatheas happy to escape from their Pygmalion. The whole scene shimmers and breaks into movement; white forms emerge from lilies, marble vases and clusters of jasmine, the mist disperses, and the swans lay their silver cloaks on the rose-bushes on the bank and turn into young dancers, forming a retinue for the Godchild of the Fairies.

Electric light makes this scene unbelievably effective. The illusion is complete; it is a real park with a real moon, and the walls of the theatre seem to have crumbled away to let in the rays of night.

This set does the greatest credit to M. Despléchin, who has created so much beautiful scenery. Nowhere can trees be found better drawn, conceived with such grandeur of style or a more poetic touch. M. Despléchin is one of the finest landscape painters in stage decoration; his work has nobility and sublimity, and his composition is admirable.

Concerning the music, we will say that it is by Adam, who wrote the delightful score of *Giselle*. For a ballet to have music by Adam is a rare piece of good fortune, for one can count on charming motifs, perfect rhythms, a graceful facility that never palls, an orchestration that is carefully constructed without being scholarly, rousing waltzes, and melodies for the dances that are light, tender, and full of passion and grace. And when the situation requires, he can also inject sentiment in what appears to have it least, pirouettes and *jetés battus*. Working with a collaborator, M. de Saint-Julien, seems to have detracted nothing from Adolphe Adam's usual qualities.

His new score is just as good as his earlier ones, our only complaint being that he slightly overdoes the use of drums and bells. There should be a good reason for such sounds, which do not mix well with those of other instru-

---

[7] In Torquato Tasso's *Jerusalem Delivered* the sorceress Armida seduces the Christian knight Rinaldo in her magic garden.

ments; for instance, the effect of a carillon or a clock striking is only charming when sparingly used.

La Filleule des fées, with Carlotta and Perrot, its prestigious moonlight and its charming music, will enjoy a long and fruitful success.

La Presse, October 15th, 1849.
L:1017.

57

Opéra: *Stella*

Stella, ou les Contrebandiers,
ballet-pantomime in 2 acts and 4
scenes, ch. Saint-Léon, mus.
Pugni, f.p. February 22nd, 1850.

It is sad to see such an ingenious mind as M. Roqueplan's neglecting the intellectual side of the ballets performed at his theatre. Ballet, more than any other work, has need of a poem or, if this word seems too ambitious, a story very clearly presented and understandable without effort. In ballet there can be no recourse to effects of literary style. The depiction of the action must never cease to be visual; verbal explanations are naturally forbidden in a mute drama; there can be no allusion to the past or the future; everything has to take place in the present, and the subject must be self-explanatory.

It is therefore no easy task to produce such a scenario. In England ballet is accepted as a framework for dances and divertissements—the dramatic side, presented in pantomime, counts for nothing there—but in France a meaning, even in the dance, is demanded; the lack of interest shown abroad in the substance of a ballet would never be allowed here, and M. Nestor Roqueplan, who is such a master of paradox, should not turn nonsense into a principle in the ballet. People in this country are too rational to admit that any pleasure can be derived from the rhythm and construction of the movements apart from interpolated *pas*. All the ballets danced by Mme Cerrito and Saint-Léon, which are composed of fragments from divertissements mixed up together, have this drawback. If only that charming ballerina's talent were deployed in a ballet that was really new, we should be much better off for it.

This is the story of *Stella*. That pretty title conceals a somewhat prosaic tale of customs men and smugglers. Stella rescues a poor devil who has lost his way in the mountains and has been seized as a revenue spy. She marries him to save him from the threatened death penalty, much as Esmeralda married Gringoire when he fell among thieves in the Cour des Miracles.[1]

Instead of taking advantage of the rights to which this sort of marriage entitles him, Gennaro, like a fool, thinks only of escaping, taking as his excuse a cousin named Luisella, whom he thinks he is in love with without quite knowing why. But just see what happens when, returning to his fiancée, he finds Stella established there as a servant and accepted as the friendly spirit of the household—not a benevolent and useful Trilby, but the most mischievous little imp that ever wriggled its way through an intrigue. She breaks the crockery, spills sauce over the black suit of the notary who has been summoned to draw up the marriage contract, and holds the candle so close to the document that it catches fire as he is reading it. In short she creates such havoc that the indignant family turns her out of the house for possessing the evil eye.

Gennaro and Luisella, who are only mildly in love with one another, are making their way to the church when Stella interrupts the procession and points to the engagement rings that she and the bridegroom had exchanged on the mountain. Gennaro had taken his off, but Stella had replaced it while he was asleep. It therefore has priority, and Luisella good-naturedly relinquishes her claim to her cousin, for whom she has only feelings of friendship, and since Petruccio, Stella's father, is now rich enough to give up smuggling and discovers that he is an old school friend of Gennaro's father, matters are arranged to everyone's satisfaction—that is to say, Gennaro, having left home with one lady on his arm, enters the church with another.

This ballet is mounted with a care and a splendour worthy of a better canvas. The costumes are picturesque and the sets are charming.

The first represents a mountain gorge, a narrow cleft of gigantic rocks which the sunrise begins to light up with a pink glow. It is not one of those sets that arouse applause, like a colonnade in perspective or the backcloth of an apotheosis, but it will be admired by artists and is worthy of being copied and preserved in a gallery.

The second is a view of the seaside near Naples, very light and delicate in tone. The third presents a rustic interior, rapidly drawn like a watercolour by Cattermole,[2] and the fourth takes us to Piedigrotta, the scene of a celebrated festival.[3] All these cloths, painted with spontaneity and luminous colouring,

---

[1] In Victor Hugo's novel *Notre Dame de Paris*, Esmeralda takes pity on the poet Gringoire, who has fallen into the hands of the truands and is being threatened with death because he has nothing on him worth stealing, and saves him by taking him away as her husband.

[2] See No. 55, note 3.

[3] The Festa di Piedigrotta was a popular Neapolitan festival, taking place each year on September 8th, and famous for the colourful national costumes of the local inhabitants. Instituted by Charles III in 1744, it was discontinued after the fall of the Bourbon dynasty in 1860.

evoke the transparent light of the open air, and are a credit to MM. Cambon and Thierry.

In the servant scene Mme Cerrito's sulky rebelliousness and provoking graces are enchanting. She knows exactly where to draw the line between comedy and buffoonery—the latter never goes down well at the Opéra—and how to remain charming when raising a laugh, a difficult thing for a woman to do. In the *tarantella* she displayed a brilliant vivacity and petulance; nothing could have been livelier, gayer, prettier, more loveable or more charming. This *pas*, in which Saint-Léon is an admirable partner, will become all the rage. In particular there is a moment that is delightfully graceful and original, when he places his foot against hers and they move together as one, as though joined at the toes.

Saint-Léon is intent, it seems, to join the ghost of Paul,[4] the former zephyr, in the flies. He rises so high that there is time to read the evening paper before he lands, and beneath his feet every plank of the stage becomes a springboard that propels him heavenwards. He fully deserves the epithet of "india-rubber man" that the English have given him, for no rubber ball ever bounced more lightly.

The Piedigrotta festival is a very entertaining sight with its merry tumult of water carriers, vendors of fried food, *aqua dolce* and maccaroni, and its *corricole* with their enormous red wheels cleaving the crowd and scattering people before them. The turbulence of Naples is very well rendered in this scene—a perpetual swarm of colours, accompanied by a racket of castanets, tambourines, clicking of heels, rattles and bells that would disperse the blackest melancholy. From footlights to backcloth everyone is jigging, coming together and parting, chasing one another and escaping, capering, jumping, stamping their feet and twisting and turning in a bustle of delirious activity.

La Presse, February 25th, 1850.
L:1043.

---

[4] Antoine Paul (1795–1871) was celebrated for his elevation and known as "Paul l'aérien". He danced at the Opéra from 1813 until his retirement in 1831.

58

Opéra: *Pâquerette*

Pâquerette, ballet-pantomime in 3
acts and 5 scenes, sc. Gautier, ch.
Saint-Léon, mus. Benoist, f.p.
January 15th, 1851.

Was it too much of an effort, seeing that we were ourself the author of
that immature narrative, dictated by the legs of Cerrito, that passes for
a ballet scenario, to go and look for a critic lurking in some dark corner to
discourse about the piece at length? If we had done so, we should have been
guilty of the worst form of modesty, modesty motivated by pride. M. de Jouy
was able to say all the good in the world about Rossini's music in *Guillaume
Tell*[1] without excessive pride, and no one thought any the worse of him for
that, so we do not see what need prevent us from admiring a charming
ballerina along with everyone else. The objection that we are the author of the
few lines that describe the scenes and the *pas* in which she displays her grace
does not seem valid, and we shall applaud her with the clearest conscience
just like the next man, even if our authorship has been announced. Is it really
necessary nowadays that everything should be signed, even the most inoffen-
sive rumour, even a ballet in which not a word is said and which will soon
provide the only occupation available to poets and writers of style?

All the *pas* of Cerrito and Saint-Léon—we can say this without a blush—
were received with enthusiastic bravos. In the first scene she is seen in a
charming peasant costume, all lace and satin and flowers, which has the merit
of being most adorably make-believe. In the second she wears male costume
with the greatest of ease and grace. In the third she appears in a haze of white

[1] Joseph-Etienne de Jouy (1764–1846) wrote the libretto for Rossini's opera
Guillaume Tell, in the foreword to which he fulsomely praised the music and dedicated his efforts to the composer.

gauze, shimmering with golden spangles. And in the fourth a smart Hungarian jacket clings tightly to her trim figure, and boots with resonant heels imprison her pretty feet. Is that not enough?

If one wanted to apply the principles of aesthetics to this choreography, if one was concerned with piercing a butterfly with a pin, it would be difficult to prove that all the precepts of Aristotle[2] were strictly observed in *Pâquerette*. Its action follows the ballerina, and in three bounds Cerrito is already far away. We start in French Flanders and finish in Hungary. Why Hungary? There seem to be two or three reasons for that, and none of them very good, but who will say, after seeing that *pas*, sparkling like a dragonfly waltzing in a sunbeam, that we were wrong to follow Cerrito to a town with a difficult spelling that perhaps no more exists than do Shakespeare's Bohemian seaports? She could just as well have asked for Lima or Timbuctu as the site of her *pas*, and we would have granted her wish. There is also a dream scene that may not be very logical, but is no worse than dreams in tragedies that have been hallowed by the Institut; instead of being declaimed in hexameters, it is composed of white tarlatan, pink tights, garlands of May lilies, gentle movements of pretty heads and beautifully rounded arms, and reeds that part to show charming smiles by the glow of an electric sun sprinkling a trail of rubies on a lake, all of which is much to be preferred.

The music is by M. Benoîst, a talented, modest man, whose services are much appreciated at the Opéra, where he is chorus master. It is clear, lively and rhythmical, as ballet music should be. It has an abundance of charming melodies for waltzes and quadrilles, and Paris will be dancing to the tunes in *Pâquerette* all winter long. However, do not dismiss M. Benoîst too quickly because he has the gift of melody, for there are two fugues in his score—yes, two fugues that are well structured and perfectly organised, something for difficult critics to get their teeth into.

The purely choreographic part has been carried out by M. Saint-Léon with rare skill and intelligence. The groups are well designed, the attitudes graceful, the evolutions of the corps de ballet well arranged—it is his masterpiece. As for the *pas*, we need say no more than that Saint-Léon was recalled twice during the evening with Cerrito. The success was complete.

To say that Cerrito danced in a charming manner is so banal that we quite lack the courage to do so, but we must mention her acting in the second act. She was born a dancer, but she has now become a mime, and a comic mime at that, which is very difficult at the Opéra. The amusing parts of the ballet were rendered by her with the greatest delicacy.

[2] The three unities which French classical tragedy had to observe in the seventeenth and eighteenth centuries were attributed to the Greek philosopher Aristotle (384–322 BC). The unity referred to here is that of place, which incidentally was not one of the precepts laid down by Aristotle.

Berthier[3] is very good in the rôle of Bridoux, and Coralli is a perfect successor to Elie, that fantastic comic mime, who has now retired.

La Presse, January 20th, 1851.
(Théâtre, 2nd. ed.,
pp. 331–333.) L:1097.

[3] Francisque Garnier Berthier (1813–75) specialised in comic rôles. He danced at the Opéra from 1847 to 1867 and from 1871 to 1874. He was *régisseur de la danse* from 1855 to 1867.

59

Opéra: Revival of *La Vivandière*

La Vivandière (see No. 53),
revived for the début of Mlle
Bogdanova, October 20th, 1851.

Mlle Nadezhda Bogdanova[1] comes to us from Russia, as her name alone implies. France has sent enough dancers to the Tsar for him to send one of his in return. This one is very delightful, and has perfected her training under Saint-Léon. And it is in a ballet by this master that she has made her début at the Opéra, in a rôle that Cerrito used to play. Such a choice, which for anyone else might have proved hazardous, has provided her with the means of success.

The young Russian dancer is small and well formed, endowed with elegantly shaped legs and dainty feet. Her expression is merry, refined, intelligent, with an arch and roguish touch that is a welcome change from the cold and stereotyped appearance of the run-of-the-mill dancer. She is remarkably nimble, rapid and precise. Everything she does is clean, full of life and correct; she darts and bounds hither and thither, then stops suddenly to turn back her head like a hunted gazelle, but one that knows full well it can never be caught. Judging her on the strength of this single ballet, and to borrow a musical term, Mlle Nadezhda will be more successful in *presto* than in *allegro*. She is an alert, light and lively dancer, possessing a grace that is impish rather than voluptuous, and capable, so long as she keeps within her nature, of cultivating a charming originality. She reminds us not of Elssler, Taglioni or Carlotta Grisi, but perhaps a little of Cerrito, which is doubtless due to the coaching of Saint-Léon. She also mimes with much intelligence and a keen feeling for a

---

[1] Nadezhda Bogdanova (1834–97) arrived in Paris with a recommendation from Fanny Elssler. She first studied under Mazilier, but it was Saint-Léon who prepared her for her Paris début. She danced at the Opéra from 1851 to 1855, and returned to Russia to become something of a national heroine for having been a forced expatriate during the Crimean War.

situation. Her success was not for a moment in doubt, and each one of her *pas* was rewarded with numerous bravos.

La Vivandière is one of those ballets conceived on the Italian and English model, with a complete lack of concern for the scenario, like all those of Saint-Léon. In spite of all its choreographic merits, it would benefit from a clearer and more coherent action. In France we apply a very strict aesthetic to ballets, and require them to be more motivated and logical than tragedies.

It is also our belief that *La Vivandière* would be more effective if everyone were not in a continual state of trepidation. It is as if the stage is red-hot and nobody can put his feet down for longer than a second. Such forced animation is fatiguing, and the eye longs to rest on a few tranquil groups. It is impossible to focus one's opera-glass for a moment to follow a dancer in that dizzy swarm, for they are always slipping away, swept along in the volubility of the movement. A few *pas sur place* would be a welcome change. It seems to us that Saint-Léon overdoes the use of space.

> *La Presse*, October 27th, 1851.
> L:1136.

60

Opéra: *Vert-Vert*

Vert-Vert, ballet-pantomime in 3
acts and 4 scenes, sc. de Leuven,
ch. Mazilier[1] and Saint-Léon, mus.
Deldevez and Tolbecque, f.p.
November 24th, 1851.

The subject of *Vert-Vert* has already been used on the stage in the form of a vaudeville,[2] in which Mlle Déjazet impersonated the twittering bird, the emerald-coloured hero of Gresset's poem.[3] We see hardly any connection between the vaudeville and the ballet, between a parrot and a smart, frisky young lad dressed in apple-green satin. It is simply a case of wanting to use a well-known label to arouse curiosity; that is quite obvious, and there can be no other explanation. Vert-Vert, the pious bird that in the course of flying from one convent to another becomes corrupted by picking up a vocabulary of swearwords from the bargemen on the Loire, offers no dramatic interest. Here it has been used merely as a symbol to suggest a young innocent sowing his wild oats and finally, angel though he is, kicking up the devil of a rumpus. Nothing of the original subject has been kept, so why lumber it with this ornithological title?

But all that is of no consequence in the light of the current vogue, introduced by Saint-Léon, for ballet-divertissements in the English or Italian manner, that is to say, lacking plan, continuity or logic, and unfolding before

---

[1] Mazilier had been released to accept an engagement in St. Petersburg, leaving *Vert-Vert*, on which he had been working for some time, unfinished. Saint-Léon revised the production and arranged the concluding ball scene.

[2] *Vert-Vert*, comedy-vaudeville in 3 scenes by de Leuven and Pittaud des Forges, f.p. Th. du Palais-Royal, March 15th, 1832. Virginie Déjazet (1798–1875) enjoyed an exceptionally long career as actress and theatre director, making her stage début at the age of seven and her last appearance a few months before she died.

[3] Jean-Baptiste-Louis Gresset (1709–77), poet and dramatist best known for his comic poem, *Ver-Vert*, recounting the adventures of a parrot flying from one convent to another.

one's eyes like the tumultuous and brilliant scenes of a muddled dream. We, however, hold the opposite view that no theatrical work has greater need than a ballet of a clear action that is well presented, well developed and never lost sight of, and is designed by a painter rather than a writer. The scenario of a ballet should be written in a series of outline sketches, like the illustrations by Retzsch for Goethe's *Faust* and Schiller's *Fridolin*.[4]

A convent cannot be presented on the stage of the Opéra, and nun's habits are too long for dancing. Moreover, all those little pieces of nonsense written in the eighteenth century by chubby *abbés* would be very much out of favour today when even the censorship[5] would pass their insipid impieties. So the funeral of Vert-Vert, who has died of a surfeit of sugared almonds, takes place in the apartment of the Queen's maids of honour. Looking comically sad and assuming poses of antique mourners, the girls all follow the crepe-covered cage in which the dead bird has been laid out on a bed of roses. It is to be buried in the garden at the foot of a myrtle tree where sings a nightingale: *Lugete Veneres Cupidinesque!*[6]

Who will take Vert-Vert's place now it is dead? Who will relieve the boredom of those long hours passed miserably under the stern supervision of their custodian, Mme de Navailles? This time it will not be a bird, but a slender good-looking boy with small feet and hands and a sweet and modest expression—the nephew of Mme de Navailles, who has no qualms in allow-ing this young chick, who will soon be growing claws and beak, into the cage. You only have to see his timid expression, with eyes hypocritically downcast, his reserve, his inhibited gestures, the walk imitated from his tutor, to understand the confidence that rather surprisingly Mme de Navailles has placed in him; you only have to see him hiding behind the skirts of Blanche, who has taken on the rôle of his protector, after every prank of the maids of honour, blushing at the slightest provocation. A poor love of a cherub still in the state of St. Agnes![7]

This innocence does not last long, thanks to the example and the talk of several bad lots among the pages who, taking no notice of the owl-like hootings of their warders, come to play hide and seek with the maids of honour behind the rose bushes. Quickly corrupted, Vert-Vert plies his tutor with drink, abducts Blanche in her petticoat and sets out on a round of the

---

[4] Moritz Retzsch (1779–1857).

[5] Censorship was in force in the French theatre at this time, all dramatic pieces having to be approved before being publicly performed. It was abolished in 1870.

[6] Grieve, ye Loves and Graces. See No. 18, note 2.

[7] St. Agnes, virgin and patron saint of girls. Refusing to marry, she was placed in a brothel, where the Roman youths left her untouched and the only client who took her was struck blind and then healed by her prayers. She was killed in one of the persecutions in the reign of the Emperor Diocletian.

taverns, in the course of which he encounters a troupe of strolling Italian players performing a harlequinade. Blanche arrives just in time to replace the leading dancer of the troupe who has sprained her foot, and performs a classical *pas* in the courtyard of the inn. M. Vert-Vert is carried away; he puts his arm round the girls' waists, fights a duel and generally behaves like a real-life dragoon. Not content with these escapades, he plans to lead his scalliwag companions in an invasion of the maids of honour's dormitory. With Blanche's connivance, he has acquired a key to this fortress, in which a long line of four-poster beds vanishes into the distance in a gallery lit by the dim glow of night-lights. The pages announce their arrival with a signal, at which each bed curtain is drawn aside to reveal first a pretty head, knowingly wide awake, then shoulder, arms, bosom, and finally the entire figure, and the bacchanalia begins. Vert-Vert forms them into couples and blesses them, and everyone dances so well that at the end there are grounds for fifty forced marriages.

All this is certainly nonsense, but the costumes are so fresh and charming, and copied with such delicacy from Eisen, Moreau and Baudouin[8] that the eye is captivated and the mind all-forgiving. It is the eighteenth century brought to life in all its piquancy and grace. The Opéra is to be congratulated for getting away from the costumes of carnival marquis and marquises that we have to be satisfied with in all other theatres. Mlle Plunkett is ravishing in the costume of a young gallant that might have been taken from Grelot's illustrations of *Angola* or *Les Matines de Cythère*.[9] But the main interest of the ballet was the début of Mlle Priora, a young Italian dancer whose reputation had aroused great expectations that were in no way disappointed.

Mlle Priora[10] is a girl of eighteen. She has regular and distinguished features such as might be found on an antique cameo. A forest of black hair and ebony eyebrows that appear to be etched with kohl like those of Moorish women

[8] Charles-Dominique-Joseph Eisen (1720–78), Jean-Michel Moreau (Moreau le jeune) (1741–1814), Pierre-Antoine Baudouin (1723–69), artists who flourished before the Revolution and were well-known through their prints of gently erotic scenes.

[9] This passage reads in the original "d'Angola, de Grelot, et des Matines de Cythère". The allusions are not at all clear. Angola may conceivably be an error, perhaps for Langlois: there were several artists of that name who flourished in the eighteenth century. Grelot may also be an error. There was an artist of that name, Guillaume-Joseph Grelot, but he worked in the previous century, and it seems more likely that Gautier was referring to Hubert Gravelot (1699–1773), who illustrated many books with drawings notable for their delicacy and fine draughtsmanship. *Les Matines de Cythère* probably refers to the painting by Antoine Watteau, *Le Voyage à Cythère*, now in the Louvre.

[10] Olimpia Priora (1831–1911), daughter of the ballet-master Egidio Priora, was said to have been fifteen when she made her Paris début but the date on her tomb in Florence suggests that she was twenty. She was engaged at the Opéra from 1851 to 1854.

give a wild touch to her beauty that is in sharp contrast to the pallid grace of ballerinas. Her arms are rounded, her waist supple, her legs strong and taut, her feet well arched. Her dancing is vigorous, precise and correct. In particular, she has an extraordinary elevation and rises very high without gathering force with her arms and solely by her spring. Her *entrechats* are beaten cleanly, and her *pointes* stab into the stage like arrow-heads. In *temps penchés* she never trembles; her body might be supported by a marble pillar. And she performs three turns as quickly and easily as a man. The originality of her style consists of a certain masculine vigour, tempered by an extreme flexibility in *renversées* and sequences of contrasting poses.

Her success was assured from her first *pas*, and grew act by act to finish with a real ovation. It is the most brilliant ballet début we have seen for a long time, and we think that the pleiad of Taglioni, Elssler, Carlotta Grisi and Cerrito is to be augmented by a new star. Yet, in spite of her success, the rôle of Blanche did not seem suitable for displaying all of Mlle Priora's resources. The charming, frothy fashions of the age of Louis XV do not go with the serious beauty and the energetic physique of this young Roman girl; powder is out of place on a medallion. We would have preferred to see her in a mythological ballet, or at least in the rôle of a Dalmatian, a Morlachian, a Spaniard or an Arab, which would have been more in keeping with her strong, pure features, her jet-black hair and her southern eyes.

As for Mlle Plunkett, she is born to wear powder, cuffs, a waistcoat of glazed taffeta, knee breeches with diamond buckles, silk stockings with golden wedges, and red heels. She belongs to the world of the pier-glass and the gouache fan. She was charming in the part of Vert-Vert. A daintier, more roguish, more arch, more prettily petulant little fellow cannot possibly be imagined.

Mlle Nadezhda Bogdanova, the graceful little Russian, danced a Hungarian *pas* with Fuchs with rousing verve and speed.

The management is to be congratulated for renovating the corps de ballet. It has been pruned of ugly dancers, and in default of talent, there are now at least fresh faces and pretty figures to look at.

La Presse, December 1st, 1851.
L:1143.

61

Opéra: Revival of *La Sylphide*

La Sylphide (see No. 17), revived
for the début of Mlle Priora,
March 5th, 1852.

It needs courage for a Director to attempt to revive a piece that, in bygone days and in other conditions, obtained a staggering success, and it takes still more for an artist to assume the leading rôle with which her predecessor was virtually identified. And indeed, no sooner were the playbills pasted on the columns in the Boulevard than the Gérontes[1] of public opinion began muttering on the asphalt and deciding that the said piece had been better staged in their younger days, and then, when the curtain rose, went out of their way to note everything that was not exactly as they had seen it before.

Then along came those with long memories, complacently pointing out that the flight is taken from right to left instead of from left to right, that a certain tree has been placed in the middle of the stage and not at the side, that a scene that used to be very effective has been cut, that another has been added, and so on, all of which, to us, first of all dates the speakers and secondly, is quite absurd, particularly as related to a ballet, which is a work of fantasy if ever there was one, and where respect for what are called the "great traditions" is totally pointless.

Being a confessed admirer of all things excellent and beautiful and having an aversion to pedantic hair-splitting, we are grateful to the Director for having staged *La Sylphide* and given it with Mlle Priora. Admittedly she has nothing in common with Mlle Taglioni, the creator of the part, but we must state, first of all, that she is very beautiful, which is good on the eyes, and secondly, that her dancing is adorably perfect, which is not to be deplored either. To this we shall add that she is full of nobility, simplicity, elegance and harmonious melancholy, and ask the old men who regret the past what more they want than the qualities mentioned above.

Here, in a few words, is the story of *La Sylphide*, the ravishing creation of poor Nourrit, who put together the scenario, and Schneitzhoeffer, who wrote

---

[1] Géronte, a ridiculous old man, a theatrical type established by Molière's *Le Médecin malgré lui* (1666) and *Les Fourberies de Scapin* (1671).

the music for it.[2] That was twenty years ago. A young Scotsman is loved by a Sylphide who draws him into the forest on his estate at the very moment he is about to marry the beautiful Effie, to whom he is betrothed. Some dreadful witches, real spoil-sports, persuade the young man to ensnare the spirit of the air in the woven folds of a magic scarf, which causes her to die immediately like those delicate necroptera that live and die in the space of a morning. As the young Scotsman is mourning the dying Sylphide clasped in his arms, the wedding procession of Effie, who is marrying his rival, is seen passing in the distance.

This very simple plot is the excuse for some most charming and effective choreography, providing Mlle Priora with poses of simple tender passion so graceful and moving that the devotees of the past could not resist joining the younger generation in lavishing the wildest applause on her, a pleasant alliance that gave Mlle Priora a fine and legitimate success.

Mlle Luigia Taglioni, who was playing the rôle of Effie, wanted to live up to her name and displayed great brilliance in her variation in the first act, so much so that several people could not understand why the Scotsman preferred Mlle Priora. There was something for everyone in this performance, every *pas* being greeted with applause. A young newcomer, Mlle Pougaud,[3] a pupil of Saint-Léon, turned up to reveal unusually beautiful shoulders and a real talent.

Mlle Quéniaux[4] once again allowed us to admire her lovely dark eyes and her elegant and correct dancing, M. Berthier made us laugh, and M. Saint-Léon amazed us.

Speaking of the Opéra, we cannot pass over in silence the dazzling début of Mlle Régina Forli[5] in *Le Violon du Diable*. This very young dancer revealed some precious qualities. She has the most expressive features, and we hope that her intelligent miming will remind the principal dancers of this very important aspect of their art. She played the scene of the second act in a remarkable way, and at last we understood the eternal enigma of woman: angel or demon?

La Presse, March 9th, 1852.
L:1163.

[2] Adolphe Nourrit (1802–39), principal tenor of the Opéra from 1831 to 1837, created the rôle of Robert in *Robert le Diable*, and shortly afterwards wrote the scenario for *La Sylphide*. He committed suicide in a fit of depression by throwing himself out of his hotel window in Naples. For Jean-Madeleine Schneitzhoeffer, see No. 36, note 5.

[3] Mlle Pougaud later married the dancer Mège, and appeared in a series of ballets by Saint-Léon at the Th. Italien in 1865–66.

[4] Constance Quéniaux (b. c. 1831) entered the corps de ballet of the Opéra in 1847 and was a minor soloist from 1853 to 1859.

[5] As Héloïse Guérinot she had played the rôle of Sarah as a child in the first act of *La Gipsy* in 1839.

62

Opéra: *Orfa*

Orfa, ballet-pantomime in 2 acts,
sc. Trianon, ch. Mazilier, mus.
Adam, f.p. December 29th, 1852.

The new ballet has the advantage of presenting a novel mythology and a geographical setting hitherto unknown at the Opéra, an advantage that is particularly welcome in the case of these wordless poems in which the idea can only be conveyed visually and plastically, and which ought to be composed by a series of outline drawings like Retzsch's illustrations for Goethe and Schiller.[1] Here we have Odin, wearing his golden helmet and with ravens perched on his shoulders to interpret the past and foretell the future; Thor, shouldering his blacksmith's hammer; Loki, breathing fire and flames; Fenrir, the god in wolf's form; Idun; Frigg; the Valkyries, pallid fiancées of the heroes, and all the fearsome deities of the wild Scandinavian Olympus drinking hydromel from human skulls beneath the branches of the ash tree Yggdrasil blanched by the eternal frost. While such figures may lack the serene beauty of ancient Greece, they possess a grandiose and mysterious originality that can be turned to good account for types and costumes. The region they inhabit, with its polar snow, aurora borealis, glaciers and ice fields, forests of pine and birch resembling concretions of quicksilver, vast white plains from which the antlers of buried moose rise like living bushes, bubbling geysers and volcanoes that the winter never extinguishes present the scene designer with new motifs and the opportunity to experiment with unexpected effects. The very choice of subject for *Orfa* reveals a scholar and a poet, for the ordinary run of ballet scenarists takes little note of the *Edda*[2] and the runes engraven on the rocks of Iceland. M. Henry Trianon[3] is both.

[1] See No. 60, note 4.

[2] The *Eddas* are a compilation of Icelandic writings, mostly dating from the thirteenth century but in part composed earlier, which provides the most comprehensive source of Teutonic mythology.

[3] Henry Trianon (b. 1811) was primarily a scholar, holding the post of librarian at Ste. Geneviève, and producing translations of Homer and Xenophon, but he became involved in theatrical affairs, not only as a writer, but also managerially, being

236

When the curtain rises, the stage represents the sparkling snow-covered countryside of the harsh poems of the North. At the back, smoke is rising from Hecla, the Icelandic Vesuvius, a white tripod-shaped peak to which Winter comes to warm its hands. The statue of the god Loki stands in the foreground, a monstrous barbaric idol sculpted in granite. Lodbrog and his fiancée Orfa arrive in a sleigh drawn by two frisky ponies at full speed across the ice, which is criss-crossed by the evolutions of skaters. Lodbrog is Petipa, and Orfa, as you have guessed, is Cerrito. Curled up in a conch shell, shivering gracefully in dazzling furs, less white than herself, made of swan's feathers and ermine, she appears like a northern Venus risen from the ice-bound sea.

Sleighs speed by, crossing one another, approaching and separating, propelled by confident skaters who smilingly lean down to their mistresses' cheeks to confide a secret or beg a kiss. The evolutions of the sleighs is followed by dancing, and the dancing by beer drinking. Cups brimming with froth are roisterously passed round as the future happiness of Lodbrog and Orfa is toasted around a flickering fire. An old man with a bald head and a long white beard approaches the revelling group to warm his shivering hands. The disrespectful and fierce young people push the old patriarch aside, but Lodbrog, who has been better brought up, greets him respectfully, offers him his seat and pours out a generous measure of liquor in his ox horn. A heavenly harmony fills the air like the vague sighs of an Aeolian harp. Everyone turns to look at the old man, but he has vanished. The priests of Loki come out of the temple to celebrate the wedding of Lodbrog and Orfa, but are interrupted by a series of bad omens; the sky darkens, there is a rumble of thunder, flames spurt from the crater of Hecla, avalanches crash down with a fearful roar, and the statue of the god shudders on its base and glows red. Lodbrog, enraged by this obstacle, draws his dagger and rushes at the granite giant, who disarms him and bending over the praying Orfa, seizes her in his arms and carries her away to his volcanic kingdom, like another Pluto abducting Proserpina.[4] The old man with the white beard reappears, and as a token of gratitude for having welcomed him, gives Lodbrog a golden arrow that will enable him to descend into the depths of Hecla's crater, break the spell of Loki and rescue his sweetheart, for the old man who was repulsed by the foolish young Icelanders is none other than great Odin himself, whose power is infinitely more potent than that of the minor deity of fire.

associated with Nestor Roqueplan in directing the Opéra-Comique from 1857 to 1859. He was the author of the libretti of two short operas produced at the Opéra; *Le Maître chanteur* (music by Limnander, 1853) and *Pantagruel* (music by Labarre, 1855).

[4] Proserpina was the Roman equivalent of the Greek goddess Persephone, daughter of Zeus by Demeter. Zeus promised her to Aidoneus (Pluto to the Romans), ruler of the Underworld, who surprised her as she was gathering flowers and carried her off.

In the second act we are in Loki's flamboyant palace in the heart of the mountain. An immense stairway leads down from the flies into his volcanic domain whose walls of crystal glitter with all the colours of the rainbow and reflections from seams of gold, silver, copper, all fused together. Rubies, sapphires, amethysts, and other marvellous subterranean outcrops sparkle like flowers amid a foliage of emeralds. The seven deadly sins, or if this expression sounds too Christian for a Scandinavian underworld, the seven passions, personified by the prettiest and ablest dancers of the Opéra, are nonchalantly grouped on the steps of the stairway, charged with the task of forcing Orfa to respond to Loki's love, for the god has little faith in his personal powers of seduction. Even with all the fire at his disposal he fears that he will never be able to melt the young girl's heart. The temptations begin with such sensuous grace and dazzling impetus that when Lodbrog arrives with his golden arrow, he is only just in time. Orfa is on the point of yielding, Gluttony is impelling her into the arms of Lust, and only a single step separates her from Loki's embrace. But at the touch of the magic arrow, all these fascinating apparitions vanish. Thwarted, Loki makes one final effort, enmeshing Orfa in a network of metallic foliage that conceals her from the view of the astonished Lodbrog, but Odin then makes his appearance, radiantly "covered with gold, from helmet to spur," driving Loki back into the depths of the earth, freeing Orfa from her cage and restoring her to the arms of her beloved, before returning to Valhalla, whose blue perspectives, peopled with groups of gods, stretch into the infinite distance, in the true apotheosis manner, glowing with the intense glare of electric light.

Mlle Cerrito dances the rôle of Orfa with the grace and sensuality of pose and attitude that we know so well. Petipa gives her perfect support, and Mlles Bogdanova, Louise Marquet, Taglioni and Robert form a charming retinue. The music is by Adam, which is to say that it is full of melody, rhythm and movement. As for the scenery, it suffices merely to name Cambon and Thierry. The success was complete, and M. Henry Trianon could not have made a happier début as a choreographic poet, in which he has found a most intelligent and able translator in M. Mazilier.

La Presse, January 3rd, 1853.
L:1201.

63

Th. Lyrique: *Le Lutin de la vallée*; *La Sténochorégraphie*

Le Lutin de la vallée, opera-ballet in 2 acts and 3 scenes, mus. E. Gautier, libr. Carré and Alboize, ch. Saint-Léon, f.p. January 22nd, 1853.

The Théâtre Lyrique has just enjoyed a real fashionable success with *Le Lutin de la vallée*, or to be more precise, with Saint-Léon and Mme Guy-Stéphan[1], for the piece is non-existent on its own and can be summed up in a few lines, but it provides a happy framework for dancing, which is all that is required of it.

Count Ulric has lost a medallion containing his mother's portrait, and has sworn to marry the girl who returns it to him. Katti, a poor dumb girl who has been brought up on the charity of Dame Bridget, has found the precious medallion, but the old lady steals it from her while she is asleep so that her own daughter can receive the "honest reward". The fraud would have passed undetected had it not been for the intervention of the sprite of the valley, a sprite like the Trilbies and the Ariels,[2] very benevolent, very virtuous, most worthy of the Prix Montyon,[3] and not at all like that malicious gang of gnomes, kobolds and dwarfs from the Emerald Isle who spend their time curdling basins of milk, tangling the manes of horses, sending skeins of wool rolling into distant corners, and frightening little girls in the woods by shaking their bells. Thanks to the sprite, who restores the stolen medallion,

---

[1] Marie Guy-Stéphan (1818–73) had danced briefly at the Opéra in 1840–41, and had then been engaged for several years in Madrid. She was to be engaged at the Opéra again later in the year.

[2] Trilby, the imp of Argyll, the central character in Charles Nodier's short novel of that name, published in 1822; Ariel, the spirit of the air in Shakespeare's *The Tempest*.

[3] Among the prizes founded by the philanthropist, the Baron de Montyon (1733–1820), was one for a virtuous deed by a poor Frenchman.

Katti becomes the wife of the powerful Count Ulric. If marriage seems a forced ending, remember that Katti is dumb, which is worth a dowry in itself, and what is more, can say such pretty things with her feet.

Having come to the end of the plot and done it justice by recording that it is neither long nor complicated, we reach the heart of the matter, which is the dancing.

A few years ago we saw Mme Guy-Stéphan in Madrid, at the Teatro del Circo, where she was all the rage. We remember that she danced a very original and fantastically effective *pas des miroirs* with such rare perfection that she would be well advised to repeat it in Paris, where it would be equally successful. We also admired her *pas de caractère*, and the *aficionadas* of Spanish dancing found that she had caught wonderfully the spirit of the *cachucha*, *bolero*, *zapateado* and *jota*, and God knows how jealously the Spaniards guard them! Since then we have often wondered why we have not seen this first class talent at the Opéra.

Among her natural qualities Mme Guy-Stéphan has an extraordinary lightness. She bounds from the stage like a rubber ball, alighting like a feather or a snowflake, her foot making no noise when it touches the ground, as if it were that of a shade or a sylphide, and her jumps are not marked by the heavy footfall of a dancer landing that brings to mind the marble heels of the Commander's statue.[4] Training has given her a clarity, a precision and a polish that are rarely seen nowadays when true dancing is neglected in favour of voluptuous attitudes and *poses penchées* in which the male dancer acts as a pivot and a springboard. Her *jetés battus* are cleanly beaten, her *pointes* firm, correct and unwavering, and she has remarkable elevation.

The *pas* which she dances in the moonlight with the sprite of the valley, who skips across the silvery foam of the waterfall, is ravishingly poetic. You could not wish for anything lighter, fresher, more suggestive of nocturnal mist, or more chastely caressing. As the girl stands poised in a dreamy attitude of innocence and love, the sprite bounds and flits about her, tracing circles of benevolent magic. It is charming. Only Saint-Léon could arrange such a *pas* and dance it, a man with a fine mind served by legs of steel, a man with a brain as well as legs, which are rarities even on their own.

The *madrileña*, danced by Mme Guy-Stéphan who wanted to display her classical and her romantic sides on the same evening, drew forth thunderous applause and was honoured with an encore. You could not find a more skilful summary of the diverse talents of Dolores Serral, Pepita Diaz, Guerrero, Espert, Oliva and Petra Cámara; no translation from Spanish into French could have been more intelligent, more accurate or more poetic. What Elssler did for the *cachucha*, Mme Guy-Stéphan has done for the *madrileña*. She

---

[4] See No. 28, note 8.

combines fire with correctness, modesty with passion, vivacity with wit. In short, she combines temperament with art.

We are certainly not guilty of indifference in such matters. We adore those passionate angry bursts, that crazy exuberance, that dreamy languor, that lascivious arching of the back, those arms that seem to be gathering up desires like a sheaf of flowers, that knee lifting a flounce of her dress as the dancer leans back as if dying of love—all that ardent, graceful and at the same time savage Andalusian poetry of tambourine, castanets, fan, sombrero and cape. Is there any greater admirer of the velvety brows and long eyes, kept lowered to open like a black cloud allowing a shaft of lightning to escape, of that sleep-walker and vampire of the dance, Petra Cámara, with her terrifying grace and her disturbing charm, as irresistible as death itself or as that Pedrina who, under the name of Inez de las Sierras, maddens Sergy and the French officers with love and terror in Nodier's charming story, whose prose we have translated into some unworthy verse?

> *Elle danse, morne bacchante,*
> *La cachucha sur un vieil air,*
> *D'un grâce si provocante,*
> *Qu'on la suivrait même en enfer.*
>
> *Ses cils palpitent sur ses joues*
> *Comme des ailes d'un oiseau noir,*
> *Et sa bouche arquée a des moues*
> *A mettre un saint à désespoir.*
>
> *Quand de sa jupe qui tournoie*
> *Elle soulève le volant,*
> *Sa jambe, sous le bas de soie,*
> *Prend des lueurs de marbre blanc.*
>
> *Elle se penche jusqu'à terre,*
> *Et sa main d'un geste coquet,*
> *Comme on fait des fleurs d'un parterre,*
> *Groupe les désirs en bouquet.*[5]

Mme Guy-Stéphan has introduced a polish, a correctness, a classical purity into that undisciplined, fiery and violent dance that in no way detracts from its character. Its native poetry is preserved intact, although arranged and distilled into a finer aroma. It is the *cachucha* made conscious of itself, improved, revised. The attitudes are more strongly delineated, the steps marked with a sharper rhythm. Inspiration has been refined by skill, nature rearranged through art. This *madrileña* will draw all Paris to the Théâtre Lyrique.

[5] Strophes 12 to 15 of Gautier's poem, *Inès de las Sierras*.

People will also want to hear the marvellous violin solo played by Saint-Léon, who, as everyone knows, is a remarkable virtuoso who can produce astonishing effects from his Guarnerius. The sprite, disguised as an old fiddler, begins by playing a simple popular tune, and when pressed to repeat it, introduces a mass of extraordinarily intricate imitations of farmyard noises. As the melody carries on unconcerned, the hen clucks, the cock crows, the turkey gobbles, the pig grunts, the donkey brays, the cow moos, the duck quacks, and way up in the sky the meadowlark sings its song to add a poetic touch to the rustic clamour. This musical joke demands prodigious skill in performance, and only a professional violinist would have the technique to attempt it. We would not have believed it possible for music to produce such a lifelike imitation; to be blunt, all the raucous din of the farmyard can be heard behind the persistent little tune.

This gives us a good opportunity to talk about a work that has been written by Saint-Léon, for the multiple skills of that old devil cover all things.

This work, which is appearing in instalments, is entitled *La Sténochorégraphie*, or, in other words, "the art of rapidly recording the dance". Until now the dance has had neither alphabet nor notation. Its fleeting steps leave no trace, and are handed on by a procedure so vague that the tradition quickly fades away. There is no record of a single ballet by Noverre, Gardel and other masters of the art. Saint-Léon intends to fill this unfortunate gap and offer a simple, easy and complete method of committing the entire choreographic part of a ballet to paper. With the aid of a few symbols he records all the *changements de pied* and all the component parts that make up the art of dancing. To write a step he makes use of five lines with four spaces in between. Above these five lines is a sixth line, representing the line of the shoulders. The spectator or reader is placed beneath the bottom line as if he were in the stalls of a theatre. In this manner the *pas* is shown as it is performed. The performer's right is the spectator's left, and vice versa, which avoids any transposition or disorientation.

Now that the lines have been drawn, we come to the symbols. Legs placed on the floor, turned out and straight are indicated by vertical strokes resting on the line and joined at the top by a thicker stroke representing the dancer's torso. The dancer's five positions are indicated by the corresponding numbers, 1, 2, 3, 4, 5. The position of the feet is marked by a dot placed alongside the number, the dot always indicating the front foot, and being placed to the right or left of the number according to whether the right or the left foot is in front.

Legs placed on the floor, turned out and bent are indicated in a similar manner, except that the two strokes are bent in an angle that approximates to the position, and so on. With each position and step given its own note, a ballet recorded in this way can be read like a musical score, and the choreographer can put his name to his work and claim it as his own property. It will be like a song book, but easier to read, which pupils should be made to study in the dance class and which will be of great help to them in practising their vocation.

To this manual of stenochoreography Saint-Léon has appended a history of the art and biographies of celebrated ballet-masters, past and present. A curious fact to be learnt from this interesting volume is that the first person to think of writing down the dance was a canon, Thoinot Arbeau, or rather Jehan Tabourot, his pen-name being an anagram, born in Dijon in 1509 and the author of a treatise on *Orchésographie*. Saint-Léon reproduces a *pas* written down by the worthy ecclesiastic, whose notation, although inadequate for current needs, is remarkable nonetheless and contains more than a fertile seed. Let us hope that the ingenious inventor of stenochoreography will now apply his invention to the charming *pas* and ballets that he composes and performs so perfectly, and thus rescue them from oblivion.

La Presse, February 1st, 1853.
(Section on Guy-Stéphan
reprinted in *L'Entr'acte*,
February 2nd, 1853.)
L:1208.

64

Opéra: Mathilde Besson in *La Fille mal gardée*, Régina Forli in *Giselle*

La Fille mal gardée, ballet-
pantomime in 2 acts and 3 scenes,
produced in its original version by
Dauberval in 1789, revised by
Aumer for the Opéra, f.p. there
November 17th, 1828, revived
February 23rd, 1853.
Giselle (see No. 27), revived
August 11th, 1852.

The passing of time sometimes imparts to a light work from another period an old-fashioned grace full of the charm of autumn colouring that is very pleasing both to the eye and the heart. *La Fille mal gardée* is a case in point. At the stage choreography has now reached, this ballet might be criticised for its ingenuous theme, its lack of spectacle and the childish simplicity of its dances bordering on the ridiculous, but it is nonetheless enjoyable and it is a pleasure to see it now and again, as it is to look again at the aquatints of Demarne and Carle Vernet.[1]

Fanny Elssler danced the rôle of the *fille mal gardée* three or four times with the most ingenuous good nature and divine rusticity.[2] She appeared like a Napaea[3] who has taken refuge in a farm to avoid the pursuit of Pan and is

[1] Jean-Louis Demarne (1754–1814) and Antoine-Charles Horace (more generally known as Carle) Vernet (1758–1836).

[2] Fanny Elssler first danced the rôle of Lise in Berlin on February 1st, 1832, at the age of twenty-one. Gautier's recollection, however, was of a maturer interpretation in Aumer's revised version for the Paris Opéra, in which she first appeared on September 15th, 1837.

[3] The Napaeae were a species of nymph that haunted woods and valleys.

condemned to churn the milk of Io, the cow with the eternally rosy udders, with her marble-white hands. From time to time she deigned to let a smile escape from her beautifully sculpted lips, the smile of a goddess who had no wish to conceal her divinity from her admirers. Then, when some character out of the commonest village pantomime entered the ramshackle room, she affected a purposeful activity as she churned her butter. Everyone understood her silent language, in which she announced with charming gestures: "For you I am the white nymph of ancient times, the silver-buskined Terpsichore, the young Greek Bacchus dipping his pink foot in the snows of Taygetus.[4] For them, however, I am merely Lise, the comely daughter in a short skirt, spinning and churning butter, although beneath my sleeves of grey-brown cloth, see, there are marble arms—the arms that the Venus de Milo lost."

That was how the great pagan ballerina played this rôle, in which, despite the apparent superficiality of the subject, she filled us with a strange sense of awe, like a sort of mysterious apprehension that comes on for no apparent reason, and which Heinrich Heine has described in his superb article, *The Gods in Exile*.[5] If Jupiter has become a merchant of rabbit pelts on a small island in the North Sea, if Bacchus is wearing the frock coat of a wine waiter and Mercury is in the export business disguised as a dealer in souls, then surely Venus, after dumping that imbecile of a knight, Tannhäuser, there, must be a dancer at the Opéra, having assumed the form and the name of Fanny Elssler—an entirely suitable occupation for a deity who has fallen from ancient Olympus. It was that same vague presentiment that sent shivers of voluptuous apprehension down our spine during this pleasant but silly little ballet, which the Goddess perfumed with the scent of ambrosia and illumined with a mythological glow. Behind the insipid figure of Lise, we sensed the holy mother of men and gods.

Mlle Mathilde Besson, a gentle creature with tiny feet, slender legs, a slim figure, the arms of a young girl, a fine delicate profile and nut-brown hair, does not give the rôle of Lise that deep, unfathomable, almost disturbing meaning that Fanny Elssler did, but she is the *fille mal gardée* to the life. She has everything the rôle requires; she is extremely young, naively coquettish, modestly forward and charmingly saucy, and her dancing is light and rapid. Even her nervousness served her in good stead, and although she did not die of stage fright on the evening of her début, as she threatened when she paid us a visit, her emotion was obvious to all and earned her general indulgence, particularly since she held herself firmly on her *pointes*, made no blunders and betrayed her anxieties only by the pallor of a fading rose.

---

[4] The mountain in Laconia on whose slopes the women of Sparta celebrated the orgies of Bacchus.

[5] Heine's essay had just been published in a French translation in the *Revue des Deux Mondes* (April 1st, 1853).

Berthier was comically gruff and pestering in the travesty rôle of Mother Simone, while M. Petit, whose name is a contradiction, for he is one of the tallest of mortals, played the imbecile who is carried into the sky by his umbrella like the drollest cardboard puppet. Every joint seemed held in place with a mere knot of thread, so incredible were the antics of which he delivered himself.

Giselle has been revived with Mlle Régina Forli. The scenery of this ballet is beginning to look threadbare. The sky needs another coat of paint, the yellow vine leaves have fallen and whirl around like the golden dust of Danzig brandy, and the castle is tottering on its rock and in danger of tumbling into the valley if not repaired with a few strokes of the brush. Giselle's roof has only two or three pieces of straw left, and what straw! as Janin[6] would say. The lake has almost run dry, its reeds now discoloured thongs, and the moonlight has lost its mystery. But all this is forgotten when the vivacious dancer darts rapidly out of the faded wings.

Mlle Régina Forli has charmingly delicate features, a complexion of opaline transparency, a frail and dainty figure, and a chaste and frothy style of dancing that enables her to tackle a rôle that Carlotta's interpretation has made almost impossible. Also, she mimes the scenes that require passion with great intelligence and sensitivity. We were delighted to see Petipa again, but we missed Mlle Adèle Dumilâtre, that beautiful queen of the shades, a moonbeam shaded in gauze, and Mlle Forster, who exuded such aristocratic charm as a huntswoman.

La Presse, April 25th, 1853.
L:1221.

---

[6] Jules Janin, dramatic critic of the *Journal des Débats*. See No. 6, note 6.

65

Th. du Gymnase: Petra Cámara

Dances inserted in *Les Folies
d'Espagne*, vaudeville by Lubize,
f.p. June 2nd, 1853.

When Petra Cámara[1] comes forward to the footlights and raises the lace of her mantilla and the dark fringe of her eyelashes, the very sun of Andalusia beats down on the stage. . . .

Her head voluptuously resting on the shoulder of her *majo*, who wraps his cape around her like a curtain, Petra circles the stage with that stamping, that *meneo*[2] of the Spanish dance that is quite impossible for our dancing automatons to imitate and can best be compared to curvets performed by a thoroughbred horse held on a tight rein. Then flinging aside her mantilla, she appears in all the fantastic splendour of her gypsy costume. To describe the colour of her dress would be quite impossible. Imagine a sparkling jumble of filigree buttons, folderols, silk tassels, ornaments, soutaches, fringes, embroidery and every fanciful decoration that a haberdasher gone wild might sew on to a bodice and basquine. Certain mule harnesses in which the animal's head completely disappears beneath a mass of feathers, embellishments and bells is the closest idea we can give of this glorious costume that will make muleteers, smugglers, knife-throwers, toreros, and all those weather-beaten fellows accustomed to smoke their cigarettes before the portals of the Caridad green with envy.[3] Goya,[4] the most Spanish of painters, could not have dressed a *maja* in a more characteristic fashion. It is coquettish, wild, crazy; it gleams,

[1] Petra Cámara was engaged at the Gymnase with a company of Spanish dancers for the months of June and July. Her partner was Manuel Guerrero.

[2] A characteristic shaking movement of the hips.

[3] The Caridad, the celebrated hospice established in Seville in 1578 and run by Sisters of Charity. Murillo painted a series of pictures for its chapel, and is buried there.

[4] Francisco de Goya (1746–1828), one of the greatest of all Spanish painters, whose enormous output has preserved the Spain of his time.

glitters, shimmers and dances before one's eyes, and even when the dancer is still, the flounces of her skirt seem to be beating *entrechats* and the colours of her trimmings indulging in a mad *cachucha*.

It is not easy to describe the *pas* which the playbill calls *Petra la Sevillana* in the chilly words of our hyperborean language. Mix salt, pepper and beetles in mercury and you will only have a word that is a very pale approximation to convey the fire, the delirium, the whirlwind, the vertigo that electrifies the house and sends it, together with its two thousand spectators, spinning like a séance table. Never has the intoxication of rhythm, the ecstasy of passion and cataleptic sensuality been taken to such extremes. When she is carried away, Petra is no longer simply a dancer, she is the very Pythia[5] of the dance. Beneath her satin slippers one can sense the shining golden tripod and the blue vapours of divine inspiration rising into the air.

Her bosom swells, her head is thrown back, her long eyes are closed, a nervous smile is hovering on her lips, her arms float about her like scarfs, and she seems to be in a trance, veiled, so to speak, in her own rapidity like a moth in the still centre of the gauze-like halo of its beating wings. Abandoning herself utterly to some divine dream, she is oblivious of the public, her only point of contact being the tip of her foot. In such moments she reminds us of the whirling dervishes of Pera, with their white eyes, their faces radiant with fragrance, their mouths half open in contemplation of the bliss of paradise. A mysterious bond links the Spanish dance and that of the Orient. The irresistible impetus of the rhythm produces similar results in Petra Cámara to those obtained by the whirlers; she enters a dizzy, spinning world, crossed with waves of sound and light, where the dance almost becomes a sacred exercise, a surrendering of the flesh to the pressure of the soul, an involuntary accompaniment to the dance of the spheres whose Platonist music has been rediscovered by Félicien David.[6]

To bring her back to reality, the *majos* shake clusters of castanets in her ears, and woken thus from her choreographic trance, she suddenly opens those black velvet eyelids of hers and releases a shaft of radiance that fills the house with a dazzling glow. Her supple body quivers, throbs and bounds forth, her hips sway, her torso arches back, her basquine flies about her in

---

[5] Pythia, the priestess of Apollo at Delphi who delivered the oracles. She was supposed to receive her inspiration from the sulphurous vapour that issued from a subterranean cavity, over which she sat on a three-legged stool, the tripod. When under this influence, her eyes sparkled, her hair stood on end and she went into convulsions as she spoke the words of the god.

[6] Félicien David was a musician greatly admired by Gautier, whose reference to Platonist music implies the idea of musical perfection, referring to Plato's theory that music echoes divine harmony, and that rhythm and melody imitate the movements of heavenly bodies and reflect the moral order of the universe. David was an active member of the Saint-Simonian community and wrote music for the cult's ceremonials. See also No. 46, note 7.

spite of the little leaden balls that weigh it down, and her legs, glimpsed through her transparent tights, take on the glow of marble. She skims along the footlights, raising the hem of her skirt as if to gather into it all the desires of the audience, and then shaking it scornfully, as if to show that she can sweep up many more; then her arms curve so as to suggest that she is clasping to her heart all the bouquets that are being thrown to her.

You may well think that the dance is now at an end, and that the gasping dancer is going to collapse, half dead, on a chair that someone will hurriedly bring to her in the wings, but not at all. A dozen *panderos* rattle their brass plates, buzzing around her like stinging flies attacking a deer, deafening her, intoxicating her, sending her out of her mind, to the accompanying clatter of all the castanets of the corps de ballet and the furious din of the orchestra in full flood, and here she is again, flying, spinning, leaping, blazing like a will-o'-the-wisp, a dreamy look in her eyes, her nostrils aquiver, her mouth illumined in a sparkling laugh, shaking her ivory crotales as a maenad of antiquity might shake her fir-cone thyrsus, before dropping to one knee, bending backwards so as to touch the floor with her shoulders, and rising again in a shower of roses, camellias and Parma violets.

What can one say of the *Rumbo* and the *Zandunga?* Here is Andalusian, gypsy and picaresque Spain condensed into a few steps, with much play of cape, fan, hat, tambourine and castanets, and all the coquetries of Triana, the Puerto de Córdoba, the Plaza de San Lucar.[6] It is like a ray of sunshine piercing through the fog, an orange in a pile of apples, the passion of the South coming to melt the ice of the North.

While Petra was dancing, we heard Spanish being spoken behind us, and were given the illusion that the embroidered elbow of a *majo's* jacket was brushing our sleeve, and imagined we were back in Seville, leaning over the balcony of a patio, watching a wild *gitana* with an amber necklace and a blue dress with white stars capering in the courtyard. A suspicion of the scent of jasmine entered our mind, and had anyone then told us we were at the Gymnase, we should certainly have been astonished.

La Presse, July 7th, 1853.
L:1227.

---

[7] According to a guide book of the time, Triana, a suburb of Seville, was "inhabited by smugglers, bull-fighters, gypsies and other picturesque rascals". The gypsy element there was responsible for a major development in Spanish dancing, for Triana was the birthplace of flamenco. The Puerto de Córdoba was one of the city gates. The Plaza de San Lucar (in the original text it appears as "*la plage* (sic) *de San Lucar*") seems to be a lapse of memory. Since Gautier is here referring to Seville, he probably meant the Plaza del Duque.

66

Opéra: *Aelia et Mysis*

Aelia et Mysis, ou l'Atellane,
ballet-pantomime in 2 acts, ch.
Mazilier, mus. Potier, f.p.
September 21st, 1853.

The cycle of romantic legends from which plots for ballets have been drawn these many years is on the point of being exhausted. The stories of Musäus, the brothers Grimm and Heinrich Heine have been widely used;[1] swan-women, elves, nixes, wilis, valkyries have brought their graceful sabbaths into the blue gleam of German moonlight. Have we not seen enough of those white apparitions, lifting the sheets of water lilies on slumbering lakes and revealing their blonde heads crowned with gladioli, arrowheads and forget-me-nots before the enchanted gaze of some noble knight who has lost his way in the magic forest? Have they not been dragged around enough, those nocturnal dancers, the hems of their dresses turned green from the moisture of damp grass that has felt the foot-prints of their fairy rounds? How many gallons of spirits of wine have been used for will-o'-the-wisps, how much lycopodium powder has gone up in demonic flames!

No doubt, it was all pleasantly funereal and sentimental in a Germanic way, but everything pales after a while, even the delightful poems of the North, and it was not a bad idea to hang up the blue gauze skirts, the emerald wings, the silver waist-bands and the coronets of acquatic plants, along with the magic horn of the ballads from across the Rhine.

---

[1] Three important figures in the preservation of traditional fairy tales. Johann Karl August Musäus (1735–87) wrote a number of fairy tales including *Libussa*, which was the inspiration for Perrot's ballet *Eoline*. Jacob and Wilhelm Grimm (1785–1863, 1786–1859) were the first to produce a scientific compilation of traditional fairy tales, which by this time had already become a classic. Heinrich Heine's survey of the "elemental spirits" of central Europe in his book *De l'Allemagne* was one of the sources that provided Gautier with the inspiration for *Giselle*.

After this *Walpurgisnacht,* it was generally felt there was a need for a Roman ballet. Why should not ballet too have its little classical revolution? And so hemlock, Lucretius, Lesbia's sparrow and Sappho now have their equivalent in mime and dance.[2]

At the rise of the curtain we are in Ostia, in the villa of the consul Messala. The stage represents an antique atrium. Trophies of African and Gallic arms hang from fluted columns painted vermilion and entwined with fronds of climbing plants. On the brown background of the Pompeian frescoes are painted graceful figures. The altar of the household gods, with its statuettes and images of ancestors, stands in one corner. It was a setting fit for a hero and his henchman to exchange tirades of alexandrines,[3] and we confess that the first sight of this interior set for a tragedy gave us quite a shock, from which we soon recovered when we realised that the characters of a ballet are, by happy necessity, deprived of the deadly gift of speech.

Reclining on an ivory bed, covered by a tiger skin, Aelia, the consul's daughter, seems prey to a deep melancholy and is responding to the antics of her jester Scurra with nothing more than a wan smile. This young patrician girl is bored, like some vapid English miss, even though she is to marry Tigranes, a handsome young Asiatic prince with a curled beard, bracelets on his wrists and pendants hanging from his ears, and wearing a robe bespangled with gold and precious stones. Perhaps that is what is distressing her, the poor child! However, this prince is very suitable and has the finest manners imaginable. In accordance with the traditions of his Negro race he has laid at the feet of the disdainful Aelia, as wedding gifts, a pile of caskets of ebony, sandalwood and cedar encrusted with mother-of-pearl, containing strings of pearls, diamond necklaces, tunics dyed with purple and crocus-yellow, silks woven with threads of gold, myrrh vases filled with the most precious perfumes of the Orient, and mirrors of polished metal in which Aelia can contemplate her beauty. But see how cold she is in the presence of these beautiful objects! It is not natural. Is the consul's daughter consumed with one of those strange passions that come from over-indulgence and caprice and were so common among the patrician beauties of the Roman Empire? Might she be secretely in love with Bathyllus, the effeminate dancer with the limp style of miming, or the gladiator Sergius, or some renowned zither player? That is what Scurra thinks, for he is a well informed scoundrel who remains a keen observer of the human passions while imbibing from

[2] Hemlock, the poison which Socrates took when he committed suicide. Lucretius and Sappho were Roman poets, who flourished in the first and sixth centuries B.C. respectively. Lesbia's sparrow was the subject of a poem by another first-century-B.C. Roman poet, Catullus (*Carm.* III; see No. 18, note 2).

[3] The verse form used in French classical tragedy.

amphoras. But it is neither Bathyllus nor Sergius, but the handsome poet Euclio, the laureate of the Capitoline Games, who is ousting the lord Tigranes in Aelia's affections, notwithstanding the latter's Persian sleeves and his title of future King of Pontus.

However, the betrothal ceremony is about to take place, and Aelia has to play a rôle in the *atellana*[4] that is to be performed for her wedding. If you are surprised that a patrician girl, the daughter of a consul, should mime alongside professional actors, let us remind you that the divine Nero did not disdain to appear on the stage and that Louis XIV danced *entrées de ballet* in Molière's interludes.[5] What a Roman Emperor and a King of France did not consider beneath them must surely be allowed to a young girl, especially if she is bored and looking for an excuse to dance.

A bell rings, and Euclio enters at the head of a procession of dancers, mimes, musicians with zithers, flutes and pipes, and other votaries of Dionysus bearing masks at shoulder height and carrying *thyrsi*.[6] Blame the scenario for this show of ancient erudition, for we are not so scholarly as that and have merely copied a line from the programme that might have been written by Dezobry between chapters of *Rome in the Century of Augustus*[7] instead of by a mere ballet scenarist.

At a gesture from Euclio the band withdraws. Mysis, a Thessalian dancer, seems to want to remain behind, her jealousy aroused by some suspicion, but the poet sends her to prepare herself quietly for the Gaditanian dance[8] she is to perform in the *atellana*.

Euclio and Aelia rehearse a very lively, passionate dance that amounts, in choreographic terms, to a declaration of love. Such a declaration seems a little premature to the proud patrician girl, who leads her Greek partner to the portraits of her ancestors whom she calls upon to witness what has happened. However, she is not so annoyed as she appears. Her breathing becomes heavy, her eyes begin to sparkle, her cheeks flush, and Master Euclio, who can recognise his good fortune when he sees it, realises that he is loved. Mysis too has no longer any doubts, for she has furtively returned; her suspicions

---

[4] The *Atellanae fabulae* were farces that took their name from the town of Atella, originally inhabited by the Oscans, situated between Naples and Capua.

[5] In the early part of his reign Louis XIV frequently danced in ballets produced at the Court. Among these were two comedies by Molière, *Le Mariage forcé* (f.p. January 29th, 1664) and *Les Amants magnifiques* (f.p. February 7th, 1670), in which he made his last appearance as a dancer.

[6] A *thyrsus* was a staff with a tip in the shape of a pine-cone, borne by Dionysus and his votaries.

[7] Louis-Charles Dezobry's *Rome au siècle d'Auguste*, published in Paris in 1835. The author's name was misspelt in the newspaper text as "Desroby".

[8] A dance originating from Gades, as the Romans called Cadiz.

have been confirmed, and she knows all. She threatens to tell Aelia's father unless Euclio will return with her to Thessaly after the *atellana* so that she can keep him in her power by her natural and magic charms, for she is something of a sorceress, as were all Thessalian women at that time.

Messala notices that his daughter is upset, but being a consular Géronte,[9] he puts it down to the unbridled movements of the dance. Prince Tigranes arrives with his colourfully dressed retinue, and the Superior of the Vestal Virgins approaches bearing the green branch of her office to preside over the betrothal. But oh, dreadful omen, there is no wine in the libation jars. Scurra has drunk it all. Let him be cast to the fishes! The poor devil, threatened with such a terrible punishment for his drunkenness, throws himself at the feet of the priestess, who extends a protective hand to him. The betrothal is then celebrated as best as it can be. Tigranes takes Aelia's hand and sits down by her side on a *biclinium*.[10]

Mysis then enters to dance the Gaditanian *pas* that Euclio had sent her away to study shortly before. The swaying of her hips and her expressive suppleness earn for the Thessalian girl the same compliment that Virgil paid to the Syrian hostess of that little cabaret where he loved to escape the heat of the day in the shade of the broad vines and the fig trees:

Crispum sub crotalo docta movere latus! [11]

a pentameter that proves how ancient is the genealogy of the *cachucha* and the castanets.

After the Gaditanian dance, Euclio announces the interlude, being preceded by heralds bearing diptychs with the inscription:

VENERIS NUPTIAE
Atellana.[12]

The curtains at the back of the stage part. Masses of volcanic rocks rise slowly from the ground. One of them opens, and out darts Scurra, dressed as Vulcan, black, begrimed, all aglitter with metallic dust, deformed and still limping from his fall from heaven on to the island of Lemnos. He summons the Cyclops, his underground workers, who come forth from their lairs striking the ground rhythmically with their golden hammers. Fed up with forging arms for heroes and tripods for the gods, Vulcan complains to Jupiter about the miserable life he leads. He wants to marry. Jupiter comes down from Heaven on an eagle and throws a handful of roses into the sea, from

---

[9] See No. 61, note 1.
[10] A reclining couch for two.
[11] See No. 5, note 2.
[12] The Nuptials of Venus.

which Venus soon emerges in a conch shell of mother-of-pearl, accompanied by Cupid and the Graces. Mythology, which is not so gallant as ballet, has Aphrodite born from the blood of the mutilated Coelus and the foam of the sea, not a very pleasant combination.

Aelia has left Prince Tigranes on her purple couch to go and play the part of Venus, who does not seem particularly keen on marrying Vulcan. To console her, Cupid introduces the god Mars, covered from head to foot in shining gold armour, which is removed by the Graces. Relieved of helmet, breast-plate and greaves, Mars partners Venus in such a suggestive *pas* that Prince Tigranes rises in a great rage and Mysis angrily reveals to Messala that his daughter and Euclio are lovers.

Aelia makes it quite plain that she will marry no one but the poet, a statement that arouses the fury of Messala to fever-pitch. The insolent actor could have been killed on the spot, but fortunately he is a better swimmer than a dancer, and he dives into the sea under a hail of stones and a shower of arrows loosed by Messala's lictors and Tigranes' archers. As for Mlle Aelia, she will go into a convent—in other words, she will become a Vestal Virgin.

The second act transports us to the *Hieron*[13] of Vesta in Rome, one of the most beautiful sets we have ever seen in the theatre. Never has the dense, fresh horror of a sacred wood been better rendered. The trees have taken on priestly attitudes, and the foliage seems to contain the secret of the mysteries. Through the dark greenery the marble temple shines with a white brilliance, like the back of the tunic of a goddess who is passing, veiled, through the fearsome shadows. The unquenchable flame flickers on the altar, like a star plucked out of the sky. We must congratulate M. Despléchin for this master-piece. Neither Poussin nor Bellel,[14] those great masters of landscape painting, could have produced a nobler composition. Here is antiquity in all its unfathomable mystery.

Her thoughts still dwelling on the poet Euclio, the novice Aelia shows little interest in becoming a pagan nun. Samnio, the Superior of the Vestal Virgins, exhorts her in vain to take the veil, and a formal order which Mysis brings from Messala has no greater effect. Aelia still resists. For Scurra's head has appeared above a long rectangular wall and a note has dropped at the girl's feet. Euclio is not dead, and is on his way to rescue his beloved. And indeed he is soon seen climbing down a rope ladder, followed by his friend, the jester. But unfortunately the wretched Mysis, who has seen everything, hacks down the ladder with her golden sickle and cuts off the lovers' means of escape.

Seizing the sacrificial knife, Euclio wants to kill Mysis, who bares her

---

[13] A holy place.

[14] Nicolas Poussin (1594–1665). Jean-Joseph-François Bellel (1816–98), a landscape artist much appreciated by Gautier.

breast. But in desperation Aelia cries out to the Thessalian, "Kill me, and your jealousy will be at an end and you will be able to save him". Moved by such devotion, Mysis takes Euclio and Scurra into the *sacellum*,[15] intending to facilitate their escape during the confusion of the *Lampteria*[16] that is about to be celebrated. In fact the priestesses are already arriving with their torches to perform the sacred dance. Mysis encourages them, and their wild evolutions become increasingly frenzied until it seems as if the very heavens are engaged in a drunken waltz with the stars against the dark blue background of the wood.

By some prophetic insight Samnio senses the presence of the intruders, and guided by the spirit of the chaste goddess, goes straight to the *sacellum* and discovers them. There is a peal of thunder, the fountains spout fire instead of water, and the temple glows red with the reflection of the flames.

Euclio and Scurra must now pay for their sacrilege with their lives. Aelia hesitates no longer. Knowing that the Vestals have the right of clemency, she puts on the veil and touches the poet and the jester with her sacred branch.

With her black eyebrows, her jet-black hair, and her statuesque profile, Mlle Priora is excellently cast as the young Roman girl, and with very good reason—she is herself young and a Roman, and her hair, as glossy as a raven's wing, frames a mask of pale marble. As a dancer, she has much elevation, and she mimes very expressively.

In the rôle of Mysis Mlle Guy-Stéphan showed remarkable suppleness, precision and agility, and proved that she is as much at home in the *danse noble* as she is in *pas de caractère*, and that she can do more than arch her back and play the castanets. In the ample white folds of the Vestal Virgin, Mlle Louise Marquet caught that rhythm and melody that are so much admired in the draperies of the Mnemosyne[17] in the Louvre. A sculptor could not have fashioned this minor character better.

Petipa mimed the character of Euclio with intelligence and passion, and Berthier is very funny as the antique jester.

M. Henri Potier's[18] music is lively, light, danceable, skilfully orchestrated,

---

[15] The sanctuary.

[16] The *Lampteria* was a festival celebrated at Pellene in Achaia in honour of Dionysus, who was given the additional name of *Lampter*, from the Greek word meaning "to shine". It took place at night, and the worshippers went to the Temple of Dionysus with lighted torches in their hands.

[17] Mnemosyne, or Memory, was the mother of the nine Muses by Zeus. However, Gautier is probably referring to the enormous statue of Melpomene, the Muse of tragedy, dating from the first century B.C. and originally in the Theatre of Pompey in Rome.

[18] Henri-Hippolyte Potier (1816–78), son of a well-known actor, and chorus master of the Opéra from 1850 to 1856, wrote a number of *opéras comiques* and ballads.

and entirely suitable for ballet, which calls for a wealth of rhythm and melody.

The success was complete, and M. Mazilier's name was announced amid applause.

La Presse, September 26th, 1853.
L:1241.

67

Th. Lyrique: *Le Danseur du roi*

Le Danseur du roi, opera-ballet in
2 acts and 3 scenes, mus. E.
Gautier, lib. Alboize, ch. Saint-
Léon, f.p. October 22nd, 1853.

Nothing could be more unbelievably absurd than this harmless piece, the first two acts of which could well be cut. Forgive me for saying so, but that would not be asking too much. It tells the story of one Cramoisi, a fanatical danceomane who can only be calmed down by great doses of ballet and being made to believe that he is the King's dancer.

The third scene, which is entirely choreographic, presents us with a bevy of fresh young *danseuses*, Mlles Lisereux, Nathan, Aranywáry, Lilienthal,[1] who comes from Berlin, and Mlle Yella, who comes from Vienna by way of England, all of whom dance a mass of *tarantellas, cracoviennes,* jigs, *cachuchas* with rousing vivacity.

Mlle Yella,[2] a very pretty girl with well shaped arms, a supple figure, and plump hips—*muy guapa y muy salada,*[3] as the Spaniards would say—mimed and danced a fiery bull-fighting *pas*, wielding the scarlet *muleta*[4] and the

---

[1] Julie Lisereux, Adèle Nathan, Emília Aranywáry, Rosalie Lilienthal. Aranywáry was later to dance in Budapest for a number of years, appearing there in *Giselle* and *Esmeralda.*

[2] Gabriele Yella (1835–57), an Austrian ballerina who came from a good family and adopted the name of Yella instead of dancing under her real name of von Spielmann. She made her début in Vienna in 1851, and also danced in Königsberg, Marienberg and Pest. Her greatest successes were in St. Petersburg, where she danced in 1854 and 1855 and played the rôle of Marguerite in Perrot's *Faust.*

[3] "Very dashing and very salty." See No. 70, note 6.

[4] The red cape used in the last stage of a bullfight.

cross-hilted sword of Chiclanero or Cúchares,[5] tantalising and playing with the bull, and then making the kill with a fine *estocada a vuela piés*.[6] Mlle Nathalie Fitzjames, who was admired at the Opéra some ten years ago, personified the art in its purely classical and traditional form amid all the swirling turmoil.

La Presse, October 31st, 1853.
L:1247.

---

[5] Two celebrated matadors of the time: Francisco Montes (1805–51), who was born in Chiclana, near Cadiz, and Francisco Arjona Herrera (1818–68), known as Cúchares.

[6] *Estocada a vuela piés*, as Gautier explained in Chapter 7 of his *Voyage en Espagne*, is the sword thrust, delivered with such rapidity that the bull receives it stationary and falls on to its front knees with the *espada* planted between its horns.

68

Opéra: Jovita

Jovita, ou les Boucaniers, ballet-
pantomime in 3 scenes, ch.
Mazilier, mus. Labarre, f.p.
November 11th, 1853.

Widow Jonas, who publishes the ballet programmes, should really claim damages from M. Mazilier, the all too intelligent author of *Jovita*, on the grounds that his work is capable of being understood on its own and that you do not have to be continually consulting the learned explanations in the scenario while watching it, as you do for some ballets that are as obscure as the coloured panels in the temples of Ipsambul and Karnac[1] and unintelligible unless you are a Champollion[2] of mime with the strength of several Saint-Léons. In *Jovita* the eye has no difficulty in following the story, and the green booklet remains virtually unopened on the red ledge of the box, almost its only function being to reveal the Hispano-Mexican names of the characters. That of Jovita, however, is announced on scrolls framed by flowers hanging from coconut palms in the plantation of Don José Cavallines, the father of the girl whose birthday the slaves are celebrating. This forest of exotic trees and rich vegetation glowing in a pinkish blue light, and providing shade for the elegant mansion with its jutting balconies, all studded with the flowers of the Mexican plantation, offers an original touch of local colour that does credit to M. Despléchin, an artist renowned for his quest for authenticity and research.

The slaves are hurriedly putting the finishing touches to the preparations for the fête before their young mistress wakes. While they are weaving garlands and arranging baskets of flowers, Jovita tiptoes down in a fresh morning dress of gauze that is more transparent than the veils of dawn. Each slave kneels before her, offering a bouquet, which she accepts as a token of

---

[1] Two of the greatest ancient Egyptian sites. Ipsambul is now generally known as Abu Simbel.

[2] Jean-François Champollion (1790–1832), who played the leading rôle in the decipherment of Egyptian hieroglyphics.

259

homage. The dancing is about to begin when the sound of a drum roll is heard. A platoon of soldiers forms up at the back of the stage, and two of the men unroll a notice bearing the following inscription: "The Viceroy offers a reward of two hundred ounces of gold to whoever rids Mexico of Zubillaga, the buccaneer chief who is committing new crimes every day". Every day without exception! What a tremendous rascal, what a hard-working villain he must be, not to rest from his life of crime on Sunday and Monday! And two hundred ounces of gold in exchange for the head of such a rogue as that! It is really a pittance considering the difficulty of catching him!

The officer in command of the detachment, Altamirano, is the fiancé, the *novio* of Jovita, but he has been so fully occupied with Zubillaga, the ferocious buccaneer, that he has forgotten that it is her birthday, a lapse of memory that earns him a pretty little pout and the threat that she might prefer Don Alvar as her partner. During this altercation, a strange figure comes on the scene, a combination of hermit and beggar, his head shrouded by a hood, his whole body concealed by his habit, and further disguised by a grey beard, walking with the aid of a long staff and carrying a beggar's bag on his back. He reads the offer of reward with a sardonic expression and sits down beneath the threatening words. Had you looked a little harder at this sort of Father Aubry,[3] whose false nose has seen better days, you would undoubtedly have noticed two bright yellow eyes shining out of his habit, eyes of a jaguar or a puma, too brilliant for such a hoary old man, and something of a suspicion would have entered your mind. In fact this old bundle of rags is none other than Zubillaga himself, who has come in disguise to scout out the ground for a daring exploit he is planning.

Altamirano, seeking to find favour in the eyes of Jovita's father, Don José Cavallines, who hopes for a more distinguished son-in-law than a junior officer of marines, wants to court danger by attacking Zubillaga in his lair. Such a brilliant deed would earn him promotion to captain. The old beggar listens to the plan and shakes his head. Zubillaga, he says, is a most dangerous man, and he would do better plunging his hand into a vipers' nest than penetrating his lair. However, if the young officer has made up his mind, he will lead him to the terrible buccaneer chief, for in the course of his travels he has discovered the whereabouts of the bandits' lair—a discovery of no danger to himself, since a beggar has nothing to fear from thieves.

With those words he moves off, but returns shortly afterwards carrying an enormous sword and pretending to be more twisted and bent than ever. When the small squad is marching off, however, he straightens himself up to his full height, pulls off his beard, throws back his hood, and with a flourish

---

[3] Probably a reference to Jean-Baptiste Aubry (1736–1809), a Benedictine scholar who wrote a number of books on philosophy. He endured great poverty when the monasteries were abolished.

of his rapier, reveals the well-known features of Zubillaga to everyone's terror. The soldiers are on the point of taking aim when they are surrounded by the buccaneers, who burst upon them from every side. "I promised to take you to Zubillaga, and I have kept my word," says the bandit with a laugh, and the looting of the plantation begins. Sacks of doubloons are carried out, chests are broken open, caskets pillaged, the slaves led away—those who are young and pretty, of course—and a placard is nailed up in the place of the other one, offering four hundred ounces of gold to whoever frees Lieutenant Altamirano.

The second scene represents the arid gorge where these mountain eagles have built their eyrie. Enormous rocks leaning against one another form the ramparts of a natural fortress whose moat is the blue valleys between the mountain ranges.

In this inaccessible spot the bandits snap their fingers at the Viceroy's troops, hiding their booty and holding their prisoners captive to extort enormous ransoms. By a stroke of good luck Jovita has escaped capture, having hidden beneath a pile of matting. She has now worked out a plan to kill Zubillaga. Disguised as a gypsy, with a tambourine and a dagger as weapons of seduction and revenge, she sets out on the rugged mountain path and arrives at the bandits' lair. At first her appearance arouses little suspicion among the fierce band, which she quickly captivates with her vivacious charms.

So voluptuously does she arch her back, giving sidelong glances with her black diamond-shaped pupils, so gracefully does she curve her lovely arms above her head, so rapidly does she rattle the brass plates of her *pandero*, and so smartly and dashingly does she handle the rifle, that Zubillaga is entranced and feels his tiger's heart beating beneath his buffalo skin to the great annoyance of Altamirano, who finds that Jovita is seducing the bandit all too well. But while she has been beating her tambourine with the tip of her foot and leaping and flitting about hither and thither, the so-called gypsy girl has discovered the whereabouts of the ammunition store. She lays a powder trail, and when the bandits assemble in the cave, sets light to it, having carefully spirited away Don José, Altamirano and the slaves. The flame reaches the gunpowder store, and a terrible explosion blows up the rocks, which fall on the heads of the brigands who are thus entrapped. Justice is done.

MM. Cambon and Thierry have shaped and sculpted those granular, flaking, crumbling rocks, roasted many times over by the sun, with a tonal strength, a thickness of texture and a truculent touch that is reminiscent of Salvator Rosa, Decamps and Guignet.[4] Stage design is not, in our opinion,

---

[4] Artists who specialised in painting wild mountain landscapes: the old master Salvator Rosa (1615–73), and two contemporary painters, Alexandre-Gabriel Decamps (1803–60) and Jean-Adrien Guignet (1816–54). Gautier wrote an article on one of Guignet's paintings in *Magasin Pittoresque*, June 1869.

sufficiently appreciated; such back-cloths stand comparison with the most esteemed paintings, and these gentlemen have brought their art to a high degree of perfection, even though the man in the street believes that it is all done by lighting and perspective. The effect of the exploding powder magazine and the collapse of the cavern was very successful, and does honour to M. Sacré[5], the former machinist of the Cirque.

The killing of the bandits concludes the melodrama, but not the choreography, and the third scene of the piece is devoted to the celebration of Jovita's triumph. She is brought to Mexico City, before the palace of the Viceroy, carried in a palanquin and escorted by a numerous and brilliant crowd in which Indian youths in feathers and shells mingle with the splendidly costumed Spanish Mexicans. The Viceroy presents Lieutenant Altamirano with his captain's commission, and his marriage with the brave Jovita is solemnly celebrated against a multitude of revolving suns.

Would it be pedantic to tell the author that he has confused buccaneers with bandits? Buccaneers were not bandits, they were men who hunted wild bulls and dried and smoked their meat for sale.[6] They had the reputation, it is true, of being fierce and unscrupulous rascals, quick on the draw with their carbines and cutlasses, but they were not brigands in the strict sense of men on the run and in open conflict with the police. But that, after all, is of little importance, and Jovita's exploit none the less commendable.

La Rosati was, one might say, unknown in Paris, although she had made an appearance at the Salle Ventadour in the opera-ballet, *La Tempesta*, when Mr. Lumley was manager.[7] Then she had injured her wing or her foot on making her first entrance, and was unable to take flight freely. This time no accident interfered with the ballerina's success, and on the boards of the Opéra Jovita found no projecting nail, nothing in fact but the petals of roses and camellias.

La Rosati—let us say so at once, for the thing is becoming a rarity—is an excellent mime, reminding us of Elssler by the expressive mobility of her features, the precision of her gestures, and the correctness of her attitudes. Her miming is clear, lively, impassioned, and always easily intelligible; she knows how to make her thoughts visible, her expression conveying at once what is passing through her mind. As for her person, she is an Italian in every

[5] Victor Sacré was chief machinist at the Opéra from 1847 to 1872.

[6] The word buccaneer (*boucanier*) was applied in the mid-eighteenth century to French hunters on the island of Saint-Domingue, and it is this meaning that Gautier is referring to, not the more general meaning of a pirate.

[7] Benjamin Lumley, who was manager of Her Majesty's Theatre in London from 1842 until 1858, was briefly director of the Théâtre Italien in Paris, where Rosati made her Paris début as Ariele in Halévy's opera, *La Tempesta*. At the first performance she caught her foot on a trap and badly bruised her knee in falling. The opera was not a success, being performed only eight times.

Petra Cámara. (*Illustrated London News*, July 26th, 1851.)

Arthur Saint-Léon and Marie Guy-Stéphan in *Le Lutin de la vallée*. Lithograph by A.F.

LEFT: Josefa Vargas dancing the *Madrileña*. Lithograph by August Off.

BELOW: Manuela Perea, la Nena, and her company. (*Illustrated London News*, November 4th, 1854.)

Orfa, Act I, Cerrito's entrance in the sleigh. (*L'Illustration*, January 8th, 1853.)

Aelia et Mysis, Act II. (*Illustrated London News*, October 1st, 1853.)

Arthur Saint-Léon in *Le Danseur du roi*.

Carolina Rosati in *Jovita*.
Water-colour by Bertrand.

Louis Mérante and Fanny Cerrito in the *valse magnétique* in *Gemma*. Lithograph from a drawing by Prudent LeRay, from a music title.

Caterina Beretta as Autumn in the ballet in *Les Vêpres siciliennes*. Anonymous lithograph, from a music title.

Amalia Ferraris. Anonymous lithograph.

Sacountala, Act I. The *pas de deux* by Amalia Ferraris and Lucien Petipa in the forest scene. Engraving by H. Linton. (*Le Monde illustré*, July 24th, 1858.)

Sacountala, Act II.

Théophile Gautier demonstrating steps to Amalia Ferraris for his ballet *Sacountala*. Caricature by Cham. (*Le Charivari*, August 1st, 1858.)

Amalia Ferraris and Lucien Petipa in *Sacountala*. Caricature by Marcelin. (*Le Monde Illustré*, October 9th, 1858.)

Théophile Gautier and Alexandre Dumas *fils* meet in St. Petersburg. Caricature by Cham. (*Journal Amusant*, October 16th, 1858.)

НА БОЛЬШОМЪ ТЕАТРѢ.

Спектакль № 22-й.

Въ Четвергъ, 6-го Ноября,

ПРИДВОРНЫМИ БАЛЕТНЫМИ АРТИСТАМИ ПРЕДСТАВЛЕНО БУДЕТЪ:

для 2-го дебюта Г-жи ФЕРРАРИСЪ, первой

танцовщицы парижскаго Опернаго Театра,

во второй разъ:

ЭОЛИНА,
ИЛИ
ДРІАДА.

Большой фантастическій балетъ въ 4-хъ дѣйствіяхъ и 5-ти картинахъ, соч. балетмейстера Г. Перро; новая музыка соч Г. Пуни; новыя декораціи: 1-й картины: Рудники — Г. Рол лера, 2-й картины: Садъ и Замокъ—Г. Шишкова (по рисунку Г. Роллера), 3-й картины: Спальня — Г. Чулкина (по рисунку Г. Роллера); 4-й картины: Лѣсъ — Г. Вагнера; 5-й картины 1-я декорація: Залъ – Г. Роллера; 2-я декорація: Горящій лѣсъ и 3-я декорація: Апотеозъ — Г. Вагнера; фигуры, писанныя на декораціяхъ Г. Егорова 1; новые костюмы (мужскіе) Г. Кальвера, (женскіе) Г. Столярова; скульптурныя вещи Г. Гаврилова; машины Г. Роллера; освѣщеніе, производимое химическими препаратами, Г. Шишко.

Роль ЭОЛИНЫ будетъ играть Г-жа ФЕРРАРИСЪ.

Playbill for the St Petersburg production of *Eoline*.

Emma Livry in *Le Papillon*. Statuette by Jean-Auguste Barre. Photograph by Felix Fonteyn.

RIGHT: Martha Muravieva as Néméa in *Néméa*. Photograph by Disdéri.

BELOW LEFT: Louis Mérante as Count Moldor in *Néméa*. Photograph by Disdéri.

BELOW RIGHT: Eugénie Fiocre as Cupid in *Néméa*. Photograph by Disdéri.

ABOVE LEFT: Léontine Beaugrand in *Le Papillon*. Photograph by Disdéri.

ABOVE RIGHT: Eugénie Fiocre as Fenella in *La Muette de Portici*. Photograph by Reutlinger.

LEFT: Adèle Grantzow.

Caricatures by Marcelin of *Le Roi d'Yvetot*. (*La Vie Parisienne*, January 6th, 1866.)

Guglielmina Salvioni as Naïla in *La Source*.

Louis Mérante as Djemil in *La Source*.

La Source, Act III, Scene II, with Salvioni and Mérante and, reclining against rocks, Eugénie Fiocre. From a music title.

The roller-skating ballet in the 1869 revival of *Le Prophète*, led by Elliot and Frederika. Caricature by Hadol. (*La Vie Parisienne*, July 17th, 1869.)

Giuseppina Bozzacchi, the first Swanilda in *Coppélia*. Photograph by Reutlinger.

sense of the word: abundant black hair, black eyes, black eyebrows, an olive complexion that whitens in a strong light, and a certain savour of antiquity in the sinews of her neck and the full, firm lines of her bosom and arms; her legs, which are somewhat sturdily built, end in small, sensitive feet, well made and well arched, with delicate ankles and toes of steel that, in *temps de pointe*, pierce the ground like javelins. And she has a sort of robust, vivacious elegance that bears no resemblance to the arch graces and mincing airs of the conventional ballet-trained dancer. Her dancing does not have much elevation, but all she does is quick and precise, and rendered with a sure touch and faultless technique. Her *pas* in the first scene, which is related in style to the *Jota* and the *Cachucha*, includes two or three very difficult movements that are excellently performed, while the *pas de fusil*, consisting mainly of a series of contrasting poses and attitudes, gave her a good opportunity to reveal her speed and precision.

In the very pretty, very captivating and very brilliant *pas du tambour de basque*, we would like to have seen more *brio* and bustle. She was not quite at her ease when handling the tambourine, and should have taken a few lessons from the prodigious *pandero* players of the Cirque.[8] A dancer as agile and sensitive to rhythm as she should have flashed like lightning amid the tornado of sound, but the *pas*, such as it is, gave pleasure none the less, and the purely Spanish disappointment which we express was not shared by the public. You have to have seen the *pandero* vibrating in the hands of a *gitana* from Albaicín or the Barrio[9] to appreciate fully what we are saying. La Rosati met with the most gratifying reception from the Parisian public, and was recalled with cheers after the fall of the curtain.

We must also mention a very pretty comic dance interspersed with kicks, performed with great deliberation by Mme Dominique and Berthier, that was honoured with an encore. Mlle Mathilde Besson, the pretty *"fille mal gardée,"* is a very golden blonde for a Mexican girl, but no one will criticise her for not looking the part when she dances with childlike grace, looking like a head by Greuze against a background of jam-roses and nopals. Petipa, as Zubillaga, was as ferocious as one could expect from a man accustomed to Prince Charming rôles, and as for Petit, he is quite the tallest mortal in existence, and played his rôle of a grotesque buccaneer with movements of a semaphore gone mad.

[8] The *pandéristes aragonais*—there were two of them—made their first appearance at the Cirque Napoléon in the Boulevard des Filles de Calvaire on January 8th, 1853. "Their number is indescribable," wrote *L'Entr'acte* two days later. "They dance while accompanying themselves on the tambourine, which they smite not only with their fingers, but with their heads, elbows, knees and feet, and their movements have such rapidity that the eye can hardly follow them." They gave their last performance there on March 3rd.

[9] Respectively the gypsy quarters of Granada and Seville. For the Barrio de Triana, see No. 65, note 7.

The music of *Jovita* is by M. Labarre,[10] a great virtuoso on the harp and a distinguished maestro. M. Labarre has lavished more care on this work than is usual, for ballet music is generally despised by composers. Is this because it demands melody and rhythm, qualities now scorned by scholars? Personally, we are very fond of the unpretentious symphony that instils a dreamlike quality into the ballet it accompanies. M. Labarre, who seems to be of the same opinion as ourselves, has composed a score for *Jovita* that is elegant, rich in motifs and perfectly orchestrated. There are many operas for which one could not say as much.

La Presse, November 15th, 1853.
L:1249.

[10] Théodore Labarre (1805–70), harpist, composer and conductor, wrote his first ballet score for Filippo Taglioni's *La Révolte au sérail* (Opéra, f.p. December 4th, 1833), hurriedly composed but containing some effective passages. It was twenty years before he returned to this field to write the music for *Jovita*, which was to be followed by *La Fonti, Graziosa* and *Le Roi d'Yvetot*.

69

Opéra: *Gemma*

Gemma, ballet in 2 acts and 5
scenes, sc. Gautier, ch. Cerrito,
mus. Gabrielli, f.p. May 31st,
1854.

In this case we find ourself both judge and defendant. This would have been
very embarrassing if we were speaking of anything else than a ballet, which
is the least literary form there is, being a wordless work that could therefore
have just as well been composed by a Chinaman, a Patagonian or a Papuan
from the Pacific Ocean. Our task was limited to tracing a few chalk lines on
the stage to serve as an excuse for the pantomime and the *pas* of Fanny
Cerrito. All the credit is due to the charming ballerina who has composed and
performed the choreography with such grace and perfection.

The only ballet we know of that has been arranged by a woman is Therese
Elssler's *La Volière*, which had little success and was only in one act. It is a
difficult task to set five great scenes, in which the stage is often filled with
more than a hundred people whose gestures have to be designed and co-ordi-
nated from the *coryphée* before the footlights to the humblest supernumerary
fluttering obscurely at the back. To discipline and manoeuvre such a crowd
the choreographer has to be poet, painter, musician and drill-sergeant all at
the same time. These are qualities difficult to find in one person, but Fanny
Cerrito has accomplished this difficult task in a way that will surprise those
who had any doubts about her talent.

The basic idea is taken from Alexandre Dumas' *Balsamo*.[1] The contrasting
feelings of a woman who, when hypnotised, is in love with the man who
fascinates her, and on coming out of her trance, finds him repulsive, seemed
to offer good opportunities both for pantomime and the dance, and the
applause lavished on Cerrito proved that our intuition was correct.

A ballet scenario is like a canvas on which the choreographer paints a

---

[1] Alexandre Dumas *père*'s *Joseph Balsamo*, published in 1848, was a historical novel
based on the life of Cagliostro, the charlatan who played a sinister rôle in the affair of
the diamond necklace, shortly before the French Revolution.

picture, and we can speak of *Gemma* as freely as Deforge, the artist's supplier,[2] can speak of a picture by Couture or Muller[3] for which he has supplied the stretcher. Any shortcomings are of our own making, either because we have not stretched the canvas sufficiently or because the one we have selected has a defective weave. The credit is entirely due to the painter.

Perhaps it is hardly necessary to explain how the Marquis de Santa Croce uses his hypnotic powers to abduct Gemma, a young heiress whose beauty and fortune would suit him very nicely, how, when she is in a trance, he obtains her signature to a marriage contract, and how Gemma, who has fallen in love with a young artist, manages to escape from the magic circle in which the Marquis has enclosed her, and is freed from his influence when the latter is killed in a duel "on the bridge over the waterfall" after the manner of a melodrama of the time of Guilbert de Pixérécourt.[4] We have chosen therefore to consider the performers without more ado.

The scene when the curtain first rises, in which Gemma is surrounded by her companions and her ladies, coquettishly trying on her jewels before an enormous mirror, is charmingly effective and of such difficulty that no one had ever attempted it before. To set ten or twelve people in motion, bending, rising, dancing, each with a double repeating their gestures in reverse, just like a mirror reflection, demands discipline, precision and cohesion that are almost impossible to realise; and to combine both precision and grace in achieving such a result required all the energy and perseverance of Cerrito, who chose as her own reflection Mlle Mercier, who was as identically blonde and pretty as one could wish.

The scene in which the hypnotised Gemma lavishes caresses that are morbidly voluptuous yet lacking in volition on the Marquis de Santa Croce whom she loathes and fears, was played by the charming ballerina with a poetry and a mimic power that she had not shown to such a degree before.

How graceful are her hesitating movements, how like those of a bird mesmerised by a snake are her circling bounds around the rose that she had at first rejected and thrown to the floor, and on which Santa Croce is now concentrating his powers to give it a stupefying perfume. Watch her gradually approach it, fearful yet fascinated, infected against her will by its insidious scent. Look how she inhales the disturbing aroma, charged with commands and desire. Note the feverish movement with which she presses to her heart

---

[2] The *Almanach-Bottin du Commerce* lists Deforge, *marchand des couleurs*, 8 Boulevard Montmartre. Gautier misspelt his name "Desforges".

[3] Thomas Couture (1815–79), Charles Muller (1815–92).

[4] Guilbert de Pixérécourt (1773–1844), the dramatist who created the form of melodrama as presented on the Paris stage. His work had a strong influence on the Romantic dramatists.

the corrupted bloom that is as lethal as the tunic of Nessus.[5] And after the jealous lover has snatched from her hand the evil rose turned red by the fires of Hell, see how the poor girl returns to her true love when she wakes from her trance, and casts a look of scorn at her diabolic seducer. But Santa Croce soon recovers his influence in a *valse magnétique*, full of seductive power.

The pale young girl in her ball dress presents a strange sight: so haggard, her pearly eyes fixed as she docilely and automatically follows her dark lord as he directs the twists and turns of her dance, for which he is the focus, now approaching her and now withdrawing, controlling the *tempi* of her movements and making her spin and stop in her tracks at his will. In this phantom dance the eminent ballerina gives an excellent rendering of the character's lack of vitality and will power; she is like a shade summoned up by a magician at a ball, a pawn in some inexorable plot. The supernatural appeal of somnambulism could not have been better understood or conveyed.

In the third scene, which is entirely dramatic and contains no dancing, Fanny Cerrito showed herself an excellent mime. When she is called back to reality, her horror at finding herself wearing a wedding dress in the sinister mansion and not knowing how she came to be there, and her despair in the face of the relentless will power of Santa Croce are most pathetically and faithfully rendered.

The *pas du tableau*, danced by Gemma when she has escaped from the vulture's clutches and taken refuge with the painter, is extremely graceful. Never has the celebrated ballerina performed *poses penchées* more sensual or more deliciously conceived. There are moments when she recalls Canova's statue of Psyche leaning over Cupid;[6] her white muslin skirt gives the illusion of white marble, and certainly no sculptor ever fashioned out of Paros or Carrara marble arms more supple, more caressing or more beautifully moulded.

The *abruzzaise*—we do not know if the formation of this word is really correct, but no matter—sparkles with southern verve, and makes a happy contrast with the vaporous character of the other *pas* danced by the ballerina. She performs it with fire, attack and rapid precision that command one's admiration. Once again there was no lack of applause, calls, and showers of bouquets and crowns, and for one moment the stage was so littered with flowers that the dancing almost had to stop.

---

[5] The tunic soaked in the blood of the centaur Nessus which Hercules' wife, Dejaneira, gave to Hercules, believing it had the power of calling him away from illicit loves. In fact, it contained a burning poison and caused Hercules' death.

[6] The statue of *Cupid and Psyche* by Antonio Canova (1757–1822) was sculpted in 1793 and is in the Louvre.

Mérante,[7] who took over, almost at the last moment, the rôle of Santa Croce that had been given up, for what reason we do not know, by a well-known mime who had come from Naples specially to play it, acquitted himself so well that no one regretted his predecessor. He managed to give it a sinister, fatal character by skilfully accentuating his young and delicate features, which are more suited to expressing tender sentiments than fierce passions. There is authority in his gestures and fascination in his glance, and this rôle has revealed an intelligent mime in a young man who until today was known only as a light and graceful dancer.

Petipa, as the sweetheart who is loved without the aid of magic, danced and mimed his part with that perfect dramatic feeling which he had already displayed in *Giselle* and *La Péri*. To be in love and declare one's passion in *ronds de jambe* is an exercise that can easily become ridiculous, but Petipa knows how to be a choreographic leading man who is always elegant, witty and passionate.

Mlle Louise Marquet, in the minor rôle of the painter's sister, looks ravishing in a charming costume that brings out her statuesque beauty, and acts intelligently in the scenes in which she takes part.

Berthier, as the major domo, gives depth to a character that is only sketched in outline. He knows how to make people laugh, a difficult and dangerous thing at the Opéra.

The *pas de deux* danced by Cerrito and Petipa is very pretty, and so is the *pas de quatre* which features M. Friant and Mlles Robert, Emarot and Legrain. Talking of Mlle Legrain, let us add that this young dancer seems to have a most brilliant future before her; she has marvellous qualities of strength, suppleness and clarity of movement. One could not wish for more boldness, strength or lightness.

The *pas de deux* by M. Beauchet and Mlle Luigia Taglioni aroused real enthusiasm. Apart from being very well conceived, designed and arranged, it was beautifully performed. Mlle Luigia Taglioni is so vivacious, quick and delicate, spins with such a whirlwind rapidity, and jumps so easily that it is a pleasure to follow her in her graceful wanderings.

If we were to do justice to everyone, we should have to write a longer litany than that printed at the head of Molière's comedy interludes, so here we shall stop.

After congratulating MM. Rubé and Nolau[8] on their beautiful set for the

[7] Louis Mérante (1828–87), who had made his début at the Opéra in 1848, had taken over the rôle of Santa Croce after the Italian mime, Girolamo di Mattia, abandoned it. Mérante was to become the principal male dancer in succession to Lucien Petipa, and fill that post until his death. From 1869 until 1887 he was chief ballet-master.

[8] Auguste-Alfred Rubé (1815–99), a pupil of Ciceri, and François-Joseph Nolau (1804 or 1808–83) designed scenery for the Opéra in partnership from 1854 to 1860. Rubé then became associated with Philippe-Marie Chaperon.

final scene, whose sheer and savage aspect adds to the horror as the Marquis, pierced through and through as a punishment for his crimes, leaps from rock to rock to fall twenty feet to his death, let us come to our collaborator, Count Gabrielli, who can claim a large share in the success.

Count Gabrielli[9], who has written the music of *Gemma*, has made a reputation in Italy as a composer of ballet music. His new score, studded with fresh melodies that are always in the spirit of the action, exudes the facility and rousing verve that is to be found in nearly all the works of the Italian school. As for his orchestration, it is handled with care, restraint and elegance that testify to the importance that Count Gabrielli gives to this type of composition, which is so often neglected even by the most celebrated composers on both sides of the Alps.

If the composer of *Gemma* sometimes gives his nationality away by the rhythm and the structure of his melodic ideas, he also manages to avoid reminiscences and to give an individual stamp to his inspiration by the colouring and variety of his orchestration. He has a thorough understanding of every instrument and its capability; he knows all the varieties of timbre, and often manages to produce effects that are full of charm and originality by means that are both simple and sound.

The opening scene of flirtation could not have been conveyed with more ingenious detail or more delicate embroidery in the music; the mimed love passage between Gemma and Massimo is accompanied by a melody on the violins and cellos of inexpressible tenderness; while the hypnotism scene between the charming ballerina and the Marquis de Santa Croce is composed with great dramatic power, the orchestra depicting with a realism and feeling that is beyond praise all the agitation and emotion that the girl goes through while under the influence of the hypnotist's power. Count Gabrielli has made such an impressive début in our leading lyric theatre that we are hoping he will be disloyal a second time to the scene of his triumphs, where he has so often been acclaimed by the applause and the bravos of his compatriots.

La Presse, June 13th, 1854.
(*Théâtre*, 2nd. ed.,
pp. 346–350.)
L:1301.

[9] According to Fétis, Nicolò Gabrielli (1814–91) wrote more than sixty operas for the Royal Theatres in Naples, but his music was "lacking in movement, vitality, colour and grace". For the Opéra he was also to write the score of the ballet *L'Etoile de Messine* (1861).

70

Th. du Gymnase: Manuela Perea. Th. du Palais-Royal: Josefa Vargas

Manuela Perea and her Spanish
company, f.p. June 2nd, 1854.
Josefa Vargas and her Spanish
company, f.p. June 7th, 1854.

The vaudeville which serves as a pretext for the Spanish dances [at the Gymnase] is no sillier than any other. It would be amusing even if that were not its purpose. But how can anyone be expected to listen when the rustle of the basquines and the muted chatter of castanets clicking away impatiently can be heard from behind the curtain?

At last the prompter's box is removed, the drop cloth is raised, and *majos* and *majas* advance towards the footlights twisting their hips. A dozen tiny feet shake their toes in the faces of the public, and arms are lifted up like the handles of Moorish *alcarrazas*,[1] rolling their little cymbals of ivory or grenadine wood with ever-increasing fury.

Tightly wrapped in her mantilla, La Nena[2] comes forward, rolling the flounces of her skirt with the purest Andalusian *meneo*[3] like a *cigarrera* of Seville on her way to join her smuggler lover at the Cristina or in the Barrio de Triana.[4] Soon she flings the mantilla aside and appears in all the extravagant splendour of her fantastic costume. Her dress is speckled with scarlet flowers,

[1] A type of pitcher made of very delicate white clay for keeping water cool. The word is derived from the Arabic word *garrasa*, meaning to cool.

[2] Manuela Perea (La Nena) was engaged with her company at the Th. du Gymnase for the months of June and July. Her partner was Antonio Ruiz.

[3] See No. 65, note 2.

[4] The Paseo de Cristina, a popular promenade on the northern bank of the Guadalquivir, to the east of the city, near the Tobacco factory. The Barrio de Triana, the gypsy quarter, lay across the river.

her bodice covered with buttons, spangles and silver trimmings like a torero's jacket. Above her sleeves the braiding is so thick as to form epaulettes that give off the sparkling, fiery light of Spanish sunshine.

The dancer is small and slender, holding herself straight, and with but the tiniest suspicion of feet and hands, just large enough to fill the tips of two satin slippers and grasp the silk ribbons of a pair of castanets. There is a mutter of tambourines, a clattering of little copper jingles; heeltaps beat out the rhythm; and Perea Nena seems to vanish in the astounding rapidity of her movements like a dragonfly in the flurry of its gauzy wings. The vague gleam of spangles, eyes and teeth disappear from view, but fortunately she drops to one knee, bending backward to touch the ground with her shoulders and unfolding above her head two dreamy arms that might have been made specially for fluttering the gold-striped handkerchiefs of Arab almehs.

Only then can you appreciate her charming head, the arched eyebrows, the wide languishing eyes, and a mouth so small that

Qu'on n'y saurait poser,
Même quand elle rit, que le quart d'un baiser,

as some poet whose name we forget once said to a girl from Granada.

But this will not do for the other *majas*. They press round their lazy companion who has now come to rest, shaking their castanets and *panderos* in her ears, and soon she is off again, more beautiful, excited, exhilarated and frenzied than before, giving herself up completely to the swirl of the rhythm. It is enough to give you vertigo, and you feel that in a couple of minutes she must inevitably drop dead like a butterfly caught in a cloudburst.

Her other dance is a sort of *Rondalla*.[5] A suitor comes to swagger beneath the window of his lady, who soon emerges to join his companions. Although it is less glittering and not so bristling with choreographic difficulties, this *pas* is more Spanish in its flavour than the first, in which the local colour of the primitive theme somewhat disappeared among all the trills and *gargouillades*.

Perea Nena is not at all like Petra Cámara. She is *salada*[6] rather than voluptuous, witty rather than passionate, her originality lying in her extreme speed and the extraordinary neatness of her footwork. She dazzles. Her success was complete.

---

[5] *Rondalla*, a serenade performed by a band of street musicians.

[6] Literally salty, referring in this context to the quality of grace spiced with wit, much admired by the Spaniards in their women, and particularly in their dancers. "It is something that is hard to define in French," wrote Gautier, "a mixture of nonchalance and vivacity, a piquancy, a combination—as painters say—that can be encountered apart from beauty and is often preferred to it. Thus one says to a woman in Spain, 'How *salada* you are,' and no greater compliment can be paid." (*Voyage en Espagne*, chapter 14.)

[Appearing at the Palais-Royal], Pepa Vargas[7] is a dark beauty with hair and eyes as black as night, arching herself and bending back with great boldness and suppleness. Her dancing is full of energy, vivacity and ardour, but is less classically polished than that of Perea Nena. La Vargas is more closely representative of what is called in Spain *el baile nacional*, which is performed between the main piece and the playlet at the end.

La Vargas has more fire, and La Nena more art, but both are charming and delightful in their own ways. Nor should we forget the partner who plays the *pandereta* with his hands, his feet, his knees and his head, and who is worth all the celebrated *pandereteros* of the Cirque[8] put together.

La Presse, June 13th, 1854.
L:1301.

[7] Josefa Vargas was appearing with her company at the Th. du Palais-Royal throughout June and into the first week of July, simultaneously with La Nena's season at the Gymnase—evidence of the popularity of Spanish dancing in Paris. Her partner was Guzman.

[8] See No. 68, note 8.

71

Opéra: *La Fonti*

La Fonti, ballet in 2 acts and 6
scenes, sc. Deligny, ch. Mazilier,
mus. Labarre, f.p. January 8th,
1855.

L a Fonti was the ballerina in vogue, as one would have said of the Carlotta
of the time, at the Teatro de la Pergola[1] a hundred years ago, give or take a
few years—dates are never very precisely specified in ballets. The ballet *Flore
et Zéphyr* is to be given, as announced on a playbill on which La Fonti's name
has been printed in characters much too small for her liking, a circumstance
that throws her into a temper, just as if she were alive today. It appears that
there is nothing new about being given star billing. Vanity is eternal, and
today's stars are even more exacting than those who have had their day.

You can see that La Fonti has no lack of admirers. A swarm of butterflies,
their silken wings sprinkled with spangles, flutter around her, attracted by the
brilliance that the footlights cast on those who come within their rays, even
those who are not beautiful, and La Fonti is really charming! Do not object
that it is not likely when we add that she is also virtuous. And why not? Such
things do happen, whatever smug folk may say, and furthermore dancing
with its violent exercise and ceaseless toil is an excellent antidote for voluptuous languor. So La Fonti is virtuous, insisting that the way into her
bedroom lies through the church, which is not to the liking of professional
womanisers.

Although she is virtuous, the young ballerina is not unsusceptible. She is in
love with the Count de Monteleone, who is himself madly enamoured of her.
The young Count knows that the only gift La Fonti will accept is a wedding
ring, and this condition does not worry him. There is also another admirer
who would gladly marry her if she wanted him to, and if he did not have a
nobleman for a rival—Carlino, the *premier danseur* of the company.

Monteleone has promised to marry La Fonti, but he has overlooked one
important detail, the consent of his august father, a sprightly old man
obsessed with his aristocratic lineage who would not look kindly on his coat

[1] The Teatro de la Pergola is the opera house of Florence.

273

of arms being quartered with a *pochette* and a *rond de jambe*. Father Monteleone, being totally lacking in romantic ideas, can understand giving girls like that palaces, settlements and caskets of jewels, but cannot contemplate making countesses of them. That is his view of the world, and he intervenes in the affair with true aristocratic scorn and forces his son to withdraw his offer of marriage.

The ballet of *Flore et Zéphyr* is performed against the background of these events, and La Fonti is a sensation. She "rises to the stars", *alle stelle*, a fine Italian expression that could not be used in London or Paris, where the sky is always shrouded in fog. The young Count, who has attended the performance on the sly and whose love grows stronger and stronger with all the applause, curtain calls and bouquets that are lavished on his loved one, gives a note to the theatre hairdresser, who passes it to the ballerina's dresser. But the letter never reaches its destination, for old Monteleone jingles a purse of gold, which is music to the ears of the maid, who hands the letter over.

It contains a proposal from the young Count that they should elope to France. The Marquis flies into a rage at his son's disobedience, and orders the ballerina to leave Florence immediately, not even giving her time to change her costume. La Fonti resists and objects, but his henchmen seize her, stifling her cries with a handkerchief, and carry her away. Things were done without ceremony in those days. Times have certainly changed since then.

Carlino, the silent and devoted lover, has witnessed the whole scene. He determines to rescue La Fonti. Disguised as a servant, he gains admittance to the prison where the ballerina has been incarcerated by an official order obtained by the Marquis. There he changes clothes with his comrade and enables her to escape under the nose of the Governor, whom he has plied with wine.

Believing that he has been tricked or rejected when the ballerina does not turn up as arranged, young Monteleone accepts the hand of the Princess Carolina Tornasari at his father's bidding, but just as the marriage contract is about to be signed, there appears a handsome young man with a most cavalier bearing, who shows the Princess some love letters that Monteleone has written to a ballerina. The young Count quickly recognises La Fonti beneath the disguise, and is completely nonplussed. La Fonti tells him how she was seized and thrown into prison, and complains that he showed not the slightest concern for her.

Monteleone makes excuses, declaring that he knew nothing of that and is only marrying the Princess because he thought he had lost La Fonti for ever. The ballerina is so annoyed that she wishes to hear no more; she brushes aside his excuses and as she is leaving the palace, comes face to face with the Marquis and the Princess Carolina. She throws herself at their feet and begs their forgiveness so humbly and gracefully that the order of banishment is revoked.

Any self-respecting heroine of a dramatic opera or ballet who is suffering from the pains of love, must, if she knows the conventions, deliver herself of a mad scene in the final tableau. La Fonti does not fail us. She enters the Corso[2] when the Roman Carnival is at its height, and there, among all the Harlequins, Punchinellos, Turks, Savages, Cassandros, Pantaloons, Scaramouches, Brighellas, Doctors from Bologna, Tartaglias, Don Spaventos, Columbines, Isabelles, shepherdesses, nymphs and Venuses, she throws herself into a dance, part melancholic and part unbridled, that betrays the state of her mind and arouses admiration and pity in the motley crowd.

At the end, exhausted by her *cabrioles*, she falls in a faint, half dead. The faithful Carlino, who has followed her in her wanderings, takes her in his arms. And one is left with the hope that with a few doses of hellebore, baths and bleedings she will be restored to her normal state of health, and that Carlino's devotion will be duly rewarded, as theatrical justice, which is stricter in such matters than human justice, demands. The curtain falls on this consoling thought, for one must never come away from a ballet with a grieving heart.

This ballet belongs to the type known as *ballets d'action*, and is more of a drama expressed in gestures than a series of choreographic poses. It has been skilfully translated by M. Mazilier, one of our best producers of mimed action, and very well acted by La Rosati, but we still contend that the *ballet d'action* lies outside the conditions of true dancing. Every art has a corresponding order of subjects which it alone can render. Sculpture expresses form; painting, form and colour; poetry, form, colour, sound and thought; music, number, tone, the infinite and the indefinite, a presentiment of what does not exist and the memory of what has never been; and dancing, the plastic quality and rhythm of movement, and—why not admit it?—physical sensuality and feminine beauty. Ballet must be a kind of painted bas-relief or sculptured painting, and should seek its themes, not from novels or short stories, but in the graceful bacchanals, processions and *panathenaea*[3] that encircle antique vases.

Mythologies of every age and every land—India, Egypt, Greece, Scandinavia—legends, fairy tales, dreams inspired by hashish and opium, all the fancies that are beyond the bounds of the possible—those form the true domain of ballet. Outside that, it is inferior to all other forms of art, for it cannot specify or develop anything, the past and the future are denied it, and its action must always be conjugated in the present tense.

---

[2] The Roman carnival took place between the second Saturday before Ash Wednesday and Shrove Tuesday. Its highlight was the daily procession in the Corso, the most fashionable street in the city, the last evening being marked by the lighting of tapers immediately after sunset.

[3] Festivals in honour of Athena, the patron god of Athens.

A few very limited gestures, some taken from nature, others based on convention, are its only means of depicting human passions. Thus a *ballet d'action* is like a drama played by a troupe of deaf-mutes, particularly since French dancers never follow the music when miming. Nevertheless, theatre managers, who lose all sense of reason in the face of theatrical tradition, are very fond of the *ballet d'action*, because it provides them with a plot, a story, a monumental, straight-forward theme.

If we ever have the honour to become Director of the Opéra, we shall not commission playwrights to compose ballets, but painters such as Decamps, Camille Roqueplan, Diaz, Gérome, Picou, Chassériau, and Gendron,[4] whose delightful picture of the Wilis shows what artists could do in this field.

The costumes are rich and the sets very fine, for artists such as Cambon, Thierry and Martin are incapable of allowing a false or clashing colour to escape from their brushes, but there is nothing particularly striking about them, and in this area the Opéra can and must perform miracles, particularly in a ballet, which is a spectacle that really lives up to its name and must be perfectly done if it is to delight the eye.

The music of M. Labarre is remarkable, full of rhythm, distinguished and elegant. The storm in the rococo ballet of *Flore et Zéphyr* was very well done; the composer treated it in part seriously and in part as a parody, with great verve and real musical skill. The score of *La Fonti* is not inferior to that of *Jovita*, although admittedly the latest production of a poet or musician is always considered his worst.

La Rosati is now the most popular ballerina in the eyes of the public. She deserves the vogue she enjoys on many counts; she has fire and expression, she is a superlative mime, and, in a word, she is full of life, a precious quality. Her dancing, which is a little lacking in elevation, is particularly brilliant in *tacqueté* movements, precision, speed, and with a touch of Montessu and Noblet, if that is not dredging up memories that are too ancient.[5]

La Presse, January 16th, 1855.
L:1332.

---

[4] A selection of painters of Gautier's day. Alexandre-Gabriel Decamps (1803–60), Camille Roqueplan (1803–55), Narcisse-Virgile Diaz de la Peña (1808–76), Jean-Léon Gérome (1824–1904), Henri-Pierre Picou (1824–95), Théodore Chassériau (1819–56), Ernest-Auguste Gendron (1817–81).

[5] This review seems to have been carelessly shortened at the printers—perhaps by Gautier himself—for two short passages, both incomplete, were left in the text. One of these described the rococo ballet ("supers disguised as flowers lightly bending their stems; Boreas, with cheeks puffed out like a regimental trumpeter sounding reveille, blowing down with his stormy breath a whole line of *coryphées* like a pack of cards, a scene that is very amusing and entertaining") and praised the effective swarming of the crowd in the Carnival scene, and the other reported the applause given to Rosati when she appeared in travesty attire in the prison scene.

72

Opéra: Revival of *Le Diable à quatre*

Le Diable à quatre, ballet-pantomime in 2 acts and 4 scenes, sc. de Leuven, ch. Mazilier, mus. Adam, f.p. August 11th, 1845, revived for the début of Mlle Beretta, February 22nd, 1855.

In *Le Diable à quatre* the rôle of Mazourka was created by Carlotta Grisi, who mimed with such an ingenuous grace and danced so perfectly that she is still unrivalled. It was an extremely bold undertaking to make a début in a work over which hovers such a charming and formidable memory, but if fortune favours brave men, it also favours brave women, and the daring of Mlle Beretta paid off—as it always does when accompanied by true talent.

Mlle Beretta[1] is extremely young, fifteen or sixteen at the most. She is small, and with a body developed by the violent gymnastics of ballet training, perhaps possesses more strength than grace. Her legs, set in a powerful network of muscles, convey vigour rather than elegance by their shape, and her figure is more that of a healthy daughter of the soil than a vaporous sylphide with shimmering, variegated wings.

But perhaps the process of growing up, which is far from complete, will lengthen lines that are at present a little too short and add a slenderness that is now lacking. Her features are lively, arch, childlike, lit by beautiful Southern eyes. So much for the physical aspect, which we have spoken of in detail because it is important for a dancer and is, so to speak, part of her essentially plastic and silent talent.

---

[1] Caterina Beretta (1840–1911) was to become one of the leading Italian ballerinas, noted particularly for her virtuosity, and in her later years a teacher of international repute. She counted many of the Russian ballerinas of the turn of the century among her pupils, including Trefilova, Pavlova and Karsavina. She directed the ballet school of the Scala, Milan, from 1902 to 1908.

As for the technical qualities of the *débutante*, they are remarkable. The daughter of a well-known Italian mime and a mother who is also on the stage, Mlle Beretta has been trained and broken in early in the hard school of dancing. She is completely versed in the principles and techniques of her art, the difficulties of which no longer exist for her. All she does is clean, precise and firm.

She does not blur a single movement of her *jetés battus*; she jumps energetically, if not to a great height; she covers the stage with speed and agility; and in *posés renversées*, she attempts positions that are so off-balance that they would break the back of a dancer who does not have the suppleness and acrobatic elasticity that distinguish Mlle Beretta. Her *double tour sur la pointe* on the left leg, executed with a dazzling rapidity, aroused much applause.

The purely mime part of the rôle was not so superbly rendered by Mlle Beretta as the dance part. There she was practising a skill that was newer to her. However, she gave proof of great intelligence in the acted scenes. Her gestures were sometimes a little haphazard, but they revealed a true feeling that experience will bring under control.

Mlle Quéniaux played the rôle of the spiteful Countess, and the puckering of her beautiful black eyebrows, while it would not have scared the wits out of Olympus like the bushy frown of Zeus, at least drew bravos from the pit. She could not have been more pleasantly insupportable or more deliciously fierce. Being shrewish and charming at the same time, striking a balance between giving a kick up the backside and making a declaration of love—these were problems that Mlle Quéniaux solved. Now we shall look forward to seeing her intelligence put to use in a new ballet.

Petipa is very distinguished in the character of the prince, and Berthier very funny—a difficult thing at the Opéra—in the comic rôle of Mazurki.

La Presse, February 27th, 1855.
L:1339.

73

Th. de la Porte-Saint-Martin: *Esmeralda*

Esmeralda, ballet in 5 scenes, ch. Perrot, mus. Pugni, f.p. Her Majesty's Theatre, London, March 9th, 1844, revived at Th. de la Porte-Saint-Martin, Paris (the first Paris performance of the ballet), December 24th, 1856.

The Porte-Saint-Martin, as is well known, has in its privilege the authority to present ballet. This it rarely uses, for it is no small matter to support a ballet company in addition to a drama troupe. *Esmeralda*, which it has presented this week, was originally performed in London at Her Majesty's Theatre; it is the masterpiece of Perrot, the last man to have danced—Perrot, who designs dances as well as he used to dance them in times gone by.

Esmeralda! The name conjures up a sparkling figure whirling like a golden bee in a sunbeam; the coldest imaginations are stirred by it, and everyone leans over the gallery of Notre Dame to watch her dancing on the cathedral square in her crazy gypsy costume and with her brass-belled tambourine, the poetic sister of Mignon and Fenella.[1] Claude Frollo's eyes are burning beneath his black hood; Quasimodo is rubbing his hands in glee, showing the stumps of his teeth as he grins; Jehan the scholar is searching his pocket for his last farthing; the stupid swell, Phoebus de Châteaupers, rides past, proud and straight, on his prancing steed; Pierre Gringoire is mixing philosophy with a balancing act; Mathias Ungaddi, Duke of Egypt and Bohemia, is stealing some passer-by's purse. Then the background takes shape behind the characters: the cathedral raising its great stone arms and its steeple that has since been lopped off; the roofs silhouetted against the sky; staircases and gables

---

[1] *Esmeralda* was based on Victor Hugo's novel, *Notre Dame de Paris*. Mignon and Fenella, heroines of Goethe's *Wilhelm Meisters Lehrjahre* and Auber's opera, *La Muette de Portici* respectively.

forming sharp angles; clocks, towers, belfreys shooting up from every side, and Gothic Paris is recreated as is the immortal book of the poet.

Who has not fallen in love with Esmeralda after reading *Notre Dame de Paris*? Is there anyone who has not dreamed of that charming phantom endowed with every beauty and perfection? It is an awe-inspiring and dangerous rôle for a ballerina, just as Célimène[2] is for an actress. Furthermore, it used to be danced by Carlotta Grisi, and no one who saw her, all white and pink and blonde, with her violet eyes and her mouth in full bloom, remembered that the poet's Esmeralda was wild and bronzed like a child of Egypt with glints of blue in her jet-black hair. She danced it as no one else will, with the grace of flight, a charm that was irresistible, and such precision and suppleness.

Mme Scotti[3] is a ballerina who comes from a good school. She is versed in all the secrets of her profession, a rarer quality than you would suppose, and mimes the dramatic passages intelligently. She was deservedly applauded in the *Truandaise*, but she is not the poet's Esmeralda, nor Perrot's. The movements composed for Carlotta require too much elevation for her. However, the public liked her. Mlle Rosita Comba reminds us a little of Cerrito with her rounded arms, the grace of her poses and her provocative manner. The male dancer, M. Paul, has good elevation; he springs up towards the flies and stays there, but today the public no longer takes any notice of men in ballet.

La Presse, December 29th, 1856.
L:1465.

---

[2] Célimène in Molière's *Le Misanthrope*, a gay and frivolous coquette, is one of the most testing rôles in French comedy.

[3] Maria Scotti was trained at the ballet school of the Scala, Milan, and probably a pupil of Carlo Blasis. She danced at the Scala until 1855.

74

Opéra: *Sacountala*

Sacountala, ballet-pantomime in 2
acts, sc. Gautier, ch. L. Petipa,
mus. Reyer, f.p. July 14th, 1858.

We are extremely embarrassed. The regular critic[1] has been released from his duties at the Opéra and is at Vichy taking a rest after the music of the winter and the spring, and enjoying the pleasure of seeing and hearing nothing of theatrical things, just like a mere mortal—a well-earned holiday, for it is a hard task to sample pleasures for others like a cupbearer tasting the wine before passing the glass to his master, and to say to the public: "Drink" or "Do not drink". Had he been here, you would have had the benefit of one of those judicious, sensible, witty *feuilletons*, well informed to the smallest detail, that make his readers impatiently look forward to Sunday. But he was not here. So what was to be done? Pass *Sacountala* over in silence? That our pride would not allow: the author of a ballet scenario is almost a stranger to his work, the credit belonging entirely to the choreographer, the composer and the designer. Also, a work performed at the Opéra, be it good or bad, arouses a curiosity that a newspaper has a duty to satisfy. Should we have looked for some young expert?[2] Alas, there no longer are any; they have all become grizzled, chiefs themselves or half dead, so there was nothing for it but to undertake the review ourselves. At first this seemed difficult, but really nothing was easier.

The original idea of the ballet was not ours. We borrowed the uncomplicated story of our ballet from the excellent dramatic poem by Kalidasa, a contemporary of Virgil[3] flourishing at the court of Vicramaditya, the

---

[1] Pier-Angelo Fiorentino della Rovere, who wrote music criticism for *Le Moniteur* under the name of A. de Rovray.

[2] Gautier uses the term "*critique blond*" to mean a young specialist, usually in musical matters, who advised him on the sections of his reviews that needed expertise that he lacked himself.

[3] Kalidasa, the great Sanskrit poet and dramatist, in fact lived several centuries after Virgil, in the fifth century A.D.

Augustus of India, only adding passages that were necessary for giving visual effect to what the drama explained in words, and only cutting the King's mythological journeys in search of the lost Sacountala, journeys that over-flowed the normal limitation of two acts. That said, we can take our seat in the stalls like an ordinary member of the audience.

After an introduction in F minor, full of charming motifs and orchestrated with a skill and mastery that one would never have expected from a young composer handling the powerful orchestra of the Opéra for the first time, the curtain rises to reveal a sacred forest in India in all its profusion of strange vegetation—strange at least to our eyes that are accustomed to a more restrained plant life.

The fig trees of the Banias,[4] with their monstrous and curiously bent trunks, form, so to speak, the pillars of this botanical pagoda. Talipot palms, mango trees and latanias spread their sturdy branches and large shiny leaves in every direction. Beneath the gigantic trees lies a tangled undergrowth of strange plants, sprouting like the multiple arms of Hindu gods bearing flowers in their hands. On every side bloom enormous flowers, brilliantly coloured and filling the air with their scent. Creepers, from whose network birds take wing, hang from age-old branches in tangled confusion. The foreground is bespattered, embroidered, festooned and perfumed with amras, malicas, madhavis, sirichas and a thousand other shrubs and flowers whose musically melodious names must sound barbaric to our ears, which are attuned to the howl of the North wind. Through an opening at the back can be seen the sparkling water of a *thirta*, a sacred lake, with here and there reed huts peeping through the profusion of the foliage. A small temple, with its triple-headed, six-armed idol, shows that the *trimourti* of Brahma, Vishnu and Shiva[5] has worshippers even in such a solitary spot apparently unvisited by man.

This beautiful scene has been painted by M. Martin,[6] a talented man who has lived in India for fifteen years and has availed himself of the hues of the blazing palette with which everything there is tinged by the sun. So no one must be surprised if his forest is unlike the Bas-Bréau and the Bois de Vincennes.[7]

There among the flowers, the scents, the sunbeams, the dew and the songs,

---

[4] One of the Indian castes, consisting mainly of traders.

[5] The triad of the three major Hindu gods, representing respectively creation, preser-vation and destruction.

[6] Hugues Martin (b. 1809) was a regular exhibitor at the Salon between 1845 and 1876, two of his paintings shown there being of Indian scenes. He designed scenery for a number of productions at the Opéra between 1853 and 1862, including the ballets *La Fonti* (1855), *Le Corsaire* (1856), *Les Elfes* (1856) and *Sacountala* (1858).

[7] The Bas-Bréau, part of the Forest of Fontainebleau.

in close contact with the plants, birds and gazelles, in perfect communion with nature, live Sacountala, Anousouya, Priyamvada and the band of young priestesses, their companions, under the supervision of the sage Canoua and the prudent Gautami.

Sacountala's pet antelope has escaped into the forest, but it is soon caught and taken back to its stable, bringing in its wake an entire royal hunting party that shatters the peaceful echoes of the forest and disturbs the devotions of the brahmins, who have retired to this spot to study their *vedas*.

King Douchmanta is not lacking in respect; he returns his arrow to its quiver, dismisses his suite, takes off his royal insignia in a gesture of submission, and raising to his feet the brahmin chief who has prostrated himself before him, casts a handful of the cousa herb[8] on the altar as an offering to the gods. The brahmins retire, leaving the King alone. At the sound of some young priesteses approaching with urns on their shoulders, he hides in the thick undergrowth so as not to scare them away. Sacountala enters to pour some of the pure water of the lake on her favourite plants. A bee flies out of the bloom of a malica, pursuing her as if mistaking her for a flower and trying to enter her rosy mouth, and the girl's agile leaps soon take her near the king, who emerges from his hiding place to chase the buzzing insect away. After their initial surprise at discovering a stranger in their midst, Anousouya and Priyamvada invite him to sit down on a mossy bank and offer him flowers and fruit, while Sacountala, blushing with emotion, goes to fetch the fresh water. Notice our force of habit! See how we are falling into the humdrum routine of analysing the story as if it were someone else's ballet, when all we need to do is to copy out the scenario.

There follows a long love scene in which Kalidasa's exhilarating verses have perhaps been translated for the first time with all their heady scent, their langorous rapture and their turtle-dove cooings. M. de Chézy[9] would have been amazed if he could have seen Mme Ferraris "reading" fluent Sanscrit, "declaiming" it with never a fault, and rendering the *slokas*[10] that gave him so much difficulty with the tips of her tiny feet. In places where he has added a footnote bristling with textual variants, the ballerina comments on the difficult passage by half shutting her eyes, letting her arms float gracefully in the air, inclining her head like a flower filled with dew, leaning on her partner's shoulder with voluptuous calm, and is understood by everyone.

Now alone, now surrounded by her companions, Sacountala flutters about the flowers like a feather fallen from a bird's nest and floating on a scented

---

[8] A kind of grass used in certain Hindu ceremonies.

[9] Antoine-Léonard de Chèzy's translation of Kalidasa (1830) was Gautier's inspiration and principal source for this ballet. He was lent a copy by his friend Maxime Du Camp.

[10] The main epic metre in Indian poetry.

breeze; then, shaking with emotion, her heart pounding, and troubled by the stirring of love that has come upon her, she sinks on to a mossy bank to come to her senses in the arms of the king—amid the rumblings of a storm, vivid flashes of lightning, the cries of the *rakshasas*,[11] and the curses of Durwasas, the awe-inspiring ascetic who is indignant at finding the holy place profaned by an impure love. Douchmanta's mind becomes disturbed, and he flings himself about like a madman; the guards lead him away, and Durwasas snatches the royal ring, the token of betrothal, from the finger of the swooning Sacountala, and casts it into the still waters of the sacred lake. In spite of the loss of her ring and the funereal phantasmagoria with which the wicked Durwasas tries to frighten her, Sacountala, robed by the *apsaras* sent by Menaca,[12] her celestial mother, and accompanied by her faithful companions, Priyamvada and Anousouya, leaves for the palace of Hastinapourou,[13] having taken leave of the birds, flowers and plants in a farewell that radiates the touching pantheistic sentimentality of India.

The whole of this act, choreographically, was one long series of ovations for Mme Ferraris and Petipa.

From the sacred forest we pass to the palace of Hastinapourou, from shadow to light, from silence to tumult, from ascetic simplicity to royal splendour, and what splendour! That of a king of the lunar dynasty, one of those fanciful princes plastered with diamonds, dripping with jewels, who dazzles the massive golden palanquin on the back of an elephant caparisoned with pearls. This set, without speaking ill of the others, is one of the most beautiful to have been seen at the Opéra for a long time. Imagine one of those tremendous architectures of John Martin,[14] ascending into the sky in a perspective that vanishes into infinity. But here there are no biblical shadows, no black cloud rent by lightning. A "gleaming, dazzlingly white" light sheds a cascade of clarity on gigantic layers of terraces, monumental stairways, tiers of colonnades with bizarre capitals that descend from the distant line of the sky to the portico of the inner courtyard.

This portico is supported by squat columns and granite elephants with tusks encircled with gold and covered in metal, some solemnly kneeling and

---

[11] Semi-divine creatures who display deplorable passions and malevolently haunt human beings.

[12] *Apsaras* are nymphs of great beauty in the Hindu Paradise, originally aquatic by nature but later supposed to dwell in trees. Menaca may be a misprint for Manasa, the serpent goddess.

[13] An ancient city, situated north of Delhi, mentioned in the Indian epic, the *Mahabharata*.

[14] John Martin (1789–1854) was celebrated for the massive architecture and limitless perspective of his paintings. Gautier was fascinated by his work, but not uncritical. "Martin," he wrote, "suffers from the nightmare of infinity. It is an *idée fixe*, a sort of sublime monomania" (*La Presse*, January 31st, 1837).

curving their trunks like Ganesa,[15] the god of wisdom, and others with trunks raised like trumpets to sound a triumphal fanfare. At either side of the stage horseshoe-form marble stairways lead to a lower platform. And among the architecture there rise palms, exotic trees, and enormous flowers whose hues of green and pink add a freshness to all these colossal buildings scorched by the sun.

In the middle of the courtyard King Douchmanta, deprived of his reason and memory as a result of the curse of the ascetic Durwasas, is sitting limply on his throne by the side of Queen Hamsati. The *antahpura* women,[16] reclining on the steps of the throne in poses of despondency, languor and boredom, seem to be waiting for their master to deign to lower his gaze on them. Madhavya, the king's favourite, plucks at her guitar—we dare not write the Sanscrit name, for there are no more a's left in the printers' cases—and slowly these sleeping bodies come to life, stretching their supple limbs and arching their slender figures, as they begin one of those lazy, sinuous dances in which the women bend and twist like snakes and with every step seem to be dying of lassitude and love. These dances, which make no impression on the king, are followed by others, lighter and more lively, which are themselves interrupted by the entrance of Sacountala and her graceful retinue of young priestesses. She has come to remind the king of the promises made in the sacred wood. Alas! lifting her veil to display her charming features, miming the scene with the bee, and her attempts to bring back his memory that an evil spell has expunged are of no avail. And what is more, the ring that would confirm the truth of her story has been snatched from her. The jealous Hamsati summons the executioners and orders a pyre to be prepared for the brazen hussy who has dared come to the steps of the throne to claim a lover who does not know her. No sooner has Sacountala been led away than a fisherman presents Douchmanta with the royal ring, which he has found in the stomach of a fish. At the sight of his ring, the king remembers everything, his reason returns, and he asks where Sacountala is. The apsara Misrakesi has saved the girl by transforming the flames of the pyre into flowers. Now nothing stands in the way of the union of Douchmanta and Sacountala, who will give birth to the great conqueror of India, the hero of the *Mahabharata*, a poem as vast as the mountains, rivers, forests and pagodas of that land where everything is oversized.

Ernest Reyer's music justifies all the expectations that have long been held

---

[15] A friendly and popular Hindu god with the head of an elephant, revered for his good sense.

[16] *Antahpura* means a harem, or women's quarters.

of this young composer, for whom we wrote the verses of *Le Sélam*.[17] Reyer has a deep understanding of Oriental music; he is second to none in the possession of its strange timbres, compelling rhythms, bizarre cadences, and its cantilenas of savage grace. He can write for dancing almehs, whirling dervishes, and the Arab dreaming at the entrance of his tent. All these qualities he has displayed in *Sacountala*, producing, without descending to puerile imitation, music that could not be more indigenous or Indian. Petipa, who had previously produced only divertissements, has become a past master at his first attempt. He possesses grace, originality, freshness, a feeling for plastic form in groups and an ease in handling masses. As for the mime passages, his own talent in this direction is already well known.

What is to be said about Mme Ferraris?[18] She danced her five *pas* with lightness, gentleness and an unimaginable suppleness. Light as a dove's feather when she rises, and firm as an arrow point on landing, she preserves the chaste and voluptuous grace of Sacountala, her gentle resignation as a victim, and her quality of half flower, half woman. If the ghost of Kalidasa had wandered into the theatre, he would have applauded her with both his spectral hands. And never did a prouder beauty than Queen Hamsati appear in robes more splendid or strikingly authentic.[19] Not a detail of the bizarre splendour of India was too much for her, and as she performed her calm, arched-back poses, she called to mind one of those cruel but graceful favourites of the seraglio who demand heads as they dance.

Coralli, who was cast as Durwasas, managed to convey an austere, sinister and awe-inspiring impression without wearing claws on his hands, bird's nests in his hair or a snake round his waist. He was very effective. Lenfant, as the good hermit, is as gentle as Coralli is surly. Ed. Cornet played the small scene of the fisherman very well. Now, if we pass on to the dancing, a catalogue longer than Homer's would be needed. The choreographic army performed its duty well. Let us single out that sparkling ballerina, Mlle

[17] Ernest Reyer (1823–1909) was to develop into an opera composer of distinction, much influenced by Wagner, his finest works being *Sigurd* (1884) and *Salammbô* (1890). He owed much to his friendship with writers such as Gautier, who wrote the verses for an early work, *Le Sélam*, *scènes d'Orient*, a descriptive symphony, f.p. Th. Italien, April 5th, 1851. Eighteen years previously, in 1833, Gautier had written a preface to a collection of pieces by contemporary writers entitled *Le Sélam*, explaining that a selam was a bouquet of allegorical flowers offered to their favourite lovers by odalisques, in which each flower represented a phrase in the language of love.

[18] Amalia Ferraris (1827–1904) had been engaged at the Opéra since 1856, when she made her début in Mazilier's *Les Elfes* (not reviewed by Gautier). Gautier probably saw her first towards the end of 1850, during a visit to Naples, for in his short story, *Arria Marcella*, he describes, no doubt from personal experience, a visit to the San Carlo, where she was supported by a corps de ballet wearing green knickers—a style imposed to satisfy the prudery of the Queen—"that made them look like frogs bitten by a tarantula".

[19] Played by Louise Marquet.

Cucchi,[20] and the pure and correct Mlle Quéniaux; Mlles Schlosser, Poussin, Cellier and Maupérin, who surround Mme Ferraris like roses and violets encircling a camellia in a bouquet; and Mérante, who managed to be applauded by the whole audience as a male dancer—a rare triumph!

Le Moniteur Universel, July 19th, 1858.
(*Théâtre*, 2nd, ed., pp. 376–381.)
L:1598.

---

[20] Claudina Cucchi (1834–1913), a pupil of Blasis, later gained an international reputation. She wrote a volume of memoirs.

75

Bolshoi Theatre, St Petersburg: *Eoline*

Eoline, ou la Dryade, grand ballet
fantasque in 4 acts and 5 scenes,
ch. Perrot, mus. Pugni, f.p.
November 4th/16th, 1858.

The curtain rises to reveal to the audience a mysterious subterranean kingdom with a rocky vault for its sky, lamps for stars, strange crystallisations of metals for its flora, black waters swimming with blind fish for its lakes, and for its inhabitants, mountain gnomes who are now being disturbed in their deep retreat by the activities of man. The mine is a hive of industry: picks are hacking minerals from the seams, cables are being wound on winches, baskets are conveyed hither and thither, and the treasure extracted from the rock is being emptied from hods into the flaring red maws of the furnaces. And once cooled, the metal is formed into ingots under the rhythmical blows of hammers. The whole scene is fascinating.

Such labour deserves its reward, and down a fragile flight of stairs, the top of which disappears through the roof of the cavern—the only means of access with the outer world—enter, like angels descending Jacob's ladder, the wives, daughters and sweethearts of the miners, clad in charming, picturesque costumes and bringing lunch to their labouring menfolk. All those tiny feet and shapely legs trip down the innumerable steps with winglike rapidity before a battery of opera-glasses, with not a false step, not a hesitation, and without shaking the lofty staircase for one moment. There could be no more graceful or daring sight than this aerial *défilé* of the entire corps de ballet.

The provisions are then unpacked from the baskets, and Lisinka, the most comely of the maidens, lovingly serves her father, the head miner, who is as skilled in detecting metal in its earthly envelope as the *telchines* of Samothrace[1] or the gnomes of the Harz Mountains. To complete everyone's

---

[1] In Greek mythology the *telchines* were supernatural creatures who were skilled metal workers and were the first to forge statues of the Gods.

happiness, Count Edgar, who owns the mines, has sent pitchers of wine and jugs of beer to his worthy workmen. The miners drink their fill, and the sober lunch turns into a merry feast.

This joyous tumult penetrates to the underground palace of Rubezahl, and awakens the king of the gnomes, the spirit of the mountain, whose domain has been invaded by the impudent greed of the mortals. An enormous mass of slag once liquefied by the fire of primitive volcanoes suddenly splits asunder, and out of it darts a supernatural creature, part god, part demon, wearing a little white cloak on his shoulders, and arrayed in a bespangled breast-plate and greaves that were surely forged by his mythical forbear, Vulcan. It is Rubezahl. At first displeased at all the noise, he soon cheers up at the sight of the dancing and descends from his rocky ledge to take part in the jollity. Possessing the gift of invisibility, as though he were wearing the ring of Gyges,[2] he circulates among the groups, causing consternation by tickling them.

Count Edgar enters the mine to compliment his workers on their labours, which have made him rich and eligible to win the hand of Eoline, the adopted daughter of the powerful Count Ratibor.

Eoline, who is curious to see this underground world, arrives shortly afterwards with her father, strewing the dark cavern, where only gold, silver and precious stones grow, with wild flowers, still damp from the dew, that she has picked on her way. Everyone gathers around her, admiring her and singing the praises of her beauty, goodness and charm. Beneath this beauty, a second beauty can be admired, shining through the layer of the first like a flame in an alabaster globe. There is a sensation of sudden glints of phosphorescence; it is as if Eoline is but an envelope, a transparent veil concealing some higher being, a goddess condemned by some fate to live among mortals. Madly in love, Edgar pursues his beloved, trying to restrain her high spirits.

While Eoline has been admiring the treasures of the mine, accepting a morsel to eat, joining in the dances, greeting the girls who crowd around her, and receiving the indiscreet confidences of a young worker who is in love with Lisinka, Rubezahl, the spirit of the mountain, has reappeared. Standing enraptured, with hands outstretched and a look of wonder on his face, he has been following every movement of Edgar's beloved. He gazes hungrily at her beauty. Never before has such a marvellous creature penetrated his dark realm; none of the ondines from the innermost lakes or the salamanders of the Plutonic depths who have tried to seduce him ever possessed such perfection of feature and form, such virginal grace, such an enchanting smile. Rubezahl is entranced by Eoline; Cupid's arrow has found its mark through the dense layers of the earth.

[2] According to legend Gyges was a shepherd—other sources have him as an army officer—who found a ring that made him invisible, and used it to seduce the queen of King Candaules of Lydia. He slayed the king and usurped the throne.

All of a sudden he transforms himself into a miner, and with an awkward, rustic manner approaches the table in spite of the scorn of the noblemen. He ignores their mockery, for concealed beneath his modest attire is a greater power than theirs. He can see clearly the seams of metal as they flow through the rock; it is he who holds the key to the treasures of the mountain, and what is the wealth of the caliphs compared with such dazzling marvels? In the simple miner who draws himself up proudly, the spectator can recognise Rubezahl, the king of the gnomes. Impervious to Edgar's anger and his sword, which strikes but empty air, the genie declares his love for Eoline. He will make her queen of the gnomes, and the earth will offer her all its riches. Thus Rubezahl has decreed, and nothing can stand in his way, for who can possibly oppose a genie, and above all one so rich!

Eoline's protests are in vain, as are Edgar's attempts to teach the insolent fellow a lesson. Rubezahl remains unruffled; he makes a gesture, and the cavern glows with a purple light, as if the walls that contain the fire in the centre of the earth had crumbled away. The genie disappears in a burst of flame. Everyone scatters in terror, and solitude reigns in the mine.

As soon as the mortals have left, the gnomes resume possession of their domain. Out of fissures in the rock emerge a multitude of small grey-clad beings, their cunning little eyes gleaming beneath their hoods. They caper about with strange movements to uncoordinated rhythms in an attempt to amuse their master, who appears troubled. The gnomes are followed by pretty creatures in dresses sparkling with the colours of minerals, who try, with no greater success, to distract the king of the mountain from his thoughts. Rubezahl pays no more attention to his page Trilby, his beloved goblin. The thoughts that fill his mind pierce the dark walls of the cavern; the thick rock becomes opaque, melts away in a vapour, becomes tinged with blue, and reveals, in a magical perspective, the interior of a Gothic chamber. In the gentle glow of a lamp, Eoline is seen sleeping peacefully on a coverlet of checkered brocade. A moonbeam shines into the chamber through the open window, and as its silvery light falls on Eoline, a metamorphosis takes place. Like a chrysalis emerging from a cocoon and flying away as a butterfly, the girl sheds her earthly form and leaves her crumpled clothes on the bed. For at night she, like her mother before her, becomes a dryad. Her companions now surround her and lead her into the forest to the oak tree to which her existence is bound. "Mortal or goddess, it matters not," cries Rubezahl, "I shall win her love." The vision vanishes, and the curtain falls.

In the following act, the pink tinge of dawn is chasing away the blue moonlight as it plays upon the high roofs of a Gothic mansion that stands at the edge of a sheet of sparkling water. All the rest of the scene is still in shadow, and in the foreground, near a ruined tower, an ancient oak tree, split by lightning, spreads its dead and twisted branches. The betrothal day of Edgar and Eoline is dawning and the miners are preparing a throne of flowers and foliage for the ceremony. "Suppose we cut down that dead tree that is in the way," says Frantz, Lisinka's sweetheart, to old Hermann, the miners' chief. "Take care never to do that, my children," replies Hermann. "There is a legend attached to that tree. The lady of the manor, Eoline's mother, was drawn by some mysterious attraction and used to rest in its shadow. Then one stormy day it was struck by lightning, and as though her life were joined to the oak tree's existence, the lady died."

While the old miner is recounting this legend, a crackle of sparks is heard and Rubezahl springs out of the ruined tower as if in pursuit of a vision. And indeed, like a bird swooping over a lake, a luminous figure is skimming above the river, its reflection spread out in the water, like a bird swooping over a lake. It is the dryad resuming her earthly form with the coming of day.

The sunrise lights the front of the mansion, sparkles in the water of the river, and gilds the foliage of the trees in the park. Workmen come marching in with their banner and tools, bearing heavy silver ingots on poles that they are to present to their lord. They are followed by the girls of the village, and Rubezahl's goblin, Trilby, who has come out of the ground disguised as a page to assist his master in his courtship, amuses himself by flirting with them and arousing the jealousy of their rustic swains.

Soon Duke Ratibor, Eoline, Edgar and the gentry who have come to witness the betrothal enter and take their places, and the festivities begin. A nobleman, wearing a bizarre yet magnificent costume, insolently pushes himself forward. There is a general stir of surprise, mingled with unease. You sense a supernatural force capable of dominating the will, overcoming resistance, exerting fascination like a snake, and drawing its victim to the abyss. Mesmerised by his gaze, Eoline rises to her feet and begins to dance with him. She is like a dove flying down from branch to branch towards a reptile lying in wait at the foot of the tree—its feathers ruffled, wings aquiver, terrified yet fascinated. It is obvious that Eoline feels no love for Rubezahl, yet this magical dance benumbs and intoxicates her. An insidious languor softens her movements, her head droops, her eyes become misty, and her lips part in a smile as her breathing quickens. Half fainting, she falls into Rubezahl's arms.

This *pas*, which is a masterpiece, sends all who watch it, on stage as well as in the audience, into raptures. Count Edgar is the only one who finds it distasteful, and frankly he has good reason to do so. He angrily rushes up to the couple brandishing his dagger, but the king of the gnomes fells him to the ground with a gesture and disappears down a star trap into his cavernous realm. The girls go to the aid of Eoline, who has fainted, and bear her away.

We now find ourselves inside the mansion, in a rich Gothic chamber, Eoline's bedroom. The girl is asleep, but her dreams are disturbed by terrors and strange visions. She shudders and sits up on the edge of her bed, thinking she hears voices and is seeing moving shadows. It is not all imagination, for Trilby, sent as a scout, has found his way into the room, and his cunning little face appears through the curtains. However, Eoline recovers her composure when she is joined by her maids, who heard her cries. She tells them of her bad dream. To banish it from her mind, she goes to her mirror—an object before which a woman can forget everything, even her love, can she not?—and smiles to see that the dream has not dulled the brilliance of her eyes or paled her cheeks. Her maids are helping her choose jewellery when suddenly her charming reflection in the mirror is replaced by the figure of Rubezahl, kneeling before her in a passionate attitude and stretching out his arms as if to clasp her to his heart. She staggers back in a swoon. The vision disappears, but the lovesick genie has purloined Eoline's reflection. Unable to possess her body, he has stolen her shadow, and the mirror no longer reproduces the girl's features. But that image of her, lifelike though it is, does not satisfy Rubezahl; he is intent on having the original, and he soon returns, more ardent and passionate than ever. Eoline defends herself as would any woman whose heart is given to another, but her situation is perilous. Trilby has frightened the maids away, and the genie is persistent. The girl throws herself on to a prie-dieu before a holy image; only prayers can save her now. Midnight strikes—the hour of her metamorphosis. A moonbeam filters into the room, and on its luminous shaft the dryad flies away, leaving Rubezahl forlorn and furious. Warned that an interloper has entered Eoline's room, Edgar runs in, sword in hand, but the king of the gnomes has anticipated the discovery of electricity. His weapon makes blue sparks fly as the two swords clash and sends a terrible spasm up Edgar's arm. And before the Count can pick up his useless weapon, the genie has vanished.

It is a daunting task, even for a king of gnomes, to pursue a woman with a dual existence, who slips away as soon as you feel her in your grasp and takes refuge in a tree trunk in a vast forest. Rubezahl, for all his skill, is at a loss. Disguising himself as a woodcutter, he inspects each one of the oak trees, young and old. Beneath which protective bark is Eoline concealed? He cannot tell. But then he has an idea—he will test each oak with his axe. As soon as the steel blade bites into the wood, a dryad appears imploring him to spare the tree to which her life is linked. Rubezahl continues this process until he comes to Eoline's oak. The poor dryad resists as long as she can. Cutting into the sapwood, the axe draws drops of rosy blood that stand out on its delicate skin before she decides to emerge. The gnome threatens to fell the tree that she animates if she persists in rejecting his love. Her graceful entreaties, her modest prayers calm the demon's anger, and he is then surrounded by her companions, who form groups that conceal her from view while she makes her escape. Edgar, who has been searching for her, takes her back to the mansion.

There the marriage festivities of Edgar and Eoline are to take place in the armoury, which is decorated with a panoply of cavalry weapons. The sound of an organ is heard from the adjoining chapel, and soon the couple emerge, joined together for all eternity in the presence of God and man. A number of dances follow. Eoline, in a superb *pas*, expresses the chaste rapture and divine joy of licit love. And meanwhile, you may ask, what is Rubezahl doing? Will he allow the girl he loves to marry his rival? Is that to be the sad fate of being king of the gnomes? But wait! See that red glow over there at the back, turning the forest to crimson. Clouds of smoke stream and twist into the sky, flames shoot up, the fire spreads, and in the inferno the oaks that the dryads inhabit contort with pain.

Eoline collapses, holding one hand to her heart and making a gesture of farewell to Edgar with the other. The fire that is destroying her oak is consuming her too; she dies, and Rubezahl suddenly appears at her side, laughing with diabolical malice. At least she will belong to no one else.

Mme Ferraris's triumph was complete, and the Russians are notoriously difficult in matters of dance. They have seen Taglioni, Elssler, Cerrito and Carlotta Grisi, not to mention their own ballerinas, a young choreographic army graduated from their ballet school, one of the best run in the world, agile, supple, marvellously disciplined, and with talents already fully formed that lack only stage experience, which will come with time.

Our article is already long, but more space is needed to finish it. There are so many blue eyes shining, so much blonde hair flying, so many tiny feet twinkling and slender legs rising and falling in this whirl of gauze, sequins, smiles and pink tights called *Eoline, ou la Dryade*! And remember that we are a foreigner who arrived only yesterday, listening with surprised fascination to all those strange feminine names, sounding like unknown birdsongs, and yet so sweet, so full of vowels and music that they might be mistaken for Sanskrit names in some unknown Indian drama by William Jones or Schlegel[3]: Prikhunova, Muravieva, Amosova, Kosheva, Lyadova, Snetkova, Makarova .. [4]. It seemed that we were transcribing from the text of *Sacountala*, for the benefit of the dancers of the Rue Le Peletier, all those beautiful names, full-bloomed and scented like the flowers of India, that caused them such alarm. Well, with your greater knowledge of all this charming world, just imagine that each one of those names signifies beauty, talent, or at least youth and hope. As for Mme Petipa,[5] her French name acts as a guide,

[3] Sir William Jones's translation of *Sacountala* into English was published in Calcutta in 1798. August Wilhelm von Schlegel (1821–68), the greatest authority of his age on comparative linguistics, translated the *Bhagavad-Gita* and other Indian classics into Latin.

[4] Anna Prikhunova (1830–87), Martha Muravieva (1838–79), Anastasia and Nadezhda Amosova (1832–88 and 1833–1903), Anna Kosheva (b. 1840), Maria Lyadova (1837–77), Maria Snetkova (b. 1831), Alexandra Makarova (1828–89). Gautier spelt one of these names "Kupieva", but it seems there was no dancer of that name and I have taken the liberty to assume that he had misread the name of Kosheva.

[5] The first wife of Marius Petipa, *née* Surovshchikova (1836–82).

although she is Russian, and we can state more specifically that she is delicate, pretty, light, and worthy to be admitted to that family of distinguished choreographers.

Journal de Saint-Petersbourg,
November 23rd, 1858 (N.S.).
(*Voyage en Russie*, ch. 12.)
L:1616.

76

Tribute to Emma Livry

Emma Livry[1] was barely twenty-one. From her début in the *pas* from *Herculanum*, she had shown herself to be a dancer of the first order, and the public's attention had never strayed from her. She belonged to the chaste school of Taglioni that transforms the dance into an almost spiritual art by its modest grace, seemly reserve and virginal translucency. Catching a glimpse of her through the transparency of her veilings, her foot barely raising the hem, one was reminded of a happy shade, an elysian apparition at play in a bluish moonbeam, for she possessed its imponderable lightness, and her silent flight shot through space without a quiver in the air. In the ballet—the only one, alas—that she created, she played the part of a butterfly. This was no banal choreographic gallantry. She could imitate its charming, capricious flight as it settled on a flower without bending its stem. But she resembled a butterfly too closely, for she too burnt her wings in the flame, and as though wishing to take part in the funeral of a sister, two white butterflies hovered ceaselessly over her white coffin during its journey from the church to the cemetery. This detail, which the Greeks would have seen as a poetic symbol, was remarked by thousands of people, for an immense crowd accompanied the hearse. On the simple tomb of the young dancer, what epitaph could be more apt than that written by a poet of the Anthology for an Emma Livry of antiquity: "Oh, earth, rest gently over me, I trod so lightly upon thee".[2]

To be sure, it was the young victim's talent, youth and tragic death, and her long suffering, that were largely responsible for the warm and affectionate

[1] Emma Livry (1842–63) was a French dancer of exceptional promise whose career was tragically cut short when she was severely burned at a rehearsal. She had made her début, not in David's opera *Herculanum* (f.p. March 4th, 1859), but in *La Sylphide* in October 1858, when Gautier was in Russia. Marie Taglioni was tempted out of retirement to see the new wonder, and was so impressed that she stayed to coach her and become teacher of the perfection class at the Opéra until 1870. She also choreographed an important ballet for her, *Le Papillon*, mus. Offenbach, f.p. November 26th, 1860. Emma Livry did not recover from her accident, dying after months of agony on July 26th, 1863.

[2] Euripides, *Alcestis*, 462.

concern of an entire population, but there was yet another cause—the desire
to honour that life of purity in a profession beset with temptations, that
modest virtue in face of which slander held its tongue, that love of art and toil
which asked for no other reward than the dance itself; the desire to show
respect for an artist who respected herself. If anything could console a
mother's grief, it would be that procession, so solemn, so affecting, so
religious in character, that followed the mourning carriage in which, seated
among the celebrities of the Opéra, were the two Sisters of Charity who had
tended the poor girl during the agony she had borne so courageously and in so
Christian a spirit.

Le Moniteur Universel, August 3rd, 1863.
(*Portraits contemporains*, pp. 429–430.)
L:1872.

77

Opéra: *Néméa*

Néméa, ou l'Amour vengé, ballet-
pantomime in 2 acts, sc. Meilhac
and L. Halévy, ch. Saint-Léon,
mus. Minkus, f.p. July 11th, 1864.

B allet is generally looked upon as something light and of little importance, and it is popularly believed that the first scenario that comes into a writer's head will do. This is a fallacy, for no other theatrical work presents such difficulty. Convention is stronger than in opera and tragedy, for it is easier to convey passion by song or verse than by *cabrioles* and *ronds de jambe*. Also, the number of subjects in which dancing can evolve, if not naturally, at least plausibly, is extremely restricted. Ballet can only be interpreted by gesture; it cannot therefore allude to past events, and its verbs can only be construed in the indicative tense. Everything in it is happening in the present, and each situation must be arranged as a tableau that can be understood without a caption.

The ideal ballet scenario would surely be an album of scenes drawn in outline, such as Retzsch's illustrations for Goethe's *Faust*, from which a child can understand the story from the pictures without reading a word of the text.[1] Ballet cannot even name its characters, and it only establishes their station in life by means of costume and outward insignia.

Everything that cannot be reduced to design, grouping and perspective is not of its essence. The true element of choreography is plastic animation, and the writer of a ballet scenario would do well to collaborate with a painter or a sculptor, who is used to presenting his ideas visually through his mute art. This preamble may seem somewhat serious for the subject of dance, but if treated seriously, choreography is capable of producing excellent effects that

---

[1] See No. 60, note 4.

are undreamed of in France, although familiar in Italy, where the traditions of antiquity and a feeling for sculptural form have been better preserved.

Viganò, whom Stendhal always refers to as the immortal Viganò without a trace of irony, and who is for him the equal of his favourite artists, Canova and Rossini, produced works of marvellous beauty in this line. His *Prometeo* is a grandiose conception instilled with the powerful breath of the primitive Melpomene. And no one has made a finer translation of Aeschylus than he.[2]

Having taken his measure against that Titan of Greek tragedy, Viganò had no misgivings about producing *Othello* as a ballet,[3] and if Stendhal's admiration is anything to go by, Shakespeare's drama only gained by this transformation. Seeing the great choreographer at rehearsal was like watching an Athenian sculptor trying out poses on his models. Not only did he arrange every attitude, but he concerned himself with the colour of the costumes and the matching of the tones in the groups. The effects he obtained were so prodigious that one could understand the frenzied enthusiasm that was aroused by the mimes Paris and Bathyllus in Imperial Rome. Does Viganò have any successors? Possibly, but one has to look hard to find them. While waiting for their discovery, let us come to *Néméa, ou l'Amour vengé*, the ballet that was performed last Monday at the Théâtre Impérial de Musique et de Danse.

When the curtain rises after a charming introduction which augurs well for the music of M. Minkus,[4] the Hungarian composer, the eyes alight on a set representing a romantic forest that has grown on the site of a classical sacred wood, where in the days when the Gods of Olympus held sway, a temple of Cupid was erected, several columns of which are still standing, symbols of elegance and beauty, amid the barbaric invasion of undergrowth. On a plinth dappled with moss and garlanded with ivy, the statue of the eternally youthful Cupid still holds, intact in its marble, the pose that Praxiteles gave it in days of old. Some miraculous power has preserved it from the ravages of

[2] Salvatore Viganò (1769–1821), the most celebrated and influential Italian choreographer of his time, noted particularly for the dramatic content of his works. He produced the only ballet for which Beethoven wrote the music, *Prometeo* (original version, 1801, revised 1813), based on *Prometheus Bound*, one of the plays of the early Greek dramatist, Aeschylus.

[3] F.p. La Fenice, Venice, during the Carnival season of 1819.

[4] Ludwig Minkus (1826–1917), composer of many ballet scores, mostly written for the Russian Imperial Theatres, by which he was employed in that capacity. *Néméa* was a reworking of a ballet Saint-Léon had earlier produced in St. Petersburg, *Fiammetta* (f.p. Bolshoi Th., February 25th (N.S.), 1864).

time and man, and the friendliest of the Gods of old has not met his iconoclast. But in what part of the world is Cupid standing on his pedestal amid the ruins of his temple?

A peasant wedding party entering in a burst of jollity gives the answer to this question by their costumes. We are in the company of Hungarians or Walachians, in the Banat, near the military frontiers[5]—geographical information that is quite sufficient for a ballet.

To ensure their happiness, the young couple observe a popular superstition that newly-weds ignore at their peril, and kneel before Cupid's statue. This duty accomplished, the revellers form a kind of bacchic procession and, with much ceremony, bring on a small barrel decorated with ribbons and garlands that contains "the marriage wine". Everyone applauds as Hermiola and Kiralfy[6] drink. Only Néméa fails to join in the general rejoicing. Is she jealous of her friend's happiness? Is she in love with Kiralfy? No, Néméa is pining of a mysterious and unattainable love, and while she has strength enough to keep her secret, she cannot conceal her melancholy. Her friends try in vain to cheer her up and suggest consulting the oracle of the flowers.

Néméa refuses, claiming that the flowers have nothing but gloomy messages for her. So the girls consult the oracle for her, and by a clever ruse, bring back a favourable reply. A wan smile plays on the lips of the unhappy girl, who allows herself to be drawn into the dancing. The friends of Hermiola and Kiralfy perform a dance so arranged as to prevent the newly-weds coming together. The boys carry off the young bride, and the girls carry off the husband, and everyone laughs at the lovers' vexation. Then Néméa executes the *pas de la berceuse* with an abandoned and melancholy grace that shows that she is in no mood for dancing.

Adjoining the forest, and separated from it only by a terrace, is Count Molder's park. The noise of the village wedding has drawn the Count out of his mansion with a retinue of debauchees and courtesans. Maybe the crude rejoicing of these good people will afford him a few minutes' amusement. And what is more, peasant girls are sometimes pretty, and a little sun-tanned face can be a welcome change from painted and made-up features, just as brown bread can be a change from white. Completely absorbed with the

---

[5] The Banat was a region of the Ottoman empire governed by a ban. The Banat of Temesvar was the area of fertile plain between Timisoara (formerly Temesvar, now in western Romania) and Belgrade. At the time Gautier was writing, this had long been disputed territory between the Austrian and Ottoman empires. In fact at this time Belgrade was still occupied by Turkish troops, who were not to withdraw finally until 1867.

[6] The names of the bridal couple seem to have been borrowed from a group of Hungarian dancers, the Kiralfy family, whom Gautier had seen at the Théâtre Déjazet only a few weeks earlier. The group consisted of three dancers, Imre and Bolossy and their sister Haniola, whom Gautier referred to in his review (*Le Moniteur*, June 27th, 1864) as Hermiola.

bride, Count Molder does not so much as cast a glance at Néméa, and yet it is he who is the object of the carefully concealed love that is the sole cause of the girl's pallor.

Count Molder is a type of Don Juan with waxed moustache and golden brandenburgs, who tipples, gambles a little, believes in neither God nor Devil, and in the prevailing custom seduces all the women by these pleasant qualities. Soon, to the great distress of Néméa, who runs into the forest so as not to witness a sight that will break her heart, the Count's attentions to Hermiola become so pressing that Kiralfy invokes the protection of Cupid, guardian spirit of young couples. At the sound of Cupid's name, the Count gives a scornful laugh. He loathes that lying God and all the illusions, languishings, ecstasies and professions of long fidelity that are associated with him. Pleasure alone has any meaning for him, and springing at the statue, he strikes it, mutilates it, shakes it, and topples it from its plinth.

As the statue falls, the sky darkens, a peal of thunder is heard, and a mighty wind sweeps through the forest. Astonished by this marvel, but still persisting in his impiety, Count Molder, like his model, Don Juan, before the monument to the Commander, has nothing to say but "Let us be off from here".[7]

To our shame we must admit that we were distressed by this fictitious sacrilege. We have preserved a sort of superstitious affection for the old Gods who were chased out of Olympus. For two thousand years they reigned over the world without opposition. They were the Gods of Homer, Hesiod, Aeschylus, Aristophanes, Plato, Socrates, Horace and Virgil. Art has given them the most perfect, majestic and charming forms. If they no longer have any power, they still live on through their beauty, and our gardens and palaces are filled with their statues. Before we saw the light, they provided a noble translation of the divine dream that humanity, being deprived of the gift of prophecy, cannot fly in the face of nature. They therefore command respect. In their white marble arms they cradled the world in its infancy, whispering in its ear the most delightful poems, the most ravishing fables, the most graceful symbols.

If, in those nameless regions where ever-expanding waves still preserve echoes of everything that has ever been but can no longer be perceived, in the mysterious depths of Hades beyond time and space, those ancient divinities known as "the Mothers", who vanished long ago and lost their cult, sleep in some aromatic or spectral existence not to be defined in human terms, imagine the immense sadness, the overpowering melancholy to which they must be prey, having once looked forward to an eternity of youth and power in a luminous paradise, inhaling, like an intoxicating nectar, the smoke of

---

[7] In the second act of Mozart's opera, *Don Giovanni*, Don Giovanni asks the statue of the Commander, whom he has killed in one of his escapades, to supper, and having done so, leaves with the words, *"Partiamo—via di qua"*.

sacrifices and distant incense rising from the earth![8] How painfully must they have felt the insults to their fallen glory, those idols of a religion that has now become myth! And again, what pleasure it must give them when a festival, a ballet or an opera procures them some vain act of adoration to satisfy the demands of the production.

We remember how impressed we were by the performance of Donizetti's *Les Martyrs*,[9] which featured a sacrifice to Jupiter. The triangular façade of the great temple seemed carved in the serenity of the azure sky. Perfumed incense burned in the bronze tripods, the victims were led to the sacrifice crowned with flowers, and the high priest, clad in white, uttered the sacred words. The illusion was complete; one might have been back in the times of polytheism. It seemed that the statue of the God nodded his head in assent, and that after this nutation, the scent of his ambrosial locks spread through the theatre. The flash that followed the sacrifice was surely not produced by lycopodium ignited and blown through a pipe, nor was there any need to rock the wheelbarrow full of paving stones in the flies to imitate the thunder.

According to Heinrich Heine, in his admirable piece on *The Gods in Exile*,[10] the Gods live on in our midst, incognito, as befits fallen rulers, but still viewed with disfavour by the authorities.

Jupiter lives in obscurity on the Island of Rabbits, an island in the North Sea, where he carries on a small furrier's business. With him are the old goat Amalthaea[11] of the ever-pink teats and his eagle, half bald but still casting thunderbolts with its eyes. Sailors have spoken to him, and were answered in very ancient Greek; a mariner from Piraeus who happened to be there understood several words of it. Bacchus has become a wine steward in a monastery. In the daytime he wears a frock coat and serves wine to the friars, who are amazed at the taste, bouquet and colour of the divine beverage that has entered into their cellars as local wine; and by night, resuming his marble-like nudity with a crown of vine leaves on his head, he leads the grand bacchanal through the forests with the likes of the maenads, Silenus, the

---

[8] In Goethe's *Faust*, Part II, Act I, "the Mothers", the most ancient of deities, beyond the knowledge and reach of the minds of man, are suggested by Mephistopheles to Faust as a source of the power by which the legendary beauty of Paris and Helen can be brought back to life.

[9] *Les Martyrs*, opera in 4 acts by Donizetti, f.p. Opéra, April 10th, 1840.

[10] See No. 64, note 5.

[11] Amalthaea, daughter of King Melissus of Crete, fed Jupiter with goat's milk. Hence some ancient authors called her a goat, maintaining that Jupiter rewarded her by placing her in Heaven as a constellation and gave one of her horns to the nymphs who had cared for him as a child. This was the horn of plenty, which had the power of giving the nymphs whatever they desired.

aegypans, and the tigers of India, intoxicated with blood and the grape.[12] Mercury, or Hermes-Pyscopompos, is a cashier in Hamburg, and on one night in the year, remembering his former occupation, he rows ghosts in a mysterious boat.[13] As for Venus, you have no doubt met her on the pavement in the Rue Notre-Dame-de-Lorette. A long cashmere shawl covers her statuesque figure from neck to heels, and as she bends her head, humiliated at the absence of her mother-of-pearl conch shell drawn by doves, a glimpse is caught of golden hair twisted into little curls beneath the brim of her hat. The corset is as becoming to her as the girdle, and her feet are shod with laced boots instead of cothurnes. She does not walk, she glides, *et vera incessu patuit dea!*[14]

MM. Meilhac and Ludovic Halévy,[15] who seem to have thought of Heinrich Heine for a moment when writing their scenario, have placed Cupid in a Hungarian forest and given him the task of bringing happiness to couples who kneel before him. But as you shall see, his usefulness does not end there.

Néméa, in despair at the coldness of the Count, of whose impiety she has no idea, returns to implore Cupid's assistance. By some inexplicable magic, the statue of the God has resumed its place on the plinth, but now larger, more beautiful, more alive. The Greek sculptor would this time have admitted defeat.

Néméa ascends the steps of the pedestal and stretches up on tiptoe to whisper her distress in the God's ear. But has she been dreaming? The marble cheek is warm, a fiery expression glows from the immobile white eyes, a scented breath comes forth from the bow-shaped lips. It is no longer a statue, but the God himself! Stepping down from the pedestal with a movement of incomparable grace and the rhythm of a Greek hexameter, Cupid approaches the girl. This movement is one of the great effects of the ballet. The substitution for the marble of the immortal flesh of the God, aglow with rose-pink light and ambrosia, could not have been carried out in a nobler, simpler or more antique fashion. The whole audience broke into applause at this walk which, from its first step, revealed the presence of the legitimate son of Venus.

---

[12] The maenads were a sect that indulged in wild orgies. Silenus was a demi-god, the attendant of Bacchus, fat, jolly and eternally inebriated. The Aegypanes were a mythological race in the centre of Africa, half man, half goat.

[13] As well as being the messenger of the Gods, Mercury rowed the souls of the dead to the Underworld.

[14] "And shows her true divinity in her step." Virgil, *Aeneid*, I 405.

[15] Henri Meilhac (1831–97) and Ludovic Halévy (1834–1908) formed one of the most successful literary partnerships in the field of operetta. Their works include the libretti for Offenbach's *La Belle Hélène* (1864), *La Vie Parisienne* (1866) and *La Grande Duchesse de Gérolstein* (1867), and Bizet's *Carmen* (1875). Halévy was also the author of an amusing series of stories partly set back-stage at the Opéra, collected under the title of *La Famille Cardinal*.

Cupid promises to avenge Néméa for the indifference of Count Molder, who has rashly defied his power and insulted his statue. He will endow Néméa with every attraction, not that this is really needed, and will pierce the Count's heart with one of his golden arrows, which will fill him with an inextinguishable passion.

At a gesture from the God, Néméa's simple peasant dress vanishes to reveal the costume of a nymph in white transparent gauze. Two little fauns come out from the wood, one carrying a polished metal mirror in which the girl sees herself more beautiful and charming than before, and the other playing on his pan-pipes a melodious air that accompanies the *pas* of Néméa, who has now been transformed, without much effort, into a perfect dancer. With a pupil like that, a teacher has little difficulty. Some little *putti* come forward to perform a dance. Electric light sweeps across the forest; nymphs gambol in the pale rays, then the shadows deepen and blue flashes, like will-o'-the-wisps, begin to flicker in the dark background of the ancient trees. This is the *pas des lucioles*.

To tell the truth, all this has a touch of witchcraft and the magic forest that we do not much care for. The authors have not made the most of their idea. If, by means similar to that which Goethe adopted in the second part of *Faust*, where he makes Helen appear at the height of the Middle Ages, they wanted to transpose the antique Cupid into modern times, they should have made the most of the contrast, which is such a good one for ballet.

The old forest, whose undergrowth obscures the ruined temple, and whose black depths have a romantic picturesque quality, ought to have vanished when the God appeared in his immortal form, giving place to an idealised Cythera, ablaze with light, in which the marble temple rose up, pure and white, among clusters of oleanders.

Venus herself and the sacred trio of the Graces should have descended from the skies to instruct Néméa in the art of feminine charms. Venus could have lent her the girdle that Juno borrowed when she wanted to seduce Jupiter. All that would have provided some appropriate choreographic ideas and made a scene that would have stood out from the rest of the piece by its brilliance. But the blue flashes, the will-o'-the-wisps, and the little fauns looking like imps give an air of *Walpurgisnacht* to this scene, which should have been bright, brilliant and serene, like everything to do with ancient mythology.

Pointing a menacing finger at the Count's mansion, Cupid leaves with Néméa, and the setting returns to its original aspect. The toppled statue still lies among the plants and flowers crushed under its weight, and when the Count returns home with his companions, he mocks the powerlessness of a God who cannot even defend his image.

In the second act, an orgy is in progress in Count Molder's mansion, quite a usual occurrence. Through an opening in an arcade can be seen a rich salon, where a supper party is coming to a rowdy end. Glasses are filled and emptied; everyone is drinking and gambling, and dice are being thrown among the bottles. However, the Count is not satisfied. The pleasure he seeks evades him, and he is finding his friends boring and his mistresses ugly. The leader of a troupe of gypsies is then announced. Perhaps some of his dancers will please Their Lordships.

This gypsy chief is none other than Cupid in a fanciful costume of blue and white that shows off the slender, graceful form of a young Greek God. But Count Molder is too drunk and unartistic to recognise Eros in this disguise.

Several gypsy couples perform dances, but vivacious and pretty though they are, the Count is no more satisfied with their dancing than with their appearance.

Then Cupid presents Néméa. Hardly has she described a few attitudes than Molder is troubled. An unknown fire runs through his body; he feels trans-fixed, afire, and shows all the symptoms described in Sappho's famous ode.[16] He is in love; Cupid's revenge is complete.

While her dancing expresses all the ardour and intoxicating sensuality of passion, Néméa assumes an air of indescribable coldness whenever the Count approaches, and this combination of fire and ice produces such a powerful attraction that the libertine, now a convert to love, falls at the girl's feet and begs her to marry him. But Eros, with an imperious gesture, makes a pretence of taking the dancer away. The Count rushes at the God with a dagger, but the weapon shatters in his hand, and with a show of annoyance Cupid reveals his identity. "You love this girl, but she will never be yours." And exercising an influence which Néméa is unable to resist, he draws her to the back of the room. The walls then part, and the temple of Cupid reappears, risen from its ruins, with the God standing on his pedestal.

Néméa goes down on her knees to beg Eros to pardon the Count, whom she still loves. The son of Venus is not a very vindictive deity; he smiles, and the girl falls into her lover's arms.

It is Mlle Muravieva[17] who plays the rôle of the girl. The qualities of her dancing are well-known—lively, spirited, original, carrying grace to the

---

[16] No. a.5 in Lobel's edition of Sappho's poems, freely translated by John Hall in 1652:

> I'me speechless, feavrish, fires assail
> My fainting flesh, my sight doth fail
> Whilst to my restless mind my ears
>   Still hum new fears.
>
> Cold sweats and tremblings so invade
> That like a wither'd flower I fade
> So that my life being almost lost,
>   I seem a Ghost.

[17] Martha Muravieva (1838–79) was one of the leading Russian ballerinas of the time. She was a pupil of Saint-Léon, and visited Paris as guest ballerina at the Opéra in the summers of 1863, making her French début in *Giselle*, and 1864. Gautier did not review her *Giselle*, but was inspired by the production to write an important article on stage design (*Le Moniteur*, May 11th, 1863).

limits of impossibility in *attitudes penchées* and sudden *renversées, pointes* driven into the ground like arrows, and rapid *tacqueté* movements. Her legs have nerves of steel that she can flex and soften, as she does in that ravishing *berceuse*, so simple and childlike, which she performs with great facility and nonchalant charm. In each of her *pas* she aroused prolonged enthusiasm which expressed itself in repeated bursts of applause.

Mlle Eugénie Fiocre[18] is Cupid, who was surely never portrayed in a more beautiful, more graceful, or more charming body. Mlle Fiocre has managed to combine the perfections both of a young girl and of a youth, and out of them to form a sexless beauty which is beauty itself. She might have been hewn from a block of Paros marble by a Greek sculptor, and animated by a miracle such as that of Galathea. To the purity of marble she adds the suppleness of life. Her movements are developed and balanced in a sovereign harmony. Each one of her attitudes offers ten profiles that an artist would be sorry not to capture. What admirable legs! They would be the envy of Diana the Huntress. What easy, proud and tranquil grace! What modest, measured gestures, always retaining a sculptural line, never forcing the expression, yet conveying everything. Her miming is so correct, rhythmical and noble that, like that of the mimes of old, it might be regulated by two unseen flute-players. If Psyche had seen this Cupid, she might have perhaps forgotten the original.

In a number of passages the music of *Néméa* reminded us of the songs of the Russian *tsygany* or the Hungarian *Zigeuner*. It has the same haunting, dreamy quality, and the harmonies contain those sweet and rather effeminate distortions that are a secret that Chopin and Glinka knew so well. Particularly deserving of mention is Néméa's theme, a delicious motif which hovers over the entire score, and which the composer, M. Minkus, has had the good taste to orchestrate with the greatest simplicity. No better choice could have been made from the rich treasure of national songs, Slav or Hungarian; we even wished that the composer had been less cautious and had borrowed more of them; it would have given the Parisian public the opportunity of discovering music that deserves to be better known. The *polonaise* and the *mazurka* of the first act were much applauded, and rightly so; their noble, clear-cut rhythms suit the talent of M. Minkus. Perhaps he found that our male dancers could not produce the energetic heel-tapping that sends the rowels of spurs vibrating, but what grace and precision was displayed by our *danseuses*!

The rather less defined action of the second act has certainly influenced the music, which, considered as a whole, is very harmonious and carefully

[18] Eugénie Fiocre (1845–1908), the younger of two sisters who both danced at the Opéra during the Second Empire, was celebrated for her beauty. The rôle of Cupid was therefore a particularly appropriate piece of casting. She played a number of rôles *en travesti* that enabled her to show off her figure, among them being those of the Colonel in *Le Roi d'Yvetot* and Frantz in *Coppélia*.

constructed, but contains fewer passages of inspiration. We must, however, mention a drinking song that is very well handled. In spite of these comments on detail, we must report that this music enjoyed a great success, and we think that every true music-lover will wish to hear such a distinguished and original work.

> *Le Moniteur Universel*, July 18th, 1864.
> L:1947.

78

Opéra: Léontine Beaugrand in *Diavolina*

Diavolina, ballet-pantomime in 1
act, ch. Saint-Léon, mus. Pugni,
f.p. July 6th, 1863, revived
November 27th, 1864.

We have no musical news to convey from the Opéra, not even a titbit about Meyerbeer's *L'Africaine*.[1] But we have to report that Mlle Beaugrand has recently made her début in *Diavolina*, a little ballet by Saint-Léon in which Muravieva used to dance. Mlle Beaugrand is a child of the house, and has risen through all its ranks—*coryphée, troisième danseuse, seconde danseuse*, and now she has become a *premier sujet*.[2] There are several dancers of that rank who are very talented and quite as good as the exotic celebrities who are brought to Paris at great expense,[3] but then we have seen them ever since they were children and the growth of a small shrub under our very nose passes almost unnoticed. Yesterday there was nothing, but today a bud is unfolding which in a few days' time will become a charming flower, and we must beware of some foreigner coming along and saying, 'What a lovely rose you have there!" To make an impression on the public, a sudden burst of brilliance is needed, an unexpected revelation, for you cannot turn a common or garden firefly into a star of the firmament. The point of all this is

[1] *L'Africaine*, Meyerbeer's last grand opera, had been eagerly awaited for some twenty years, and was eventually produced at the Opéra on April 28th, 1865, nearly a year after his death.

[2] Léontine Beaugrand (1842–1925) was trained from childhood in the Opéra ballet school and, as Gautier says, rose through the ranks. This was her first performance in a principal rôle. In the later years of the Second Empire she was overshadowed by foreign guest artists, but after the Franco-German War she came into her own as the leading exponent of the pure French style, remaining one of the most popular stars of the company until her retirement in 1880.

[3] Marie Petipa (in 1861 and 1862), Martha Muravieva (in 1863 and 1864), Amina Boschetti (in 1864).

that Mlle Beaugrand would enjoy great success in London, Milan, St. Petersburg, or wherever she might take her graceful, correct and light style of dancing.

> *Le Moniteur Universel*, December 5th, 1864.
> L:1967.

79

Opéra: Revival of *La Muette de Portici*, with Eugénie Fiocre

La Muette de Portici, opera by
Auber, f.p. 1828, revived on
February 17th, 1865, with Mlle E.
Fiocre as Fenella.

No one has forgotten the sweet, poetic and lovely Marie Vernon, who was so moving in the rôle of Fenella.[1] Her modest, timid, beseeching grace, which almost seemed to crave pardon for her charm, her large, plaintive blue eyes, which shone so brightly when she raised them to the sky, her delicate, immaterial, smooth beauty, her attitude of a bending flower and air of a tender victim made her an ideal choice for the character. She mimed the rôle of the young girl who is seduced and betrayed with such feeling, passion and sadness that her misfortune ought to have rendered her sacrosanct and sheltered her from every outrage. Her mute despair drew tears from the hardest eyes. But the stage will never see that adorable Fenella again, for a happy marriage has concealed her forever beneath the veil of private life.

Now it is Mlle Eugénie Fiocre, the avenging Cupid of *Néméa* who has taken over the rôle of the dumb girl. With her the character assumes features that are still charming but in complete contrast. Marie Vernon's resigned and touching sadness is no more. Anger and indignation are to be found in Mlle Fiocre. She rebels against the misfortune that overwhelms her. Several drops of Masaniello's blood flow in her veins, and although she allows her vengeance to be disarmed by the Duchess's entreaties, one is aware of how much this effort has cost her and how, being a daughter of the people, her heart would delight in humiliating the great lady who is her rival. This love and its fatal consequence have come to disturb a happy, carefree existence, enlivened

---

[1] Marie Vernon's real name was Marie Renon, and according to Janin, she was Gautier's goddaughter. She made her début in September 1862, and was cast as Fenella in *La Muette de Portici* after Emma Livry's accident. She danced at the Opéra until the end of 1864, when she abandoned her career to marry.

by the rhythm of tambourines and the throbing of trumpets, and *tarantellas* danced beneath the branches of the vineyard. Dumbness is no great embarrassment in Naples, the land of mime *par excellence*, where speech is so often replaced by gestures that are more rapid and quite as comprehensible, and before her catastrophe Fenella could not have been melancholy. Melancholy is a delicate Northern flower, which a hot sun burns away. This is how Mlle Fiocre has understood the rôle, and by so doing the young dancer has given proof of her intelligence.

Her naturally smiling features are formed to express the joys and passions of love rather than sad feelings. In the rôle of Fenella her usual expression is a kind of sad astonishment at finding herself involved in all those dark, violent and heart-rendering happenings that shock her more than they move her. As for her physical appearance, if the picturesque costume of the girls of Nisida,[2] with its heavy skirt, rough cloth blouse, and thick, gaily striped apron, are not so becoming to her sculptural beauty as the short tunic of Eros, at least it allowed us to follow the harmonious lines of her beautiful body without being deceived by a corset or crinoline. Every movement of Mlle E. Fiocre's miming might, if arrested in its flow, provide a subject for a drawing or a statuette. She does not seek this effect; it comes to her unwittingly, through the natural elegance of her limbs, the perfection of her proportions, and the purity of her form, which from every angle offer the felicitous profiles, charming curves and harmonious proportions that the sculptors of antiquity discovered. Apart from her beauty, we greatly admired Mlle Eugénie Fiocre's perfect simplicity of gesture and pose. She is nature itself, as artists say. In short, Mlle Eugénie Fiocre is a charming Fenella whom we shall be delighted to see again when, for the hundredth time, we listen to Auber's delicious music that never palls.

Add to these attractions a new *pas* very well arranged by Petipa, the skilful choreographer, and no less well danced by Mlle Fonta.[3]

> *Le Moniteur Universel*, February 27th, 1865.
> L:1972.

---

[2] An island in the Bay of Naples, lying about a mile off shore between Naples and Pozzuoli.

[3] Laure Fonta (b. 1845), who danced at the Opéra from 1863 to 1881, was also very interested in the dances of the past and wrote an introduction on the dances of the sixteenth century for the French edition of Arbeau's *Orchésographie*, published in 1888.

80

Opéra: *Le Roi d'Yvetot*

Le Roi d'Yvetot, ballet-
pantomime in 1 act, sc. de Massa,
ch. L. Petipa, mus. Labarre, f.p.
December 28th, 1865.

*L*e Roi d'Yvetot was given its first performance at the pension fund gala. It had a great success that evening and again at the second performance, which was the press night.

Béranger's song[1] has popularised that little kingdom which its monarch can cross on a donkey in less than half an hour, wearing, not a crown but a simple cotton bonnet with gold edging that has been stitched on by his maidservant, Jeanneton. This is an elective kingdom, and although the reign lasts only for a day, ambitions in the village compete for it with unparalleled ferocity. Factions struggle furiously around this ephemeral throne. For it is good to be a king even if only for twenty-four hours. You are acclaimed, addressed, carried in procession and blessed by the people, you issue decrees, and you are surrounded by sycophants. Delightful! Of the candidates, Maître Crochu the lawyer and Maître Guillaume the innkeeper seem the most likely contenders. But, to the great chagrin of the man of law, it is the innkeeper who wins the day, thanks undoubtedly to his clientele of drinkers and some timely distributions of barrels of cider.

So much for the political background, but politics alone are not enough for a ballet. Choreography must have a female element, a love interest. Exactly, and Maître Crochu and Maître Guillaume each has a daughter, "a ripe young filly",[2] as our forebears used to say, both of them charming and both in love with Jeannot. Happy Jeannot to be favoured by two such fresh, comely and trim young girls! But it is a difficult and perplexing happiness. For if he

[1] Pierre-Jean de Béranger (1780–1857) was a highly popular *chansonnier*, whose songs looked back nostalgically to the Napoleonic era and satirised the restored Bourbon monarchy, for which he was sentenced to a prison sentence in 1821. His poem, *Le Roi d'Yvetot*, written as Napoleon's empire was crumbling, extolled the pleasures of living under a peace-loving king.

[2] The old French phrase that Gautier quotes here is *"de l'âge d'un vieux boeuf"*.

chooses one, he is liable to regret the other, and Jeannot, who is not so stupid as he seems, pays court to both Thérèse and Rosette, separately of course, as Molière's Don Juan did to Mathurine and Charlotte.[3] If it were in Turkey or China, the affair might be resolved by a double marriage, but we are in France where, according to the learned authors, polygamy is a hanging offence. Jeannot is really most embarrassed.

However, the triumphal procession sets off, followed by all the men and boys of the village, with the sole exception of Jeannot, who has arranged to meet Thérèse and Rosette at the same time. Which appointment will be kept? It is a difficult question. Rosette is very pretty, and Thérèse very charming. While he is trying to make up his mind, as unsure as Buridan's ass[4] between his two hay-stacks, the village is invaded by the most delightful regiment of hussars that can possibly be imagined. Hussars without moustaches, if you please, and played by the slenderest, most shapely and most attractive women of the Opéra. Their colonel is Mlle Fiocre, their captain Mlle Louise Marquet. You can judge the rest of the troop by their officers. The village raises no objection to this graceful invasion, and the hussars, discovering Jeannot, who is the only man in the town, blindfold him and lock him up in Maître Crochu's cellar. Having got rid of this awkward witness, the officer in charge orders the bugle to be sounded, and in the windows there appear a host of pretty heads in high *cauchois*[5] bonnets with lace edging, a rustic memory of the wimples of the Middle Ages.

The bonnets come pouring into the village square, and the gallant *colbacks*[6] pursue them with the greatest exuberance. The bevy scatters, although not very much frightened, and takes refuge among some willow trees, wishing, like Galathea, to be seen by their pursuers before disappearing into the transparent foliage. Rosette is the only girl who manages to escape from the charge of the hussars, and left alone in the square, she begins to think of Jeannot. From a cellar window she hears a groan. It is Jeannot begging to be let out from his prison. Rosette frees him, but at that moment a corporal enters, a breaker of heads and hearts, who has no friendly feelings for anyone except girls. Jeannot is not much of a hero, and hides behind the courageous Rosette, who decides to risk a kiss to save her friend, but the young girl slips

---

[3] In *Don Juan, ou le Festin de Pierre*, f.p. Th. du Palais-Royal, February 15th, 1665.

[4] Jean Buridan, a celebrated French philosopher of the fourteenth century, posed the question, in a discussion on free will, what an ass would do if it were equally thirsty and hungry and at an equal distance from a pail of water and a ration of oats.

[5] From the *Pays de Caux*, a region of France, north of the Seine in eastern Normandy, of which Yvetot is the principal town.

[6] A type of military headgear that had been introduced into the French army during Bonaparte's campaign in Egypt, and adopted for the mounted chasseurs of the Consular Guard. It was shaped like an inverted truncated cone, with a high bristle and a loose pocket-like attachment falling down to one side.

away and it is pretty Jeanneton, Maître Guillaume's maid, who receives it instead, lightly brushing her apple-fresh cheek. Before long Thérèse has replaced Jeanneton, and the colonel has sent the corporal packing. It is very dangerous to flirt with a colonel of hussars with such a good figure as Mlle Fiocre. Thérèse discovers this at her peril and at the cost of a smacking kiss that can be heard throughout the village. A merry throng of cavalrymen and young women and girls come running on, and soon dances are being organised. But the festivities are interrupted by the return of the King of Yvetot and his procession. What will the fathers, husbands, brothers, cousins, and every man responsible for a woman in any capacity, say when they see the female population on such intimate terms with this unexpected garrison? The hussars suggest that the village girls should pretend to be resisting them under the leadership of Jeannot, and arm them with flails, pitchforks, rakes, crooks and other weapons. Never did Amazons look so fierce!

The male population of Yvetot is enchanted by this display of heroism, which reveals a Hyrcanian bravery[7] that can face any danger. As a reward for organising such a brilliant defence, the King gives Jeannot the privilege of marrying the girl of his choice. Maître Crochu objects. Jeannot's hat has been found in his cellar, and Thérèse has been compromised; Jeannot must marry his daughter. But the distraught Rosette puts forward a promise of marriage that the village Alcibiades[8] has made to her. Somewhat perplexed, the King of Yvetot scratches his head. Fortunately, he remembers the judgment of Solomon. He proposes to slice Jeannot down the middle and award half of him to each of the claimants. The very idea makes Thérèse, who is more a flirt than a girl in love, roar with laughter, but Rosette takes it seriously. She begins to weep, and throwing herself at the feet of fat old Maître Guillaume, declares that she would rather abandon her sweetheart to her rival than see him sliced in two. And just like Solomon, who in similar circumstances recognised the real mother, the King of Yvetot perceives from this generous renunciation where true love lies, and awards Jeannot entirely to Rosette.

This judgment, notwithstanding that it is very just and based on biblical precedent, infuriates Maître Crochu, who is somewhat pacified when fat Guillaume offers to abdicate as king of Yvetot in his favour. A reconciliation, a marriage and a succession to the throne—what more does a ballet want to set everyone dancing from the backcloth to the footlights? And so the ballet ends with a general *ballabile*.

To this gay, amusing and lively scenario Petipa has designed some charming *pas* and graceful ensembles to a score by M. Labarre, a composer with a

---

[7] See No. 24, note 7.

[8] Alcibiades, an Athenian general noted as much for his philandering as for his professional prowess.

real talent—lively, bright music, full of rhythm and melody, which would be pleasant to listen to on its own without the charm of the dances, pink tights, gauze skirts and pretty faces. The elegant uniforms of the hussars form a happy contrast to the fresh village costumes, and everything is cheerfully set against a coquettishly rustic set by MM. Cambon and Thierry that possesses the delicate blue tones of a Boucher pier-glass.

Mlle Fioretti[9] and Mlle Fonta are both delightful, and we share Jeannot's embarrassment in deciding who is the prettier and the better dancer.

Colonel Eugénie Fiocre, with her slender figure and proud bearing, is like a heroic Amazon queen disguised as a gallant hussar.

Le Moniteur Universel, January 1st, 1866.
L:1986.

[9] Angelina Fioretti (1846–79) danced at the Opéra from 1863 to 1870.

81

Opéra: Revival of *Le Dieu et la bayadère*

Le Dieu et la bayadère. (see No. 10),
revived January 22nd, 1866.

S cribe's libretto . . . certainly made a pleasing canvas, a charming point of departure for an opera or a ballet, and perhaps he did all that could have been expected of a skilled dramatist such as himself. He was obviously hampered by the mute character of the Bayadere that was composed for Mlle Taglioni. The success of Fenella in *La Muette de Portici*[1] might have led him to expect the same sort of success with *Le Dieu et la bayadère*, but Fenella really has lost her voice and it was not just a whim that made her resort to gestures. Dancing and miming are Fenella's only means of communication, while Zoloé's way of speaking is to perform a *pas*; her *ronds de jambe* are phrases and her *jetés battus* the equivalent of words. She conveys love, passion, sorrow and fear by her steps and gestures, as a singer does with arias and notes. This is the convention of her art, and one's mind easily accepts it. There is nothing in pure opera or pure ballet that offends against logic, once the mode of transmitting ideas has been accepted. But the mixture of the two means comes as a shock and puts one off, almost producing the effect of one of those productions in which a great foreign actor plays in his own language while the characters he talks to reply in their native tongues. This was how we once heard Ira Aldridge, the negro tragedian, performing Othello in St. Petersburg,[2] delivering threats in English to a Desdemona who was imploring his pity in German. A dialogue between song and dance produces the same sort of ill-assortment . . . .

Mme Taglioni, a slender, diaphanous figure in white, was nothing like the

---

[1] *La Muette de Portici*, with its famous mime rôle of the dumb girl Fenella, had been given two years earlier, in 1828, with Lise Noblet.

[2] Ira Aldridge (1805–67) was visiting St. Petersburg when Gautier was there in the winter of 1858. Gautier saw him at the Teatr-Cirk in *Othello*, speaking his part in the original while the rest of the cast, who were German, spoke in Schiller's translation.

real *bibiaderis* who dance before the doors of the choultries and temples, as we learnt when we saw Amany, Saoundiroun and Ramgoun. With complete disregard for local colour, she scorned the sandalwood covering that confines and perfumes the bosom, the pink brocade pantaloons, the metal bracelets tinkling on the ankles like the bells of Vasantasena,[3] the cap incrusted with gems and reflecting glass, the ring in her nose set with diamonds that add sparkle to a pearly smile, the long tresses hanging down at the back and exuding the scent of lotus blossom, and the length of cashmere that serves as a scarf, its ends tucked into a golden waist band. No, it was enough for her to be the Sylphide and dance in her accustomed style, adorable, chaste and modest.

Mlle Salvioni,[4] who has been cast in the rôle of Zoloé, has greatly developed its dramatic side. She mimes and sketches it with Italian passion. As played by her, the Bayadere is no longer, so to speak, a mute character. Her gestures speak. As a dancer, she has strength, precision and *parcours*.[5] Poised firmly on the *pointe*, she performs the most daring *renversées* and tosses off every kind of choreographic difficulty with marvellous ease. She was recalled after the fall of the curtain along with the beautiful and elegant Mlle Eugénie Fiocre, whose movements and attitudes and the design of whose poses are like danced sculpture.[6]

Le Moniteur Universel, January 29th, 1866.
L:2025.

---

[3] The courtesan Vasantasena was the heroine of the Sanskrit play, *Mrcchakatika* (The Little Clay Cart), by Sudraka, written in the fourth century A.D. Adapted for the Paris stage by Méry and de Nerval, and f.p. Th. de l'Odéon, May 13th, 1851 under the title *Le Chariot d'enfant*, it revealed to Gautier the dramatic possibilities of Hindu drama. (See Edwin Binney 3rd, *Les Ballets de Théophile Gautier*, pp. 320–322.)

[4] Guglielmina Salvioni, Italian ballerina who danced at the Opéra from 1864 to 1867.

[5] The ability to cover the stage.

[6] Jean-Baptiste Carpeaux (1827–75), who created the famous group, *La Danse*, for the new Opéra, also sculpted a number of portrait busts, one of the finest of which was of Eugénie Fiocre, now in the Musée de l'Opéra.

82

Opéra: Revival of *Giselle* with Adèle Grantzow

Giselle (see No. 34), revived for
the début of Mlle Grantzow,
May 11th, 1866.

Giselle has just been revived at the Opéra for the début of Mlle Grantzow. This young dancer, in spite of her Russian name, is said to come from Hanover, but she received her ballet training in St. Petersburg.[1] *Giselle* has already served to introduce us to Muravieva. . . . The dancers from the North love this melancholy ballet, in which a whole act takes place in moonlight, bringing Heinrich Heine's pretty legend of the Wilis to life. The childlike grace, the naive charm and the moving warmth that Carlotta Grisi brought to the part when she created it is well-known. How light, aerial, impalpable, vaporous she was! And how perfectly she danced! She has remained its ideal interpreter.

Mlle Grantzow is neither blonde nor blue-eyed like Carlotta. Her hair is black, her eyes dark too, but her features are nevertheless charming and have the innocent and tender expression that the rôle demands. She has a gentle suppleness, a facility, and a sort of sensuality in her dancing which we prefer to those somewhat graceless *tours de force* that never fail to draw applause. She knows how to find natural and graceful poses for her arms. Her miming is intelligent, expressive, without violent gestures; her features interpret well the workings of her soul. At the end, when the tomb claims its prey and Giselle disappears beneath the flowers, she was very moving and stirred one's feelings in a way that ballets seldom manage to do. Mlle Grantzow's success grew as the ballet progressed; she was applauded during every *pas* and

---

[1] Adèle Grantzow (1845–77) had in fact received much of her early training in Paris, under Mme Dominique. She had gone to St. Petersburg as Saint-Léon's *protégée*, and was therefore trained in the French school. She was at her peak when she danced in Paris between 1866 and 1868. She was originally chosen to create the rôle of Swanilda in *Coppélia*, but had to abandon it through illness.

recalled. It is a long time since a dancer has been so warmly received at the Opéra.

Mlle Fioretti danced the *valse* in the first act very well, but perhaps a little coldly, and Mlle Fonta is a Queen of the Wilis who might have stepped out of Gendron's painting.[2] Mérante mimes and dances with his accustomed superiority, and Coralli presents the forester Hilarion as a sinister and characteristic figure.

Le Moniteur Universel, May 14th, 1866.
L:2029.

---

[2] Auguste Gendron's painting, *Les Wilis,* exhibited in the Salon of 1846, made a deep impression on Gautier, who referred to the artist in many of his articles on the Salons of later years.

83

Opéra: Adèle Grantzow in *Néméa*

Néméa (see No. 77), revived
May 25th, 1866.

Mlle Grantzow, who was given such a favourable reception in *Giselle*, is continuing her début performances in the rôle of Néméa with equal success. Without being completely a star of the first magnitude, Mlle Grantzow stands out in the choreographic firmament, which is somewhat dim these days, and sparkles in a very distinctive manner; there is no need for a telescope to find her in her corner of the sky. She is neither an Elssler, a Taglioni, nor a Carlotta Grisi, but she has qualities that are both inborn and acquired. She is a pleasing dancer whom it is possible to applaud and who is in fact applauded. She is of medium height, neither too tall nor too short. She has elegant legs, pretty feet and charming arms. Her features are not lacking in expression, and she mimes with truth and feeling. Her dancing is correct and light, and seems to cost her no effort, although she executes extremely daring and rapid *renversées*. In *Néméa*, standing on a sort of plinth with her toe pointed like an arrow, she attempts with unusual success one of those dangerous attitudes to which we admit we prefer a simple graceful and voluptuously modest pose. Dancing, like playing the piano, has its regulation *tours de force*, its difficulties, that are expected of the virtuoso, who is obliged to attempt them to prove she can conquer them, even though she may find such violent gymnastics distasteful. Mlle Eugénie Fiocre plays Cupid—not the pink, chubby little Cupid of the eighteenth century, but the beautiful Greek Eros of antiquity, the divine adolescent who might be the husband of Psyche and who has reawakened after many centuries in all the purity of his Paros marble on his bramble-covered pedestal. Never was a rôle better filled. The very sight of Mlle Eugénie Fiocre makes one feel in the presence of one of those beautiful young godlike Apollos in which sculptors delighted to combine the beauties of both young man and girl.

Le Moniteur Universel, June 4th, 1866.
L:2052.

84

Opéra: *La Source*

La Source, ballet in 3 acts and 4
scenes, sc. Nuitter, ch. Saint-Léon,
mus. Minkus and Delibes, f.p.
November 12th, 1866.

This title, *La Source*, inevitably reminds one of M. Ingres' delightful
picture.[1] The imagination immediately depicts that young, virginal figure
in the flower of adolescent beauty, whose marble body, with a light glow of
pink, stands, so pure, fresh and delicate, against the grey background of rock,
pouring a stream of silvery water from the tilted urn on her shoulder into a
clear pool reflecting her feet as in a mirror. However, after a moment's
thought one realises that in the present state of our moral standards such a
subject, with its chaste nudity, is out of the question at the Opéra. Only the
Greeks, who applauded Phryne emerging from the sea in the costume of
Venus Anadyomene and the naked young Sophocles leading the chorus of
ephebes, were capable of accepting such a spectacle. So we have to forget the
masterpiece of our great painter and accept the ballet of MM. Charles
Nuitter[2] and Saint-Léon in the form in which it has been given to us.

When the curtain is gathered up beneath the cloak of Harlequin, the rosy
light of dawn, shining through a vanishing morning mist, is revealing a site
whose exotic and luxuriant vegetation denotes an Oriental landscape, and
releasing into the air all the charming, fantastic population of winged insects
that the light of day sends flying into the blooms of flowers, into rocky
crevices, and into the pearly hammocks of spider's webs. Making its way
through the plants flows a fresh, crystalline spring, murmuring and sparkling. Naturally this spring has a nymph, who is called Naïla and is portrayed
by Mlle Salvioni. Djemil, a mountain huntsman, quiver slung across his

[1] Painted in 1856, and now in the Louvre, Ingres' *La Source* was the subject of an
article by Gautier in *L'Artiste*, February 1st, 1857.

[2] Charles Nuitter (1828–99) was the author of numerous pieces for the theatre,
including translations of several of Wagner's operas, but his greatest achievement was
the establishment of the archives of the Paris Opéra.

shoulders and bow in hand, tracking some wild creature, enters to prevent Morgab, a tall, beautiful girl, half gypsy, half witch, a sort of Asiatic Canadie (*sic*), from soaking some poisonous plants she has picked by moonlight in the spring water to concoct a potion. Naïla is touched by this act and falls in love with the handsome huntsman, whom she regards tenderly through her crystal curtain.

Suddenly a kind of march, blaring out on strange instruments, kettle-drums, Dervish flutes, rebecks and nakers, breaks the silence of the empty landscape. A caravan emerges with outriders, footmen, slaves, palanquins, and *ataticbes*, a kind of cage covered in striped silk, made to contain women instead of birds. All that is lacking to complete the local colour are two or three *maharis* or dromaderies. It is a favourable spot, offering shade, cool air and water, and the caravan comes to a halt. The curtains of the palanquins are drawn aside, the veils of the *ataticbes* part, and like jewels pouring from an overturned casket, the mysterious beauties of the harem invade the stage. This procession is taking Nouredda, the Pearl of the East, under the protection of her brother Mozdok, to the Khan of Gengeh.

Morgab, annoyed at being disturbed while preparing her evil spells, has threatened the huntsman Djemil that she will take her revenge by making him conceive a fatal passion for an object he can never attain. The prediction is soon realised. Djemil catches a glimpse of Nouredda nonchalantly reclining in her hammock, her radiant beauty shining, like a flame in an alabaster lamp, through the transparent veils that cover her, and his heart is filled with an overpowering love. While rocking in the hammock, Nouredda has seen a marvellous flower with a purple bloom and golden pistils, more dazzling than the rubies of Jamshid,[3] glinting at the end of a branch on the edge of a precipice. Pointing to it, she makes it clear that she wants it, that she must have it. And Nouredda is one of those women for whom a man would pluck sun, moon and stars from the sky if asked. However, not a soul in her numerous suite stirs. Djemil, who until then has remained hidden, springs out and with three leaps reaches the flower, but the branch snaps and he falls into the chasm. After a few anxious moments, he reappears with the flower in his hand and presents it to Nouredda. For his reward he asks to look on the features of her for whom he has risked his life, and with a trembling hand he lifts the girl's veil. In Europe this would be an impertinence, but in Asia it is a crime. At such an outrage, her ferocious brother, Mozdok, orders his slaves to seize Djemil, and in spite of his struggles, they bind his arms behind his back with creepers and cast him on a rocky bank, unable to move, to die of hunger and thirst by the side of the spring, in a solitude where seldom a

---

[3] A legendary King of Persia in Ferdowsi's *Shah-nameh*, the possessor of a great treasure store.

traveller passes. The caravan then moves on, and Nouredda can do no more than cast a sad and piteous glance at poor Djemil.

By wriggling in his bonds Djemil, who seems to be a pupil of the Davenport brothers,[4] manages to free his arms. He yearns to quench his burning thirst in the clear waters of the spring. As if understanding his need, the water swells, foams, broadens out and courses through its bed, and Naïla appears to loosen the remaining cords. She thanks him for preventing the purity of her water from being polluted, but chides him for allowing himself, at a woman's whim, to pluck the flower that is the talisman of the valley. If Djemil were not in love with another, he would see that the spirit of the spring is in love with him, and that Naïla is far worthier than Nouredda, a mere mortal destined for the seraglio of some ridiculous *mamamouchi*[5]. His only response to the nymph's advances is to cry out for revenge. He is intent on killing Mozdok and rescuing Nouredda, and with a sigh the good Naïla places her power at the disposal of this huntsman who has rejected her. She even gives him a guide, Zaël, her household goblin, the Puck of this aquatic Titania.

The second act transports us to the abode of the Khan of Gengeh, who is expecting the arrival of his betrothed. As soon as Nouredda appears, the old Khan indulges in extravagant expressions of joy and love. But this great passion is short-lived, for Naïla, exerting all her charm and glowing with a magical brilliance, appears to entertain him, and the Khan of Gengeh no longer has eyes for Nouredda, whom he dismisses in disgrace, together with her brother. The harem walls cannot confine Naïla, who vanishes as soon as she has succeeded in freeing her rival for Djemil's heart.

The gypsy Morgab conducts Mozdok and Nouredda to her tent, where the three of them are plotting some diabolical act of vengeance in the glow of red, blue and green fire, when Djemil arrives, heaping reproaches on Nouredda for being so cool towards him. Mozdok is about to deal roughly with him when the long-suffering Naïla appears to rescue the ungrateful huntsman for the second time. She even goes so far as to give him the flower she wears at her waist, a flower that contains the essence of her life-force and has the power to inflame the heart of any mortal whose breast it touches.

Djemil tests its power, and Nouredda softens as the flame that burned in Naïla is transferred to her own heart. But if she has gained a soul, it has been at the expense of the poor nymph, and what a change has come over the once delightful landscape when Djemil conducts his bride through the valley where he had come across her caravan! The brilliant vegetation, in which

---

[4] Ira and William Davenport (b. 1839 and 1841), American escapologists, had appeared at the Salle Herz on September 12th, 1865, preceded by a blaze of publicity. The Paris public was not greatly impressed; their agility at extricating themselves from ropes was recognised, but the "spiritualist" side of their act was exposed as trickery.

[5] A mock-Turkish title, from Molière's *Le Bourgeois Gentilhomme*.

flowers once sparkled like butterflies of light, has withered to a pitiful state. Dead creepers hang limply over the rocks like the cast-off skins of snakes. The spring, almost dry, trickles along its sandy bed with barely the strength to dislodge a pebble. No longer is there any green moss, any fontinalis. The dry sand of the desert has taken over, the oasis has vanished, and the mysterious life that once animated plants, flowers and trees has been quenched. Naïla lies dead, surrounded by the little genii and charming fairies who composed her court. Djemil, his arm around Nouredda's waist, passes without even a glance at the spirit who gave her life for him.

Mlle Salvioni dances and mimes the rôle of the Spring in a very talented way. She is pure, correct and noble, but bearing in mind the nature of the character, one would have preferred something a little more gentle, more fluid, more pliant in her bearing and her poses. It would suit her type of beauty, which is more that of Diana than of a naiad.

Mlle E. Fiocre is quite the prettiest blond houri that ever wore the bonnet and pearl corset in the Mohammedan paradise. Her charming body, vaguely glimpsed through flimsy gauzes speckled with gold, is revealed with exquisite grace in the *pas de la Guzla*, one of the prettiest dances in the ballet.

Mlle Beaugrand is becoming a dancer of the front rank, yet the powers that be still persist in borrowing stars of lesser worth from distant skies.

Mlle Louise Marquet makes a proud and beautiful gypsy, her performance in the witchcraft scene admirably bringing out the picturesque nature of the rôle.

The music is the work of two composers, MM. Minkus and Léo Delibes.[6] The former has already given proof of a certain exotic originality in the ballet *Néméa*; the latter is no less talented for being a Frenchman and carried out his allotted task well. We thought we recognised in the score a few recollections of Mendelssohn's *Midsummer Night's Dream*, perhaps not sufficiently concealed, but they fit into place very well, for is not ballet a mimed symphony?

Le Moniteur Universel, November 19th, 1866.
L:2084.

[6] Léo Delibes (1836–91) was at this time second chorus master at the Opéra. His music for Act II and Act III, Scene I of *La Source* established his reputation as an exceptionally gifted composer of ballet-music, but he wrote only two complete ballet scores, for *Coppélia* and *Sylvia*.

85

Opéra: Adèle Grantzow in *La Source*

La Source (see No. 84), revived
May 10th, 1867.

It will be remembered that the leading rôle in *La Source* was originally destined for Mlle Grantzow. But an engagement that could not be changed obliged her to return to Russia, and her departure would have meant interrupting the success after the first few performances. So Mlle Salvioni was charged with the character of Naïla, a sort of nymph or Oriental naiad in love with a fierce huntsman. She brought to the part the elegance, the distinction and the serious qualities that are hers, but it was plain to see that the rôle had not been created for her, for one can write for the legs just as one writes for a voice. There are sopranos, mezzo-sopranos and contraltos in the dance. Mlle Salvioni is a contralto, while Mlle Grantzow is a soprano. Naïla was a little high for Mlle Salvioni; Mlle Grantzow performs it without transposing it. . . .

Mlle Grantzow played the rôle of Naïla with much grace and feeling. She is supple and light, and performs the *temps penchés* and *renversées* and the *retirés*[1] *sur les pointes* in a wonderful manner. Her movements are harmonious, well linked, and infused with a softness that is voluptuous as well as being modest. She has clearly been very well trained. She has talent and charm, and her success was not for a moment in doubt . . . .

Le Moniteur Universel, May 13th, 1867.
L:2119.

---

[1] Gautier, whose use of ballet terminology is occasionally suspect, used the word "*retraites*".

86

Opéra: Revival of *Le Corsaire* with Adèle Grantzow

Le Corsaire, ballet-pantomime in
3 acts and 5 scenes, sc. Saint-
Georges, ch. Mazilier, mus. Adam,
f.p. January 23rd, 1856, revived
October 21st, 1867.

The revival of *Le Corsaire* . . . was a brilliant success. The subject is based vaguely on Lord Byron's *Corsair*. In it Conrad, Medora, Gulnara are all to be found, but mixed up with the most amusing Turkish effects imaginable. Puppets with massive turbans from *The Arabian Nights* jostle amusingly with Uscoques, Klephts, Pakhares and the melodramatic heroes imagined by the English poet.[1] Visually nothing could be more amusing: in particular there is an old pasha, an ideal Schahabaham,[2] a fantastic caricature of the Orient, worn out by pleasure, stupefied with opium, a Cassandre of the seraglio, half paralytic, puerile and savage, somnolent and violent, a kind of childhood Ali Pasha, admirably played by Dauty.

Mlle Granzow renders the poetic character of Medora with exquisite grace. Her dancing is light, elegant, precise, and irreproachably correct, which in no way detracts from her charm. She is a *ballerina di primo cartello* in the full acceptance of the term. As Gulnare, Mlle Fioretti is vivacious,

---

[1] Races hostile to Turkish rule. Uscoques were Slavs who were notorious pirates until the Venetians chased them from the Adriatic; they later settled in Croatia. Klephts were mountain bandits. Pakhares seems to be a corruption of the Paliakars referred to in canto II, verse LXXI of *Childe Harold's Pilgrimage*:
> Each Paliakar his sabre from him cast
> And bounding hand in hand, man link'd to man,
> Yelling their uncouth dirge, long daunced the kirtled clan.
The word Paliakar is derived from Παλικα′ζι, a general name for a soldier in use among Romaic-speaking Greeks and Albanians.

[2] Probably a reference to Eugène Gautier's one-act *opéra bouffe*, *Schahabaham II*, f.p. Th. Lyrique, October 31st, 1854, and reviewed by Gautier in *La Presse*, November 7th, 1854.

piquant, lively, witty, and made a graceful foil for Medora. Mérante is a very fine Conrad.

The production, which is new or renovated, is very rich in spectacle, and the decor of the ship act attains the furthest limits of scenic effect. When the curtain rises, the pirates' ship is floating happily on a calm sea, and all is laughter, singing and dancing. Gradually the sky darkens, the sea swells, waves form into mountains and valleys, and clusters of foam drop on to the bridge, where cries of anguish have succeeded the joyous clamour. Livid flashes now cast their sulphurous gleam on the banks of black clouds. The ship splits in two and sinks, disappearing into the monstrous jaws of the deep, and then, in the distance, under a dazzling beam of electric light, Conrad and Medora are espied, their strained hands grasping the steep side of an islet against which the waves are breaking. No longer does it resemble a painted canvas, but the sea itself in all its convulsive fury.

Adam's music is excellent ballet music. It has spirit, rhythm, speed, and here and there some charmingly nonchalant phrases and motifs and melodies that would be a credit to more than one opera.

Le Moniteur Universel, October 28th, 1867.
L:2144.

87

Opéra: Return of Adèle Grantzow in *Le Corsaire*

Le Corsaire (see No. 86), revived
April 17th, 1868.

*L*e *Corsaire* has just been revived at the Opéra. It is a grand spectacular
ballet with a dramatic and varied action that is suited to that vast stage.
Something of Lord Byron's poem, a certain epic and lyric touch, remains in
the scenario. An idea can be sensed behind the pantomime, and an idea never
comes amiss, even in a ballet. Lord Byron is barely read nowadays, but his
shadowy brilliance shines in the recesses of memory like the afterglow of a
vanished meteor. His touching heroines have not been forgotten—Haidée,
Gulnara, Medora, graceful figures endowed with immortal life like Ophelia,
Desdemona and Miranda, and akin to Marguerite, Claire and Mignon.[1]
Byron shares with Shakespeare and Goethe the privilege of creating types of
womanhood that are the stuff of dreams and inspire man's love. Happy the
poet who can add a sister to that ideal and divine family!

No sight could be more entertaining than the picturesque costumes of
modern Greece mingled with those of the East—braided jackets, fustanellas,
greaves, red skullcaps with long tassels of blue silk, waistbands bristling with
yataghans, kandjars and pistols, pelisses, dolmans, haiks, burnous, chachias,
turbans, babouches, scimitars, blunderbusses, rifles chased with silver,
mother-of-pearl and coral, Circassian shields and helmets, all the old
Museum of Elbisei-Atika[2] set in motion, without mentioning what the
women wear, the taktikos worn tilted over one eye, sequins in the hair,
diamond aigrettes, corsets of brocade or velvet studded with precious stones,

---

[1] Byron's heroines, Haidée in *Don Juan* and Medora and Gulnara in *The Corsair*,
compared with the heroines in Shakespeare's *Hamlet*, *Othello* and *The Tempest*, and
Goethe's *Egmont*, *Wilhelm Meisters Lehrjahre* and *Faust*.

[2] The Museum of Ancient Costumes, or of the Janissaries, in the At Meidan, Constantinople. Gautier described it in one of his series of articles on that city, published in
La Presse, October 28th, 1853.

cashmere scarfs, Bursa silk interwoven with gold and silver, transparent gauzes streaked with flat stripes, jackets stiff with embroidery, silk pantaloons flecked with gold, silk fleshings taking on the sheen of marble in the light, flowers, pearls, sequins and all the wealth that the Bezesten[3] of Constantinople, the bazaar of Smyrna and the shops of Damascus can provide. All those gems and gauzes and glittering trimmings, set in motion by beautiful dancers, produce a dazzling effect. The wild and picturesque landscape of the Cyclades, where the action takes place, has provided the designers with a subject for superb sets that form a most appropriate background for this story of a Romantic corsair.

Mlle Grantzow appears as the graceful figure of Medora, and it can be said that she is not inferior to the idealised figure that charming name evokes. Of her dancing, praise is superfluous, for everyone knows how light, pure and correct she is. To her talent as a dancer she brings that of an intelligent, expressive and moving mime. We stress this point, for it is fashionable nowadays to decry pantomime, the *récitatif* of ballet without which it would have no meaning. What would the immortal Viganò, author of *Mirra*, *Prometeo* and *Il noce di Benevento*, to which Beyle attached such great importance,[4] have said of those modern ballets which are no more than a succession of *pas* which lead out of nothing and have no connection with one another.

But the main attraction of the ballet is still the ship . . . . It is impossible to imagine a more beautiful final scene.

Le Moniteur Universel, April 20th, 1868.
L:2178.

---

[3] The central section of the bazaar district of Stamboul, dating back to Byzantine times.

[4] See No. 77, note 2. *Il noce di Benevento* (1812) and *Mirra* (1817) were ballets by Viganò, to which Stendhal referred enthusiastically in his *Rome, Naples et Florence en 1817*.

88

Opéra: Revival of *Le Prophète*

Le Prophète, opera by Meyerbeer,
f.p. 1849, revived June 28th, 1869.

A somewhat unimportant detail in such a serious work as *Le Prophète*, but one that will have a certain curiosity appeal, is the addition of M. Elliot and Mlle Frederika to the skaters' ballet that is so original and rousing. This couple was said to have been a great attraction at the Alcazar,[1] as they will not fail to be at the Opéra. It is difficult to imagine anything more light, more graceful, more elegant and at the same time more daring than the sort of *mazurka*, which is glided, or rather skated by this young man and the slender, pretty blonde with imperturbable equilibrium, who seem in no way hampered by the steel rollers on the rubber soles of their boots. They dart forward, stop in their tracks, grasp and release one another, describe curves, lean forward, and change direction with such agility, ease and precision that they might be skimming over the ice of a real lake. How awkward and heavy the other dancers appear by comparison, going to and fro with the noise of velocipedes against that foggy background on which an electric sunset flickers through the evening mist.

> *Le Journal Officiel de l'Empire Français*,
> July 5th, 1869.
> L:2265.

[1] The Alcazar was a café concert situated in the Faubourg Poissonnière in the winter months and in the Champs Elysées in the summer, presenting music-hall numbers such as singers, clowns, gymnasts, tight-rope dancers and other specialty acts. Thérésa made her reputation there.

89

Opéra: Revival of *Robert le Diable*

Robert le Diable, opera in 5 acts,
mus. Meyerbeer, libr. Scribe, ch.
F. Taglioni, f.p. November 21st,
1831, revived with new
choreography by Saint-Léon,
March 7th, 1870.

Those who did not see the first performance of *Robert le Diable* can have no idea of how novel this great work appeared at that time . . . .

The scenery, which, while not entirely new, has at least been touched up to give the appearance of being painted yesterday, is a marvellous framework for the legendary drama . . . . The set for the cloister scene seems to have been somewhat modified, but it has lost nothing by that. At the left side the long cloister still extends back with its arches and pillars casting shadows on the flagstones in the moonlight. To the right is the cemetery with its white tombs, among which can be recognised the monument of St. Rosalie, lying in her marble shroud holding the magic branch that Robert is to take.

Now that we are in the cloister, let us stay to watch the funereal bacchanalia. Bertram's cavernous voice has just pronounced the irresistible incantation that rouses the guilty nuns from the depths of their coffins, those pretty sinners who, when the purple fluid of life brought colour to their now frozen veins, deserted the pure joy of Heaven for the profane sensuality of the world. The slabs of the tombs open, and the phantoms rise and form vague shapes in the shadows. A slight rustling is heard, like the beating of dragon-fly's wings. Indistinct forms stir in the darkness, emerging from every pillar and rising from every flagstone like wreathes of smoke. A bright beam of light, produced by an electric burner, shoots its brilliance through the arches, picking out in the shadows female forms moving beneath the white pallor of their shrouds with deathly sensuality. This scene is admirably composed; the groups are well arranged, and the soft lighting does not divest those dancers of the tomb of their poetry and their mystery. But at the moment when they have to seduce Robert, the lamps hanging down from on high light up by themselves, electric light floods down from every side, and the shades vanish. Daylight has come to the cloister, and its atmosphere has disappeared.

It is true that pretty Mlle Fonta would otherwise have had to dance in the dark with weak moonlight playing on her white gauze skirts, which would have been a pity from the choreographic point of view, since she is elegant, light and a joy to behold. This rôle of the Abbess, played in earlier times by Mlle Taglioni, has a strange appeal. The young dancer exerted all her charm, and it was possible to understand how Robert would have been so fascinated as to let himself be tempted to seize the green branch from the pale hand of St. Rosalie, whose name reminds him of his mother. This fantastic bacchanalia, which has been staged, it is said, from notes left by Meyerbeer, produces an irresistible impression, and will be a significant factor in the success of the revival.

Journal Officiel de l'Empire Français, March 15th, 1870. L:2288.

90

Opéra: *Coppélia*

Coppélia, ou la Fille aux yeux
d'émail, ballet in 2 acts and 3
scenes, sc. Nuitter, ch. Saint-Léon,
mus. Delibes, f.p. May 25th,
1870.

*D*er *Freischütz* was followed by the new ballet by MM. Nuitter, Saint-Léon and Delibes, *Coppélia*, in which the début was to take place of Mlle Bozzacchi,[1] a young Italian dancer who realised all the good things that were being said of her.

Everyone knows Coppélius, that strange, twisted character from the tales of Hoffmann, that Prometheus of a dummy who endeavours to give life to a doll. Indeed, Olympia is very much like a young girl.[2] She raises and lowers her eyes, a clockwork movement ticks in her side where her heart should be, she can reply to a few simple questions about the weather, she plays her sonata on the piano like a professional, and in the ballroom she waltzes to perfection and is never out of time. Her regular beauty seems to have been formed from a mould, and it can be said without any suggestion of metaphor that she has well turned arms. Her enamel eyes are shaded by long lashes, and she has the scarlet smile of a wax figure. We have spoken of her as Olympia, but it is Coppélia that she is called in the new ballet. Coppélius places her at the window every morning, and she can be seen from the street apparently deeply absorbed in a book, the pages of which are never turned.

Frantz, the sweetheart of Swanilda, a charming girl who owes none of her

---

[1] Giuseppina Bozzacchi (1853–70), an Italian-born dancer who was trained by Mme Dominique and selected by Saint-Léon to create the rôle of Swanilda in *Coppélia* when Adèle Grantzow, the original choice, fell ill. The ballet's première was her first stage appearance, and her career consisted only of the first eighteen performances of the ballet, for she died of smallpox the following winter, during the Siege of Paris.

[2] In Hoffmann's tale, *Der Sandmann*, the hero becomes obsessed with the beautiful Olympia, reputed to be the daughter of Professor Spalanzani but in reality a clockwork doll he has made. But the Professor has failed to pay Coppelius (or Coppola) for supplying the eyes, and in a horrific tussle between the two men the doll is smashed. This story provided the basic idea for the plot of *Coppélia*, but the scenarist Nuitter removed virtually all trace of the sinister element of the original.

graces to mechanical means, passes Dr. Coppélius's house every day, and is astonished that the strange creature never returns his look. She is always there, beautifully dressed, impassive and seemingly never bored. Frantz's curiosity is aroused by this mystery, for it seems unnatural that a handsome lad like himself cannot even extract a glance from this haughty creature. Swanilda, for her part, is puzzled that her fiancé Frantz should make advances beneath the balcony, and she finds her way into the house of Master Coppélius, followed by her companions. On entering the learned old man's workshop the inquisitive visitors are presented with a very baroque and fantastic sight—a jumble of dummies in rigid poses, their angular gestures making awkward attempts at imitating real life but managing only to produce a frightening and laughable sort of tableau of the dead. Behind a curtain, seated on a stool as if it were a throne, stiff, immobile, her eyes fixed, is Coppélia, whom the old savant has forgotten to put away. So Swanilda has been jealous of a doll! Her mischievous companions have found the keys that wind up the mechanisms of these dummies, and in no time the whole collection is gesticulating in a strange fashion with a whirr of cogs, pulleys and counterweights. One of them is trying to raise a glass to its lips, another to put on its spectacles, and all are rolling their eyes like the negro with a pendulum in his chest. A tumbler is making the most amusing grimaces. But now Master Coppélius returns, soon to be followed by Frantz. The girls make their escape—all of them, that is, except Swanilda, who wants to see how the adventure will end and hides behind the curtain concealing the doll.

Coppélius offers Frantz a glass of wine, in which he has mixed a drug, and the youth soon slips into a state of somnolence. When he is fast asleep, the learned old man leans over him and makes hypnotic passes as if to draw out his life-force. By transferring this energy into his inert creation, an absolute wonder of machinery lacking only a soul, he believes he can bring it to life. The miracle of Master Coppélius's dreams seems to be achieved. The curtain parts, and a slender creature with eyes shining and a graceful smile springs lightly off the doll's pedestal, and darting and bounding hither and thither, overturns the dolls, creates all manner of mischief and pokes fun at Coppélius, who would much prefer his doll, once so tranquil, to come to life in a less boisterous manner. Frantz is woken up by the din. Swanilda grabs him by the arm and they make their escape, leaving the doctor bewildered by the adventure, but none the wiser. Already he is working out a better adjusted mechanical contraption, with an infusion of mysterious substances that will take the place of blood. This monstrous chimera of a child not born from a mother's womb, *prolem sine matre creatam*, was the obsession of the Middle Ages. In those days there was not an alchemist or a *famulus* Wagner[3] that did not possess a *homunculus* in a bottle.

[3] Wagner was Faust's assistant. Famulus, an archaic term for a student who assists a University professor.

Anyone without the slightest notion of the poetry of ballet would have long since gathered that Frantz and Swanilda are now to be married and that their marriage will be the pretext for dancing and celebration.

La Bozzacchi, to use the Italian way of speaking, is a charming girl of sixteen, possessing a pretty face, with witty black eyes that are neither too large nor too small, perfectly built, very light and very loose-jointed. Her movements are rapid, but blended and with no rough edges. Her *pointes* are very clean, and to use a technical ballet term, she has good *parcours*.[4] Worthy of special praise are the graceful movements of her arms, which are naturally rounded and well formed. All this adds up to the most charming combination of person and talent. Also, she was received with an enthusiasm that is seldom shown today for the dance. In addition she mimes most intelligently. In the first act, the *pas de la paille*, in which she questions an ear of corn to discover her sweetheart's secrets, is a little poem in itself. Following what the ear of corn tells her, her charming features express in turn unease, joy, anger, love with an extreme delicacy of shading.

In the grand divertissement are featured, in the suite of Father Time, Dawn, Prayer, Work, Hymen, Discord, War, Peace and Pleasure, represented by the prettiest dancers of the Opéra. La Bozzacchi symbolises Pleasure, and never was allegory more pleasingly personified. A *czardas*, a series of Hungarian dances, performed by the corps de ballet with an attack and an energy that reminded us of great evenings in St. Petersburg, was very warmly applauded. It had a rare success for a *pas d'ensemble*.

M. Delibes' music is full of happy motifs, among which we thought we detected several Russian or Bohemian melodies. It has been orchestrated, set to rhythm and wrought with much greater care than is normally devoted to ballet music. It played an important part in the success of *Coppélia*, the dances of which have been arranged with perfect taste by Saint-Léon, one of the masters of his craft. The sets are truly pictures signed by the most painstaking masters, and the costumes, which seem to have been inspired by the albums of Valerio,[5] are rich, elegant and picturesque.

Mlle Eugénie Fiocre, the charming Cupid in *Néméa*, is Mlle Bozzacchi's fiancé in the ballet. She wears travesty clothes to perfection, and Frantz and his Swanilda make a graceful couple.

Le Journal Officiel de l'Empire Français,
May 30th, 1870.
L:2305.

---

[4] See No. 81, note 5.

[5] Théodore Valerio (1819–79), well known for his scenes of Eastern Europe, on which Gautier wrote three articles when they came out (*La Presse*, March 11th and 18th, May 7th, 1854).

91

Opéra: Revival of *Coppélia*

Coppélia (see No. 90), revived
October 16th, 1871.

Coppélia ... completed the evening on a happy note. *Coppélia* was the
ballet produced for the début of Bozzacchi, that pretty Italian dancer,
such a clever and charming girl, who died of smallpox during the siege, a
delicate flower with the scent of a violet that was withered by the storm and
the pestilence that raged about us.[1] Her tomb might well be inscribed with the
epitaph of the young Roman dancer, "*Saltavit biduo et placuit*"[2] (She danced
for two days and gave pleasure), which sums up her ephemeral and graceful
life so well. She gave pleasure: that phrase says everything, and the memory
she has left behind her, so fresh and pure, has not been effaced by the great
cataclysm. Time was found, beneath the rain of bombs, to spare a tear and
say a few words of farewell, an honour that more illustrious figures than she
have not always obtained.

The subject of *Coppélia* is taken from *Master Coppélius*, one of
Hoffmann's fantastic tales, also known as *The Sandman*, that is full of a
breathtaking horror. But Olympia, the doll that the student Nathanael
mistakes for a real woman—it is possible sometimes to be so deceived—is not
the creation of the terrible, satanic barometer maker, who only provided the
eyes for the learned Professor Spalanzani's automaton. *Coppélia* is not
therefore the mechanical daughter of Coppélius or Coppola.[3] But no matter!
Ballet has the right to try anything and arrange matters to suit itself. And
furthermore, a tale of Hoffmann is not a sacred text.

---

[1] Nearly seventeen months separated the two performances of *Coppélia* that Gautier
saw. In the interval France had been humbled by her defeat in the Franco-German
War, and Paris had been through the agonies of the Siege and the Commune. Saint-
Léon, the choreographer of *Coppélia*, had died of a heart attack early in September
1870, Bozzacchi had fallen a victim to smallpox during the Siege, and Dauty, the first
Dr. Coppélius, had also died.

[2] The correct quotation is "*Antipoli in theatro biduo saltavit et placuit*". *Inscrip-
tiones*, Corp. XII 188.

[3] See No. 90, note 2.

Coppélia is a charming ballet, lively, gay, witty—yes, witty, even though some people seem to doubt whether wit can be found in *ronds de jambe*—and realises an ideal that is very difficult to achieve, graceful comedy . . . .

It was Mlle Beaugrand who played the rôle of Swanilda.[4] She has earned her stripes on the boards of the Opéra, where she was seen as a child, then as an adolescent, as corps de ballet girl, *coryphée* and ballerina, always hard-working and making progress year by year. All she lacked was a star's sudden brilliance, borrowed from a strange sky, that dazzles and fascinates the eye. She does not have a foreign name, and it might well be said of her, adapting the well-known proverb, "No one is a goddess in her own country". But certainly there has been no better dancer since Carlotta Grisi for finish, attention to detail, clarity and perfection. Talent can go no further. Mlle Beaugrand is as light as a feather, as rapid as a bird, poising as firmly on her skilful *pointes* as though they were arrowheads of iron. She mimes wittily and amusingly, but . . . Yes, there is a but, as there is at the end of every eulogy. Find it out for yourselves, for we shall not tell you what it is.

La Gazette de Paris, October 23rd, 1871.
L:2329.

---

[4] Here Gautier inadvertently wrote "Coppélia".

Appendix

Notices not translated in full

Titles of newspapers are indicated by the letters in parentheses at the end of each item: M, *Le Messager*; JO, *Journal Officiel de l'Empire Français*; MU, *Le Moniteur Universel*; P, *La Presse*.

Items marked with an asterisk have been partially translated in the main text. Except where specifically stated otherwise, all events are at the Opéra. For other theatres the following abbreviations have been used: AMB, Ambigu-Comique; CCE, Cirque des Champs-Elysées; CH, Châtelet; CO, Cirque-Olympique; DEJ, Déjazet; FN, Folies-Nouvelles; GAI, Gaîté; GYM, Gymnase; IC, Th. Impérial du Cirque; LYR, Th. Lyrique; MONT, Montansier; OC, Opéra-Comique; PR, Palais-Royal; PSM, Porte-Saint-Martin; TF, Th. des Fleurs, Pré Catalan; TI, Th. International (in the grounds of Exposition Universel, 1867); VAR, Variétés; VAUD, Vaudeville.

1837

July 24th. The sisters Fabiani, Spanish dancers, at PR, much inferior to Dolores Serral. Approving comments on Spanish dance costume. (P)

October 9th. Continuing success of Fanny Elssler's *Cachucha*, which has been encored. (P)

October 13th. *Cachucha* still being encored. *La Chatte métamorphosée en femme* saved only by Elssler's presence. (P)

1838

January 1st. Shortage of good ballets. Excessive thinness of Louise Fitzjames, "hardly suitable to play the part of an asparagus in a ballet of vegetables". (P)

January 29th. Odry's parody of the *Cachucha* in *Les Saltimbanques* at VAR. (P)

February 5th. Progress of Nathalie Fitzjames, whose technique is improving although her features need more expression. (P)

February 19th. Mélanie Noblet, "vivacious, sparkling and light, although a little robust", has been given a *pas* in *Le Diable boiteux*. Success of Lise Noblet and Mme Alexis Dupont in *El Jaleo de Jerez*, danced with "a furious attack, much bold arching of the back and unbelievable exuberance". (P)

March 5th. Untidy dress of the corps de ballet at a rehearsal, most of them wearing grey stockings and "clogs that were somewhat jointed". (P)

March 12th. Mazilier's first attempt at choreography, a *pas de deux* by Mme Alexis Dupont and himself: "too disturbingly exuberant, lacking quiet and sensuality". (P)

March 26th. Lise Noblet's benefit, a very long and boring evening, including scenes from *Clari* and *La Servante justifiée*. On another evening Nathalie Fitzjames danced a new *pas* with Guerra. (P)

April 9th. Nathalie Fitzjames to dance the *Jota aragonese*, arranged specially for her. (P)

April 23rd. Revival of *Le Carnaval de Venise*. Success of Nathalie Fitzjames in the *Jota aragonesa*, with Mabille. (P)

*May 4th. Advance information of the programme for the Elsslers' benefit. (M)

*May 7th. Non-dance items in the Elsslers' benefit, including the *tableaux vivants*. (P)

*May 21st. Second performance of *La Volière*. Nathalie Fitzjames obtaining a success in London with the *Jota aragonesa*. (P)

June 6th. *Capsali*, a heroic ballet produced at PSM. Mlle Bertin attractive but "dances rather badly". On male dancers: "we are repelled and revolted by *danseurs nobles* .... Strength is the only grace a man may have. Mazurier was adorable, M. Frémolle is nauseating." (P)

June 18th. The threadbare scenery of *La Révolte au sérail*. Negligent performance by the corps de ballet, but Adèle Dumilâtre stands out—"two velvety black eyebrows, a limpid glance, a charming smile, a cameo profile atop a bust that is firm yet dainty". Nathalie Fitzjames' *Jota* and the Noblet's *Jaleo* compensating for Elssler's absence in London. (P)

*August 7th. Nathalie Fitzjames as Cupid in *Le Carnaval de Venise*. Elssler's return imminent. Mme Alexis Dupont's resignation. Mlle Nathalie dances the *cachucha* with Mmes Grassot and Virginie Goy at GYM. (P)

August 15th. Spanish dancers at PR. Marianna and Escudero. (P)

*August 27th. Elssler's return in *Le Diable boiteux*. Lucile Grahn continuing her débuts. Nathalie Fitzjames. (P)

September 10th. Progress of Nathalie Fitzjames. Elssler to appear in *La Sylphide* to the disapproval of the Taglioni faction. Gautier not worried about her. (P)

October 1st. Fanny Elssler's second appearance in *La Sylphide*. Maria as Fenella in *La Muette de Portici*. (P)

*November 2nd/3rd. How the public's obsession with a great name inhibits promising performers. (P)

December 24th. Three great stars appear on the same night for the benefit of the widow of the singer Lafont—Fanny Elssler, Duprez and Mario. Both Nathalie Fitzjames and Maria claim the right to dance a *pas* of Mme Alexis Dupont, and Mazilier gives it to Adèle Dumilâtre to the annoyance of Mlle Fitzjames, who offers her resignation, which is not accepted. Success of the Elssler sisters in a *pas de deux*. (P)

December 31st. Arrival of a troupe of Spanish dancers in Paris. Success of Mlles. Noblet in Bordeaux. (P)

1839

January 28th. The Spanish dancers at the Opéra balls. The general rehearsal of *La Gipsy*. (P)

March 5th. Spanish dancers at VAR (Srs. M. Camprubí, Piatoli, Garcia; Sras. Manuela, Lopez, Alonzo). Début of Mélanie Duval. Nathalie Fitzjames, Elise Varin. Duponchel in Milan trying to engage Cerrito, "an astonishing ballerina who . . . can perform the most daring and dangerous feats. She darts, hell for leather, from one side of the stage to the other, stopping short like one of those Arab steeds whose riders gallop them towards a wall—a rare sight that is both terrifying and graceful." (P)

April 15th. Divertissement in Auber's opera, *Le Lac des fées*, produced by Jean Coralli as a bacchanal from ancient times, with the dancers in tiger or leopard skin costumes. Maria as Erigone, Coustou as Bacchus, and the Noblet sisters in a *pas de deux*. Rôle of Silenus, created by Barrez, omitted after the first performance, to Gautier's regret. (P)

May 6th. *La Sylphe d'or* at GAI contained a ballet of rabbits. (P)

May 19th. Dolores Serral dancing better than ever at PR. (P)

June 9th. Continued success of *Le Diable boiteux* and the *Cachucha*. *La Gipsy* beginning to lose its novelty; the *Cracovienne* lacks the sensual appeal of the *Cachucha*. (P)

June 18th. Lucien Petipa's début. Gautier's first impression is that, despite his good jump, he was inferior to Louis Bretin, whom the Opéra had thought of engaging. (P)

July 14th. Reappearance of Lucile Grahn. Noblet sisters in *Las Boleras de Cádiz*. (P)

July 21st. Continuation of Lucile Grahn's début performances. (P)

July 28th. The Spanish dancers appear in a performance of *Don Juan*. Mme Alexis Dupont and Noblet in *El Jaleo de Jerez*. Nathalie Fitzjames' *bolero*. Manuela Dubinon arranges *Las Seguidillas de Andalucía* to music by Schneitzhoeffer. (P)

August 14th. Lucile Grahn's success continues. Maria to appear in *La Fille du Danube*. *Las Seguidillas de Andalucía*. (P)

September 9th. Victorine Capon, formerly of the Opéra, in *Les Filles de l'enfer* at AMB. (P)

October 7th. News of Lucile Grahn, Nathalie Fitzjames and the *Cachucha*. (P)

November 4th. Elssler in *La Tarentule* compared to Miss Smithson. Barrez's talent as a comedian. (P)

1840

March 9th. Lucile Grahn succeeds Elssler in *La Gipsy*. (P)

March 18th. Début of Mme Desmaziers from Naples. (P)

April 6th. Elssler and Barrez in London. (P)

December 7th. Albert's *pas de six* in *La Favorite*. (P)

December 28th. Barrez and Maria in *Annette et Lubin* in a benefit performance at PR. (P)

1841

January 7th. Début of Achille Henry, "a monstrous fat boy with a torso like a sack of nuts, arms that could smash the Tivoli dynomometer, and a bull neck surmounted by a small fat head shaped like a fist." (P)

January 25th. A harlequinade by Barrez at VAR. (P)

March 7th. Début of Carlotta Grisi. "Her strength, lightness, suppleness and originality place her at once between Elssler and Taglioni. Perrot's teaching is there for all to see." (P)

April 5th. Adèle Dumilâtre in *La Sylphide*. (P)

June 15th. Début of Caroline Beaucourt. Statuette of Nathalie Fitzjames and Mabille in *Le Diable amoureux*. (P)

June 22nd. *Giselle* in preparation. Habeneck and the orchestra enchanted with the music. (P)

July 12th. Publication of the score of *Giselle*. Success of Grisi and Nathalie Fitzjames. (P)

July 20th. Nathalie Fitzjames sings in a concert. (P)

September 9th. Revival of *La Tarentule* with Maria. The romantic grace of Mlle Forster. (P)

October 30th. Dolores Serral and Camprubí at VAUD. A parody of *Giselle* at PR. Emile Thomas' statuette of Grisi in *Giselle*, suspended on one foot. (P)

1842

January 24th. Grisi to replace Leroux in *La Rosière* [later *Jolie Fille*] *de Gand*. Maria in *La Tarentule*. (P)

April 19th. Mabille as James in *La Sylphide*. Louise Weiss's début performances interrupted by injury. (P)

May 22nd. Nathalie Fitzjames as a singer.   (P)

June 13th. *Le Fils mal gardé* at PSM.   (P)

June 21st. *La Jolie Fille de Gand* in rehearsal.   (P)

July 26th. Grisi's continuing success in *La Jolie Fille de Gand*.   (P)

August 14th. Tom Mathews' parody of the *Cachucha*. Grisi and Petipa in Rouen.   (P)

December 20th. Début of Delphine Marquet.   (P)

1843

January 16th. Grisi and Petipa reappear.   (P)

March 1st. Thoughts on the cancan.   (P)

March 8th. Grisi to sing in a concert.   (P)

March 21st. Grisi sings Adam's trumpet song in a concert.   (P)

April 19th. Mariano Camprubí and Dolores Serral at VAR.   (P)

May 6th. Grisi and Petipa dance a *tarantella*. Grisi's "little feet . . . disappeared in the rapidity of their movements, like the gossamer wings of a dragonfly in its swirling flight."   (P)

May 12th. Grisi in a mime rôle in Grétry's *Un Quart d'heure de silence* at a concert.   (P)

May 24th. Grisi's *tarantella*.   (P)

July 5th. Dolores Serral, Manuela Garcia, Juan and Mariano Camprubí, with the singer Cáceres, at VAR.   (P)

*August 30th. Return of Blangy and Maria.   (P)

November 13th. Success of Grisi and Petipa in *La Péri* in London. Her famous leap encored every evening.   (P)

December 4th. *L'Ombre* at PSM, with Mlle Camille ("the Carlotta of the place").   (P)

1844

February 19th. *Lady Henriette* in preparation. Grisi engaged in London at 30,000 fr. and to appear in *Esmeralda*. She and her sister Ernesta go first to Rouen.   (P)

March 18th. The polka rage.   (P)

March 25th. A book on the polka.   (P)

*April 1st. E. Coralli and Maria dance the polka at the Opéra.   (P)

May 8th. Grisi's rapid journey from London.   (P)

*June 3rd. *Les Beautés de l'Opéra*.   (P)

August 26th. Grisi's reappearance. La Reine Pomaré, the polka dancer.   (P)

October 7th. *Le Diable à quatre* in preparation.

November 18th. *Le Diable à quatre* postponed. Fabbri in *La Sylphide*.   (P)

December 2nd. Vogue for the mazurka.   (P)

December 9th. The divertissement in *Marie Stuart*. *Le Diable à quatre* in preparation.   (P)

1845

January 13th. Grisi returns in *La Péri* with a new hair style.   (P)

*January 20th. *Le Diable à quatre* in preparation. Engagement of Plunkett.   (P)

January 27th. Success of the Viennese Children. Leroux's benefit. Postponement of *Le Diable à quatre*.   (P)

February 17th. Benefit of the Viennese children.   (P)

*March 31st. *Le Diable à quatre* to be given in July.   (P)

April 21st. Grisi dances a new *pas* in *La Péri*.   (P)

May 12th. News of Grisi. Possibility of a ballet by Perrot.   (P)

June 23rd. *Le Diable à quatre* to be given shortly. Problems of a heatwave.   (P)

September 22nd. The Moorish dancers at CO.   (P)

September 29th. *Les Moresques* at PSM.   (P)

October 27th. Grisi slightly injured.   (P)

November 2nd/3rd. Grisi's return.   (P)

December 1st. Grisi's "gay sparkle and brilliant footwork" in *Le Diable à quatre*.   (P)

*December 8th. Plunkett replaces L. Fitzjames in *Robert le Diable*.   (P)

1846

January 12th. Ragaine's ballet *Trilby* at PSM, with Mlle Richard, "the Carlotta of the place".   (P)

January 19th. Spanish dancers at VAR.   (P)

February 9th. Grisi injured by stabbing her foot on a nail.   (P)

February 16th. Grisi, S. Dumilâtre and Maria away, and Plunkett holding the fort.   (P)

*February 23rd. Grisi dances at Versailles.   (P)

May 4th. The Scandinavian mimes at AMB. Carlotta re-engaged at the Opéra. (P)

May 11th. Camille Leroux dances a *pas des quatre nations* on horseback at the CCE. (P)

May 25th. *Betty* in rehearsal, doubts about the wisdom of turning plays into ballets. (P)

August 17th. The *Pas des déesses* at Her Majesty's Theatre, London.

September 7th. Grisi returns from England and Ireland. (P)

September 28th. *Tableaux vivants* at PSM. (P)

December 7th. Plunkett dances the *manola*. She and Elssler "the most authentic Andalusians we have ever come across". (P)

December 21st. Grisi engaged in Rome, her new ballet postponed. (P)

1847

January 11th. Grisi and Plunkett in Italy. (P)

January 18th. M. Camprubí and Serral at VAUD. (P)

March 8th. Grisi in Rome, her return to Paris. Plunkett's *manola*. (P)

May 31st. Plunkett in *Le Diable à quatre*. Grisi's success in London, where she is to appear as a female Mephistopheles in Heine's ballet. (P)

June 21st. Début of Thérèse Ferdinand, whom Gautier had seen in Madrid in 1846. Sr. de Vegas expected in Paris shortly. (P)

August 23rd. An effective mirror dance at VAR, recollections of Marie Guy-Stéphan and T. Ferdinand in a similar dance at the Teatro del Circo, Madrid.

September 13th. Perrot negotiating with the Opéra. (P)

September 20th. Grisi's return to Paris. (P)

September 27th. A performance at Compiègne. (P)

October 4th. Josefa Soto dances the *Jaleo de Jeréz* in *La Muette de Portici*. A. Dumilâtre. Grisi in *La Favorite*. Cerrito rehearsing *La Fille de marbre*. (P)

October 11th. Plunkett in *La Péri*. (P)

*October 25th. Grisi to spend her month's leave in Belgium and Holland. (P)

November 8th. Cerrito's continuing success. *Les Cinq Sens* (later *Griseldis*) in preparation for Grisi. Grisi's success in Brussels in *La Jolie Fille de Gand*, revived by Barrez. (P)

November 22nd. Grisi's success in Brussels. (P)

November 29th. News of the ballet. (P)

December 27th. A parody of *La Fille de marbre* at PR. (P)

1848

March 20th. Theatres doing better as Paris settles down after the revolution. Grisi's success. (P)

April 10th. A play about Vestris at MONT. (P)

April 17th. Grisi dances a new *pas*. (P)

May 1st. Grisi making her final appearances. (P)

May 15th. Grisi and Esther Aussandon in London. (P)

June 5th. News of dancers. Contracts of A. Dumilâtre and Fleury not renewed. Grisi's success in London in Perrot's *Les Eléments*. (P)

June 19th. A. Mabille's Spanish divertissement in *L'Apparition*. A new ballet in preparation. (P)

December 18th. *Le Violon de Diable* in rehearsal. (P)

1849

*January 22nd. Début of Mlle Néodot. (P)

February 5th. Success of Cerrito and Saint-Léon in *Le Diable à quatre*. (P)

March 5th. Grisi has returned from Berlin. (P)

April 23rd. The divertissement in *Le Prophète*. Petipa and Plunkett dance a *redowa*. (P)

July 16th. Theatres in Paris beginning to recover from the cholera epidemic and political disturbances. Grisi has a slight attack of cholera. Fuoco and Clara Galby in the opera *Dom Sébastien*. (P)

September 17th. Début of Alexandre Paul. *La Filleule des fées* in active preparation. (P)

September 24th. Fuoco's extraordinary *pointe* work in *La Favorite*. Regret that Grisi did not dance her usual *pas*. (P)

December 3rd. The Viennese Children at PSM. (P)

December 10th. Lerouge's ballet *Les Trois Fêtes* at PSM, featuring the Viennese Children. Mlle Camille "graceful, light and taglionesque"; Espinosa "bounding in the footsteps of Mazurier and Ravel, whom he will soon surpass". (P)

December 31st. Cerrito and Saint-Léon return in *Le Violon du Diable*. (P)

1850

January 29th. The ballet in *Le Pied de mouton* at GAI. Amélie Laporte. (P)

February 18th. Léon Espinosa in *Jocko* at PSM. (P)

May 6th. Plunkett and Petipa in *Le Diable à quatre*. Zélia Lacoste. (P)

October 2nd. Augusta Maywood in Brescia. (P)

December 9th. The ballet in *L'Enfant prodigue*. Plunkett and Elisabeth Robert. (P)

1851

May 12th. Foreign tour of a troupe of Spanish dancers headed by Petra Cámara. (P)

May 19th. Petra Cámara at GYM, with Sra. Guerrera, Sr. Ruiz. (P)

August 18th. Rosa Espert and Joaquina Segura at VAR. (P)

September 15th. Lola Montez has benefited from studying with Mabille. A note on authentic costuming: "In *La Péri* all the costumes were designed by Marilhat, but only one dancer, Delphine Marquet, had the intelligence to accept hers." (P)

December 30th. Clara Galby in a ballet of the hours in *L'Imagier de Harlem* at PSM. (P)

1852

January 14th. Plunkett's *Aldéana*. She shows signs of having assimilated the nonchalance and fire of Petra Cámara. (P)

April 26th. The ballet of Aristée and the bees in the opera *Le Juif errant*. (P)

November 22nd. A Spanish dancer at GYM. (P)

1853

February 21st. Galby at PSM. (P)

April 25th. Cerrito's return in *Orfa*. (P)

May 10th. L. Petipa's ballet in the opera *La Fronde*, with L. Taglioni, Forli and Bogdanova. (P)

May 30th. Guy-Stéphan dances the *Jaleo de Jerez* with Massot as her partner at LYR. Petra Cámara expected shortly at GYM. (P)

August 8th. Grisi to reappear in Paris. (P)

August 15th. Grisi recalled to Warsaw and St. Petersburg. Flexmore and Auriol at VAUD; the former's "extraordinary agility and suppleness". (P)

September 19th. Louise Marquet in *Les Huguenots*. (P)

October 24th. Grisi about to leave for Warsaw and St. Petersburg. (P)

December 14th. Rosati's farewell performance. Her extraordinarily expressive pantomime. (P)

1854

January 19th. Cerrito in *Orfa*. Grisi in Warsaw.   (P)

February 14th. *Les Etoiles* at LYR.   (P)

March 21st. The ballet in the opera *La Vestale*. Priora. Début of Mlle Guichard.   (P)

April 4th. Rosati has returned from Turin. A new ballet in preparation for Cerrito.   (P)

May 16th. The dances in the opera *La Reine de Chypre*. Robert dances *La Cypriote*.   (P)

July 11th. La Nena in a new dance at GYM.   (P)

September 16th. Cerrito returns in *Gemma*, dancing a Spanish *pas* with Petipa.   (P)

1855

February 6th. *Idalia* at PSM, with Fabbri.   (P)

May 5th. Cristina Mendez and Sr. A. Martinez at VAR.   (MU)

June 4th. Concepción Ruiz at PSM, with Blick.   (MU)

July 16th. Concepción Ruiz at FOLN. Her *Gallegada* with Maldonado. (MU)

1856

July 14th. *L'Oiseau de paradis* at GAI, with Guy-Stéphan.   (MU)

1857

March 9th. Mlle Emma in the ballet in *Le Petit Cendrillon* at FN.   (MU)

June 3rd. Revival of *Jocko* at PSM, with Blick.   (MU)

June 8th. *Nella* at TF, with Paul Legrand and Spanish dancers, Romero, Maria and Pepita Barrios, Cámara and Osario.   (MU)

July 27th. *La Naiade* at TF, with Spanish dancers.   (MU)

1858

February 15th. The ballet in the drama *La Moresque* at PSM. Mlle Coustou, "a Frenchwoman who made herself 'more Spanish than the Spanish' for the occasion".   (MU)

June 28th. *Claribella* at TF.   (MU)

July 5th. *Claribella* at TF.   (MU)

1859

July 5th. Espinosa and Adèle Monplaisir dancing at PSM. (MU)

1860

September 11th. Carlotta de Vecchi at PSM. (MU)

December 3rd. Italian dancers engaged at IT: Teofonia Amicali, Fransquitta Barba, Carlotta and Emilia Perla, Teresa Toledo. (MU)

1861

May 13th. Barre's statuette of Emma Livry. (MU)

1862

March 3rd. The lace ballet in *Rothomago* at IC, with Mlle Coustou. (MU)

1863

May 11th. Thoughts on stage design after seeing the new production of *Giselle*. (MU)

June 1st. Espinosa in *Les Pilules du Diable* at PSM. (MU)

1864

June 27th. The Kiralfy family at DEJ. (MU)

August 1st. Corrects oversight of not mentioning Saint-Léon in his notice of *Néméa*. (MU)

October 7th. The divertissement in the opera *Roland à Roncevaux* with Fonta, Fioretti, Beaugrand and Baratte. (MU)

November 21st. The ballet company at IT, led by Ernestine Urban, Elise Troisvallets and Mme Grédelue-Mérante. (MU)

December 12th. Revival of the opera *Moïse*. Beaugrand, Baratte, Fonta, Fioretti, and Louis Mérante.

1865

June 26th. Petra Cámara, more buxom than before, at VAR. A "*tango-américain* amusingly performed with simian gestures" by two performers made up as negroes. (MU)

July 3rd. The ballet of amazons in *Le Biche au bois* at PSM. (MU)

July 24th. Negligent performance by the corps de ballet in *Les Huguenots*. (MU)

November 20th. Fonta in *Robert le Diable*. (MU)

November 27th. *Il Basilico* at IT, with Mmes Urban, Rossi, Pougaud-Mège; Grédelue and Mérante. (MU)

1866

February 26th. *Gli elementi* at IT, with Mmes Grédelue-Mérante, Rigl, Diani, Pougaud. (MU)

March 26th. *La fidanzata valacca* at IT, with Urban and Grédelue. (MU)

April 9th. The dances in *Bas de cuir* at GAI. (MU)

June 25th. The dances in *Jean la poste* at GAI. Esther Austin performs a jig "with marvellous precision and complete authenticity". (MU)

July 9th. Saint-Léon's divertissement of the bees, originally composed for *Le Juif errant*, interpolated in the revival of *La Juive.* (MU)

July 23rd. Mlle Roséryi dances in *Salvator Rosa* at PSM. (MU)

October 29th. Esther Austin in the divertissement in *Le Major Trichman* at GAI. (MU)

1867

July 22nd. La Nena at GAI. (MU)

July 29th. Moorish dancers at TI. (MU)

November 2nd. Revival of *Guillaume Tell* with Fioretti, Beaugrand, Pilatte and Villiers dancing the *tyrolienne.* (MU)

December 16th. The ballet in *Gulliver* at CH. (MU)

1868

January 6th. Angelina Fioretti in *La Source.* (MU)

March 16th. The divertissement in *Hamlet*, with Fioretti and E. Fiocre. (MU)

April 27th. *La Comédie bourgeoise* at VAR, with Zina Mérante dancing *La Pifferari.* (MU)

July 6th. Revival of *Herculanum* with Fonta. (MU)

December 7th. Revival of *Les Huguenots.* (MU)

1869

May 3rd. The divertissement in *Faust.* (JO)

August 18th. Revival of *La Chatte blanche* at GAI. (JO)

1870

June 20th. Revival of *Lalla Rookh* at OC, with Mlle Trevisan.   (JO)

August 1st. *Le Kobold* at OC, with Mlle Trevisan.   (JO)

Index

Adam, Adolphe xxi, 9, 94, 95, 102, 103, 111, 189, 197, 215, 220, 236, 238, 277, 325, 326, 341
Aeschylus 298n
Agrippa 216
Albert (François Decombe) 103, 111, 340
Alboize de Pujol, J.E. 239, 257
Albertine [Albrié or Coquillard] 70, 81, 84, 92, 93
Albrié, Sophie 81n
Albrié, Victorine 81
Alboni, Marietta 182, 213
Aldridge, Ira F. 315
Aline [Dorsé] 199
Allom, Thomas 212
Alonso, Señora 337
Amany xxiii, 3n, 40–46, 48, 49, 135, 136, 160n, 316
Amicali, Teofonia 347
Amosova, Anastasia or Nadezhda 293
Andreyanova, Elena 163
Angel (Angel-Jean-Robert Eustache) 13n
Anicet-Bourgeois, August 48n
Antier, Benjamin 88n
Aranawary, Emilia 257
Arbeau, Thoinot 243, 310n
Ariosto, Ludovic 15n, 159n
Aristotle 226
Artois, Comte d', later King Charles X 2n
Auber, Daniel 17, 29, 89, 279n, 309, 310, 339
Aubry, Jean-Baptiste 260
Aumer, Jean 59n, 244
Aurangzeb 172
Auriol, Jean-Baptiste 138
Auriol, Francesca 345
Aussandon, Esther 213, 214, 344
Austin, Esther 348

Balfe, Michael 165
BALLETS (choreographer's name in parentheses, where known; unperformed ballets attributed to scenarist)
Aelia et Mysis (Mazilier) 250–256
Annette et Lubin (Dauberval) 340
Bacchante, La (Perrot) 171, 172
Betty (Mazilier) 54n, 65n, 175–177, 343
Brézilia (F. Taglioni) 10
Capsali (Ragaine) 338
Carnaval de Venise, Le (Milon) 38, 51, 338
Chatte métamorphosée en

femme, La (Coralli) 25–27, 51, 58, 337
Clari (Milon) 59, 338
Claribella (Lanner) 346
Cléopâtre (Gautier, unperformed) xxin, 58n
Coppélia (Saint-Léon) xxiv, 188n, 305n, 317n, 323n, 332–336
Corsaire, Le (Mazilier) 9n, 59n, 282n, 325–328
Dansomanie, La (P. Gardel) 159
Diable amoureux, Le (Mazilier) 65n, 91, 92, 94, 120n, 152, 340
Diable à quatre, Le (Mazilier) 197, 277, 278, 342–344
Diable boiteux, Le (Coralli) 3n, 37, 52, 54, 56, 58, 65, 75n, 80, 92, 181, 337–339
Elementi, Gli (Saint-Léon) 348
Eléments, Les (Perrot) 344
Elfes, Les (Mazilier) 282n, 286n
Eoline (Perrot) 250n, 288–294
Esmeralda (Perrot) 257n, 279, 280, 341
Etoile de Messine, L' (Borri) 269n
Etoiles, Les (Barrez) 346
Eucharis (Coralli) 129n, 146–152
Faust (Heine, unperformed) 164n
Faust (Perrot) 257n
Fiammetta (Saint-Léon) 298n
Fidanzata valacca, La (Saint-Léon) 348
Fille de marbre, La (Saint-Léon) 182–188, 201–203, 343
Fille du Danube, La (F. Taglioni) 9n, 52, 56, 57, 339
Fille du roi des Aulnes, La (Gautier, unperformed) xxin
Fille mal gardée, La (Dauberval) 51, 59, 244–246
Filleule des fées, La (Perrot) 9n, 59n, 215–221, 344
Fils mal gardé, Le 341
Flore et Zéphyr (Didelot) 142
Fonti, La (Mazilier) xxiii, 198n, 264n, 273–276, 282n
Gemma (Cerrito) xxi, xxvi,

80n, 265–269, 346
Gipsy, La (Mazilier) xxiii, 54n, 58–65, 165n, 235n, 338
Giselle (Coralli, Perrot) xxi–xxiii, xxvi, 9n, 59n, 67n, 70n, 94–102, 113, 119, 121, 144n, 340, 347
Gottin Diana, Die (Heine, unperformed) 164n
Graziosa (L. Petipa) 264n
Griseldis (Mazilier) 54n, 189–197, 343
Idalia (Bretin) 346
Jolie Fille de Gand, La (Albert) 9n, 59n, 103–111, 140, 143, 144, 155, 340, 341, 343
Jovita (Mazilier) 259–264
Jugement de Pâris, Le (Perrot) 343
Kermessen i Brugge (Bournonville) 104n
Lady Henriette (Mazilier) 54n, 59n, 124–129, 341
Lalla Rookh (Perrot) xxiv, 171–173
Manon Lescaut (Aumer) 83
Marcobomba, El (Ragaine) 76, 77
Mariage à Séville, Le (Gautier, unperformed) xxin
Mars et Vénus (J.B. Blache) 142
Mirra (Viganò) 328
Mohicans, Les (Guerra) xx, 9–14, 30, 51
Moresques, Les 342
Naiade, La 346
Napoli (Bournonville) 122n
Nathalie (F. Taglioni) 20, 21
Nella 346
Néméa (Saint-Léon) 188n, 297–306, 319, 323, 347
Nina (Milon) 82, 84, 85
Nisida (A. Mabille) 65n, 71n, 198–200
Noce di Benevento, Il (Viganò) 328
Noces de Gamache, Les (Milon) 91
Ombre, L' (Berthier) 341
Ombre, L' (F. Taglioni) 140, 143
Orfa (Mazilier) 9n, 54n, 236–238, 345, 346
Otello (Viganò) 298
Ozaï (Coralli) 75n, 178–181
Papillon, Le (M. Taglioni) 295n
Pâquerette (Saint-Léon) xxi, 65n, 188n, 225–227
Paquita (Mazilier) xxiii, 54n,

129n, 166–170, 197
Pas de quatre (Perrot) 171n, 182
Pas des déesses, Le (see *Jugement de Pâris, Le*)
Péri, La (Coralli) xxi, xxiii, xxvi, 70n, 112–121, 139, 153n, 161, 341, 342, 345
Preneur des rats de Hameln, Le (Gautier, unperformed) xxin
Prometeo (Viganò) 298, 328
Révolte au serail, La (F. Taglioni) 153n, 264n, 338
Sacountala (L. Petipa) xxi, xxiii, xxv, xxvi, 70n, 281–287
Servante justifiée, La (P. Gardel) 338
Somnambule, La (Aumer) 51, 59
Source, La (Saint-Léon) 188n, 320–324, 348
Stella (Saint-Léon) 188n, 222–224
Sylphide, La (F. Taglioni) xxi, 1n, 17n, 51–55, 78, 122n, 131–133, 140–143, 144n, 215, 234, 235, 338, 340, 342
Sylvia (Mérante) 323n
Tarentule, La (Coralli) xxv, 66–75, 91, 92, 340
Tempête, La (Coralli) 3n, 15, 16
Tempête, La (Hansen) 65n
Toreadoren (Bournonville) 122n
Trilby (Ragaine) 342
Trois Fêtes, Les (Lerouge) 344
Vert-Vert (Mazilier, Saint-Léon) 54n, 129n, 230–233
Violon du Diable, Le (Saint-Léon) 188n, 203, 205, 207–211, 235, 344
Vivandière, La (Saint-Léon) 188n, 204–206, 228, 229
Volière, La (T. Elssler) xxv, 33–36, 51, 75n, 265, 338
Yanko le bandit (Honoré) xix, 129n
Baratte, Marie 347
Barba, Fransquitta 347
Barre, Jean-Auguste 3, 4, 49, 347
Barré, Mlle (Louise-Arthémise Lointier) 199
Barrez, Jean-Baptiste 74, 76, 82–84, 92, 111, 121, 129, 339, 340, 343
Barrios, Maria 346
Barrios, Pepita 346
Baudouin, Pierre-Antoine 232

Bayaderes, The xxiii, 39–50, 135
Bazin, François 88n
Beauchet, Magloire 268
Beaucourt, Caroline 340
Beaugrand, Léontine xxiv, 120n, 307, 308, 323, 336, 347, 348
Beaumarchais, Pierre 135
Beethoven, Ludwig Van 44, 298n
Bellel, Jean-Joseph-François 254
Bellini, Vincenzo 142n
Bendemann, Eduard Julius Friedrich 19
Benoist, François 58, 65, 95n, 198, 200, 225, 226
Béranger, Pierre-Jean de 311
Beretta, Caterina 277, 278
Berlioz, Hector xixn, 64n
Berry, Duc de 91n
Berthier, Francisque Garnier 197, 227, 235, 246, 263, 268, 278
Bertin, Louise 88n
Besson, Mathilde 244, 245, 263
Binney, Edwin, 3rd. xixn, 58n, 120n, 316n
Bizet, Georges 302n
Blache, Jean-Baptiste 142n
Blangy, Hermine 92, 341
Blasis, Carlo 287n
Blessington, Countess of 213n
Blick 346
Bogdanova, Nadezhda 228, 229, 233, 238, 345
Boïeldieu, Adrien 89n
Boileau, Nicolas 2n
Boissard, Fernand 117n
Boisselot, Xavier xixn, 58n
Boschetti, Amina 307n
Boucher, François 83, 314
Bougainville, Louis-Antoine 178
Bournonville, August 104n, 122n
Bozzacchi, Giuseppina xxiv, 120n, 332, 334, 335
Bretin, Louis 339
Brohan, Suzanne 22n
Brueghel, Jan, the elder 117, 211
Burat de Gurgy, Edmond 3n, 37, 52, 58
Burdin, Claude 67n
Burger, Gottfried August 99n
Burgmüller, Frédéric 112, 116, 121, 129
Buridan, Jean 312
Byron, Lord 2, 325, 327

Cáceres 341

Cagliostro, Alessandro, Conte di 265n
Calderón de la Barca, Pedro 135
Cámara, Petra xxiii, 240, 241, 247–249, 271, 345–347
Camargo, Marie-Anne Cupis de 82
Cambon, Charles-Antoine 10n, 118, 185, 200, 212, 220, 224, 238, 261, 276, 314
Camille, Mlle 341
Camprubí, Juan 76n, 341
Camprubí, Mariano 5, 6–8, 19, 71, 339–341, 343
Canova, Antonio 267, 298
Capon, Victorine 339
Carafa, Michele Enrico 20
Cardano, Gerolamo 216
Carey, Edouard 92n
Caroline [Vennettozza] (Mme Dominique) 120, 199, 263, 317n, 332n
Carpeaux, Jean-Baptiste 316n
Carré, Michel 239
Castil-Blaze (François-Henri-Joseph Blaze) 86n
Cattermole, George 212, 223
Catullus 57n, 251n
Cavaignac, General 202n
Cazotte, Jacques 95
Cellier, Francine 287
Cerrito, Fanny xxiv, xxv, 80, 150n, 165, 171n, 173, 174, 176, 182–184, 187, 188, 201, 202, 204, 205, 211, 214, 222, 224–226, 228, 229, 233, 237, 238, 265, 267, 293, 339, 343–346
Cervantes, Miguel de 91
Champollion, Jean-François 259
Chaperon, Philippe-Marie 268n
Chassériau, Thèodore 276
Chénier, André 151
Chézy, Antoine-Léonard de 283
Chopin, Frédéric 305
Ciceri, Pierre 68n, 102, 118n, 146, 268n
Cinti-Damoreau, Laure 22n, 33n
Colon, Jenny 22n
Comba, Rosita 280
Cooper, James Fenimore 10
Coralli, Eugène 123, 129, 151, 181, 227, 286, 318
Coralli, Jean xxi, 3n, 15, 37, 66, 94, 101, 102n, 112, 116, 120, 146, 151, 178, 179, 339
Corneille, Pierre 215n
Cornet, Edmond 286

Costa, Michael 182
Coustou, Guillaume 38, 339
Coustou, Mlle 347
Couture, Thomas 266
Creuzer, Georg Friedrich 116
Cucchi, Claudina 287
Cuvier, Baron Georges 108, 135

Dabbas, Julie 120
DANCES
  Aldeana, L' 188, 345
  Boleras de Cádiz, Las 130, 339
  Cachucha xxiv, 3, 16, 18, 37, 45, 52, 56, 70, 240, 263, 337, 339–341
  Cracovienne 63, 70, 88, 108, 339
  Cypriote, La 346
  Dagger Dance 49
  Dance of the Doves 45, 49
  Gallegada, La 346
  Jaleo de Jerez, El 18, 36, 337–339, 343
  Jota aragonesa, La 338
  Madrileña, La 240, 241
  Malapou, Le 44, 48, 49
  Manola, La 343
  Ollia, L' 130
  Pifferari, La 348
  Robing of Vishnu, The 44, 48
  Seguidillas de Andalucía, Las 339
  Smolenska, La 83, 84, 88
  Tarantella 70
  Zéphyre, pas de 38
Danseuses Viennoises, Les 155–158, 342, 344
Dante (Alighieri) 194n
Dauberval, Jean 59n, 244
Dauty, François Edouard 325, 335n
Davenport, Ira and William 322
David, Félicien 171, 173, 248, 295n
David, Jacques-Louis 151n
Debay, A. 150
Deburau, Jean-Gaspard 19, 73, 92
Decamps. Alexandre-Gabriel 92, 113, 118, 261, 276
Deforge 266
Déjazet, Virginie 230
Delacroix, Eugène 113
Deldevez, Ernest 129, 146, 152, 170, 230
Delibes, Léo 320, 323, 332, 334
Deligny, Eugène 198, 200, 273
Demarne, Jean-Louis 244
Dennery, Adolphe 48n

Desmaziers, Mme 340
Desplaces, Henri 128
Despléchin, Edouard-Désiré-Joseph 68, 117, 149, 212, 220, 254, 259
Deveneyagorn 40n, 44, 48, 49
Devoir, Louis-Lucien-Victor 10, 12
Dezobry, Louis-Charles 252
Diani, Mlle 348
Diaz de la Peña, Narcisse-Virgile 276
Diaz, Pepita 240
Didelot, Charles 142n, 144n
Didier, Charles 119n
Diéterle, Jules-Pierre-Michel 68, 117, 149, 212
Di Mattia, Girolamo 268n
Dimier, Aurélie 120
Doche, Eugénie 161n
Donizetti, Gaetano 53n, 132n, 301
Dorus-Gras, Julie 82
Dorval, Marie 22n, 64
Dubinon, Manuela 339
Du Camp, Maxime 283n
Ducrow, Andrew 138
Dumanoir (Philippe-François Pinel) 189
Dumas, Alexandre, *père* 265
Dumilâtre, Adèle 70, 92, 99, 101, 103, 128, 151, 170, 177, 246, 338–340, 343, 344
Dumilâtre, Sophie 70, 108, 120, 129, 137, 151, 342
Duponchel, Henri 46, 47, 69, 182, 339
Dupont, Mme Alexis 1n, 17, 36, 54, 71, 162, 337–339
Dupré, Louis 82
Duprez, Gilbert 17, 33n, 82, 339
Dupuis, Rosa 33n
Duret, Francisque-Joseph 43
Duval, Alexandre 175
Duval, Mélanie 339
Duveyrier, Charles 25, 26, 51

Eberhardt 76n
Eisen, Charles-Dominique-Joseph 232
Elie, Georges 13, 20, 54, 65, 76, 92, 111, 170, 227
Elliot 329
Elssler, Fanny xxin, xxiii–xxv, 3, 4, 15–19, 22–24, 26–28, 31–33, 35–37, 40, 50–57, 58n, 59, 62, 64, 66, 69, 71, 74, 75, 78, 79, 82–85, 88, 96, 101, 119, 157, 162, 165, 174, 176, 182, 197, 228, 233, 240, 244, 245, 262, 293, 319, 337–340, 343

Elssler, Therese 33, 35, 36, 54, 62, 65, 70, 82–84, 265, 339
Emarot, Célestine 199, 296
Emma, Mlle 346
Enfantin, Father 25n
Escudero 339
Espert, Rosa 240, 345
Espinosa, Léon 344, 347
Euripides 19, 190n

Fabbri, Flora 342, 346
Fabiani, Manuel Rojas 76n
Fabiani, Maria 76, 337
Falcon, Cornélie 22n
Fénelon, François Salignac de Lamotte 146, 147n
Ferdinand, Thérèse 343
Ferraris, Amalia xxiv, xxv, 283, 284, 286, 287, 293
Feuchères, Léon 68
Fiocre, Eugénie 305, 309, 310, 312–314, 316, 319, 323, 334, 348
Fiorentino, Pier Angelo xx, 281
Fioretti, Angelina 314, 318, 325, 347, 348
Fitzjames, Louise 13n, 29, 337, 342
Fitzjames, Nathalie 13, 20, 29n, 51, 60, 67n, 71, 82, 85, 88, 258, 337–341
Fjeldsted, Caroline 122, 123
Fleury, Louise 344
Flexmore, Richard 345
Flore, Mlle 49
Florian, Jean-Pierre Claris de 21
Flotow, Friedrich von 124, 129
Fonta, Laure 310, 314, 318, 331, 347, 348
Fontana, Uranio 86, 90
Forli, Régina (see also Guérinot, Héloïse) 235, 246, 345
Forster, Caroline 67, 82, 84, 101, 246, 340
Fourier, Charles 146
Franck, Célestine 199
Franconi, Laurent 13
Frederika, Mlle 329
Frémolle, Louis 338
Friant, Charles-Albert 268
Fuchs, Alexandre 233
Fuoco, Sofia 175–177, 200, 344

Gabriel, J. 13n
Gabrielli, Count Nicolò 265, 269
Galby, Clara 199, 344, 345
Gallenberg, Robert von 10n
Gambardini 159n
Garat, Pierre-Jean 2
Garcia, Manuela 339, 341

Garcia, Pauline 82
Garcia, Señor 339
Gardel, Pierre 159, 242
Garnier, Robert 159n
Gautier, Eugène 239, 257, 325n
Gavarni, Paul 87, 89
Gendron, Ernest-Auguste 276, 318
George, Mlle (Marguerite-Joséphine Weymer) 22n
Gérard, François, Baron 33n
Gérome, Jean-Léon 276
Gide, Casimir 3n, 33, 66, 75, 178, 181
Glinka, Mikhail 305
Goethe, Johann Wolfgang von xxin, xxii, 61, 65n, 106n, 134, 135n, 141, 231, 236, 279n, 297, 301n, 303
Goy, Virginie 338
Goze, Maria 76
Goya, Francisco de 160, 247
Grahn, Lucile 38, 78, 79, 122, 165, 171, 172, 338, 340
Grantzow, Adèle xxiv, 120n, 317–319, 324, 325, 327, 328, 332n
Grassot, Mme 338
Gravelot, Hubert 232n
Gredelue, Emile 348
Gredelue-Mérante, Mme 347, 348
Grelot, Guillaume-Joseph 232n
Gresset, Jean-Baptiste-Louis 125n, 230
Grétry, André-Ernest-Modeste 205n, 341
Greuze, Jean-Baptiste 263
Grimm, Jacob and Wilhelm 164, 250
Grisi, Carlotta xxii–xxv, 86–89, 96, 101, 102, 111, 116, 118–120, 139, 153n, 155, 157, 161, 165, 169, 170, 171n, 174, 176, 181, 182, 188, 192, 194, 196, 212, 219, 221, 228, 233, 246, 273, 280, 293, 317, 319, 336, 340–346
Grisi, Ernesta xxiv, 341
Grisi, Giulia 22n, 142
Gros, Antoine-Jean, Baron 185n
Guérin, Pierre-Narcisse 151
Guerra, Antonio 9, 10
Guerrera, Señora 240, 345
Guerrero, Manuel 247n
Guët, Charlemagne-Oscar 65n
Guichard, Marie 346
Guignet, Jean-Adrien 261
Guimard, Madeleine 30
Guy-Stéphan, Marie 239, 240, 241, 255, 343, 345, 346

Guzman 272n
Gyrowetz, Adalbert 20

Haafner, Jacob 39
Habeneck, François-Antoine 340
Hafiz 134
Halévy, Fromental 17n, 75n, 262n
Halévy, Ludovic 297, 302
Hall, John 304n
Harel, François-Antoine 47
Hauser, Kaspar 47
Heine, Heinrich 39, 94, 113, 142, 164, 213n, 245, 250, 301, 302, 317, 343
Henneville, Baron d' 60n
Henry, Achille 340
Hérold, Ferdinand 244
Herrera, Francisco Arjona (Cúchares) 258
Hesiod 134
Hoffmann, E.T.A. 13, 95, 209n, 332, 335
Hoguet-Vestris 151
Homer 134
Hugo, Victor xix, xx, 50, 51n, 56n, 61n, 86n, 88n, 98, 105, 112n, 113, 192n, 223n, 279n

Iamblicus 216
Ingres, Jean-Auguste-Dominique 151, 320
Isabel II, Queen of Spain 179n
Ivanov, Lev 76n

Jacotot, Jean-Joseph 146
James, Elisabeth 199
Janin, Jules 19, 134, 246, 309n
Jarente, Bishop of Orleans 30
Joinville, Prince de 3n
Joly, Anténor 86, 90
Jonas, Veuve 116, 125n, 259
Jones, Sir William 293
Jouy, Joseph-Etienne de 225

Kalidasa xxiii, 281, 283, 286
Karr, Alphonse 60
Karsavina, Tamara 277n
Kaufmann, Angelica 67
Kircher, Father Athanasius 216
Kosheva, Anna 293

Labarre, Théodore 237n, 259, 264, 276, 311, 313, 314
Lacoste, Zélia 344
Lafont, Marcellin 30, 339
Lafont, Pierre 30n
Lafontaine, Charles 150
Lamartine, Alphonse de 50, 113

Lancret, Nicolas 83
Laporte, Amélie 344
Laurent, Pauline 199
Lawrence 80, 138
Lefebvre, François-Charlemagne 91
Legrain, Victorine 199, 268
Legrand, Paul 346
Lenfant, Louis 286
Lépicié, Nicholas-Bernard 83
Lerouge, Emile 344
Leroux, Camille 343
Leroux, Pauline 30n, 120, 152, 340, 342
Leuven, Adolphe de 230, 277
Lilienthal, Rosalie 257
Limnander de Nieuwenhove, Armand-Marie-Gislain 237n
Lind, Jenny 182, 212
Lisereux, Julie 257
LITERARY WORKS (NON-DRAMATIC)
Aeneid (Virgil) 83n, 92n, 217n
Allemagne, De l' (Heine) 94
Arabian Nights, The 113
Arria Marcella (Gautier) 286n
Astrée, L' (d'Urfé) 83n, 127n
Aventures de Télémaque (Fénelon) 146n
Beautés de l'Opéra, Les (Gautier and others) 96n, 98n, 344
Bhagavad-Gita 293n
Book of Beauty, The 213n
Bride of Lammermoor, The (Scott) 53
Candide (Voltaire) 164
Clarissa Harlowe (Richardson) 67n
Club des hachichins, Le (Gautier) 117n
Corsair, The (Byron) 325, 327
Divina commedia, La (Dante) 194n
Don Juan (Byron) 327
Eclogues (Virgil) 83n, 100n
Eddas 236
Elementargeister (Heine) 213n
Etat actuel de la danse, De l' (Saint-Léon) 158n
Famille Cardinal, La (L. Halévy) 302n
Fantômes (Hugo) 98n
Fortunio (Gautier) 41
Fridolin (Schiller) 231
Gods in Exile, The (Heine) 245, 301
Golestan (Sa'di) 213n
Gott und die Bajadere, Der (Goethe) 134n

Histoire de l'art dramatique en France depuis vingt-cinq ans (Gautier) xx
Inès de las Sierras (Gautier) 241
Inès de las Sierras (Nodier) 241
Jehan de Paris 172n
Jerusalem Delivered (Tasso) 220n
Jettatura (Gautier) 153n
Joseph Balsamo (Dumas père) 265
Keepsake, The 213n
Lalla Rookh (Moore) 172
Leiden des jungen Werther, Die (Goethe) 164
Lenore (Bürger) 99
Mademoiselle de Maupin (Gautier) xx, xxiv
Mahabharata 284n, 285
Militona (Gautier) 117n
Mystères du sommeil, Les (Debay) 150
Notre Dame de Paris (Hugo) 61n, 192n, 223n, 279n
Nuits du Caire, Les (Didier) 119n
Ondine et le pêcheur, L' (Gautier) 88n
Orchésographie (Arbeau) 243, 310n
Orientales, Les (Hugo) 98
Orlando furioso (Ariosto) 15n, 159n
Pamela (Richardson) 67n
Pantagruel (Rabelais) 198n
Péri, La (Gautier) 115
Rat Krespel (Hoffmann) 209n
Rayons et les ombres, Les (Hugo) 105
Romantische Schule, Die (Heine) 95n
Rome au siècle d'Auguste (Dezobry) 252
Sandmann, Der (Hoffmann) 332n, 335
Satyricon (Petronius) 192
Shah-nameh (Ferdowsi) 321n
Song of Solomon, The 45, 49, 136, 195n, 196n
Sous les Tilleules (Karr) 60n
Sténochorégraphie, La (Saint-Léon) 242, 243
Symbolik und Mythologie der alten Völker (Creuzer) 116n
Système universel (Thilorier) 150
Trilby (Nodier) 239
Ver-Vert (Gresset) 125n, 230
Voyage en Espagne (Gautier) xix, 130n, 160n, 166n, 258n, 271n
Voyage en Russie (Gautier) xix
Wilhelm Meisters Lehrjahre (Goethe) xxin, 61n, 141n, 279n, 327
Zend-Avesta (Zoroaster) 208, 216
Livry, Emma xxii, 3n, 120n, 295, 296, 347
Lopez, Señorita 339
Louis XIV, King of France xviii, xxiv, 48n, 252
Louis-Philippe, King of the French 1
Lovenjoul, Sperlberch de xviii
Loyo, Caroline 159
Lubbert, Emile-Timothée 8
Lucretius 251
Ludwig I, King of Bavaria 130n
Lumley, Benjamin 164, 165, 187, 212n, 262
Lyadova, Maria 293

Mabille, Auguste 71, 79n, 82, 87, 108, 120, 151, 198, 200, 338, 340, 344, 345
Mabille, Charles 79n
Mahmud I, Ottoman Sultan 114
Mahmud II, Ottoman Sultan 117
Maintenon, Mme de 64
Makarova, Alexandra 293
Maldonado 346
Malevile, Claude de 66n
Malibran, Maria 132
Maria [Jacob] 60, 71, 92, 111, 129, 148, 177, 198, 338–342
Marianna, Sta. 338
Marie-Antoinette, Queen 2n
Marilhat, Prosper-Georges-Antoine 113, 120, 345
Marliani, Marco Aurelio 58, 65
Mario, Giuseppe 339
Marquet, Delphine 120, 129, 148, 341, 345
Marquet, Louise 120n, 199, 238, 255, 268, 286n, 312, 323, 345
Marquet, Mathilde 120n, 219
Mars, Mlle (Anne-Françoise-Hippolyte Boutet) 22, 33n, 47, 142
Marsollier des Vivetières, Benoît-Joseph 172n
Martin, Hugues 276, 282
Martin, John 284
Martinez, Ambrosio 346
Massa, Marquis de 311
Massenet, Jules xxin
Massot, Pierre 345
Mathews, Tom 341
Maupérin, Virginie 287
Maywood, Augusta 79–82, 85, 345
Maywood, Robert 79n
Mazilier, Joseph xxi, 54, 58, 59, 60, 65, 175, 189, 228n, 230, 236, 238, 250, 256, 259, 275, 277, 286n, 325, 338, 339
Mazurier, Charles xxv, 138, 338, 344
Médard, St. 205n
Mège 235n
Mehemet Ali 119, 120n
Méhul, Etienne-Nicolas 159
Meilhac, Henri 297, 302
Mélesville 13n, 25
Mendelssohn, Felix 323
Mendez, Cristina 346
Mérante, Francis 348
Mérante, Louis xxin, xxvi, 268, 287, 318, 326, 347
Mérante, Zina 348
Mercier, Pauline 266
Méry, Joseph 48n, 217, 316n
Meyerbeer, Giacomo 17n, 86n, 307, 329, 331
Milon, Louis 59n, 82, 91
Minkus, Ludwig 297, 298, 305, 320, 323
Molière (Jean-Baptiste Poquelin) 22n, 59n, 82, 234n, 252, 268, 280n, 312, 322n
Monnier, Henri 69
Monplaisir, Adèle 347
Montes, Francisco (Paquiro) 130n, 258
Montez, Lola 130, 159, 160, 345
Montyon, Baron de 240n
Moore, Thomas 172
Moorish dancers 342, 348
Moreau, Jean-Michel 232
Mozart, Wolfgang Amadeus 109n, 300n
Muller, Charles 266
Muravieva, Martha 293, 304, 305, 307, 317
Murillo, Bartolomé Esteban 77, 247n
Musäus, Johann Karl August 250
MUSICAL WORKS
Désert, Le (David) 173
Midsummer Night's Dream, A (Mendelssohn) 323
Sélam, Le (Reyer) 286
Symphony No. 1 in C major (Beethoven) 44
Musset, Alfred de 113

Napoleon III, Emperor of the French xxvi, 3n, 202n
Narai, King of Siam 48n
Nathan, Adèle 257
Nemours, Duc de 92n
Nena, La (see Perea, Manuela)
Néodot, Mlle 344
Nerval, Gérard de xviii, 48n, 112, 125n, 148, 316n
Nézel, Théodore 88n
Nielsen, Augusta 122
Noblet, Lise 17, 18, 36, 40, 54, 162, 337, 338
Noblet, Mélanie 337
Nodier, Charles 239n, 241
Nolau, François-Joseph 268
Nourrit, Adolphe 15, 17, 37, 51, 234, 235n
Noverre, Jean-Georges 242
Nuitter, Charles 320, 332

Odry, Charles 5, 61n, 337
Offenbach, Jacques 302n
Oliva, Pepita de 240
OPERAS
  Africaine, L' (Meyerbeer) 307
  Apparition, L' (Benoist) 344
  Belle Hélène, La (Offenbach) 302n
  Bohemian Girl, The (Balfe) 165n
  Carmen (Bizet) 302n
  Chalet, Le (Auber) 20n
  Dame blanche, La (Boïeldieu) 89
  Danseur du roi, Le (E. Gautier) 257, 258
  Dieu et la bayadère, Le (Auber) 1n, 29–30, 47, 88, 134–137
  Dom Sébastien de Portugal (Donizetti) 344
  Don Giovanni (Mozart) 109n, 300n, 339
  Enfant prodigue, L' (Auber) 345
  Esmeralda, La (Bertin) 88
  Faust (Gounod) 348
  Favorite, La (Donizetti) 119, 340, 343, 344
  Freichütz, Der (Weber) 86n, 143, 332
  Fronde, La (Niedermeyer) 345
  Grande Duchesse de Gérolstein, La (Offenbach) 302n
  Guillaume Tell (Rossini) 17, 225, 348
  Gustave (Auber) 111, 130
  Hamlet (Thomas) 65n, 348
  Herculanum (David) 295n, 348

  Huguenots, Les (Meyerbeer) 17, 345, 347, 348
  Juif errent, Le (Halévy) 345, 348
  Juive, La (Halévy) 17, 348
  Kobold, Le (Guiraud) 349
  Lac des fées, Le (Auber) 339
  Lalla Rookh (David) 349
  Lucia di Lammermoor (Donizetti) 33n, 53n
  Lutin de la vallée, Le (E. Gautier) 239–242
  Maître chanteur, Le (Limnander) 237n
  Marguerite d'Anjou (Meyerbeer) 86n
  Maria Stuarda (Donizetti) 132n, 342
  Martha (Flotow) 129n
  Martyrs, Les (Donizetti) 301
  Mignon (Thomas) 65n
  Moïse (Rossini) 347
  Muette de Portici, La (Auber) 17–19, 89n, 338, 343
  Norma (Bellini) 142n
  Otello (Rossini) 82
  Pantagruel (Labarre) 237n
  Prophète, Le (Meyerbeer) 71n, 329, 344
  Quart d'heure de silence, Un (Grétry) 341
  Reine de Chypre, La (Halévy) 346
  Robert le Diable (Meyerbeer) 163, 235n, 330, 331, 342, 347
  Robin des bois (Weber) 86n
  Roland à Roncevaux (Mermet) 347
  Rosière de Salency, La (Grétry) 205n
  Salammbô (Reyer) 286n
  Schahabaham II (E. Gautier) 325n
  Sigurd (Reyer) 286n
  Tempesta, La (Halévy) 262
  Tentation, La (Auber, Halévy, Gide) 75n
  Vestale, La (Spontini) 346
  Vie Parisienne, La (Offenbach) 302n
  Zingaro (Fontana) 86–90
Orléans, Duc d' 3n
Osages, The 48
Osario, Sra. 346
Ostade, Isaak van 105
Ozy, Alice 89n
Ozy, Caroline 89

Paganini, Nicolò 6, 209
Pandéristes aragonais, Les 263, 272
Paquita, Mlle 81

Pasta, Giuditta 141n
Paul, Alexandre 280, 344
Paul, Antoine 224
Paulus, Mlle 199
Pavlova, Anna 277n
Perea, Manuela (La Nena) xxv, 270–272, 346, 348
Perla, Carlotta 347
Perla, Emilia 347
Perrot, Jules xxiii, xxv, xxvi, 76n, 80, 86, 87, 89, 94, 102, 122n, 138, 164n, 171, 206, 215, 219, 221, 279, 280, 340, 342–344
Persiani, Fanny 82
Persuis, Louis de 82
Petipa, Jean 76n
Petipa, Lucien xxiii, xxv, xxvi, 70, 76n, 82, 87, 96, 102, 116, 119, 122, 123, 129, 133, 143, 144n, 151, 170, 177, 197, 205, 219, 237, 238, 263, 268, 278, 284, 286, 310, 311, 313, 339, 341, 344–346
Petipa, Marie S. 293, 294, 307n
Petipa, Marius 76n
Petit, Louis 246, 263
Petrarch 32
Petronius 192
Phidias 114
Philastre, Humanité-René 10n, 118, 200
Piatoli, Señor 339
Picou, Henri-Pierre 276
Pigeaire, Mlle 67
Pilatte, Marie 348
Pixérécourt, Guilbert de 266
Pittaud des Forges 230n
Plato 215
PLAYS
  Amants magnifiques, Les (Molière) 252n
  Bajazet (Racine) 194
  Bas de cuir (Montépin, Dornay) 348
  Biche au bois, La (Cogniard, Blum, Toché) 347
  Bourgeois Gentilhomme, Le (Molière) 82
  Bradamante (Garnier) 159n
  Chariot d'enfant, Le (Méry, de Nerval) 316n
  Chasseur noir, Le (Antier, Nézel) 88
  Chatte blanche, La (Cogniard) 348
  Cinna (Corneille) 215
  Colonel d'autrefois, Le (Mélesville, Gabriel, Angel) 13n
  Comédie bourgeoise, La (Clairville, Cogniard) 348

Concert à la cour, Le 33n
Dame aux camélias, La (Dumas *fils*) 161n
Don Juan (Molière) 312
Egmont (Goethe) 327
Faust (Goethe) xx, 106n, 327
Filles de l'enfer, Les (Desnoyer, Dupeuty) 339
Fourberies de Scapin, Les (Molière) 234n
Gaspard Hauser (Anicet-Bourgeois, Dennery) 48n
Goetz von Berlichingen (Goethe) 65n
Gulliver 348
Hamlet (Shakespeare) 327
Hernani (Hugo) xviii, 56
Imagier de Harlem, L' (Méry, Nerval, Lopez) 345
Jean de Paris (Marsollier) 172n
Jean la poste (Boucicault, Nus) 348
Jeunesse d'Henri V, La (Duval) 175
Jocko (Rochefort, Lurieu, Merle) 344, 346
Major Trichman (Bourgeois, Blum) 348
Malade imaginaire, Le (Molière) 187, 214n
Mariage de Figaro, Le (Beaumarchais) 33n
Mariage forcé, Le (Molière) 252n
Marie Tudor (Hugo) 51
Médecin malgré lui, Le (Molière) 234n
Misanthrope, Le (Molière) 22n, 280n
Mithridate (Racine) 215
More de Venise, Le (de Vigny) 56
Moresque, La (Hugelmann) 346
Mrcchakatika (Sudraka) 316n
Oiseau de paradis, L' (Masson, Gabriel) 346
Othello (Shakespeare) 56n, 327
Petit Cendrillon, Le (Bridault, Legrand) 346
Phèdre (Racine) 89n
Pied de mouton, Le nouveau (Cogniard) 344
Pilules du Diable, Les (Laloue, Bourgeois, Monnier) 347
Plaisirs de l'île enchantée, Les (Molière) 59n
Princesse d'Elide, La (Molière) 59

Rothomago (Dennery, Clairville, Monnier) 347
Ruy Blas (Hugo) 86n, 112n
Saltimbanques, Les (Dumersan, Varin) 5n, 337
Salvator Rosa (Dugué) 348
Sapajou (Dupetit-Méré) 138n
Sylphe d'or, La (Meyer, Lemoine-Montigny, Lefort) 339
Tempest, The (Shakespeare) 239n, 327
Vert-Vert (de Leuven, Pittaud des Forges) 230n
Winter's Tale, A (Shakespeare) 95n
Pleshcheyev, A.A. 76n
Plunkett, Adeline 161, 162, 170, 177, 181, 198–200, 232, 233
Pomaré, La Reine (Elise Sergent) 342
Pompadour, Marquise de 83
Potier, Henri-Hippolyte 250, 255
Pougaud, Mlle (later Pougaud-Mège, Mme) 235, 348
Pourchet, Michel 10, 12
Poussin, Laure 287
Poussin, Nicolas 254
Praxitiles 298
Prikhunova, Anna 293
Priora, Egidio 232n
Priora, Olimpia 232–235, 346
Pugni, Cesare 171, 182, 204, 207, 222, 279, 288, 307

Quéniaux, Constance 199, 235, 278, 287
Quériau, Germain 184

Rabelais, François 176, 198
Racine, Jean 89n, 190n, 194n
Ragaine, Jean 76, 342
Ramalingam 40n, 45, 48, 49
Ramgoun 30, 43–46, 49, 135, 316
Raphael 87, 114
Ravel, Gabriel 344
Rébard, Jean-Baptiste-Hippolyte 49
Reber, Napoléon-Henri 95n
Redisha 80, 135
Retzsch, Moritz xxii, 231, 236, 297
Reyer, Ernest 281, 285, 286
Ricard, J.J.A. 150
Richard, Mlle 342
Richardson, Samuel 67n
Risley family (Richard, John and Henry) 138
Rigl, Betty 348
Rittner 4

Robert, Elisabeth 120, 238, 268, 345, 346
Romero 346
Roqueplan, Camille 276
Roqueplan, Nestor 182, 222, 237n
Rosa, Salvator 261
Rosati, Carolina 213, 262, 263, 275, 276, 345, 346
Roséryi, Mlle 348
Rossi, Mlle 348
Rossini, Gioacchino 17n, 50, 82, 225, 298
Rousseau, Jean-Jacques 52, 83n, 85, 135
Rubé, Auguste-Alfred 268
Ruiz, Antonio 270n, 345
Ruiz, Concepción 346

Sacré, Victor 262
Sa'di 213n
Saint-Georges, Henri de 58, 59, 94, 95, 101, 103, 124, 128, 215–218, 325
Saint-Julien, Adolphe de 215, 220
Saint-Léon, Arthur xxvi, 80n, 158n, 174n, 182, 183, 188, 202–207, 211, 222, 224–226, 228–230, 235, 239, 240, 242, 243, 257, 259, 297, 304n, 307, 317n, 320, 330, 332, 334, 335n, 344, 347, 348
Saint-Simon, Henri de 25n
Saint-Victor, Paul de 89n
Saint-Ybars (Isidore de Latour) 208
Salieri, Antonio 2n
Sallé, Marie 83n
Salvioni, Guglielmina 316, 320, 323, 324
Sand, George 136
Saoundiroun 40, 43–46, 48, 49, 135, 316
Sappho 251
Sauvage, Thomas 86
Savaranim 44, 48
Schlegel, August Wilhelm von 293
Schiller, Friedrich 231, 236, 315n
Schlosser, Eugénie 287
Schneitzhoeffer, Jean-Madeleine 15, 51, 142, 234, 339
Schubert, Franz xxin
Scott, Sir Walter 53
Scotti, Maria 280
Scribe, Eugène 25, 29, 33, 66, 68, 124, 134, 135, 315, 330
Séchan, Charles 68, 117, 149, 212
Segura, Joaquina 345

Serral, Dolores xxii, xxiii, 5–8, 18, 36, 71, 130, 160, 162, 240, 337, 339–341, 343
Sévigné, Marquise de 83n
Shakespeare, William 64n, 95, 134, 226, 239n, 298
Simon, François 54, 65
Smirnova, Tatiana 144, 145
Smithson, Harriet 64, 85, 340
Snetkova, Maria 293
Soto, Josefa 343
Stendhal (Marie-Henri Beyle) xx, 298, 328
Sudraka 134, 316n
Susse 4

Taglioni, Filippo 10n, 20, 29, 51, 143n, 264n, 331
Taglioni, Luigia 199, 200, 235, 238, 268, 345
Taglioni, Marie xx, xxiii, xxiv, 1, 2, 3n, 15, 39, 47, 52–57, 78, 80, 82n, 101, 119, 131–137, 140–145, 157, 163, 165, 171n, 174, 176, 182, 197, 199n, 213n, 228, 233, 234, 293, 295n, 315, 319, 331, 338, 340
Taglioni, Marie, the younger 213
Taglioni, Paul 213n
Taglioni, Salvatore 199n
Tamburini, Antonio 82
Tardival, E.C. 40n
Tartini, Giuseppe 203
Tasso, Torquato 220n
Teniers, David, the younger 105, 193
Theocritus 44
Théodore, Thérèse 199
Thérésa 329n
Thierry, Edouard 134
Thierry, Joseph-François Désiré 185, 200, 220, 224, 238, 261, 276, 314
Thilorier, Jean-Charles 150
Thomas, Ambroise 58, 65, 175, 177
Thomas, Emile 340
Tillé 40n, 43, 45, 48
Titian 114
Tolbecque, Jean-Baptiste 230
Toledo, Teresa 347
Trefilova, Vera 277n
Tresse 116
Trevisan, Mlle 349
Trianon, Henry 236, 238
Troisvallets, Elise 347
Turner, Joseph Mallord William 212

Urban, Ernestine 347, 348
Urfé, Honoré d' 83n, 127n

Valerio, Théodore 334
Vargas, Josefa xxiii, 270, 272
Varin, Elise 339
Vecchi, Carlotta de 347
Vegas, Señor de 343
Venua, Frédéric-Marc-Antoine 142n
Vernet, Carle 244
Vernon, Marie 309
Véron, Louis 1n, 8n
Veronese, Paolo 193
Vertpré, Jenny 25
Vestris, Auguste 344
Veydoun 43, 48
Viganò, Salvatore xxii, 298, 328
Vigny, Alfred de 56n, 113
Villiers, Adèle 348
Virgil 16, 83n, 92n, 99, 100n, 217n, 281
Voiture, Vincent 66n
Voltaire, Arouet de 82, 83n, 85, 135

Wagner, Richard 286n, 320n
Watteau, Antoine 83, 84, 148, 232n
Webster, Clara 153, 154, 161n
Weiss, Josephine 155–157
Weiss, Louise 340
WORKS OF ART
  Corinne au cap Mysène (Gérard) 33n
  Cupid and Psyche (Canova) 267
  Don Quixote and Sancho Panza (Decamps) 92
  Danseur napolitain (Duret) 43
  Faust (Retzsch) 231, 297
  Fridolin (Retzsch) 231
  Garden of Eden (J. Brueghel) 211
  Jeremiah on the Ruins of Jerusalem (Bendemann) 19
  Marriage at Cana (Veronese) 193
  Marriage of the Virgin (Raphael) 87
  Napolitain dansant la tarantella (Duret) 43
  Source, La (Ingres) 320
  Supplice des crochets, Le (Decamps) 118
  Voyage à Cythère (Watteau) 232n
  Wilis, Les (Gendron) 318

Yella, Gabriela 257, 258

Zoroaster 208